Young

Unwed

Fathers

Young
Unwed
Fathers

Changing Roles
and Emerging Policies

Edited by
Robert I. Lerman and
Theodora J. Ooms

TEMPLE UNIVERSITY PRESS
PHILADELPHIA

Temple University Press, Philadelphia 19122
Copyright © 1993 by Temple University. All rights reserved
Published 1993
Printed in the United States of America

Library of Congress Cataloging-in-Publication Data
Young unwed fathers : changing roles and emerging policies / edited
by Robert I. Lerman and Theodora J. Ooms.
    p.   cm.
   Includes bibliographical references (p.   ) and index.
   ISBN 1-56639-048-6 (alk. paper)
    1. Unmarried fathers—United States. 2. Unmarried fathers—
Government policy—United States.   I. Lerman, Robert I.   II.
Ooms, Theodora, 1939–
HV700.7.Y68   1993
362.8—dc20   92-39617

Chapter 4 first appeared in *The Annals of the American Academy of
Political and Social Science*, vol. 501 (January 1989), "The Ghetto
Underclass: Social Science Perspectives," ed. William Julius Wilson.
© 1989 by the American Academy of Political and Social Science.
Reprinted by permission of Sage Publications, Inc.

Contents

Acknowledgments

The seeds for this book were sown in discussions in 1985 with Linda Mellgren and Jerry Silverman, both policy analysts at the Office of the Assistant Secretary for Policy and Evaluation, Department of Health and Human Services. They pointed out the neglect of unwed fathers in federal policy. The immediate outcome was the Young Unwed Fathers Project, a collaboration between the Family Impact Seminar and the Center for Youth Development at Catholic University. The Young Unwed Fathers Symposium held in October 1986 provided the initial stimulus for Chapters 2, 3, 8, 14, and 15. The authors of these chapters substantially revised their original conference papers for this book. Chapter 4 by Elijah Anderson previously appeared in *The Annals of the American Academy of Political and Social Science*, vol. 501 (1979). We are grateful to Sage Publications for permission to reprint his work.

We wish to thank Linda Mellgren and Jerry Silverman for their insights and encouragement; Jacqueline Smollar for her painstaking work as colleague and coauthor of the report on the Young Unwed Fathers Project; and the many officials from the Department of Health and Human Services and the Department of Labor who provided partial funding for the unwed fathers project and for funds that helped support Robert Lerman's research.

Our special thanks to Allen S. Downing and Jason Thomas, two caring and responsible young unwed fathers, and to their sons, Johnathon Allen Downing and Jake Thomas; to Josie Thomas for reminding us of the importance of family support; and to Ralph Smith and Tom Henry of the Responsive Fathers Program of the Philadelphia Children's Network.

We much appreciate the incisive editorial pen of Michael Ames and his guidance throughout the process of assembling this volume. Finally, our thanks to our contributors whose high-quality work inspired us to produce this volume.

Young

Unwed

Fathers

1 Introduction: Evolution of Unwed Fatherhood as a Policy Issue

ROBERT I. LERMAN AND THEODORA J. OOMS

After centuries of anonymity unwed fathers are emerging from the shadows into the harsh spotlight of public scrutiny. The dramatic increase in children growing up without fathers and in the public costs of out-of-wedlock childbearing have led federal and state governments to take an increasingly active role in requiring unwed fathers to face up to their paternal responsibilities. In 1989 over one-quarter of all births were outside marriage, but new paternities constituted only about 30 percent of the number of out-of-wedlock births.[1] About four of five young unmarried mothers report going on welfare within a few years of their first child's birth (U.S. Congress, Congressional Budget Office 1990).

The declining presence of fathers is particularly serious because of the associated impacts on child poverty. Most of the rise in U.S. child poverty rates between 1970 and 1989 can be attributed to the declining proportion of children living in married couple families.[2] The one-parent families most subject to poverty—those headed by never-married mothers—have also increased rapidly. Between 1970 and 1989 the share of children living with never-married mothers jumped over eightfold, from 0.8 to 6.7 percent. Poor children of never-married mothers accounted for nearly 1 in 4 poor children in 1989, up from only about 3 percent in 1970 (Lerman 1991).

Federal and state governments have responded to these developments with several initiatives.[3] In 1988 Congress passed the Family Support Act

The authors wish to thank Daniel Scott Smith and Maris Vinovskis for their helpful comments.

1

(FSA) in a new effort to reduce welfare dependency by helping mothers heading families increase their earnings and collect additional child support from absent fathers. Although the law directed most employment and training funds toward mothers on welfare, it also authorized demonstration projects to provide training for noncustodial fathers, including unwed fathers.[4]

Since mothers and children are the visible actors in one-parent families, absent fathers receive limited attention from welfare laws. After all, mothers typically raise the children, interact with welfare programs, select living arrangements, manage family expenses, and respond to national surveys. Only recently have researchers and policymakers taken a serious interest in fathers, at least in their child support obligations and their willingness to pay what they owe. The emphasis on child support has meant a corresponding focus on divorced, separated, and remarried fathers, mainly because married or formerly married fathers are more likely than unwed fathers to be subject to support orders.

Reliable research on never-married fathers has lagged far behind and left policymakers with inadequate information. Too often, judgments about unwed fathers are formed on the basis of unrepresentative anecdotes that tell of young men fathering large numbers of children and then failing to acknowledge any responsibility. Even basic facts—such as the size and characteristics of the unwed father population—have been largely inaccessible. The current volume is an effort to lessen the information gap and to present to the public an array of findings and policy perspectives about unwed fatherhood among American young men.

Several contributors to the volume address key empirical questions, such as: Who are the young unwed fathers? What causes young men to become and remain unwed fathers? How do unmarried young men respond to fatherhood? How often do unwed fathers provide financial support and take an active parenting role? What is the impact on children of growing up without a father?

Others ask: What are the appropriate legal and moral responsibilities of unwed fathers towards their children? How should they be enforced? What are the rights of unwed fathers? To what extent do their rights come into conflict with the rights of their children and their children's mothers?

Still others consider how to improve public policy by asking: How can programs and policy best encourage and enhance young fathers' ability to be responsible parents? Do service and counseling programs attract unwed fathers to become involved with their children? Should public programs provide special employment and training assistance to unwed fathers?

A decade ago this book could not have been written. Too few systematic studies and too little data were available. Today we have studies based on nationally representative data on unwed fathers, serious ethnographic work on unwed fathers in two cities, research that has tracked the children of unwed fathers, analyses of the changing legal status of unwed fathers, and several reviews of programs and policies dealing with unwed fathers. While the scope of research and policy initiatives dealing with unwed fathers is still modest, many findings have emerged that separate fact from fancy and that are thus important to share with a wide audience. This volume brings together many of these new findings.

The Historical and International Context

Although the book concentrates on young unwed fathers in the contemporary United States, we should remember that illegitimacy is hardly a new phenomenon, nor one exclusive to this country. The social meaning of unwed parenthood, the rights of unmarried parents and their children, and even the language and analytical categories have differed significantly over time and across countries. Community disapproval of unwed parents has varied in intensity, depending largely on prevailing religious attitudes. For example, early New England Puritans responded to nonmarital births with moral outrage, while their Chesapeake Anglican contemporaries were only concerned about how the potential dependency of such children affected the community's purse (Vinovskis 1986).

Whatever their attitudes, nearly all societies have tried hard to limit the community costs of raising children born outside marriage. Bastardy in England prior to the sixteenth century was quite common and clearly deviant, but was not considered to be a shameful status. In the Middle Ages children born out of wedlock were raised in families with their half brothers and sisters with little hint of disgrace. However, they did suffer from having no legal rights of inheritance (Laslett, Oosterveen, and Smith 1980).

Begetting or conceiving a child was not against the law in England. If the parents were able to support the "bastard" offspring, the community gave little overt disapproval. But if the child became a public charge, the parents became the object of the community's scorn and punishment (Macfarlane 1980). Historian Lawrence Stone relates how justices of the peace in late sixteenth- and early seventeenth-century England would condemn both the unwed mother and father to public whipping, and to sitting in the stocks if their child lacked financial support. The justices were determined to impress on young people the costs of fornication. Stone reports that "tremendous pressure was put on the mother to reveal the identity of the father, who could then be required to pay for the child's maintenance" (Stone 1979, 401).

Echoing our own time, the purpose of many laws was to force fathers to pay support for their children. For example, a 1733 English law made any man identified by the mother as the father of an illegitimate child liable for payment of the child's upkeep. It is striking that this law also established an incentive to marry. When the alleged father was too poor to provide support, marrying the mother gave him eligibility for a child's allowance from the poor rate (taxes) in his own parish (Stone 1979, 398).

English common law considered a child whose parents were not married as an "illegitimate" child, because in Sir William Blackstone's summary "he cannot be heir to any one . . . for, being nullius filius (the son of no one), he is therefore of kin to nobody. . . ." The bastard child therefore had neither a legal father nor a legal mother. Such provisions meant that illegitimate children could not inherit property from either parent and that they faced widespread discrimination.

The legal treatment of illegitimacy varied significantly across countries. In the late eighteenth and early nineteenth centuries English society dealt ever more harshly with unwed mothers and their offspring as attitudes towards out-of-wedlock childbearing hardened. "Illegitimate" children were regarded with shame and derision, and their parents, especially the mother, were shunned and often punished by various religious and civil authorities. The Poor Law of 1834 fastened responsibility for illegitimate children almost entirely on the mother. Unmarried mothers were viewed as sinners and their children as illegitimate or "bastards." In general, the fathers escaped serious notice and appear to have gotten off scot free.

In Bavaria, however, the harsh penalties against illegitimacy of the seventeenth and eighteenth centuries gave way to a significant liberalization, beginning with an 1808 edict that abolished all fines for nonmarital pregnancies (Lee 1980). The removal of a variety of legal constraints, perhaps together with an increasingly liberal attitude about sexual activity, led to a rapid increase in illegitimacy and premarital conceptions over the 1750–1850 period (Shorter 1980). Similar growth in illegitimacy took place in many parts of Western Europe. At the same time women becoming pregnant by a man of equal social status were expected to marry the father. Thus, increasing rates of nonmarital conceptions legitimated by marriage occurred alongside the growth in illegitimacy.

By the late nineteenth century and early twentieth century the ratio of illegitimate births to total births had leveled off across most of Europe. Declines occurred in England, Scotland, Italy, Switzerland, and Norway, but increases took place in France and Germany. As of 1921–25, the proportion of illegitimate to total live births varied from about 2 percent in the Netherlands, 4–5 percent in England, Switzerland, and Italy, to 11 percent in Germany and 15 percent in Sweden (*Encyclopaedia Britannica* 1929, 12:84–85). In the United States the decline appears to have begun nearly fifty years earlier (Smith and Hindus 1980).

A cyclical pattern of illegitimacy rates and premarital conception is apparent in the United States as well as in Europe (Smith and Hindus 1980). In New England the proportion of births conceived out of wedlock rose from 10 percent of first births in the mid-seventeenth century to 30 percent a hundred years later. By the mid-eighteenth century, the pendulum had swung back toward declining out-of-wedlock births. Still, the U.S. experience is distinctive because of the clear racial differentials in illegitimate births. In the 1920s, 12.6 percent of black births, but only 1.4 percent of white births, were out of wedlock (*Encyclopaedia Britannica* 1929, 12:85).

Overall, despite variations across countries, illegitimacy was a marginal phenomenon by the early twentieth century, usually affecting one in twenty children or fewer. Legal restrictions had become liberalized, but serious social and economic barriers remained. Not only did unmarried mothers lack welfare benefits, they faced a near-impossible situation in keeping their family. If they remained at home, they were not able to support their families. If they worked, officials would see them as irresponsible for leaving their children.

The process of giving birth involved considerable stigma for unmarried mothers. In the United States a white unmarried pregnant woman would often choose to enter a maternity home located far away from her hometown, where she would receive shelter, medical care, and support until she gave birth. The social worker would provide some counseling and help her give up her baby for adoption. She would usually go through this whole experience in secrecy from her family and most of her friends (Young 1954). The social work literature of this period makes virtually no mention of the pregnant woman's sexual partner, the baby's father.

Between the 1920s and 1950s momentous events shook the world, but the tendency to have children outside marriage was unaffected. In fact, the illegitimacy ratios (the proportion of children born to unmarried mothers) broadly declined in Western countries. As of 1960, out-of-wedlock births constituted about 4–6 percent of total live births in Germany, France, Finland, Norway, the United Kingdom, Canada, and the United States. The illegitimacy ratio was even lower in Italy and the Netherlands (Kamerman 1991).

This trend was not to last beyond the 1950s. The sixties saw the beginning of a sharp rise in sexual activity and soaring illegitimacy ratios in the United States as well as in many other countries. Note in Table 1-1 that the U.S. proportion of births that took place outside marriage doubled

TABLE 1-1 Percentage of Births Out of Wedlock in
Selected Countries, 1960–1986

	1960	1970	1986
United States	5.3	10.7	23.4
Canada	4.3	9.6	16.9
Austria	13.0	12.8	21.8
Denmark	7.8	11.0	43.9
Finland	4.1	5.5	15.0
France	6.1	6.8	24.0
West Germany	6.3	5.5	9.6
Italy	2.4	2.2	5.6
Netherlands	1.3	2.1	8.8
Norway	3.7	6.9	24.0
Sweden	11.3	18.4	48.4
United Kingdom	5.4	8.5	21.0

Source: Kamerman 1991, table 5.

between 1960 and 1970 and then more than doubled from 1970 to 1986. By the late 1980s over one in five births were outside marriage in the United States, Austria, Denmark, France, Norway, Sweden, and the United Kingdom. Since birthrates were declining among married couples, not all of the growth in illegitimacy ratios was the result of a greater tendency of the unmarried to have children. Moreover, in some countries—especially Sweden and other Scandinavian countries—the rise in out-of-wedlock births partly represented a longer period of cohabitation prior to marriage.

The jump in the U.S. proportion of out-of-wedlock births took place among blacks and whites, but the patterns and magnitudes differed considerably by race. Between 1960 and 1989 the chances of a black child being born to an unmarried woman rose from about one in five (22%) to over three in five (64%); at the same time, the white child's chances increased from about one in fifty (2.3%) to almost one in five (19%) (U.S. Bureau of the Census 1985, 62, and 1992, 69). These increases can come about via several mechanisms, including a declining marriage rate, a falling birthrate among married women, and/or a rising birthrate among unmarried women.

Some analysts have viewed the rising share of out-of-wedlock children, especially among blacks, as largely the result of a trend in which married women are having fewer children.[5] To isolate the impact of changing birthrates, we calculated what the 1960–89 illegitimacy ratio would have been under two scenarios: (1) constant (1960) proportions of married and unmarried women with changing (actual) marital and nonmarital birthrates; and (2) constant (1960) marital and nonmarital birthrates with changing (actual) proportions of married and unmarried women. These decompositions reveal that one-third of the rise in the black illegitimacy ratio and about half of the rise in the white ratio can be attributed to the declining birthrates among married couples.[6]

In any event, with the rise in nonmarital births has come a profound shift in law and social attitudes. The Uniform Parentage Act of 1973 and other similar state laws now have the effect of giving the nonmarital child complete legal equality with the legitimate child, as long as paternity was legally established. Several Supreme Court decisions in the late sixties outlawed most discrimination against children born outside marriage on grounds of equal protection. However, out-of-wedlock children can take advantage of the same rights as marital children only if paternity has been established.

Meanwhile, unwed motherhood no longer carries the same stigma, partly because of the increasingly liberal attitudes toward premarital sexual activity. Legalized abortion has given unmarried mothers an added way to avoid unwed parenthood. Although each year about 400,000 teenage women choose this option, many young mothers decide to keep and raise their babies on their own. Young people, their parents, and their communities no longer view marriage as necessarily the best solution to an unwed pregnancy, and some have actively discouraged marriage (Chase-Lansdale and Vinovskis 1987). To some experts, teenage marriages are inherently unstable, married teenage mothers are less likely to complete their education than if they remain unmarried, and their babies receive better care if teen mothers live with their parents.

Still, public institutions in the United States are increasingly providing unwed mothers with financial help and services. Prior to the 1935 enactment of the Aid to Dependent Children (ADC) program as part of the Social Security Act, unwed mothers rarely qualified for any public aid. Although the primary goal of ADC was to help widows, the program did explicitly provide public support for the children of divorced, separated, and never-married mothers. By the late 1960s only about 6 percent of assisted children received support on the basis of a widowed parent and 28 percent were in families with unmarried mothers. Since then, the proportion of welfare children with unmarried parents has continued to rise and reached 53 percent in 1989.

The shifts in the availability of services for unwed mothers are also significant. Before the last two decades, high schools usually suspended or expelled pregnant students. Today many school districts offer alternative school programs, on-site day care, and other special services to unmarried mothers or pregnant students. In 1978 Congress set up the Office of Adolescent Pregnancy Programs (now the Adolescent Family Life Office), which funded community-based programs to provide comprehensive services to pregnant teenagers and adolescent mothers.

A New Policy Focus

Particularly worrisome to policymakers and the public has been the problem of children (teenagers) having children. Teen pregnancy and parenthood rose high on the list of policymakers', foundations', and advocates' concerns, as reports documented an epidemic of teenage pregnancy (Hayes 1987; Moore and Burt 1982). The high proportion of out-of-wedlock births and of mother-headed families has created a serious dilemma for American social policy. As more of the nation's children live in one-parent families and face serious economic hardships, the need for social benefits expands. Indeed, reducing child poverty directly would require substantially increasing benefits to one-parent families. Yet, despite the lack of convincing evidence connecting welfare benefits to illegitimacy, the public has been uncomfortable providing generous income support to one-parent families, especially to young, unmarried mothers. Leaders across the political spectrum have called for limiting welfare benefits to a short time period. In the early days of his administration President Bill Clinton proposed a two-year maximum for the receipt of cash welfare. Welfare programs have repeatedly attempted to impose work requirements on recipients, including unmarried mothers raising young children, and to draw these mothers into training programs so that they can work their way off welfare.

Beginning in the 1960s, with the explosive growth in one-parent families and the tripling of the welfare rolls, studies and policy initiatives dealing with one-parent families began to proliferate.[7] Virtually all the research and program activities dealt with mothers and their children.[8] The only interest in fathers was in their status before a divorce or separation.[9] The fact that problems associated with unmarried fatherhood were especially serious among blacks was one factor that inhibited research.[10]

In the mid-1970s Senator Russell Long drew attention to another aspect of fatherhood—the tendency of many absent fathers to avoid paying child support. At the time, Long's legislative initiative to exact added child support payments from absent fathers was controversial. But only a few years later the idea of intensifying enforcement of child support obligations became widely supported across the political spectrum.[11]

Apart from analyses related to the new child support policies, researchers and policymakers did little to understand the experiences of absent fathers, especially fathers who never married the mother of their children.[12] Data on even the most basic issues were lacking. No one knew the number of unwed fathers or their characteristics, the factors influencing their fatherhood, their employment and schooling patterns, nor how many subsequently married the mother of their child or formed second families. Teen pregnancy programs seldom had any contact with the young fathers. Few policy discussions of the 1970s and early 1980s even mentioned unwed fathers (Ooms 1981).

Suddenly, starting in the mid-1980s, articles, reports, and books on teen fathers began to surface; a few teen father demonstration programs were set up, and national organizations such as the National Urban League and the Children's Defense Fund held forums and promoted "male sexual responsibility" media campaigns designed to prevent adolescent pregnancy.

The popular media began to take an interest in unwed fathers and to note their contribution to rising proportions of out-of-wedlock births and unmarried mothers. In a prime-time television documentary produced by Bill Moyers, one of the central figures was a young black unwed father who expressed no responsibility for his several children born to several different women.[13] Young Timothy nonchalantly, even proudly, boasted he had sired several kids, was supporting none of them, and was in fact himself being supported by the welfare checks received by the various mothers of his children. The same portrait of irresponsibility also emerged from the series of *Washington Post* articles by Leon Dash.[14]

In contrast to these images some researchers and health care professionals were describing a type of young unwed father who was both anxious and eager to be a good father and who provided intermittent financial support to his child's upkeep when he could and brought diapers when he could not. This father visited his child regularly, sometimes baby-sat, and occasionally cared for his child over the weekend in his own home or his parents' home. Some program operators reported young unwed fathers who were themselves raising their babies as single parents, often with the help of their parents (see Elster and Lamb 1986; Parke and Neville 1987).

No one knew how many young unwed fathers fit into either stereotype and what kind of range of behavior there was in between. And no one had figured out how policymakers should respond to these fathers' behavior or their needs although a few in the federal government were beginning to ask the questions.

Policymakers began to take seriously the data showing that the rapidly growing share of female-headed families was the result of nonmarital births, not of divorce or separation. By 1989 children of never-married mothers constituted the majority of children receiving AFDC and an even higher proportion of children at greatest risk for long-term welfare dependency.[15]

Several studies have attempted to calculate the public costs of teen parenthood. One estimated that 40–50 percent of AFDC dollars went to mothers who were teenagers or who first gave birth as teenagers (Moore and Burt 1982). Another study projected that in 1985 the total federal and state public outlays for AFDC, Medicaid, and food stamps attributable to teenage childbearing was $16.65 billion (Burt and Levy 1987).

Policymakers and researchers have increasingly blamed the nonpayment of child support as a factor contributing to the persistent poverty of female-headed families. But child support enforcement efforts have largely concentrated on increasing support payments from separated or divorced fathers. Child support enforcement officials generally assumed that never-married fathers had few financial resources and that pursuing them for support would not be cost-effective.

Recently policymakers have started to see the earnings of unwed fathers as an untapped source of financial support, especially over the long run. They learned that only about one-quarter of out-of-wedlock children's fathers have established legal paternity. Even fewer officially pay child support, although some may provide informal support. In 1988 sponsors of the Family Support Act used scanty data on the earnings of unwed fathers to argue for provisions to stimulate state agencies to attach a higher priority on the establishment of paternity. The final law mandates that states establish paternity in a certain percentage of out-of-wedlock births.[16]

New Viewpoints

The rise of an ecologically based systems framework for understanding social problems has also contributed to the growing interest in young unwed fathers. (This book is an example of this approach.) In the sixties and seventies, health care professionals viewed the problems of unwed pregnancy and childbearing as an issue solely concerned with the well-being of individual pregnant women and their babies. This view justified targeting health and social services on sexually active and pregnant women and on young mothers and their babies. Professionals taking this stance simply reflected the predominant medical and disease model of social problems. Unfortunately, such models resulted in a system of fragmented services designed to prevent or remedy particular problems (symptoms) experienced by particular categories of (diseased) individuals.

Social workers echoed these views of health care professionals. Leontine Young, a social worker and author of the influential book *Out of Wedlock* (1954), had a clear idea of the origins of teenage pregnancy. She was convinced that a young woman's pregnancy was no accident, but a result of pathological relationships with her parents. In this view there was little reason to consider anyone other than the teen mother and her baby to be the focus of intervention. Both needed practical services and the young mother needed individual casework dealing with dynamic intrapsychic issues to help her resolve her psychological problems.

As researchers and service providers probed more deeply into the causes and consequences of teenage pregnancy, they learned that the problem was complex, that the young fathers, their peers, and their families were all involved (Ooms 1981). This new focus led to a shift away from the medical model to what became known as the "systems paradigm" in the psychological and social sciences.

The systems view emphasizes that the causes of nonmarital pregnancy have as much to do with attitudes and situations of young men as with the circumstances of young women. While the female partner is the person most seriously affected by her pregnancy, her male partner's behavior and feelings often have a considerable degree of influence on decisions she makes about the pregnancy and, if she carries it to term, about the future well-being of their child. The unwed father's own future may also be affected by the birth of his child. A systems framework highlights multiple, interacting forces in the family, social, institutional, cultural, and community environment that help shape both young men's and young women's sexual behavior and their response to becoming parents. The ethnographic papers by Mercer Sullivan and Elijah Anderson in this volume (Chapters 3 and 4) deal with how individual young men are affected by a rich interplay of forces, including the attitudes of families and peers and the state of the job market. Both papers offer insights into ways unwed fatherhood develops within the black community.

Another reason for the new emphasis on unwed fathers is an increased focus in some quarters on the moral dimensions of public policy. In recent debates about welfare reform and the nature of poverty, conservatives and liberals have raised traditional questions of social obligation and individual responsibility and argued that the government can and should require work from those who benefit from public support (Novak 1987) and that noncustodial as well as custodial parents should bear the primary financial responsibility for children.

The Family Support Act explicitly promotes family responsibility as part of a new social contract. Under this contract the government provides income support and services to the custodial parent in exchange for each parent assuming specific duties. The AFDC custodial parent must now enroll in job training or education and move toward economic independence once the baby becomes three years old, or even earlier in some states. The noncustodial parent must cooperate in setting a support award and make the appropriate support payments.

As Linda Mellgren points out in Chapter 9, the Family Support Act does not explicitly identify unwed fathers as a separate group, but the provisions mandating standards for establishing paternity are clearly aimed at raising substantially the amount of support payments coming from unwed fathers. In recognition of the potential job market problems faced by noncustodial fathers, the act encourages up to five states to mount a demonstration employment and training program specifically for noncustodial fathers.

One result of the feminist questioning of traditional gender roles within the family has been to increase research on the role of fathers (rather than just mothers) in their children's development (Lamb and Sagi 1983). Today a range of cultural and media influences exhorts men to become more involved in the nurturing of their children at home, as women become more involved in life and achievements outside the home (see Pruett 1987).

Although the first books and conferences on fatherhood did not mention unwed fathers specifically (Lamb and Sagi 1983), the initial programs targeting unwed fathers drew on the new emphasis on fatherhood and included a strong focus on helping these young men learn to interact with and care for their children (Elster and Lamb 1986). Joelle Sander, in Chapter 15 of this volume, describes a multiple-site demonstration program of counseling, parenting skills classes, and prenatal education aimed at encouraging unwed fathers to develop a constructive fathering role.

The Rights and Obligations of Unwed Fathers

Ironically, attempts to strengthen paternal financial responsibility and fathers' increased nurturing of their children have prompted some divorced men to create a fathers' rights movement—a development greeted with ambivalence by feminists. As long as single mothers faced nearly all the obligations, issues about the rights of the noncustodial fathers were marginal. However, now that fathers are less able to avoid paying child support, some are insisting that they should have rights to go along with their responsibilities.

George Harris, in his contribution to Part II of this volume (Chapter 8), argues for taking the rights of unwed fathers as seriously as their obligations. He reviews the circumstances under which it may be morally appropriate for the unwed father to claim certain rights with respect to his child—for example the rights to procreate, to notification of an abortion request, to paternity determination, to custody or to visitation, and to consent to adoption. Since the analysis by Harris shows that the law is a blunt instrument for resolving conflicts among the rights of fathers, mothers, children, and society, the distinctions that should determine the morally just course of action may be difficult to write into the law.

Nevertheless, the nation's statutes and case law have confronted and will increasingly confront questions dealing with the legal rights of unwed fathers. Chapter 7, by Ruth-Arlene Howe, provides a comprehensive review of the current legal status of unwed fathers. Howe sees a contradiction facing unwed fathers between the legal basis of their obligations and the legal basis of their rights. The obligations of unwed fathers depend entirely on a blood tie with their children irrespective of the degree of interest the father shows in the child. On the other hand, their rights to seek custody or veto an adoption exist only when they can demonstrate showing a strong paternal interest in their children. Howe predicts that the law will continue to evolve on this subject.

In Chapter 14 Arthur Shostak tackles the rarely examined subject of men's reactions to abortions. Drawing on his interviews with men waiting in abortion clinics, Shostak writes about how unmarried men, both in law and in practice, are excluded from the abortion decision and from the processes of obtaining an abortion. He discusses proposed legal reforms, recommends many reforms in clinic practice and in broad community education and for males themselves to assume more equal responsibility with their partners to prevent pregnancy.

Who Unwed Fathers Are

Most unwed fathers do not fit the stereotype of a young man who takes no responsibility for his children. Half or more visit their children often and provide support payments. As the children age, visits become less frequent, but the child support payments continue, at least according to the fathers. These and other results are found in Chapter 2, by Robert Lerman, which uses data from a large national survey of youth to provide the first national estimates of the trends in unwed fatherhood, the number and characteristics of young unwed fathers, their fathering activities, and the factors causing young men to become unwed fathers, to marry, or to delay fatherhood and marriage.

The close association between early sexual activity and unwed fatherhood—even among young men with the same racial, family, and personal characteristics—makes it important to learn about the sexual and contraceptive experience of unmarried adolescent males. Chapter 5, by Freya Sonenstein, Joseph Pleck, and Leighton Ku, presents the first national estimates of these activities. The authors find that sexual activity increased between 1979 and 1988 for those 17 and over, but so did the use of contraception. Of the 17–19-year-olds who were sexually active, most had only one partner during the year and only about 20 percent had more than two. The low percentage is inconsistent with the common image of these young men having multiple sexual partners.

Data from national surveys are useful, but they cannot substitute for in-depth ethnographic research to capture the feelings of young men who might become unwed fathers. In the two ethnographic studies in Part I, Mercer Sullivan and Elijah Anderson draw on their close and continuing relationships with small groups of inner-city young men to examine attitudes and behavior with regard to becoming a father, to taking care of their child, and to marrying their child's mother. The two authors come up with very different images of the process.

Sullivan reports that the young men in his sample from white and Hispanic neighborhoods in Brooklyn tended to marry the young woman they made pregnant, while black young men rarely did so. In fact, black young men did not face strong community pressure to marry, but were expected to find work, engage in education or training, and assist the mother through financial or in-kind help. The black unwed fathers Sullivan interviewed showed a willingness to acknowledge paternity, at least on an unofficial basis, and to try hard to help care for their child. One young man even suggested that those who did little to take care of their children lost their respect within the community. Sullivan traces the lack of fatherly support and infrequent marriage largely to the instability of jobs and low pay faced by unwed fathers. Anderson paints a much more disturbing picture of early unwed fatherhood in the inner city. Many of the black young men he interviewed were strongly committed to peers who boasted about sexual exploits and derided conventional family life. In this world, young men gained status among their peers by conquering young women and by not admitting paternity.

A major concern about out-of-wedlock childbearing is the long-term impact on children. We know that children of young, never-married mothers are most likely to experience long-term poverty and welfare dependency (Ellwood 1988) and that growing up in one-parent families reduces children's school achievement and family stability (McLanahan 1988). The links between the father's absence and social problems have led some researchers to believe that involving fathers—even noncustodial fathers—in their children's upbringing can mitigate the likely harmful effects of marital disruption or illegitimacy.

In Chapter 6 Frank Furstenberg, Jr., and Kathleen Harris ask how the extent and the quality of paternal involvement influence a child's educational and employment attainment, teenage childbearing, imprisonment, and/or depression. Furstenberg and Harris draw on data from a special sample of children born to black teenage parents in Baltimore during the mid-1960s. The children's involvement with fathers varied from having their biological father live with them during their entire childhood (9%) to having no father figure at all (8%). On average, children in this sample spent about one-third of their childhood living with their biological father. About half of the children had strong bonds to biological fathers living in the home, but only 13 percent had such bonds with absent fathers. The most striking finding from the Furstenberg and Harris results is that the quality of the paternal bonds was more important than the simple presence of fathers. Although strong bonds were more likely to occur when biological fathers lived with the mother and child, often close relationships developed with resident stepfathers and with absent fathers who continued to visit their children.

Public Policies and Programs

How have public policies and programs responded to out-of-wedlock childbearing? As the chapters in Part III discuss, some responses have concentrated on raising the incomes of children through the establishment of paternity, support awards, and the collection of support payments. A few programs have attempted to go beyond the economic dimension and increase the involvement of fathers in raising their children.

Esther Wattenberg (Chapter 10) points out that having paternity determined legally can bring many benefits to the child, and indirectly to the mother, and therefore is nearly always in the best interest of the child. Wattenberg reports on interviews in Minnesota conducted with service providers, teen mothers, and their partners that explore the attitudes and barriers to establishing paternity. Responses revealed widespread ignorance of the law and the benefits of paternity as well as young couples' reluctance to get involved in what was perceived as a punitive child support system.

Unfortunately, administrative practices in the state agencies charged with establishing paternity and collecting child support have often fallen far short of the tasks. In Chapter 11 Sandra Danziger, Carolyn Kastner, and Terri Nickel detail the numerous barriers in procedures and practice in this complex system including, in many jurisdictions, punitive court procedures. At the same time, the authors point out that many states and localities have embarked on new approaches, such as the state of Washington's efforts to inform young parents about paternity and family responsibility, New Hampshire's school-based teen awareness program dealing with the financial consequences and other responsibilities of parenthood, and Illinois's successful efforts to establish paternity by increasing funds for blood testing and promoting an informal "consent process" that takes place outside the courts.

One innovative child support program in Indianapolis has attempted to improve the long-term prospects that unwed fathers will develop a close relationship with their children and will earn enough to provide children with adequate financial support. Young unwed fathers can receive credit in lieu of actual support payments by visiting their children, attending parenting classes, assisting mothers with child care and other assistance, and/or enrolling in education or training. The idea is to promote long-term responsibility by offering relief from short-term financial obligations.[17] Maureen Pirog-Good (Chapter 12) presents an evaluation of this program and gives it a mixed review.

The federal government has played a key role in sponsoring research and demonstration projects aimed at encouraging unwed fathers to become involved in parenting and to fulfill their financial responsibilities to their children. Linda Mellgren describes how the planning and evaluation office of the Secretary of Health and Human Services created a Young Unwed Fathers Project in 1985 to stimulate research, to assist in the development of demonstration projects, and to raise the awareness of the issue in other parts of the federal government. The vehicle chosen was a conference and subsequent report that was widely disseminated (Smollar and Ooms 1987). In 1992 the office sponsored a major conference on policies aimed at establishing paternity (see Institute for Research on Poverty 1992).

Joelle Sander (Chapter 15) and M. Laurie Leitch, Anne Gonzalez, and Theodora Ooms (Chapter 13) examine the experience of a range of outreach and service programs for unwed fathers. Sander reports on the pioneer multisite demonstration program to specifically target adolescent fathers with services designed to meet their needs. The lessons of these programs—such as the importance of outreach and male staff—have not been heeded in subsequent efforts to serve young fathers (Association of Maternal and Child Health Programs 1991). Leitch, Gonzalez, and Ooms find that operators of teen pregnancy and parenting programs are enthusiastic about the idea of involving unwed fathers, but that they are encountering a range of barriers to doing so. While some programs have been successful in attracting fathers, there is little concrete evidence about which practices are most effective and whether the results of program-induced involvement by fathers ends up helping the children.

A major thrust of policies for unwed fathers is to raise their earnings, largely so they can increase support contributions to their children. Robert Lerman examines the rationale for such policies and the context of recent demonstrations by analyzing the reasons for the low earnings of unwed fathers. The evidence points to the need for programs to promote responsibility among unwed fathers as well as to improve their skills.

Looking toward the Future

Society is only beginning to cope with the reality that one of every four U.S. children is born out of wedlock. Research is still in its early stages about whether the phenomenon is an inevitable part of modern societies or whether improved education, the availability of jobs, and strict child support enforcement can begin to reverse the trend. For example, most studies in this volume focus on unwed fathers in urban, low-income, and largely black communities, in which nonmarital childbearing results in high social costs. But the problem extends far beyond these groups. Sensible policies require that we know more about the causes and consequences of unwed fatherhood among suburban, rural, and other groups of young people.

More sophisticated research is needed if we are to gain a deeper understanding of unwed parenthood. Instead of simply studying unwed mothers and unwed fathers independently of each other, researchers should examine the relationships between young men and women before and after pregnancies and childbirth. They should also study those young parents who marry and stay married. And of course it will be important to study the implementation of the 1988 welfare reforms, the impacts on out-of-wedlock childbearing, and the potential effects on the relationships between absent fathers and their children. Finally it is still not well understood why so many young people, especially African-Americans, are delaying or forgoing marriage but not parenthood. William J. Wilson's (1987) explanation of the declining number of marriageable young black males, because of unemployment, incarceration, or premature death, is plausible but far from proved (see, for example, Ellwood and Crane 1990; Lerman 1989; and Mare and Winship 1991).

Presently, much of the demonstration and evaluation money is invested in improving the employment and earnings potential of noncustodial parents. Although these programs are an important investment in human capital, their success in recruiting and retaining unwed fathers depends largely on whether paternity has been established and on both parents' (and often both families') attitudes toward the fathers' involvement. This suggests devoting more resources to interventions around the time of birth, when, studies indicate, the willingness of both unwed parents to have the father involved is greatest.[18] Success at this stage may well make it easier to accomplish the goals of expanded employment and support payments. Strategies to establish paternity at birth address the needs of all out-of-wedlock children, not solely those dependent on public welfare.

The problems arising out of paternal irresponsibility continue to attract public and congressional attention. Proposed legislation introduced in 1992 by Congressmen Thomas Downey and Henry Hyde calls for federalizing the child support system and setting up demonstrations to test the concept of a minimum assured child support. Under this system, the custodial parent would receive some minimum payment in the event the government was unable to collect support payments due from the noncustodial parent. The proposed bill calls for "establishing paternity at birth (with as few exceptions as possible) for each child born in America, regardless of welfare status." Custodial parents would not qualify for the assured support payment without the establishment of paternity. In many senses the bill is another reminder of the significance of the unwed fatherhood phenomenon.

Dr. Leon Sullivan, former Secretary of the U.S. Department of Health and Human Services, has said that "the greatest family challenge of our era is fatherhood . . . male absence from family life."[19] The country will need to confront this issue and other intimate aspects of family life. Coping with these problems in a sensible way will require sensitivity, wisdom, and common sense, but also knowledge about the attitudes, roles, and activities of young men and women before and after they become parents.

Notes

1. Births to unmarried mothers as a proportion of all births rose from 18 percent in 1980 to 27 percent in 1989. The numbers vary widely by race and Hispanic origin. In 1989 nonmarital births constituted 36 percent of Hispanic births, 16 percent of births to white, non-Hispanic women, 66 percent of births to black, non-Hispanic women (Monthly Vital Statistics 1991).

2. Measuring the precise impact of family structure changes on child poverty is a complex and controversial task. The approach used by Lerman (1991) was to calculate child poverty rates in 1970, 1979, and 1989 by holding constant the child poverty rates within family categories at 1989 levels, while taking account of the actual shifts in the proportion of children across family categories. Using these results, one can attribute virtually all of the 1970 to 1989 increase in child poverty rates, and about 80 percent of the 1979 to 1989 increase, to the changing family situations of children.

3. The current volume is a product of this new interest. All the authors focus

on young unwed fathers between ages 14 and 25. They use a number of common terms, which we can define here. *Unwed fathers* are men who have never married. *Teenage* or *adolescent* refers to persons between age 13 and age 19. *School-age* or *minor parents* are mothers or fathers who have not yet reached their eighteenth birthday. *Absent parents* includes separated, divorced, and never-married parents who are not living with their children.

4. Fathers living in welfare families, under the AFDC–Unemployed Parent (AFDC–UP) component, have long been subject to work requirements and have long had access to employment and training programs. However, little research is available on the impacts of these programs on AFDC–UP fathers. For a review of findings on the way work programs affect mothers on welfare, see Gueron and Pauly 1991.

5. For example, David Ellwood (1988) concludes, "The reason for the changed proportion for nonwhite children born out of wedlock is not that more and more babies are being born to unmarried nonwhite women. The reason is that fewer and fewer babies are being born to married nonwhite women."

6. The data for this analysis come from Ellwood and Crane 1990.

7. The number of families receiving Aid to Families with Dependent Children (AFDC) increased from 992,000 in 1964 to 3 million in 1972.

8. Researchers studied the impact of welfare programs on work, marriage, psychological well-being, and poverty; the duration of poverty and the time mothers spent on welfare; the mechanisms by which mothers escaped poverty and left the welfare rolls; and the long-term effects on children of growing up in a one-parent family. Government policies have emphasized work requirements, day-care services, training, and other mechanisms to stimulate mothers to take jobs and ultimately leave welfare. Other programs have also tried to provide counseling services, prenatal care, and food in order to reduce the incidence of low-birth-weight babies.

9. A notable example was Daniel Moynihan's report on the black family, which highlighted the role of male joblessness in causing divorce, separation, and the growth in one-parent families and reliance on welfare.

10. To quote William J. Wilson (1987,4), "The controversy surrounding the Moynihan report [on the Negro family] had the effect of curtailing serious research on minority problems in the inner city for over a decade, as liberal scholars shied away from researching behavior construed as unflattering or stigmatizing to particular racial minorities." The link between family disruption and race continues to be a highly charged issue. Vice President Quayle related the Los Angeles riots to family disruption (Suro 1992). On the other hand, Marian Wright Edelman, President of the Children's Defense Fund, sees welfare bashing as a substitute for race baiting (Toner 1992).

11. In 1984 and 1988 Congress passed by wide margins increasingly tough measures to raise support awards, to establish paternity, and to collect payments owed by noncustodial parents.

12. A few studies on the subject did appear in the social work literature (see, for example, Pannor, Nassarik, and Evans 1971; and Hendricks 1980).

13. The program, "The Vanishing Black Family—Crisis in Black America," appeared as a two-hour CBS Special Report on 25 January 1986.

14. The findings appear in expanded form in Dash 1989.

15. Between 1969 and 1989 the proportion of AFDC mothers who were unmarried increased from 29 percent to 53 percent (Committee on Ways and Means 1991). Bane and Ellwood (1983) found mothers receiving AFDC who gave birth out of wedlock as teenagers were the group at highest risk of becoming long-term welfare recipients.

16. The precise figure depends on the state. Federal requirements are that a state must achieve a paternity establishment rate that (1) is 50 percent; (2) is the average of all states; or (3) has increased by 3 percentage points from fiscal year 1988 to fiscal year 1991 and by 3 points per year thereafter.

17. Since the father's support payments supplant AFDC benefits after the first $50, mothers would lose at most $50 per month from the substitution of in-kind credits for support payments.

18. The state of Washington and a few other communities are mounting vigorous and apparently successful efforts to establish paternity on a voluntary basis in the hospital at the time of birth (see Ooms and Owen 1990). Also, see the analysis of the Wisconsin experience by McLanahan, Monson, and Brown (1992).

19. Secretary Sullivan used this phrase in a speech delivered to the Council on American Families, Institute for American Values, in New York City, 9 January 1992.

References

Association of Maternal and Child Health Programs. 1991. *Adolescent Fathers: Directory of Services*. Washington, D.C.: National Center for Education in Maternal and Child Health.

Bane, M., and D. Ellwood. 1983. *The Dynamics of Dependence: The Routes to Self-Sufficiency*. Prepared for and available from the Assistant Secretary for Planning and Evaluation. Department of Health and Human Services. Washington, D.C.

Burt, M., and F. Levy. 1987. "Estimates of the Public Costs for Teenage Childbearing: A Review of Recent Studies and Estimates of 1985 Public Costs." In *Risking the Future: Adolescent Sexuality, Pregnancy and Childbearing*. Vol. 2, *Working Papers and Statistical Appendixes*, 264–293. Washington, D.C.: National Academy Press.

Chase-Landsdale, L., and M. A. Vinovskis. 1987. "Should Adolescent Mothers Be Discouraged from Marrying?" *Public Interest* 87: 23–27.

Dash, L. 1989. *When Children Want Children: The Urban Crisis of Teenage Childbearing*. New York: William Morrow.

Ellwood, D. 1988. *Poor Support*. New York: Basic Books.

Ellwood, D., and J. Crane. 1990. "Family Change Among Black Americans: What Do We Know?" *Journal of Economic Perspectives* 4: 65–84. Fall.

Elster, A. B., and M. E. Lamb, eds. 1986. *Adolescent Fatherhood*. Hillsdale, N.J.: Lawrence Erlbaum.

Garfinkel, I., and S. McLanahan. 1990. "The Effects of the Child Support Provisions of the Family Support Act of 1988 on Child Well-Being." Discussion paper no. 901-89. Madison, Wis.: Institute for Research on Poverty. March.

Gueron, J. and E. Pauly. 1991. *From Welfare to Work*. New York: Russell Sage Foundation.

Hayes, C. D., ed. 1987. *Risking the Future: Adolescent Sexuality, Pregnancy, and Childbearing*. National Research Council Panel on Adolescent Pregnancy and Childbearing. Washington, D.C.: National Academy Press.

Hendricks, L. E. 1980. "Unwed Adolescent Fathers: Problems They Face and Their Sources of Social Support." *Adolescence* 15: 862–869.

Institute for Research on Poverty. 1992. Paternity Establishment: A Public Policy Conference. Special report no. 56B. Vols. 1 and 2. Madison, Wis.: Institute for Research on Poverty.

Kamerman, S. 1991. "Gender Role and Family Structure Change in the Advanced Industrialized West: Implications for Social Policy." Conference Paper for Poverty, Inequality, and the Crisis of Social Policy. Washington, D.C.: Joint Center for Political Studies.

Krause, H. D. 1986. *Family Law in a Nutshell*. 2d ed. St. Paul: West Publishing.

Lamb, M. E., and A. Sagi. 1983. *Fatherhood and Family Policy*. Hillsdale, N.J.: Lawrence Erlbaum.

Laslett, P., K. Oosterveen, and R. M. Smith. 1980. *Bastardy and Its Comparative History*. Cambridge: Harvard University Press.

Lee, W. R. 1980. "Bastardy and the Socioeconomic Structure of South Germany." In *Marriage and Fertility: Studies in Interdisciplinary History*, edited by R. Rotberg and T. Rabb, 121–143. Princeton: Princeton University Press.

Lerman, R. I. 1989. "Employment Opportunities of Young Men and Family Formation." *American Economic Review* 79: 62–66. May.

———. 1991. "Policy Developments Affecting the Economic Support of Children." Paper presented at the Annual Research Conference of the Association for Public Policy and Management. Washington, D.C. 24 October.

Macfarlane, A. 1980. "Illegitimacy and Illegitimates in English History." In *Bastardy and Its Comparative History*, edited by P. Laslett, K. Oosterveen, and R. M. Smith, 71–85. Cambridge: Harvard University Press.

McLanahan, Sara. 1988. "The Consequences of Single Parenthood for Subsequent Generations." *Focus* 11: 16–21. Fall.

McLanahan, S., R. Monson, and P. Brown. 1992. "Paternity Establishment for AFDC Mothers: Three Wisconsin Counties." Special report no. 56B. Madison, Wis.: Institute for Research on Poverty.

Mare, R., and C. Winship. 1991. "Socioeconomic Change and the Decline of Marriage for Blacks and Whites." In *The Urban Underclass*, edited by C. Jencks and P. Peterson, 175–202. Washington, D.C.: Brookings Institution.

Monthly Vital Statistics Report. 1991. Vol. 40, no. 8. December.

Moore, K., and M. Burt. 1982. *Private Crisis, Public Costs: Policy Perspectives on Teenage Childbearing*. Washington D.C.: Urban Institute.

Novak, M., et al. 1987. *The New Consensus on Family and Welfare*. Washington, D.C.: American Enterprise Institute for Public Policy Research.

Ooms, T., ed. 1981. *Teenage Pregnancy in a Family Context: Implications for Policy*. Philadelphia: Temple University Press.

Ooms, T., and T. Owen. 1990. *Encouraging Unwed Fathers to Be Responsible: Paternity Establishment, Child Support and JOBS Strategies*. Background briefing report. Washington, D.C.: Family Impact Seminar. November.

Pannor, E., F. Nassarik, and B. Evans. 1971. *The Unmarried Father*. New York: Grove & Stratton.

Parke, R. D., and B. Neville. 1987. "Teenage Fatherhood." In *Risking the Future: Adolescent Sexuality, Pregnancy, and Childbearing*. Vol. 2, *Working Papers and Statistical Appendices*, edited by S. Hofferth and C. D. Hayes, 145–174. Washington, D.C.: National Academy Press.

Pruett, D. D. 1987. *The Nurturing Father: Journey Towards the Complete Man*. New York: Warner Books.

Shorter, E. 1980. "Illegitimacy, Sexual Revolution, and Social Change in Modern Europe." In *Marriage and Fertility: Studies in Interdisciplinary History*, edited by R. Rotberg and T. Rabb. Princeton: Princeton University Press.

Smith, D., and M. Hindus. 1980. "Premarital Pregnancy in America, 1640–1971: An Overview and Interpretation." In *Marriage and Fertility: Studies in Interdisciplinary History*, edited by R. Rotberg and T. Rabb. Princeton: Princeton University Press.

Smollar, J., and T. Ooms. 1988. *Young Unwed Fathers: Research Review, Policy Dilemmas and Options*. Summary Report. Available from Assistant Secretary for Policy and Evaluation. Department of Health and Human Services. Washington, D.C.: Government Printing Office.

Steiner, G. 1981. *The Futility of Family Policy*. Washington, D.C.: Brookings Institution.

Stone, L. 1979. *The Family, Sex and Marriage in England, 1500–1800*. Abr. ed. Hammondsworth, England: Penguin Books.

Suro, E. 1992. "For Women, Varied Reasons for Single Motherhood." *New York Times*, 25 May.

Toner, R. 1992. "New Politics of Welfare Focuses on Its Flaws." *New York Times*, 4 July.

U.S. Bureau of the Census. 1986. *Statistical Abstract of the United States: 1986*. Washington, D.C.: Government Printing Office.

U.S. Bureau of the Census. 1992. *Statistical Abstract of the United States: 1992*. Washington, D.C.: Government Printing Office.

U.S. Congress. Congressional Budget Office. 1990. *Sources of Support for Adolescent Mothers*. Washington, D.C.: Government Printing Office. September.

U.S. Congress. House. Committee on Ways and Means. 1991. *Overview of Entitlement Programs: 1991*. Washington, D.C.: Government Printing Office. May.

Vinovskis, M. A. 1986. "Adolescent Sexuality, Pregnancy, and Childbearing in Early America: Some Preliminary Speculations." In *School-Age Pregnancy and Parenthood: Biosocial Dimensions*, edited by J. B. Lancaster and B. A. Hamburg, 303–322. New York: Aldine.

Wilson, W. J. 1987. *The Truly Disadvantaged*. Chicago: University of Chicago Press.

Young, L. 1954. *Out of Wedlock: A Study of the Problems of the Unmarried Mother and Her Child*. New York: McGraw-Hill.

I

Who Young Unwed

Fathers Are

2 A National Profile of Young Unwed Fathers

ROBERT I. LERMAN

Most studies of young unmarried parents have focused on the characteristics of young mothers, the childbearing decisions by young unmarried women, and the consequences of early motherhood.[1] Relatively little has been done on young fathers. In the absence of solid information vivid images have emerged portraying the typical unwed father as a high school dropout, unemployed or working in the underground economy, having a number of children with several partners, and bearing little or no responsibility for the outcomes.[2]

Is this picture accurate? Do young unwed fathers differ significantly from their contemporaries in terms of family background, education, employment, criminal activity, and drug use? Do large numbers of young unwed fathers have many children outside marriage, remain single, and pay little or no child support? Or is unwed fatherhood largely a temporary phase that evolves into responsible parenting? To what extent does a scarcity of jobs discourage marriage and generate unwed fatherhood? Do young unwed fathers participate in raising their children? How often do they visit their children and provide them with stable financial support?

This chapter attempts to answer these questions. I use information from a national sample of youth, ages 14–21 in 1979, to present national estimates of fatherhood patterns of the cohort of American young men who reached their 20s during the 1980s. The results go beyond prior

The author thanks the Department of Health and Human Services, Office of the Secretary for Planning and Evaluation for grant funds that helped support this research. Thanks also to Theodora Ooms and Michael Ames, whose advice helped improve this chapter.

27

studies that rely on anecdotes, a few case studies, or samples of young fathers who happen to enter health clinics.

Data and Concepts

The marital and fatherhood circumstances of young men are often complex. A young man may become a father, marry his child's mother or some other woman, start a second family, and divorce. While simple definitions cannot capture the variety of paths of marriage and fatherhood, they can establish categories that specify a young man's status at a point in time. We use four terms to describe states of fatherhood.

Unwed fathers are young men with living children who, as of a specific time, have never married. *Absent fathers* are unmarried or married fathers who live away from all of their children. *Resident fathers* live with all their children. *Absent and resident fathers* live away from at least one of their children and live together with at least one child.

Data limitations have been a primary reason for the absence of literature on young unwed or absent fathers. Surveys of a representative group of young unwed fathers are difficult to undertake because of the high costs involved in finding them. On the other hand, data based on young fathers entering a program or based on referrals from unmarried mothers are unlikely to be representative of all young fathers.

One alternative is to utilize household surveys conducted for other purposes. Although obtaining enough cases from these surveys requires large samples, the Bureau of the Census frequently conducts surveys of the size necessary. Unfortunately, these large census household surveys generally include questions only about individuals who are normally members of the household and not about children living in other households. As part of its Current Population Survey (CPS), the Census Bureau did collect information on absent fathers for a few months through supplements to the monthly questionnaires. Yet even these data provide little or no information about the individual's family and work status over time, or about the detailed characteristics of the father. In some instances, analysts dealing with questions about the job, school, and crime patterns of young men have ignored the issue of absent parenthood.[3]

Fortunately, data from the National Longitudinal Survey of Labor Market Behavior (NLSY) can fill much of the gap in basic information about young absent fathers. The NLSY provides information on childbearing, household and family status, educational attainment, employment and earnings, and family background for a national sample of 12,686 youths who were 14–21 years old in 1979. The National Opinion Research Center conducted initial interviews with these youths in 1979 and follow-up interviews in every subsequent year. The rate at which youths remained in the sample has been remarkably high. For example, about 95 percent of those interviewed in 1979 completed surveys in 1984. We use NLSY data from 1979 through 1988.

Because the NLSY oversampled blacks, Hispanics, and poor whites, the survey included a higher absolute number of young absent fathers than would have resulted from a representative national sample. Of the 12,686 young men and women interviewed, the sample contained 6,413 young men, including about 1,613 blacks, 994 Hispanics, 742 poor white males, and 3,048 other white males. The NLSY also included a special sample of 14–21-year-olds in the military as of September 1978. We estimated national averages by using weights that reflect the probability of each young person's inclusion in the sample. Given its size, survey, and sample design, the NLSY has adequate cases to come up with a profile of young absent fathers.

A key concern is the accuracy of reports about absent fatherhood. Although it is difficult to establish certainty about responses concerning parenthood of these young people, the NLSY seems to be a particularly good source. The survey deals mostly with youth labor market experience and training and avoids calling attention to the questions about fatherhood. The interviewers are experienced professionals that usually establish rapport with the respondents. The interviewers often obtain considerable information about the household of the respondent from parents or other family members. Except for questions asked during the first survey, the questions about childbearing generally cover only the prior year.

Determining how well the NLSY data measure births to young men is not easy. Frank Mott (1983) found a large number of inconsistencies in the reporting of the dates at which children were born. But he was unable to determine whether young men consistently underreported births in all survey waves.

Although one would expect that the males in the survey are drawn from the same pool as the men fathering children of young women in the survey, we must still make assumptions about the age differences between men and their female partners. I developed comparisons of births to young men and women in the NLSY for one year (1984) based on the assumption that young men in the survey fathered about as many children as young women of the same race of Hispanic origin who were two years younger. Under this assumption, underreporting appears substantial among unmarried men, but not among other groups. Table 2-1 shows that the numbers of children reported by young black and Hispanic married men were about the same as the numbers reported by young black and Hispanic married women two years younger. Similarly, no discrepancy in

TABLE 2-1 Children Reported by Sex, Race or Ethnicity, and Marital Status, 1984 (unweighted number reported by respondents)

	Number of children		Children per youth	
	Men	Women	Men	Women
Hispanic				
Never married	60	122	0.14	0.32
Married, spouse present	249	297	1.00	1.19
Divorced/separated	58	64	1.05	1.23
Black				
Never married	362	547	0.40	0.66
Married, spouse present	270	265	1.09	1.23
Divorced/separated	72	67	1.26	1.31
White				
Never married	76	168	0.05	0.13
Married, spouse present	871	749	0.79	0.84
Divorced/separated	141	200	0.71	0.92

Note: The men were ages 21–26 and the women were ages 19–24.

Source: Unpublished tabulations by author from National Longitudinal Survey of Youth (NLSY) data.

reporting of children appears among black men and women who were divorced or separated. However, unmarried black men reported only two-thirds the number of children born to unmarried black women. Underreporting was even higher among white and Hispanic men, as unmarried men reported only half the number born to unmarried white and Hispanic women. In all likelihood young unmarried fathers are more than two years older than unmarried women. However, it is also likely that young men underreport births.

The underreporting might arise either because young fathers do not report any births or because young men understate the number of births. To the extent the reporting problem prevents us from identifying many young fathers, we end up with an unrepresentative group of fathers, especially absent fathers. Young men who admit having fathered a child that lives elsewhere are likely to be more stable and more concerned about their child than young fathers who say they never had children.

The potential bias should make us cautious about our findings. Still, there is much to learn from the data on the large number of unmarried young men who report fathering a child. At a minimum, results drawn from these data should display less bias than other studies of unwed fathers, especially those based on young men who enter health clinics. The typical young father is more likely to report having a child in an impersonal interview than to enter a health clinic with his partner and child.

Who Becomes a Young Unwed Father?

Young men may become fathers or delay having children. Those who become fathers may or may not marry and may or may not live with the mother and their child or children. Following this volume's emphasis on young unwed fathers, we generally divide young men into two fatherhood categories (fathers or childless) and three marital status categories (never married; married, spouse present; or divorced or separated). In practice, categorization based on fatherhood or marital status resembles but is not identical to that based on residence of fathers and their children. In 1984 only 5 percent of married fathers lived away from any of their children. However, nearly 20 percent of unmarried young fathers reported living with all their children.

The first step is to describe fatherhood and marriage patterns by age and race. Major changes take place as young men age from their late teens to their late 20s. We track this process as of 1984 and 1988. The second step is to examine the characteristics of young unwed fathers. Here we ask to what extent young unwed fathers differ from other young men in terms of ability, achievement in school, work experience, and involvement in crimes, drugs, or alcohol.

Early Fatherhood and Marriage Patterns

First marriages and fatherhood take place for most young men during their 20s. In 1984, as Table 2-2 shows, over half of young men had married and about 40 percent had become fathers by age 26. Most young fathers were married and living with their spouse as of 1984, but a sizable minority were either never married, divorced, or separated. Of the 3.6 million fathers, ages 19 to 26, over 1 million or about 31 percent were not currently married. As these young men aged over the 1984 to 1988 period, more became fathers and most of the new fathers were married. By 1988 the proportion of married fathers reached about 31 percent of 23–31-year-olds and 50 percent of 31-year-olds. Fatherhood among never-married men remained about a constant 4 percent, while divorced or separated fathers increased from 2 to 8 percent of young men.

The age pattern is interesting in several ways. Unwed fatherhood is not confined to teenagers and young men in their early 20s. The proportion of never-married fathers remained a constant 4 to 5 percent of the population in 1984 and reached about 7 to 8 percent of young men aged 20 through 26. At the youngest ages the unwed fathers account for a sizable share of all fathers. For example, nearly half of all 19–20-year-

TABLE 2-2 Fatherhood and Marital Status by Age, 1984 and 1988 (percentages)

	Not father			Father		
Age in 1984	Never married	Married	Divorced or separated	Never married	Married	Divorced or separated
19	92.0	3.5	0.0	2.3	2.1	0.1
20	86.0	4.1	0.8	3.9	4.2	1.0
21	76.8	7.2	1.7	4.3	8.6	1.4
22	71.7	10.4	1.7	4.8	9.0	2.4
23	63.3	13.3	1.8	5.2	13.5	3.0
24	54.6	13.4	3.0	5.0	21.2	2.8
25	47.8	18.3	2.7	3.9	23.7	3.6
26	38.9	18.8	2.9	5.3	31.2	3.0
Total N	10,975	1,972	344	748	2,545	390
Percent	64.7	11.6	2.0	4.4	15.0	2.3
Age in 1988						
23	60.0	14.7	3.1	7.0	12.6	2.6
24	53.2	14.9	2.7	7.3	19.4	2.4
25	47.1	20.0	2.4	5.7	19.4	5.4
26	39.3	19.9	2.5	8.0	26.8	3.6
27	38.3	15.6	4.7	6.4	27.0	7.9
28	31.1	19.1	5.0	6.3	31.6	6.9
29	30.6	15.1	4.0	4.0	38.8	7.5
30	23.9	17.5	3.1	5.0	43.1	7.4
31	18.0	16.2	3.6	3.6	50.3	8.2
Total N	6,277	2,941	594	1,009	5,230	1,017
Percent	36.8	17.2	3.5	5.9	30.6	6.0

Source: Unpublished tabulations by author from NLSY data.

old fathers were unwed fathers. This startling statistic is troubling, but it largely reflects a trend in which those who expect to form traditional families increasingly delay marriage and having children. By age 31 married fathers accounted for about 80 percent of all fathers.

The overlap between unwed fatherhood and absent fatherhood is considerable but far from complete. In 1984, 80 percent of 19–26-year-old unwed fathers were also absent fathers. By 1988, when the cohort was 23–31 years old, almost one of four unwed fathers reported living with all his children and 71 percent lived away from all their children. Unwed fathers made up only about half of all young absent fathers. Of the approximately one million 19–26-year-old absent fathers in 1984, over 40 percent were married, separated, or divorced.

Table 2-3 reveals how many young absent fathers were part of second families as of 1984 and 1988. Overall, 2.1 million fathers were living

TABLE 2-3 Overlap of Fatherhood and Marital Status, 1984 and 1988

	Never married	Married, spouse present	Divorced or separated
Young men, ages 19–27 in 1984			
No children (000s)	11,060	1,978	347
Percent of total cohort	93.6	43.7	46.9
Fathers (percentages)			
Absent	80.1	3.1	80.2
Resident	17.0	91.8	18.0
Absent-resident	2.9	5.1	1.8
Fathers (000s)			
Absent	539	130	303
Resident	136	2332	71
Absent-resident	16	80	7
Total	755	2,548	393
Young men, ages 23–31 in 1988			
No children (000s)	6,274	2,940	592
Percent of total cohort	86.1	36.0	36.9
Fathers (percentages)			
Absent	71.2	3.5	79.6
Resident	24.2	90.0	17.0
Absent-resident	4.6	6.5	3.4
Fathers (000s)			
Absent	718	181	782
Resident	244	4,707	157
Absent-resident	46	340	73
Total	1,008	5,228	7,986

Source: Unpublished tabulations by author from NLSY data.

away from at least one child in 1988. Of this group, nearly 30 percent either lived with at least one of their own children or were married. About one in five lived with at least one child and most of these fathers were married. Another 8.5 percent were married and living with their spouse, but had none of their own children in the household.

Unmarried fatherhood could be a short phase that some men go through before marrying the mother of their children, or before marrying and starting a new family in which they live with their children. To determine the duration of unwed fatherhood, I examined how fatherhood and marriage patterns changed over two five-year intervals (1979 to 1984 and 1983 to 1988) and one ten-year interval (1979 to 1988). In general, never-married fathers remained in that status for many years. Of the

200,000 never-married fathers in 1979, 70 percent had not married as of 1984, and 60 percent still had not married as of 1988. Similarly, about two-thirds of the 672,000 never-married fathers in 1984 were still unmarried in 1988. Over these five- and ten-year periods, only 12–14 percent of never-married fathers became married fathers living with all their children. By 1988 about 20–25 percent of the never-married fathers had started second families either by marrying and living with other children (8–15%), by marrying but not living with any children (1–5%), or by remaining unmarried while still living with a child (8–14%).

Racial differentials in marriage and fatherhood are striking. As Table 2-4 reveals, the incidence of unwed fatherhood among black young men was dramatically higher than among all other young men. Fully 20 percent of black 19–27-year-olds were unwed fathers in 1984. This rate was four times the average rate of unwed fatherhood (4.4%) and nearly 4 times as high as the next highest rate (5.7% among Hispanics). In 1984 blacks made up about 13 percent of the young men, but accounted for most of the nation's unwed fathers. Young men of Asian origin and from white, moderate-income families showed the lowest rates of absent fatherhood (1.4 and 1.6%). Although low-income whites[4] and American Indian young men were twice as likely to be unwed fathers as other white young men, their 3.3–3.5 percent rates were only a fraction of the 20 percent unwed father rate among blacks. Some black young men become unwed fathers as teenagers, but their peak rates do not occur until ages 24–26, when about one of four are never-married fathers.

As these young men age from 19–26 to 23–31 years old, large increases take place in the proportions of married fathers and fathers who are separated or divorced. In 1988 about one of three young men in most ethnic groups were fathers who were married and living with their spouses. Blacks and Asians were the two unusual cases. The extent of fatherhood was higher for blacks than other groups, but 60 percent of black fathers were either never married, separated, or divorced. Among Asians the overall rate of fatherhood was much lower than for other groups (about 25% as compared to 40–54%), but a sizable 40 percent of young Asian fathers were unmarried.

Comparing fatherhood across the four ethnic groups with the largest proportions of economically disadvantaged groups, we see a similar situation among Hispanics, poor whites, and American Indians, but striking differences between those groups and young black men. Nearly one in three black young men was an unmarried father in 1988, double to triple the proportions showing up in other groups.

In contrast to some images of unwed fathers, having several children

TABLE 2-4 Fatherhood by Race or Ethnicity and Marital Status, 1984 and 1988 (percentages)

	Not father			Father		
	Never married	Married, spouse present	Divorced or separated	Never married	Married, spouse present	Divorced or separated
1984						
Hispanic	60.3	8.1	1.8	5.7	19.9	4.2
Black	60.6	4.0	1.0	20.1	11.8	2.6
Poor White	53.7	14.7	2.5	4.0	20.1	5.0
Other White	67.0	13.3	2.0	1.4	14.5	1.8
American Indian	59.2	11.7	6.0	2.2	18.6	2.4
Asian	85.5	2.5	1.5	1.0	4.8	4.7
1988						
Hispanic	33.7	10.3	2.9	9.4	35.8	7.9
Black	35.3	8.1	1.8	23.3	22.8	8.7
Poor White	28.1	15.0	3.8	4.3	38.1	10.8
Other White	38.1	20.2	3.7	2.1	31.2	4.7
American Indian	36.6	13.2	6.7	4.9	31.8	6.9
Asian	47.9	23.9	3.2	3.9	14.6	6.5

Note: The men were ages 19–26 in 1984 and 23–31 in 1988.
Source: Unpublished tabulations by author from NLSY data.

from different women is highly unusual. Only about one-quarter of black and Hispanic young unwed fathers had more than one child as of 1984. Among whites the proportion was less than 7 percent. Race matters somewhat less for absent fatherhood than for unwed fatherhood. The black share of absent fathers was 47 percent, well below the 60 percent figure for unwed fathers. This is because very few young black absent fathers had married, but most white and Hispanic absent fathers married and later became separated or divorced.

Another way of viewing unwed fatherhood is to examine the *flow* into unwed fatherhood. Beginning with a sample of 14–18-year-olds who were neither married nor fathers, I calculated the proportions entering fatherhood and marriage. Each proportion shown in Table 2-5 represents the share of unmarried, childless men entering one of the three marriage-fatherhood categories during 1979 to 1982, 1982 to 1984, 1984 to 1986, or 1986 to 1988. As young men aged through their early and mid-20s, the proportion who entered unwed fatherhood remained constant. Flows into unwed fatherhood were much higher among blacks than among whites and Hispanic young men. Note, however, that the proportions of young

TABLE 2-5 Percentage Flows into Fatherhood and Marriage by Race or Ethnicity, 1982–88

Flows into (by age, year)	Hispanic	Black	White
Unwed fatherhood			
17–21, 1982	3.1	10.4	1.1
19–23, 1984	4.1	9.1	1.0
21–25, 1986	4.4	11.3	0.9
23–27, 1988	6.3	10.4	2.3
Marriage, no children			
17–21, 1982	6.2	1.4	4.6
19–23, 1984	7.1	3.6	9.2
21–25, 1986	9.1	6.4	13.7
23–27, 1988	13.1	9.9	21.2
Marriage, fatherhood			
17–21, 1982	5.7	1.8	2.6
19–23, 1984	5.9	2.5	3.0
21–25, 1986	6.9	3.6	4.9
23–27, 1988	7.9	5.6	5.5

Note: The flows represent the proportion of never-married non-fathers in the initial year who marry and/or have children two years later.

Source: Unpublished tabulations by author from NLSY data.

men who became married fathers were as large among blacks as among whites.

One fear is that unwed fathers become so invisible within communities that they do not even fill out or respond to census forms. The high census undercount of minority males might be related to high minority rates of unwed fatherhood; for example, welfare rules might discourage reporting the location of young fathers in households of the mother of their children or with others. The NLSY panel data allow a look at this potential phenomenon. To the extent unwed fatherhood contributes importantly to the undercount, one would expect unwed fathers to have exhibited higher than average attrition.

Tabulations revealed no such pattern. The attrition rates of 1982 unwed fathers and 1984 unwed fathers are actually lower than among nonfathers and even among married fathers. Only about 11–12 percent of unwed fathers were missing from sample in 1987. By comparison, the attrition rates were over 25 percent among married fathers and about 13 percent among single men who were not fathers. Black unwed fathers also showed low attrition; of the 309 observed in 1984, all but 32 reported to the sample in 1987.

Educational and Employment Backgrounds of Young Unwed Fathers

Joblessness and educational deficiencies might discourage young men from marrying and living with their children and might reduce the mother's interest in marrying the father of her children. Alternatively, unwed fatherhood might reduce a young man's incentive to do well in school and in the job market, at least in comparison to fatherhood within marriage. A third possibility is that some young men may have a characteristic (say, short time horizons) that causes them both to do poorly on the job and to become unwed or absent fathers. Finally, it may be that no association exists between unwed fatherhood and education and employment.

The first question is, did young men who became unwed and/or absent fathers do more poorly in school and in the labor market than other young men? To answer this question, we compared the employment and educational situation of 18–21-year-olds in 1979 by their subsequent fatherhood in 1984, when the young men were ages 23–26. Table 2-6 shows that high school dropout rates and unemployment rates were substantially higher among those who became unwed fathers sometime between 1979 and 1984 than among those who had not become unwed fathers. The largest and most consistent education gaps showed up among whites. Of whites who became unwed fathers in 1982 or 1984, nearly 50 percent were high school dropouts in 1979. This rate was over four times as high as among other white young men. In contrast, the dropout rate among unwed black fathers was about 1.5 times the rate for other black young men.

Employment backgrounds showed a similar pattern. Men who became unwed fathers in 1982 or 1984 were much more likely to have been unemployed in 1979 than other young men. Again the unemployment differential was greater among whites and Hispanics than among blacks.

In addition to their below-average educational and employment backgrounds, young unwed fathers also had lower math, reading, and other academic abilities, as measured by the Armed Forces Qualifying Tests.[5] However, the measured differences in abilities between unwed fathers and nonfathers were often small, especially among young blacks.

Use of Drugs, Alcohol, and Criminal Behavior

Some suspect that becoming an unwed father is symptomatic of a broad range of socially undesirable behavior. If this speculation is true, then we

TABLE 2-6 Educational and Employment Background, by Race, Fatherhood, and Marital Status, 1984 (percentages)

	Educational status in 1979				Employment status in 1979			
	High school dropout	Attending high school	Attending college	High school grad (nonstudent)	Employed	Unemployed	Not in labor force	Military service
Hispanic								
Never married	23.1	17.4	24.2	35.3	58.0	8.4	28.6	5.0
Unwed fathers	36.0	13.1	20.4	30.5	54.6	16.5	22.8	6.1
Married, no children	19.2	16.5	31.7	32.7	63.7	9.9	12.7	13.8
Married with children	34.9	17.1	18.7	29.3	65.7	14.9	9.9	9.5
Black								
Never married	23.0	20.4	22.6	33.9	48.4	19.4	24.3	7.9
Unwed fathers	30.9	21.1	11.8	36.2	48.9	25.2	19.1	6.7
Married, no children	19.7	7.6	29.1	43.5	60.1	11.3	8.7	19.9
Married with children	19.0	15.6	19.8	45.7	52.3	12.9	18.1	16.7
White								
Never married	9.9	13.5	39.1	37.5	63.6	8.7	23.4	4.2
Unwed fathers	48.7	2.1	14.6	34.6	56.0	19.3	19.9	4.9
Married, no children	11.0	6.1	33.6	49.3	73.4	5.3	14.2	7.1
Married with children	20.2	9.0	16.8	54.1	82.0	5.5	5.7	6.7

Note: Men were ages 18–21 in 1979.
Source: Unpublished tabulations by author from NLSY data.

TABLE 2-7 Drug Use and Criminal Activity in 1982
among Young Men Who Became Unwed Fathers by 1988,
by Race or Ethnicity

Drug or criminal involvement, by marital status and fatherhood	Hispanic	Black	White
Used hard drugs			
Not married, no children	19.4	13.6	26.2
Unwed father	27.2	18.2	58.3
Married, no children	17.1	20.9	21.9
Married, children	12.9	13.3	18.3
Missed school or work because of alcohol			
Not married, no children	54.4	35.7	66.5
Unwed father	55.5	49.9	73.1
Married, no children	50.0	40.5	62.0
Married, children	56.0	41.4	60.6
Charged in adult court			
Not married, no children	4.9	5.0	5.3
Unwed father	11.9	11.5	31.9
Married, no children	10.0	2.3	8.5
Married, children	6.5	7.8	10.3

Source: Unpublished tabulations by author from NLSY data.

should observe unwed fathers engaged in higher-than-average drug abuse, alcohol abuse, and criminal behavior. What does the evidence from the NLSY show?

Unwed fathers did exhibit more drug use and criminal behavior than other young men, but the patterns vary widely by type of behavior and by race. Note in Table 2-7 that virtually no differences showed up between unwed fathers and other young men in alcohol-related school or work problems. On the other hand, the incidence of hard drug use was much higher among unwed fathers, especially among white and Hispanic unwed fathers. The differences were smallest among blacks.

Criminal activity is another area in which young men who became unwed fathers showed less social responsibility than their contemporaries. The rate at which young men were charged in adult court (for other than traffic violations) was much higher among those becoming unwed fathers than among other young men. The differentials were apparent for all groups, but again, the gaps were many times wider among whites than among minority young men. Two other indicators of criminal behavior—convictions and served time in prison—revealed a similar pattern of higher rates among unwed fathers and larger differentials among whites.

Determinants of Fatherhood Patterns in Young Men

Early fatherhood depends directly on premarital sexual activity, precautions against unprotected sex, and on marriage outcomes.[6] But these in turn may have roots in the economic environment, social background, and current peer pressure facing young men as well as their individual capabilities in school, the job market, and the marriage market. The focus of this section is to examine the independent impacts of an array of individual characteristics, family background, and socioeconomic conditions on fatherhood.

The existing literature on young men and women having children has largely concentrated on the rising numbers of never-married mothers. William J. Wilson (1987) and his colleagues see the worsening job conditions facing young black men as a major cause of the decline in black marriage rates and the associated increase in black mother-headed families. The flight of jobs away from central cities, high incarceration rates, and other demographic factors have lowered the ratio of employable black young men to young black women. The smaller pool of marriageable men has, according to Wilson, inevitably reduced the marriage rate. As fewer young women expect to marry, more are willing to have children outside marriage, and more young men become unwed fathers.

Many have questioned the dominant role of joblessness in increasing illegitimacy and unwed fatherhood (see, for example, Lerman 1989; Ellwood and Crane 1990; and Jencks 1991, 89–93). One fact casting doubt on the importance of the employment explanation is that marriage rates declined as rapidly for well-educated and high-earning black men as for the less-educated and less-employable. However, other analyses see employment as a central force in affecting fatherhood outcomes.[7]

If employment patterns played a major role in fatherhood outcomes, we would expect that the substantial improvement in employment conditions during the 1980s (including those affecting young disadvantaged and minority men) would alter fatherhood patterns. Between 1982 and 1988 the nation's unemployment rate fell from 9.5 to 5.2 percent, and the employed share of the nation's adult population increased from 58.2 to 62.6 percent. Among teenage males the unemployment rate dropped from 21.7 to 13.9 percent for whites and from 48.9 to 32.7 percent for blacks; and the proportion of black men over 20 holding jobs rose from 50.9 to 57.4 percent. Despite the marked improvement in job opportunities, unwed fatherhood remained as high in the late 1980s as in the early 1980s. For example, the percentage of black 24–25-year-olds who were unwed fathers was about 26 percent in 1988 and in 1982. And as Table 2-5 shows, flows into unwed fatherhood increased or stayed the same between 1982 and 1988, even though job opportunities improved with age and with the economic expansion of the late 1980s.

These figures cast doubt on the idea that job opportunities are critical determinants of unwed fatherhood. However, these national trends do not control for individual and family factors; perhaps changes in family backgrounds and individual behaviors were increasing the tendency to become unwed fathers just as improved employment conditions were influencing a reduction in unwed fatherhood. An analysis of individual patterns can both test for the net effect of job market variables and answer questions about individual and family influences on unwed fatherhood, such as: Is unwed fatherhood closely associated with such family background factors as family income, growing up without a father, and living in a family receiving welfare? Do racial differences persist, even after taking account of family background differences? Are young men with poor reading ability more or less likely to become unwed fathers?

With the use of discrete-time-event history analysis,[8] I estimated the determinants of the flow from being never married and childless to either (1) unwed fatherhood; or (2) marriage, with or without children. My analysis traces the experiences of young men, ages 15–19 in 1980, over four time periods, 1980 to 1982, 1982 to 1984, 1984 to 1986, and 1986 to 1988. The sample for each period consisted of young men who were neither married nor fathers at the beginning of the period. The estimating equations used each risk of a young man becoming either an unwed father or married; thus young men might be entered as more than one observation. Once they married or became a father, they generated no further observations since they were no longer at risk of flowing into unwed fatherhood. The flow approach permits us to see the influence of employment conditions in the very period a young man is at risk of becoming an unwed father.

The analysis begins by examining the effects of race net of age (which changes for each two-year period) and year of birth. Table 2-8 shows that the probability of becoming an unwed father in a typical period ranged from 1 percent among nonpoor whites to 11 percent among black young men. (To ease the interpretation of the nonlinear logit estimates, Tables 2-8 and 2-9 present predicted probabilities for specific categories of young men.) The black rates are more than double the rates among Hispanics and poor whites. Compared to nonpoor whites, Hispanic and poor white young men were at least as likely to marry in a typical period. The black flow into marriage was only about half that of other young men.

Taking explicit account of individual, family, and area variables substantially lowers the apparent effects of race. However, as Table 2-9 reveals, the flow into unwed fatherhood was about four times larger among

TABLE 2-8 Predicted Flows into Unwed Fatherhood and
Marriage by Race (percentages)

	Unwed fatherhood	Marriage with or without children
White	1.0	19.1
Hispanic	5.1	18.5
Black	11.3	10.6
Poor White	4.1	24.1
Indian	3.6	19.9
Asian	1.6	13.4

Note: The sample is young men, ages 15–19 in 1980, who were at risk of marriage or fatherhood between 1980 and 1982, 1982 and 1984, 1984 and 1986, and/or 1986 and 1988. Each predicted flow represents the proportion of unmarried childless young men in the base year who marry and/or have a child two years later. For example, among poor whites, the equation estimates that 4.7 percent of the unmarried, childless men become unwed fathers and 24.1 percent marry in the typical two-year span in the process of aging between 15–19 and 23–27. The equations hold constant for age at the beginning of each two-year period and for the year of birth. All the variables are statistically significant at the 1 percent level.

Source: Multinomial logit estimates derived by author.

blacks than among whites, even controlling for age, birth cohort, family income, welfare backgrounds, area-unemployment rates, sexual activity, and religious attendance.

If job opportunities exerted a dominant impact on unwed fatherhood and marriage, we would have expected a large impact from local unemployment rates. But the results in Table 2-9 cast doubt on this hypothesis. An extremely large area-unemployment differential (moving from 6% to 11%) only slightly increased unwed fatherhood but also slightly raised the proportion who became married.

A number of other individual and family variables exerted much larger impacts than employment conditions on the flows into unwed fatherhood and marriage. Armed forces active duty was associated with a substantial reduction in the risk of unwed fatherhood and a doubling of the flow into marriage. Having lived in a welfare family in 1979, even controlling for family income, both raised the flow into unwed fatherhood and reduced the likelihood of marriage. High family income lowered the chances of unwed fatherhood and marriage. Not surprisingly, those at higher ages were more likely to marry or become unwed fathers. More recent birth

TABLE 2-9 Determinants of Flows into Unwed Fatherhood and
Marriage between 1979 and 1988 among Young Men, Ages
14–18 in 1979

	Predicted percentage flows into:	
	---	---
Variations from baseline	Unwed fatherhood	Marriage with or without children
White	1.3	17.9
Hispanic	3.0	15.1
Black	5.2	7.0
Black, other baseline characteristics plus:		
Military service	3.3	11.2
Unemployment rate, 11%	6.0	7.9
In welfare family, 1979	6.5	6.1
Religious attendance, once per week	3.9	8.0
Reading test, 25th percentile	7.1	7.7
Reading test, 75th percentile	3.7	6.3
8 years of sexual activity	11.4	9.2
1979 family income, $20,000	4.4	6.4
Age 19	2.8	1.6
Age 26	6.4	12.1
Born in 1959	3.7	5.8
Born in 1963	7.2	8.4

Note: See note to Table 2-8. The baseline characteristics are age
24, born in 1961, 6 percent area-unemployment rate, not in armed
forces, a 1979 family income of $10,000, reading score 50 per-
cent correct, 3 years of sexual activity, and infrequent attendance
at religious services. The impact of variables other than race equal
to the estimated flows for say, blacks in the Armed Forces (3.7
and 14.1%), relative to the flows for blacks with baseline characteristics (5.1 and 7.4%). All the variables are statistically significant at the 1 or 5 percent level.
Source: Multinomial logit estimates derived by author.

cohorts showed a higher tendency to enter unwed fatherhood, but also a
higher tendency to marry.

Frequent religious attendance was associated with significantly higher
marriage rates and lower rates of unwed fatherhood. One measure of
academic ability, tests of reading comprehension, indicated that more ac-
ademically capable young men avoided unwed fatherhood but were more
likely to marry. More years of sexual activity went together with much
higher rates of unwed fatherhood but with higher rates of marriage as
well.

Overall, these results point to large and systematic differences in the chances of a young man becoming an unwed father or entering marriage. Job opportunities showed little impact, while individual and family factors were important. Young men who were capable or engaged in constructive activities tended to avoid unwed fatherhood, as did young men from high-income families or families not on welfare.

Fathering Activities of Young Unwed Fathers

The primary concern about increases in unwed fatherhood is the potential negative impact on children. Evidence is accumulating that growing up in a one-parent family damages children's chances for success in school, in the job market, and in family life.[9] These problems of children might be mitigated if fathers provide mothers and children with an adequate income and with significant help in child rearing. Unfortunately, many fathers fail in both respects. Popular accounts convey an image of young unwed fathers who feel little responsibility for the economic or emotional support of their children.

Is this image accurate? Separate ethnographic studies presented in this volume yield conflicting answers. Mercer Sullivan (Chapter 3) came to know young unwed fathers who frequently visited their children and who paid child support when they were able to find jobs. Elijah Anderson (Chapter 4) witnessed a more cavalier and cynical attitude among young unwed fathers and their peers, which discouraged support payments and close emotional involvement.

These ethnographic studies offer insights about the thinking of young unwed fathers, but yield data on the actions only of small numbers. With the NLSY data we can examine the financial support and involvement in fathering among a nationally representative group of over 600 unwed fathers. Although large-scale surveys do not capture the quality of the relationship between unwed fathers and their children, they provide information on four questions: What proportion of absent fathers return to live with their children? When fathers are absent, how frequently do unwed fathers visit their children? What proportion of unwed fathers pay child support and how much do they pay? Are fathers who visit more frequently also the fathers most likely to pay child support, or do fathers compensate for their inability to pay support by visiting their children frequently?

About three-fourths of young fathers who lived away from their children at birth never lived in the same household with them. However, as Frank Mott (1990) demonstrates, the proportion of fathers moving away each year after the child's birth was only slightly higher than the proportion returning in those years.[10]

While unwed fathers remained away from their own children, only a small proportion lived in their own households. As of 1984 about one in four lived with both parents and about 30 percent lived with one parent. In fact, unwed fathers were more likely to reside with a parent than young men who had never fathered a child. Nearly two-thirds lived with another relative, about 12 percent with a partner of the opposite sex, 8 percent with another nonrelative, and about 16 percent lived alone. Living with parents or other relatives was more common among black than among white unwed fathers. In 1984 nearly 60 percent of black unwed fathers, but only 43 percent of white unwed fathers, lived with at least one parent. On the other hand, white unwed fathers were more likely than black unwed fathers to live with a partner of the opposite sex (18% versus 9%).

Many unwed fathers remain in close contact with their children, at least according to their own reports. In 1985 nearly half visited their youngest child at least once per week and nearly one in four said they visited almost every day. Only 13 percent admitted they never visited and another 7 percent reported visiting only once in the last year. These reports by fathers show a higher amount of visitation than do responses provided by mothers for a slightly different sample. Using mothers' reports on a sample of children under age 4 born to NLSY mothers, Mott estimated that nearly 40 percent visited once per week but that about one-third either never visited or visited only once per year.

How frequently fathers visit is closely related to how close fathers live to their children. As of 1985 one of four fathers lived more than 100 miles away from his child, and these fathers accounted for 52 percent of the fathers that never visited. Of the 20 percent of fathers who lived close to their children, nearly 80 percent visited every day or several times per week. Of course the data could imply that fathers who happen to live near their children chose to visit frequently and/or that fathers who want to visit often chose to live nearby.

Fathers apparently lose contact with their children as the children age. In 1986 the proportion who visited more than once a week was 57 percent among fathers with a child 2 years or younger, 40 percent for ages 2 to 4.5 years, 27 percent for ages 4.5 to 7.5, and 22 percent for 7.5 years and older. Almost one in three unwed fathers whose oldest child was 7.5 or older reported never visiting those children. The decline in visitation is evident when we examine the activities of a specific group of fathers. Between 1985 and 1986 the proportion never visiting rose from 14 to 22 percent, while the group making the most frequent visits declined from 36 to 30 percent.

Those unwed fathers who rarely or never visit their children are also least likely to pay child support. In 1985, when 37 percent of unwed fathers reported paying child support, only about 20 percent of those fathers who never visited paid support. It is clear that fathers do not substitute one form of support (financial) for another form (help in child rearing). Still, visitation and child support are only partly correlated. Those who visited less than once per month were as likely to pay child support as those visiting more than once per week. About 40 percent of each group reported making support payments.

The NLSY data reveal some variation by race in visitation but very little difference in the support payments. Of the young unwed fathers in the sample, blacks were more likely to live close to their children and to visit them than were white and Hispanic fathers. For example, in 1985 only about 12 percent of black unwed fathers rarely or never visited their children, as compared to about 30 percent of Hispanic fathers and 37 percent of white fathers. The black fathers' apparently closer involvement with their children translated into a slightly higher frequency of support payments. About 39 percent of black and 34 percent of white unwed fathers reported making support payments; of those making payments, the average level for whites was nearly $1,900, well above the approximately $1,400 figure among blacks.

Overall, we see two broad patterns of fathering. Half or more of unwed fathers live near their children, visit them often, and make child support payments. Most of the remaining group only rarely visit and usually make no payment whatever. How one views these numbers depends on one's perspective. Certainly the results show large numbers of unwed fathers doing little or nothing for their children. At the same time, the extent of visiting and financial help is higher than expected on the basis of census reports.[11] Unfortunately, many unwed fathers lose contact as their children age. By the time children reach 6 or 7 years old, over one-third have stopped visiting. Still, most unwed fathers report continuing to pay child support at about the same rates at least through ages 9 and 10.[12]

Conclusions

The findings in this paper reveal several conclusions about unwed fatherhood in the United States. First, unwed fatherhood has generally not been a benign shift toward having children first and then marrying and living with them. In the 1980s most young unwed fathers became and remained absent fathers. However, few unwed fathers reported having several children. Among black, unwed 24–27-year-old fathers, about 45 percent had more than one child, but only about 12 percent had more than two children. One implication is that unwed fatherhood is spread widely among the black youth population. As of 1988 nearly one in four black 23–30-year-olds was an unmarried father.

Young unwed fathers were generally less well educated, had lower academic abilities, started sex at earlier ages, and engaged in more crime than did other young men. However, the differences were much larger among white than among black unwed fathers. Put another way, black unwed fatherhood is less concentrated among those with the weakest life prospects than is white unwed fatherhood. For example, white unwed fathers were several times more likely to have engaged in criminal activity than other whites. Similarly, wide education and employment gaps separated white unwed fathers from other white young men. In contrast, black unwed fathers showed only moderately poorer performance in school and work. The proportion of high school dropouts of black 18–21-year-olds in 1979 was about 30 percent among those who later became unwed fathers. But this was only moderately higher than the 23 percent rate among those who had not become unwed fathers by 1984. Taken together, the data indicate that unwed fatherhood is a mainstream phenomenon more frequently for young blacks than for young whites.

Evidence on the flows into unwed fatherhood or marriage revealed several factors exerting independent effects. Family background significantly influenced the chances of unwed fatherhood. Independently of other factors low family income and having lived in a welfare household (holding income constant) increased flows into unwed fatherhood substantially. Personal characteristics and behavior also exerted significant effects on unwed fatherhood. Starting sex five years earlier nearly doubled the flow (over two years) into unwed fatherhood. Those who attended church at least once per week had a 20 percent lower likelihood of becoming an unwed father. Young men in the armed forces were nearly 30 percent less likely to enter unwed fatherhood.

The findings concerning the role of employment opportunities are mixed. Higher reading scores, which may be an indicator of the job quality that young men will attain, reduce the likelihood of unwed fatherhood. On the other hand, two key results cast doubt on the employment opportunities explanation. First, unwed fatherhood showed no tendency to decline in spite of the dramatic improvement in the employment opportunities of young men between the early 1980s and the late 1980s. Second, the flow into unwed fatherhood was virtually no lower among young men living in counties with low county unemployment rates than in more depressed counties.

Family, individual, and job market factors reduced but did not eliminate the large racial differentials in unwed fatherhood. Blacks showed four times the flow into unwed fatherhood that whites did, even among those with similar family income, prior welfare status, sexual activity, reading ability, area unemployment rates, and involvement in the armed forces.

The fathering and family patterns of young unwed fathers varied widely. Once young men became unwed fathers, they rarely returned to live with their children. Instead, they usually continued to live with their parents and/or other relatives. Their involvement with children varied across individuals and with the age of children. Unwed fathers typically both visited and paid child support, or they did neither. However, even some of those who never visited still reported providing financial support to the child. By far the most extensive involvement took place soon after the child's birth, with much lower involvement taking place as children grew older. For the entire sample the proportion visiting at least once per year fell from nearly 60 percent within the first two years of birth to only about 20 percent with children over 7. Although over one-third of unwed fathers reported paying child support, even the stated contributions were extremely low. The mean payments were only about $110–150 per month.

The high rates of unwed fatherhood are clearly disturbing and unfortunately; they show no sign of abating. Recent cohorts were more likely to enter unwed fatherhood than previous cohorts. It is disappointing that the expanded employment opportunities of the late 1980s failed to reverse the trend of unwed fatherhood. The difference between a 6 percent and an 11 percent unemployment rate had little impact on entry into unwed fatherhood.

The racial differences are too large to ignore. Unwed fatherhood is most widespread among young black men, even in comparison to other young men from disadvantaged backgrounds. It is crucial that black leaders and others continue their efforts to reorient young blacks away from these patterns and the resulting serious disadvantages imposed on black children.

One implication of the results is that those working with unwed fathers should understand the family context of these young men. Most young unwed fathers live with one or both parents and few head their own household. Because of their access to family resources, unwed fathers can afford to contribute more than their incomes might suggest. Parents of unwed fathers might be held partially responsible for this support and might assist in counseling and other service programs.

Finally, it is encouraging that young men who involve themselves in constructive activities are much less likely to become unwed fathers. Thus, enhancing certain values that are positive in themselves—such as learning, volunteerism, and religious activity—may be the best means for discouraging unwed fatherhood.

Notes

1. See, for example, the National Academy of Sciences report (in Hayes 1987), which provides little analysis of the unwed fatherhood of young men. Recently researchers have been turning their attention to the male role in premarital childbearing. See, for example, Testa et al. 1989 and Mare and Winship 1991.

2. The CBS Special Report, "The Vanishing Black Family—Crisis in Black America" (25 January 1986), put forward this image in a powerful way. Elijah Anderson's essay (Chapter 4 of this volume) reveals a complex picture of the issues, but still points to a frequent lack of responsibility on the part of young unwed fathers. Leon Dash (1989) describes cases in Washington, D.C., where young women have nonmarital births in the hope of marrying the young father.

3. A special survey of inner-city black men conducted for the National Bureau of Economic Research did not include questions about whether the young men had children.

4. The NLSY explicitly oversampled for white youths from poor families. The poor white youths in Table 2-4 are drawn from this special sample.

5. Nearly all respondents took the Armed Services Vocational Aptitude Battery (ASVAB) tests as part of the NLSY.

6. In Chapter 5 of this volume, Freya Sonenstein, Joseph Pleck, and Leighton Ku report the trends in sexual activity and contraception among adolescent males.

7. See Testa et al. 1989 and the essays by Mercer Sullivan and Elijah Anderson (Chapters 3 and 4) in this volume. Also see Olsen and Farkas 1990, which analyzes the impact of job opportunities on the rate at which women have children outside marriage or consensual unions.

8. Paul Allison (1984) describes the use of logit equations for discrete-time-event history analysis. For a discussion of multinomial logit, see Pindyck and Rubinfeld 1981.

9. The work of Sara McLanahan and her colleagues provides powerful evidence of these negative effects. See, for example, McLanahan 1985, McLanahan and Bumpass 1988, and Manski et al. 1990.

10. Mott developed these numbers in an excellent and detailed analysis of the movement of fathers using reports of mothers in the NLSY on their children born between 1979 and 1983.

11. Over 35 percent of unwed fathers in the NLSY sample reported making support payments in 1985. In contrast, only about 13 percent of never-married mothers reported to the Census Bureau that they received child support payments in 1985. The large difference may be due partly to the differences in reporting by fathers and mothers but mostly to the fact that the NLSY includes *all* payments by fathers, while the Census Bureau includes only those payments provided as part of a court order or voluntary agreement.

12. Judy Seltzer (1991) finds broadly similar patterns for formerly married fathers. Using data from the 1987–88 National Survey of Families and House-

holds, Seltzer reports that the frequency of visits declined rapidly with the number of years of separation but that the proportions of fathers making child support payments remains constant.

References

Allison, Paul. 1984. *Event History Analysis: Regression for Longitudinal Event Data*. Beverly Hills, Calif.: Sage Publications.

Anderson, Elijah. 1993. "Sex Codes and Family Life among Poor Inner-City Youths." Chapter 4 in current volume.

Clark, Samuel D., Laurie S. Zabin, and Janet B. Hardy. 1984. "Sex, Contraception, and Parenthood: Experience and Attitudes among Urban Black Young Men." *Family Planning Perspectives* 16(2): 77–82. March/April.

Dash, Leon. 1989. *When Children Want Children: The Urban Crisis of Teenage Childbearing*. New York: Morrow.

Ellwood, David, and Jonathan Crane. 1990. "Family Change among Black Americans: What Do We Know?" *Journal of Economic Perspectives* 4(4): 65–84.

Furstenberg, Frank, Jr. 1976. *Unplanned Parenthood*. New York: Free Press.

Hayes, Cheryl, ed. 1987. *Risking the Future, Adolescent Sexuality, Pregnancy, and Childbearing*. Vol. 1. Washington, D.C.: National Academy Press.

Hogan, Dennis P., Nan Marie Astone, and Evelyn M. Kitagawa. 1985. "Social and Environmental Factors Influencing Contraceptive Use among Black Adolescents." *Family Planning Perspectives* 17(4): 165–169. July/August.

Hogan, Dennis P., and Evelyn M. Kitagawa. 1985. "The Impact of Social Status, Family Structure and Neighborhood on the Fertility of Black Adolescents." *American Journal of Sociology* 90(4): 825–855.

Jencks, Christopher. 1991. "Is the American Underclass Growing?" In *The Urban Underclass*, edited by Christopher Jencks and Paul Peterson, 28–102. Washington, D.C.: Brookings Institution.

Lamb, Michael E., and Arthur Elster, eds. 1986. *Adolescent Fatherhood*. Hillsdale, N.J.: Lawrence Erlbaum.

Lerman, Robert. 1989. "Employment Opportunities of Young Men and Family Formation." *American Economic Review* May: 62–66.

McLanahan, Sara. 1985. "Family Structure and the Reproduction of Poverty." *American Journal of Sociology* 90(4): 873–901.

McLanahan, Sara, and Larry Bumpass. 1988. "Intergenerational Consequences of Family Disruption." *American Journal of Sociology* 94(1): 130–152.

Manski, Charles, et al. 1990. "Alternative Estimates of the Effect of Family Structure during Adolescence on High School Graduation." Discussion paper no. 929–90. Madison, Wis.: Institute for Research on Poverty.

Mare, Robert, and Christopher Winship. 1991. "Socioeconomic Change and the Decline of Marriage for Blacks and Whites." In *The Urban Underclass*, edited by Christopher Jencks and Paul Peterson, 175–202. Washington, D.C.: Brookings Institution.

Moore, Kristin, and Martha Burt. 1982. *Private Crisis, Public Cost*. Washington, D.C.: Urban Institute Press.

Mott, Frank. 1983. "Fertility-related Data in the 1982 National Longitudinal Surveys of Work Experience of Youth: An Evaluation of Data Quality and Some Preliminary Analytical Results." Report. Columbus: Ohio State University. December.

———. 1990. "When Is a Father Really Gone? Paternal-Child Contact in Father-Absent Homes." *Demography* 27(4): 499–517. November.

Olsen, Randall, and George Farkas. 1990. "The Effect of Economic Opportunity and Family Background on Adolescent Cohabitation and Childbearing among Low-Income Blacks." *Journal of Labor Economics* 8(3): 341–362.

Pindyck, Robert, and Daniel Rubinfeld. 1981. *Econometric Methods*. 2d ed. New York: McGraw-Hill.

Salkind, Neil J. 1983. "The Father-Child Postdivorce Relationship and Child Support." In *The Parental Child-Support Obligation*, edited by Judith Cassetty, 173–192. Lexington, Mass.: Lexington Books.

Seltzer, Judy. 1991. "Relationships between Fathers and Children Who Live Apart: The Father's Role After Separation." *Journal of Marriage and the Family* 53(1): 79–101. February.

Sullivan, Mercer. 1993. Young Fathers and Parenting in Two Inner-City Neighborhoods." Chapter 3 in current volume.

Testa, Mark, et al. 1989. "Ethnic Variation in Employment and Marriage Among Inner-City Fathers." *Annals of the American Academy of Political and Social Science*, February: 79–91.

U.S. Bureau of the Census. 1977. *Fertility of American Women: June 1976*. Current Population Reports. Series p-20, no. 308. Washington, D.C.: Government Printing Office.

———. 1984. *Child Support and Alimony: 1983*. Current Population Reports. Special Studies. Series p-23, no. 148. Washington, D.C.: Government Printing Office.

———. 1985. *Money Income and Poverty Status of Families and Persons in the United States: 1984*. (Advance data from the March 1985 Current Population Survey.) Current Population Reports. Series p-60, no. 149. Washington, D.C.: Government Printing Office.

———. 1987. *Statistical Abstract of the United States: 1986*. Washington, D.C.: Government Printing Office.

———. 1989. *Fertility of American Women: June 1988*. Current Population Reports. Series p-20, no. 436. Washington, D.C.: Government Printing Office.

Wallerstein, Judith, and Dorothy Huntington. 1983. "Bread and Roses: Nonfinancial Issues Related to Fathers' Economic Support of Their Children following Divorce." In *The Parental Child-Support Obligation*. edited by Judith Cassetty, 135–155. Lexington, Mass.: Lexington Books.

Wilson, William J. 1987. *The Truly Disadvantaged: The Inner City, the Underclass, and Public Policy*. Chicago: University of Chicago Press.

3 Young Fathers and Parenting in Two Inner-City Neighborhoods

MERCER L. SULLIVAN

The fathers of the children of unwed teenage mothers are rightly the source of serious public concern. Their children, the mothers of their children, and society at large all have a stake in these young males' development of stable careers and responsible behavior. Although young fathers have recently begun to attract the attention of policymakers and social service providers, little systematic knowledge has been gathered about their participation or nonparticipation in providing financial support or care for their children. Unlike young unwed mothers, who are more easily studied because they often must turn to social programs and public support, young unwed fathers tend to remain out of public view. They have often felt unwelcome at social programs, and like criminals from the point of view of the legal system. As a result, little has been understood about the extent to which some of them do accept some paternal responsibilities or the extent to which their failure to accept full responsibility is based on their unwillingness or their inability to do so.

The relationship between the ability and the willingness of young unwed fathers to accept paternal responsibility poses a major challenge for public policy. Early, out-of-wedlock childbearing is particularly prevalent in poor communities. Yet the relationship between community economic conditions and early, out-of-wedlock childbearing is not clear. If high

The research for this chapter was supported by grants from the Ford Foundation and the W. T. Grant Foundation. The author is indebted to Adalberto Mauras and Carl Cesvette for their help in collecting ethnographic data.

rates of poverty and welfare dependency among households headed by unwed teenage mothers are merely the result of the unwillingness of the unwed fathers to provide support, then the public policy imperative is simply to identify the fathers and enforce child support. If, on the other hand, the young fathers do not marry or provide support because they are unable to do so, public policy must also address questions of economic opportunity within poor communities.

This paper reports on ethnographic research with young fathers in poor urban neighborhoods with high rates of welfare dependency. The process by which the young men decided to accept or not to accept responsibility for their children is described, along with the ways in which some of them attempted to act responsibly.

Methods

The ethnographic methods employed in this study have some limitations but also some important advantages for examining the public policy dilemma of how to deal with young unwed fathers. The limitations derive primarily from the small size and nonrandom nature of the sample. Most of this paper is based on case studies of twenty-four individuals, ranging in age from fifteen to twenty-two at the time they were interviewed. Fourteen of these individuals lived in a low-income, primarily black neighborhood. The other ten lived in a low-income, primarily Hispanic neighborhood.

The individuals studied were recruited through community-based networks of friendship and acquaintance. The recruitment of the samples began among contacts established during a prior study of employment and crime in the careers of inner-city teenagers (Sullivan 1983, 1989b). Some of the respondents from that study were fathers. We began by recontacting them; they then introduced us to friends and neighbors who also had fathered children. Because in our original study we had deliberately sought out youths who were criminally involved, we were concerned at the beginning of this study that our sample would be too heavily weighted towards those who were criminally involved. In order to correct for this, we specifically sought out some young fathers who were not heavily involved in drugs or crime. We also consciously attempted to include in our samples a mix of both more and less supportive young fathers. Consequently, sample recruitment for this study was guided by intentional sampling of qualitative types rather than by randomized selection procedures. Because of these sampling characteristics, statistical generalizations are not appropriate or attempted here, although some distributions are noted for purely descriptive purposes.

These same sample characteristics, however, are very helpful for addressing questions of the relationships between individual responsibility and community-specific structures of opportunity. The in-depth data provided by the case study method allow for an examination of behavior and attitudes in some detail. This approach can reveal more complexity of behavior and attitudes than is possible with the more cut-and-dried results from broader sample surveys or aggregated official records. Sample recruitment through community-based networks, although it obviates the possibility of analytic techniques associated with random sampling, also confers some benefits. The first difficulty in studying teenage fathers, or, indeed, inner-city males generally, is locating them. The young men to be described here were not chosen from a self-selected population of program users or on the basis of participation in any official institution, such as the schools, the court system, or the welfare system. Some participated in each of these institutions at various times, some did not, and several moved in and out of such participation over time.

One of the most important advantages of a community-based sample of young fathers is directly related to the problem of describing individual moral choices in the context of the structures of opportunities within disadvantaged communities. Ethnographic methods describe individuals in the context of naturally existing communities. Individual choices are described with reference to the norms of a specific community. Individual behavior is described as it emerges through interaction with other members of the community. This is the approach we employed to describe how some young men decided whether to acknowledge paternity, and how they conceived and enacted the rights and duties of paternity when they did. The recognition of paternity is described as both an individual and a social process. Our data include not merely the self-reports of these young men but also our observations of their interactions with the mothers of their children and with other members of their families and communities. All of the young men were contacted several times over a period of months, or, in some cases, years.

All the members of these communities recognize the difficulties that most of them face in finding jobs and decent housing and the particularly severe labor market difficulties of young people. Yet they also recognize the difference between responsible and irresponsible behavior in confronting these commonly shared difficulties. Childbearing by teenagers who are poorly equipped to set up and support independent households is common enough in these neighborhoods that informal support systems have been developed. These "folk" systems (Stack 1974) for providing child care and child support operate, of necessity, within the parameters of the legal, educational, employment, and welfare systems of the wider society, but these societal institutions do not completely determine processes within a particular community. One of the aims of our analysis is to describe the interaction of community-based processes with the constraints and resources provided by the institutions of the wider society.

The ethnographic research reported here was carried out over a period of about two years with a focus specifically on young fathers (Sullivan 1985).[1] Research in these neighborhoods began five years before that, however, in an extensive study of relationships between crime, employment, and schooling involvements in the careers of young males (Sullivan 1983; 1989b). These career patterns will be shown to be closely tied to decisions about acknowledging paternity and attempting to carry out paternal responsibilities.

The most extensive data reported here were collected in the neighborhood that we refer to as Projectville,[2] a low-income, predominantly black neighborhood in Brooklyn in which rates of childbearing by unmarried teenagers are among the highest in New York City. Examining data from this neighborhood, we describe first the social process by which young males decide to acknowledge paternity and then the patterns of support and care for their children. We compare different cases of support and nonsupport and of varying patterns of support to show a range of variation within the neighborhood, and identify community norms in the reported reactions of others to various types of behavior by young fathers.

We then compare community patterns in Projectville to patterns in a low-income Puerto Rican neighborhood, La Barriada, exploring similarities and differences between these communities in the recognition of paternity and in the provision of care and support for the children of young males. These comparisons are intended to highlight differences in community norms and in ways of dealing with the constraints and resources provided by institutions of the wider society.

Finally, we discuss implications of our findings for public policy, and we examine the ways in which young fathers take or do not take responsibility for their offspring in light of their own choices, the norms of their communities, and the opportunities available to them in those communities.

Projectville

Census statistics show that Projectville is one of the poorest neighborhoods in New York City. In 1980 over 60 percent of the households were classified as female-headed and over half received some form of public assistance. These statistics, however, conceal as much as they reveal about the dynamics of family composition and the relationship between welfare and work. Many households do contain a working adult male.

Many other families break up and re-form over time. In addition, although the percentage of households receiving public assistance at any one time is high, there is considerable movement on and off welfare rolls.

Four of fourteen youths for whom we have developed extensive life histories grew up in two-parent households in which their fathers had stable work histories. Two of these sets of parents were legally married. Two other sets of parents had been together in common-law marriages for over twenty years. Several other youths had lived with their fathers when they were young and had seen their parents' relationships break up when they were small children. Several of those who had lived most of their lives in households headed by their mothers had nevertheless maintained regular relationships with their fathers. They saw their fathers regularly and were accustomed to receiving some money when they did see them.

Most of these households had been supported by public assistance at some point when the young men were growing up. By the time they reached their late teens, however, most of their mothers were not on public assistance. As their children had gotten older, the women had found jobs, most often as home care attendants. Some families in Projectville are chronically dependent on public support, but welfare dependency tends to be concentrated at certain points in the domestic cycle, when young children are present in the household. The high rate of public assistance in the neighborhood reflects the fact that this is a young population, with a median age of about twenty years.

Most adults in Projectville have worked, although not steadily. Many of the marital breakups mentioned above, for example, were precipitated by the male's loss of employment. Access to employment is difficult for most Projectville residents, but particularly so for teenagers. In our earlier study of the relationship between crime and employment among young males in this neighborhood (Sullivan 1983, 1989b), we found that government-subsidized employment programs accounted for more than half of their employment experiences before they reached the age of eighteen. During their late teens, they still experienced considerable labor market difficulties, but the situation began to improve as some of them managed to acquire high school diplomas and to move into clerical and service sector jobs.

The struggle for education among these youths is intense, characterized by recurrent difficulties but also by frequent renewal of efforts. Most attend school sporadically at some point in their mid-teens and few earn regular high school diplomas. Many return to school, however, often in alternative programs, and manage to earn General Equivalency Diplomas by their late teens. Those who do so usually continue to seek additional job training or begin to attend community colleges. During the mid-teens, when many are attending school sporadically and have little access to employment, some become involved in street crime. These street crime activities taper off in the late teens for many, however, as the costs of crime mount and job opportunities increase.

The family backgrounds and modal career patterns of young men from Projectville establish the context in which many of them confront paternity. Whether or not they grew up in households headed by a married, adult couple and supported by stable employment, none of these youths grew up in an environment in which stable family and employment patterns were the norm. Instead they had all seen families shift and re-form and households with shifting and mixed sources of support from public assistance, wages, and, in some cases, the underground economy. Another important aspect of household economies in Projectville is the extensive reliance on sharing, as described by Stack (1974). Networks of extended kin are the locus for most of this sharing. Household items, money, and children move frequently from place to place, as one relative runs short this week, and another the next week.

When these young men discovered that they had impregnated someone, their responses to the situation were powerfully influenced by these networks of extended kin and by their current involvements in schooling and the labor market, legal or illegal. Some acknowledged and others refused to acknowledge paternity. Patterns of child support varied widely.

Acknowledgment of Paternity

Most of the youths we interviewed directly acknowledged paternity, both within their own communities and to researchers in the course of consenting to be interviewed. This sampling bias should not be taken to imply that there is no denial or neglect of paternity going on among young men in Projectville. In fact, all of those we interviewed reported that they knew of many such cases. Their accounts of their own experiences or those of others in the neighborhood, however, made clear that the denial or acknowledgement of paternity was part of a social process and not simply an individual decision rooted in the psychology and morals of each individual.

The case material below illustrates several aspects of the social process of the recognition of paternity in Projectville. "Folk" rather than legal norms dominated this process (Stack 1974). Most of the crucial negotiations determining the recognition of paternity and associated rights and duties occurred within community-based networks. Legal recognition of paternity, through marriage and/or the signing of the birth certificate, occurred only as the culmination of these community-based processes.

The social negotiation of the recognition of paternity began with the assessment by the pregnant female and her male sex partner of the actual probability that he had been the one who had impregnated her. Those we interviewed described cases in their own and others' experience in which there was legitimate doubt. Two of the males we interviewed described cases in which females had first told them that they had made them pregnant and then had retracted those claims. Others admitted that they had had casual sexual encounters in which they might have impregnated their partners and never known because there had been little or no subsequent contact.

In cases where there had been an ongoing relationship, however, the absolute denial of paternity within the neighborhood might not be possible, as expressed in the following statement from an interview:

TOM: It's hard to hide. People know things about you, how long you been with her, or who she's been with or not. Plus, if it looks like you and she says it's yours, then nobody's going to believe it isn't yours.

Although most of those we interviewed knew of cases of doubt or disagreement over the basic facts of paternity, only one reported having undergone a blood test. In this case, he was the one who insisted on the procedure. He shared his doubts about paternity with his older sister, who explained blood tests to him and advised him to get one. He did so, even though it caused a fight with the mother of his child. Only after the test indicated his paternity did he fully acknowledge the child and sign the birth certificate. At this point, the social process of establishing paternity had begun to involve the young father's own kin, an important aspect of the process in many other cases as well.

In cases where both the young parents are agreed on the facts of paternity, and this basic knowledge is also shared in other parts of the community, the next step in the social process of establishing paternity concerns the father's response to the situation. He must decide whether he wants to acknowledge paternity publicly, in which case he will have to negotiate a set of associated rights and duties. Those we interviewed all knew of cases in which the facts of paternity were acknowledged but the father had abdicated his responsibilities, as in the following example:

STAN: He got five kids, but he only claim one. That's the first one. He got to claim that one because he signed the birth certificate. After that, he learned better and he didn't sign no more.

The young men we interviewed were very clear in their judgment of community norms towards this sort of behavior. They referred to neglect of paternal responsibilities as "stepping off." This phrase is also used to refer to backing down from a physical confrontation with another male or, more generally, to backing down from any challenge that a person cannot handle. Such behavior is acknowledged to be fairly common but is also widely condemned within the adolescent male peer group and throughout the community. The following examples illustrate these norms:

INTERVIEWER: Do you know guys who make babies and don't care?

HAROLD: Yeah, I know quite a few who say, "I got a daughter who lives over here and a son who lives over there," and the way they say it, it seems like they don't care. When you ask them about it, they may say, "Well, I don't know how long I'm going to live, so I'm looking to have as many as I can while I'm able to."

INTERVIEWER: Do they seem proud when they say it?

HAROLD: Let's put it this way. They don't get no respect from me on that. I can understand if it happens, but it ain't nothing to brag about.

INTERVIEWER: Have you known guys who make babies and don't take care of them?

TOM: Yeah, I seen it, but I don't like it. I've seen what happens on both sides of that situation. There's the girl. She's got nobody to take care of her or the baby. And the guy too. He loses his self-respect. Not only that but everyone else loses respect for him too. Sometimes it makes him go out and start ripping everybody off. I mean, even if he was doing that before, it makes him worse, it makes him get real bad and nasty. If one of my friends did that, I wouldn't talk to him any more.

Despite the disrespect associated with the neglect of paternal responsibilities, we have found little evidence of a willingness to involve the courts either in adjudicating paternity or in attempting to enforce paternal obligations, at least for young fathers in this community. The only two cases of court-ordered child support we documented involved older men, the fathers of the young men we interviewed. Tom's father had paid child support for years. Stan's father used to pay support but stopped after his mother had applied legal pressure. These court orders, however, had been entered against employed, adult males who had been married for several years prior to marital disruption and cessation of support.

Only one of those we interviewed even knew of a case in which a peer had encountered court-ordered child enforcement. Stan reported that a close friend of his had committed suicide when faced with a child support order. Harold told of a case in which the courts had been involved, but for the purpose of keeping a young father away from his child and his child's mother:

HAROLD: He's twenty, and his daughter's about two now. In the beginning his girl's mother didn't mind for him to see the baby, but when she started realizing he wasn't doing anything for the baby, she took him to court, and I don't know exactly what happened when they were in court, but what it led up to was that either he took care of the baby or he stay away from the baby and right now he has no visitation rights. he can't see the baby, be around the baby, you know. I don't know if he couldn't bother to take care of it or he really wasn't ready for it. See, he didn't have a job, and maybe he didn't want to, you know, put his foot in his mouth and say he was gonna do something even though he couldn't do it. Right now I'm quite sure he's regretting it, and I know he wants to see the baby. But the girl and her mother moved to Queens, and right now she's staying with some other guy, so . . .

Others also mentioned cases in which young fathers they knew had lost rights to see their children, although as a result of folk rather than legal processes. Zap told of a dispute that had occurred downstairs in his building just before an interview:

ZAP: I know this one guy name Rich and he got a baby by this girl. He don't take care of the baby right. This other guy, you know, he is taking care of the baby, and he be looking out. Rich came back, and I saw their hands up in the hallway: "That's my baby." "I ain't going for it," and all of that. Meantime, Rich, you know, he probably just wanted to have sex with her, that's all.

As this last example indicates, whether or not the courts have been involved, a young father who does not demonstrate some willingness to provide support or care for his child risks losing his rights to see the child or the mother. Another male is as likely as the courts to block his access.

These examples indicate the considerable variation—even within this small sample—in the extent to which different individuals acknowledge paternity and provide support for their children. While there is much bragging about sexual exploits within peer groups, there is much more ambivalence when it comes to talking about absent fatherhood. Some individuals may refer to unsupported children as proof of their virility, but their peers are not likely to respect these claims. Further, these young men do not form and validate all their attitudes only with peer groups. Their own families of origin are also crucial reference groups. When they interact with their mothers and sisters, their expressed attitudes about paternal obligations are much less likely to be flippant. Further, in individual interviews, many of them revealed considerable anger at having grown up without the presence and support of their own fathers.

Patterns of Support

Most of our sample members had in fact demonstrated their intentions to provide some child care and support. Many had been with the mothers at the hospital at the time of birth and most, although not all, had signed the birth certificates. Yet almost none of them were married to or living with the mothers of their children at the time of the interviews.

The young men had negotiated a set of rights and responsibilities before the birth took place. These negotiations usually included not only the young parents but also their own parents. In most cases agreements were reached before the birth of the child concerning the contributions the father would make to the support and care of the child. These arrangements were often fragile, however, and in some cases turned out to be unstable, with the fathers "stepping off" after a failed attempt to take responsibility.

In several cases arrangements for the support and care of the child began during the pregnancy with an explicit decision not to seek an abortion. The young father and his kin, usually his mother, were involved in the decision to have the child in the first place. If both members of the young couple wanted to have the child, the two families tried to work out arrangements together that would provide for the child's care and support. The young father was expected to seek employment and make financial contributions. He was also expected to provide some child care, usually with the assistance of his own kin.

In this neighborhood early marriage and coresidence were usually not considered possible or advisable by either of the families. As Stack (1974) also found, part of this reluctance to encourage early marriage stemmed from the fact that cooperative networks of female kin were not anxious to lose members to males of uncertain employability. Further, there was considerable support for helping either or both of the young parents continue in school. If either young parent wished to stay in school, it was considered more practical to delay marriage and formation of an independent household. If the father continued with his schooling, however, he was still expected to seek part-time employment.

These general features of planning for child support and child care—absence of marriage and coresidence; support for continued education; and expectations of some contribution of money and child care from the young father and his kin—worked out in practice in a wide variety of ways. Everyone recognized the difficulty of finding employment and the instability of available jobs. If the relationship between the young parents had been of short duration and the young father could not find work, he risked losing access to his child. Those we interviewed were quite clear that inability to find work was a frequent cause of "stepping off":

OLLIE: Some of them, they say they just stepped off. In order not to step off, you got to have a job, got to get you a job. 'Cause, if you don't get a job, and you're not supporting the baby, you ain't see the baby. You going to want to buy the baby Pampers, food, clothes, or whatever. You ain't got the money. You know the baby's mother and the baby's mother's mother, I know they're going to have money to kick out for the baby, and if you ain't got no money, you got to step off.

ZAP: Sometimes a guy got a nice job, you know, he don't mind trying, but if he ain't got no job, maybe he's afraid to try.

If the relationship between the young couple was more substantial, not being able to find a job might more easily be forgiven by the young mother and her family, especially if the young father demonstrated his commitment in other ways, such as providing regular child care, attempting to invest in education and training in order to be better able to provide support in the future, and staying clear of heavy drug use and incarceration.

Even among our small sample, a wide variety of arrangements for child care and child support was apparent. We followed some of these young men for a long enough period of time to see these arrangements for child care and support shift according to shifting involvements in school, in employment, in the welfare system, and, for some, in crime and incarceration.

Only two of the Projectville respondents both married the mothers of their children and established a common residence. In one case the mother and child received Aid to Families with Dependent Children (AFDC) payments steadily. The father was known to AFDC officials and held a series of short-term jobs. When he worked on the books, his contributions were deducted from AFDC payments. When he worked off the books, his contributions all provided extra family income. In a second case the mother and child enrolled very briefly for AFDC, until the father found steady employment and became able to support them.

In another case the young parents established a common residence for a period of about six months, although they did not get married. The father supported them through employment at a dry cleaners. Then he lost and found work several times over the next two years. The couple lost their apartment twice while the father was out of work, and the mother moved back in with her relatives each time. She did not begin to receive public assistance until the child was a year old and the father had been out of work for several months. Subsequently, he made contributions from short-term stints of off-the-books employment.

Three of the young fathers continued in school for a time after their children were born. Two of these young men had no involvement in criminal activities and found employment sporadically. One found two separate part-time jobs in fast-food restaurants and contributed about twenty-five dollars a week when he was working. His child did not receive public assistance. A second continued in school for a short time and finished his high school diploma. He then found a job in a department store and made contributions, until he was laid off. The mother of his child continued in school in a special program for young mothers, and received public assistance for herself and the child. The father had signed the birth certificate, but his occasional contributions from short-term, off-the-books jobs were not known to welfare officials. A third continued in school while the mother of his child left school and worked full-time. Their child did not receive public assistance. The young father was a part-time dealer of marijuana and made regular small contributions from his sales.

Some of the young mothers also continued with their education. They enrolled in a special program in an alternative high school with services for young mothers. In one case the young father was unemployed and not in school and provided child care while the mother attended school.

In all these cases the fathers and their families provided regular child care. The young parents still resided primarily with their own parents, but the babies moved frequently back and forth between the two households. The young fathers from Projectville reported considerable participation in direct child care. When their children were at their homes, their parents expected them to provide care. When they visited the homes of the mothers of their children, they were also frequently expected to provide direct care.

Involvement in drug use, drug sales, and other criminal activities was more prominent in the careers of some of the respondents. In one case the young father was in jail when he learned of the pregnancy. He continued to sell drugs for the first year of his child's life but also worked occasionally and made regular contributions from either wages or drug sales. He finished school and became more responsible. He joined a military reserve unit and decreased his involvement in street life.

In other cases involvement in crime and/or drug use interrupted initial attempts to provide child care and support. One young father was incarcerated when his child was only a few months old. He had known the mother only a short time and appeared unlikely to resume his initial commitments. One of the married, coresident fathers mentioned above became involved in using "crack" after two years of marriage and abandoned his family. Another father, who had been providing regular child care and irregular financial support, disappeared after becoming involved in a dispute over stolen drugs.

These case studies, from a small sample, reveal a wide variety of strategies for providing child care and support. Support came from various and shifting combinations of public assistance, employment, and, in some cases, crime. Survival strategies also shifted frequently in response to opportunities or crises. Some individuals were more involved in dishonest activities than others, but even those who tried to find stable employment were not easily able to do so. In an earlier study not focused specifically on young fathers (Sullivan 1983, 1989b), we also documented shifting patterns of involvement in work, school, and the underground economy. We observed that many became involved in illegal activities at some point in their teens but tended to move out of such involvements as they got older, achieved some kind of education and training, and found employment more easily. The young fathers in this study were still involved in these career processes and their provision of child care and support at any given time was closely tied to the rest of their career development.

La Barriada

La Barriada is a predominantly Puerto Rican neighborhood of Brooklyn with income levels and rates of welfare dependency generally similar to those in Projectville. Although the larger neighborhood is more economically and ethnically heterogeneous than Projectville, over half the households in the part of La Barriada that we studied were officially headed by females receiving AFDC. This neighborhood also had a young population, with a median age of about twenty.

The two neighborhoods displayed some important similarities and differences in the career patterns of young men. The relationships between criminal activity and employment were similar: many teenage boys had some involvement in crime but then moved on into legitimate jobs starting in their late teens. Their paths into the labor market differed, however. Very few young men finished high school in La Barriada, and, when they did find jobs, they tended to find unskilled manufacturing jobs that are less dependent on educational credentials. In comparison with Projectville, young men from La Barriada tended to stay in school for less time and to enter the labor market somewhat earlier, but fewer of them were able to use education to attain the more desirable jobs that some Projectville residents eventually managed to find. Both these differences in labor market patterns as well as differences in cultural norms relating to family and household formation affected local patterns of dealing with early childbearing.

As in Projectville, we found a range of situations and behaviors among the young fathers from La Barriada. We contacted primarily those who had been making some attempts at support, but all of them knew peers who had abandoned their children. There was no indication of respect for those who fathered children and did not attempt to support them. There was considerable variation in the levels of support the fathers provided. The strength of the relationship between the young parents, the ability of the father to find employment, and the destructive involvement of some fathers in crime and/or drug use all affected the contributions of the young father to child care and support.

The families in La Barriada differed from those in Projectville in their patterns of marriage and coresidence and in community support for continued education for young parents. More marriage and coresidence took place among the young couples in La Barriada, despite the similar difficulties encountered by the young fathers in finding stable employment that would allow them to support their new families. Five of ten young fathers married the mothers of their children. Three of the unmarried fathers were living with their children and the mothers. A further difference is that several of the young couples were living together in the residence of the father's family, a pattern that was rare in Projectville.

These differences in patterns of marriage and coresidence appear to be related to cultural norms with respect to gender and generation roles. A father who acknowledges paternity in La Barriada is expected to marry the mother of his child. Young mothers are also under tremendous pressure to move out of their parents' households. These patterns appear to be related to a high valuation of a daughter's virginity and consequent family strain if she becomes pregnant. Unlike in Projectville many of the young mothers in La Barriada became pregnant as a result of running away from home. Unmarried daughters who became pregnant were uncomfortable remaining at home, particularly if their father was present, since his honor had been severely compromised by his daughter's pregnancy. The young father's family, however, received confirmation of his virility and was not disgraced in this way. As a result, the young couples who did try to stay together and could not find their own housing were more likely to move into the father's household.

Yet these newly formed households were extremely fragile, due to many of the same structural influences affecting Projectville. The labor market difficulties faced by the young men were formidable, and some were involved in criminal activities that put them at risk of incarceration.

The effects of the welfare system in making jobless men marginal to the household were also similar in both neighborhoods. Despite the stronger cultural emphasis on marriage and coresidence, men in La Barriada often became unemployed or were employed at such low-level or unstable jobs that their financial support for the family was secondary to that provided by AFDC. Under these circumstances, they could not fulfill the bread-winner role validating their masculine identity and authority. This situation led to marital strife and frequently to their separation from the household. The fragility of marital ties was apparent among the parents of the young fathers. Seven out of ten of the young fathers grew up partially or entirely in female-headed households. All of their parents had been married, but the marriages had been disrupted, often by the men's employment problems.

Another difference between the neighborhoods which appears to be rooted in cultural norms is that the young fathers from La Barriada reported less participation in direct child care than the young fathers from Projectville. Child care was more likely to be defined as exclusively a female responsibility in La Barriada. Thus, even though the La Barriada fathers were more likely to be married and living with their children, they were less likely to provide direct child care.

Despite broad similarities in the labor market difficulties of young men from Projectville and La Barriada, their somewhat different labor market paths affected community expectations for young fathers. None of the young fathers from La Barriada considered staying in school in order to be able to increase support for their children later on. If they wished to acknowledge paternity and provide support, they were expected to forget about school and try to find work immediately. In fact, some of them appeared to be more successful in finding work than their counterparts in Projectville, as low-level jobs are somewhat more plentiful in their neighborhood. These jobs are generally off the books and do not last very long, however, and thus do not allow them to provide steady support. As a result, the relationships among work, welfare, and, in some cases, crime as sources of household income are similar to the patterns in Projectville. There is considerable movement on and off AFDC, as males find and lose work. Some households also combine short-term, off-the-books wages with AFDC support for a period of time. Some fathers receive criminal income, which they contribute to family support for a period of time, although these fathers are also the most likely to be incarcerated and thus to become unable to provide any support.

Young Fathers and Community-based Support Systems: A Summary

The case material just presented adds to our knowledge of the roles actually played by young fathers of the children of teenage mothers. Two aspects of these roles deserve particular attention. The first is the developmental nature of these young males' abilities to provide care and support for their children. The second is the range of variation among communities in the expectations of what young fathers should contribute and how they should share responsibilities with others.

Developmental Factors

Most young fathers in this study assumed some but not all of the full set of paternal responsibilities. They were not yet capable of assuming full responsibilities because of the ongoing tasks of their own development. These tasks included not only physical and psychological maturation, but social maturation through the completion of schooling and a difficult period of entry into the labor market. For many young males from the inner cities, labor market entry is a protracted and painful process. Some may never establish stable employment. Others may try and fail repeatedly for several years between the completion of formal schooling and eventual success. During this period some become involved in drug abuse and crime.

Yet it is a mistake to look at a particular youth at a given moment and say that he is a "dropout," a nonparticipant in the labor market, or a "criminal," and is likely to remain in these categories indefinitely. Available statistics indicate that many will come through these difficulties. Arrest rates, for example, peak during the teen years and decline sharply in the early twenties. Likewise, unemployment rates, even within inner-city neighborhoods, are much higher for teens than for older people. Many of these youths will earn a General Equivalency Diploma after a period of interrupted education. Despite repeated attempts by social scientists, no one has ever found an accurate method of predicting which youths will and will not survive the stresses of inner-city adolescence. Opportunities and choices along the way make differences that are not predictable. Early parenting itself is a positive opportunity for some and, for others, an additional arena for failure.

Community Factors

The responsibilities of young fathers were defined differently in the two communities. In La Barriada there was considerable pressure for young fathers to marry, establish coresidence, and find full-time employment, but little support for their continuing to invest in education and training. They were not necessarily expected to provide hands-on child care. In Projectville young fathers were not expected to marry and establish co-residence right away. They were expected to try to find work, but they were also given considerable support if they tried to invest in education and training. The combination of ongoing schooling and part-time work was frequently considered ideal. They provided a great deal of direct child care.

Additional data from a third community, a white working-class neighborhood, suggest other community-based patterns. In that neighborhood, early pregnancy frequently precipitates marriage. The young father then finds a desirable blue-collar job through a family connection to a business or a labor union. Such a job allows him to support his family as a primary wage earner and makes it possible for the young family to find an apartment and establish an independent household. This seems to be a traditional pattern in this community, but one that is disappearing along with the unionized, blue-collar jobs that give this community and its families a stability unknown to most residents of Projectville and La Barriada. Some of the younger males are becoming involved in drugs and crime to a greater extent and this irresponsibility extends to their children. Some of them are "stepping off" also, and allowing their children to become AFDC recipients.

Policy Implications

Other studies have pointed to the existence of informal support systems but disagreed about the implications of these systems for policies intended to increase child support (Rivara, Sweeney, and Henderson 1986; Danziger 1988). Stack and Semmel (1973) claimed that child support enforcement could disrupt informal support systems and actually be to the detriment of poor children. Haskins and his colleagues (1985) disputed this inference and documented continuing participation in informal support systems by men under child support orders instituted under the provisions of Title IV-D of the Social Services Amendments of 1974. No existing studies, including this one, offer any conclusive evidence of the actual effects of Title IV-D enforcement activities on informal support systems. Such studies would be difficult or impossible to conduct, given the difficulty of obtaining reliable statistical data on deviant activities such as concealing paternity or withholding child support.

Whatever the effect of enforcement actions on young fathers' participation in informal support systems, the current child support enforcement system clearly fails to recognize or take advantage of the positive aspects of the developmental and community-specific factors described here. Young fathers are treated punitively, if they are sought out at all. More frequently, they are simply neglected. The child support enforcement system, as it now exists, tends to recognize only cash payments as child support. The internal workings of the system also frequently relegate young, poor fathers to the lowest priority for attention (Rivera-Casale, Klerman, and Manela 1984). In New York City, for example, young fathers who are themselves AFDC recipients, as were several of those we studied, are automatically excluded from enforcement proceedings (Kohn 1986). None of the young fathers in our study had ever been involved in an enforcement action. Yet several of these fathers were making occasional cash contributions, and some were continuing to invest in their own education and training, to the possible long-term benefit of the child. These positive activities were not effectively linked to the official establishment of paternity.

The current child support enforcement system is narrow, punitive, and frequently ineffective, particularly in its treatment of young fathers. The current exclusive focus on securing immediate monetary contributions offers little incentive to young fathers to acknowledge paternity, or to young mothers to cooperate with official attempts to identify fathers. Our research points up some of the particular disincentives to marriage and official paternity for young fathers. Young males have especially severe labor market difficulties and are still at an age when schooling may contribute more than work experience to their long-term ability to support themselves and their children. Most of their actual work experience consists of sporadic off-the-books jobs that allow them to make cash contributions which cannot be traced and deducted from AFDC benefits.

Yet, official paternity is indisputably to the long-term advantage of the child (Wattenberg 1987; Chapter 10 in this volume). Even if the father never achieves stable employment and/or dies at an early age, official paternity can provide his children access to a wide range of benefits from the military, Social Security, or inheritance (Everett 1985). These long-term benefits are currently in conflict with the short-term advantages of concealing paternity for young fathers like those we have studied. With the passage of time the difficulties of establishing official paternity increase. The father's chances for obtaining on-the-books employment become more favorable, increasing the likelihood that his contributions will be deducted. Also, the relationship between the young parents may deteriorate, decreasing the father's willingness to contribute.

The structure of the current child support enforcement system interacts with the developmental trajectory of youthful career patterns in unfavorable ways. The exclusive emphasis on securing immediate monetary contributions is ineffective in the short run and deleterious in the long run because it provides disincentives to establishing official paternity. Research shows that, even within inner-city neighborhoods, employment prospects increase as young men age past their teens (Sullivan 1989b; Sviridoff with McElroy 1984; Williams and Kornblum 1985). Yet the fragile commitments between young parents often do not last. The emotional commitments of young fathers are likely to be strongest at exactly the time that the structural incentives to acknowledge paternity officially are weakest.

These contradictions in the operation of current policies suggest that the most productive way to encourage the establishment of official paternity for young fathers may be to seek nonpunitive measures that build upon the strengths of informal, community-based support systems rather than to ignore or possibly even undercut such systems. A number of specific suggestions are offered below.

Paternity Benefits

Many of the benefits conveyed by official paternity pose no threat to anyone. Many young fathers we studied had little awareness of the provisions of the Social Security System and the military that could benefit their children. Their decisions to acknowledge paternity officially or not were often based on sentiment rather than on practical information about the consequences of the choice they were making. Information on these benefits could be disseminated through schools, the mass media, and youth agencies.

Employment, Education, and Training

A growing body of research indicates that the perception of "life options" (Dryfoos 1988), or the lack of options, strongly influences the decisions that young people make concerning fertility control and parenting responsibility. The data presented here suggest that many young fathers want to take long-term responsibility for their children but are hampered by their lack of educational and employment opportunities. The current child support enforcement system allows no mechanism for recognizing these aspirations. Indeed, to the extent that the current system demands immediate cash contributions, it may actually discourage continued investment in education and training by forcing young fathers to leave school and seek work.

It makes much more sense in the long run for child support agencies to encourage young fathers to invest in education and training. Enrollment in employment and training programs or continued education could be recognized by the child support enforcement systems as a valid commitment to paternal responsibility, as long as such a commitment is accompanied by other demonstrations of paternal responsibility, such as providing child care and other noncash resources. Access to employment, training, and education should be facilitated for those young fathers who are motivated to take advantage of such opportunities and who are otherwise behaving responsibly toward their children. Making such resources available would reverse the current structure of incentives by encouraging the official acknowledgement of paternity. The recent experiments along these lines in Marion County, Indiana, and elsewhere should be watched carefully and replicated (see Pirog-Good, Chapter 12 in this volume).

Child Care Credits

Even with expanded employment and training resources the labor market problems of inner-city youths are unlikely to disappear in the near future. In the meantime many young men, often with the help of their own kin, are providing substantial child care for their children. They should be given credit for child care by the child support enforcement system. This is one resource they can provide, whether or not they are able to find employment. Giving them such credit might encourage official acknowledgement of paternity. Child support orders for young fathers could include agreements to provide child care.

Expanded Disregards of Paternal Contributions to AFDC Households

Since 1984, the first fifty dollars of a father's contributions are not deducted from the AFDC budget, although food stamps and other related benefits are affected (Everett 1985). This policy change is a small step in the right direction. The current situation, in which fathers without officially established paternity and those who work off the books can make contributions that increase AFDC children's welfare, while those with official paternity and on-the-books jobs cannot, creates a set of perverse incentives. Since AFDC budgets are below the official poverty level, it would make sense ultimately to allow paternal contributions in amounts up to the difference between the AFDC budget and the poverty level. As a more preliminary measure, an experimental program could be tried in which an expanded disregard could be tried in one area. Rates of paternity acknowledgement could then be measured against a closely matched area.

Sensitivity to Local Family and Labor Market Patterns

Our research points to some significant differences in community values and expectations concerning the proper behavior of young fathers and the roles they are expected to play in community-based support systems for young mothers. The current child support enforcement system ignores these differences and is blind to the different types of contributions that young fathers do or could make. Child support orders should be designed to recognize these differences and to build upon, rather than undercut, community-based support systems. For example, efforts to encourage and give credit for continued education and child care would probably be better received in a community like Projectville, and efforts to encourage immediate employment would be better received in La Barriada, given the existing family and career patterns in these neighborhoods. Local child support officials could seek meetings with community leaders to explore ways in which the goals of the child support system could be communicated to local residents and applied most effectively in the context of the cultural norms and political and social organization of the community.

Conclusion

Not all young fathers are responsible, and many are too young, psychologically and socially, to be capable of undertaking full paternal responsibilities. Yet most are capable of making some contribution. At present these partial contributions are recognized and supported at the community level much more effectively than at the level of official institutions. Public policy needs to develop ways to recognize and reward positive contributions other than immediate financial support.

Notes

1. A later report on this research can be found in Sullivan 1989a, which also includes data on a working-class white neighborhood.

2. All names of individuals and neighborhoods are pseudonymous, honoring pledges of confidentiality made to respondents.

References

Danziger, Sandra. 1988. "Child Support Among Young Families: Adolescent Mothers, Paternity Adjudication, and Father Involvement." In *Child Support Services for Young Families: Current Issues and Future Directions,* edited by

Carolyn Kastner et al., 41–56. Washington, D.C.: Center for the Support of Children and Children's Defense Fund.

Dryfoos, Joy. 1988. *Putting the Boys in the Picture*. Santa Cruz, Calif.: Network Publications.

Everett, Joyce E. 1985. "An Examination of Child Support Enforcement Issues." In *Services to Young Families: Program Review and Policy Recommendations*, edited by Henriette McAdoo and T. M. Jim Parnham, 75–112. Washington, D.C.: American Public Welfare Association.

Haskins, Ron, et al. 1985. "Estimates of National Child Support Collections Potential and Income Security of Female-Headed Families." Final report to the Office of Child Support Administration, Social Security Administration. Bush Institute for Child and Family Policy. Frank Porter Graham Child Development Center. Chapel Hill: University of North Carolina.

Kohn, Margaret. 1986. Personal communication from Irwin Brooks, Deputy Administrator, Office of Income Administration, New York City Human Resources Administration.

Rivara, Frederick P., Patrick J. Sweeney, and Brady F. Henderson. 1986. "Black Teenage Fathers: What Happens When the Child Is Born?" *Pediatrics* 78(1): 151–158.

Rivera-Casale, Cecilia, Lorraine V. Klerman, and Roger Manela. 1984. "The Relevance of Child-Support Enforcement to School-Age Parents." *Child Welfare* 63(6): 521–532.

Stack, Carol B. 1974. *All Our Kin: Strategies for Survival in a Black Community*. New York: Harper & Row.

Stack, Carol B., and Herbert Semmel. 1973. "The Concept of Family in the Poor Black Community." Studies in Public Welfare. Paper no. 12, pt. 2. Washington, D.C.: Government Printing Office.

Sullivan, Mercer L. 1983. "Youth Crime: New York's Two Varieties." *New York Affairs* 8(1): 31–48. Urban Research Center, New York University.

———. 1985. "Teen Fathers in the Inner City." A report to the Ford Foundation. New York: Vera Institute of Justice

———. 1989a. "Absent Fathers in the Inner City." *Annals of the American Academy of Political and Social Science* 501: 48–58.

———. 1989b. *Getting Paid: Youth Crime and Work in the Inner City*. Ithaca, N.Y.: Cornell University Press.

Sviridoff, Michele, with Jerome E. McElroy. 1984. "Employment and Crime: A Summary Report." A report to the National Institute of Justice. New York: Vera Institute of Justice.

Wattenberg, Esther. 1987. "Establishing Paternity for Nonmarital Children." *Public Welfare* 45(3): 9–13.

Williams, Terry, and William Kornblum. 1985. *Growing Up Poor*. Lexington, Mass.: Lexington Books, D. C. Heath.

4   Sex Codes and Family Life among Poor Inner-City Youths

ELIJAH ANDERSON

Sexual relations and out-of-wedlock pregnancy among poor black inner-city adolescents is a major social problem, yet we know little and understand less about these phenomena. To be sure, many studies deal in whole or in part with the subject, and they offer valuable insights into the dynamic of sexual interaction between youths in the ghetto and other socioeconomically circumscribed settings (Rainwater 1960; Rainwater 1966, 172–216; Rainwater 1969, 129–140; Rainwater 1970; Liebow 1967; Hannerz 1969; Furstenberg 1976; Hammond and Ladner 1969, 41–51; Green 1941, 343–348; Arensberg 1937; Whyte 1943, 24–31; Williams and Kornblum 1985; Schultz 1969; Horowitz 1983; Stack 1974; Staples 1971, 1973; Edelman 1987; Walter 1978, 117–129; Ladner 1973). The wealth of information, however, tends to be fragmented and has led to differing, even contradictory, assessments of the state of such relations. My purpose in this chapter is to present a holistic account of the situation in the form of an informal ethnographic essay that focuses on actual behavior and the motivation behind it.

To this end, I interviewed some forty people who are personally involved with this issue, including teenage mothers, pregnant teenagers, teenage fathers, and prospective teenage fathers, and grandmothers, grandfathers, sisters, brothers, fathers, and mothers of youthful parents. I conducted those interviews in what could be described as natural settings: on stoops, on trolleys, in respondents' homes, in restaurants, and in other

The author acknowledges the support of the Department of Health and Human Services, Office of Minority Health.

74

neighborhood places. Through these conversations my goal was to generate a conceptual essay on the general subject of sex and pregnancy among poor inner-city black young people ranging in age from 15 to 23.

Sexual conduct among poor inner-city black youths is to a large extent the result of the meshing of two opposing drives, that of the boys and that of the girls. For a variety of reasons tied to the socioeconomic situation in which they find themselves, their goals are often diametrically opposed, and sex becomes a contest between them. To many boys, sex is an important symbol of local social status; sexual conquests become so many notches on one's belt. Many of the girls offer sex as a gift in their bargaining for the attentions of a young man. As boys and girls try to use each other to achieve their respective ends, the reality that emerges in the eyes of the participants sometimes approximates their goals, but it often results in frustration and disillusionment and the perpetuation or even worsening of their original situation.

In each sexual encounter there is generally a winner and a loser. The girls have a dream, the boys a desire. The girls dream of being taken off by a Prince Charming who will love them, provide for them, and give them a family. The boys often desire sex without commitment or, if they do impregnate a girl, babies without responsibility for them. It becomes extremely difficult for the boys to see themselves enacting the roles and taking on the responsibilities of conventional fathers and husbands on the basis of the limited employment opportunities available to them. Yet the boy knows what the girl wants and plays the role in order to get her to give him sex. Receptive to his advances, she may think that she is maneuvering him toward a commitment or, even better, that getting pregnant is the nudge the boy needs to marry her and give her the life she wants. What she does not see is that the boy, despite his claims, is often incapable of giving her that life. For, in reality, he has little money, few prospects for gainful employment, and, furthermore, no wish to be tied to a woman who will have any say in what he does, for his loyalty is to his peer group and its norms. Consistent with this, when the girl becomes pregnant, the boy tends to retreat from her, although she, with the help of local social pressure from family and peers, may ultimately succeed in getting him to take some responsibility for the child.

Sex: The Game and the Dream

To an inner-city black male youth, the most important people in his life are members of his peer group. They set the standards for his conduct, and it is important for him to live up to those standards, to look good in their eyes. The peer group places a high value on sex, especially on what many middle-class people call casual sex. Although the sex may be casual in terms of commitment to the partner, it is usually taken quite seriously as a measure of the boy's worth. Thus a primary goal of the young man is to find as many willing females as possible. The more "pussy" he gets the more esteem accrues to him. But the young man must not only get "some"; he must also prove he is getting it. Consequently, he usually talks about girls and sex with every other man who will listen. Because of the implications sex has for local social status and esteem for the young men, there are many of them willing and ready to be regaled by tales of one another's sexual exploits. The conversations include graphic descriptions of the sex act.

The lore of the streets says there is something of a contest going on between the boy and the girl even before they meet. To the young man, the woman becomes, in the most profound sense, a sexual object. Her body and mind become the object of a sexual game, to be won over for the personal aggrandizement of the young man. Status goes to the winner, and sex becomes prized not so much as a testament of love but as testimony of control of another human being. Sex is the prize and sexual conquests are a game, the object of which is to make a fool of the other person, particularly the young woman.

The young men variously describe their successful campaigns as "getting over [the young woman's sexual defenses]." In order to get over, the young man must devise and develop a "game," whose success is gauged by its acceptance by his peers and especially by women. Relying heavily on gaining the confidence of the girl, the game consists of the boy's full presentation of self, including his dress, grooming, looks, dancing ability, and conversation, or "rap."

The rap is the verbal element of the game, whose object is to inspire sexual interest in the boy. It embodies the whole person and is thus extremely important to the success of the game. Among peer-group members, raps are assessed, evaluated, and divided into weak and strong. The assessment of the young man's rap is, in effect, the evaluation of his whole game. Convincing proof of the effectiveness of one's game is in the "booty": the amount of pussy the young man appears to be getting. Young men who are known to fail with women often face ridicule at the hands of the group, thus having their raps labeled "tissue paper," their games seen as inferior, and their identities discredited.

After developing a game over time, through trial and error, a young man is ever on the lookout for players, young women with whom to try it out and perhaps to perfect it. To find willing players is to gain a certain affirmation of self, although the boy's status in the peer group may go up if he is able to seduce a girl considered to be "choice," "down," or streetwise. When encountering a girl, the boy usually sees a challenge: he attempts to "run his game." Here the girl usually is fully aware that a game is being attempted; however, if the young man's game is sophisticated, or "smooth," or if the girl is very young and inexperienced, she may be easily duped.

In many instances the game plays on the dream that many inner-city girls evolve from early teenage years. The popular love songs they have listened to, usually from the age of seven or eight, are filled with a wistful air, promising love and ecstasy to someone "just like you." This dream involves having a boyfriend, a fiancé, a husband, and the fairy-tale prospect of living happily ever after in a nice house in a neighborhood with one's children—essentially the dream of the middle-class American life-style, complete with the nuclear family. It is nurtured by a daily involvement with afternoon television soap operas, or "stories," as the women call them. The heroes or heroines of these stories may be white and upper middle class, but for many, these characteristics only make them more attractive as role models. Many girls dream of the role of the comfortable middle-class housewife portrayed on television, even though they see that their peers can only approximate that role.

When approached by a boy, the girl's faith in the dream helps to cloud or obscure her view of the situation. A romantically successful boy has the knack for knowing just what is on a girl's mind, what she wants from life, and how she wants to go about obtaining it. In this regard he is inclined and may be able to play the character the script calls for. Through his actions he is able to shape the interaction, calling up those resources needed to play the game successfully. He fits himself to be the man she wants him to be, but this identity may be exaggerated and only temporary, until he gets what he wants. He shows her the side of himself that he knows she wants to see, that represents what she wants in a man. For instance, the young man will sometimes "walk through the woods" with the girl: he might visit at her home and go to church with her family, showing that he is an "upstanding young man." But all of this may only be part of his game, and after he gets what he wants, he may cast down this part of his presentation and reveal something of his true self, as he reverts to those actions and behavior more characteristic of his everyday life, those centered around his peer group.

In these circumstances the girl may see but refuse to accept evidence of the boy's duplicity. She may find herself at times defending the young man to her friends and family who question her choice of a boyfriend. In those cases in which the male is successful the young woman may know she is being played, but, given the effectiveness of his game, his rap, his presentation of self, his looks, his wit, his dancing ability, and his general popularity in the peer group, infatuation often rules. Many a girl fervently hopes that her boy is the one that is different, while some boys are very good actors and can be extremely persuasive.

In addition, the girl's peer group supports her pursuit of the dream, implicitly upholding her belief in the young man's good faith. But it is clear that the goals and interests of the girl and boy often diverge. While many girls want to pursue the dream, the boy, for the immediate future, is generally not interested in "playing house," as his peer-group members derisively refer to domestic life.

While pursuing his game, the boy often feigns love and caring, pretending to be a dream man and acting toward the girl as though he has the best intentions. Ironically, in many cases the young man does indeed have the best intentions. He may experience profound ambivalence on this score, mainly because of the way such intentions appear to relate to or conflict with the values of the peer group. At times these values are placed in sharp focus by his own deviance from them, as he incurs sanctions for allowing a girl to "rule" him or gains positive reinforcement for keeping her in line. The peer group sanctions its members with demeaning labels such as "pussy," "pussy-whipped," or "househusband," causing them to posture in manners that clearly distance themselves from such characterizations.

At times, however, some boys earnestly attempt to enact the role of the "dream man," one with honorable intentions of "doing right" by the young woman, of marrying her and living happily ever after, according to their versions of middle-class norms of propriety. But the reality of the poor employment situation for young black males of the inner city makes it extremely difficult for many to follow through on such intentions (Anderson 1978; Wilson 1978; Anderson and Sawhill 1980; Anderson 1980; Wilson 1987).

Unable to realize himself as the young woman's provider in the American middle-class tradition, which the peer group often labels "square," the young man may become ever more committed to his game. With ambivalence many young men will go so far as to "make plans" with the women, including house shopping and window shopping for items for the prospective household. A 23-year-old female informant who at 17 became a single parent of a baby girl said the following:

> Yeah, they'll [boys will] take you out. Walk you down to Center City, movies, window shops (laughs). They point in the window, "Yeah, I'm gonna get this. Wouldn't you like this? Look at that nice livin' room set." Then they want to take you to his house, go to his room: "Let's go over to my house, watch some TV." Next thing you know your clothes is off and you in bed havin' sex, you know.

Such shopping trips carry with them important psychological implications for the relationship, at times serving as a kind of salve that heals wounds and erases doubt about the young man's intentions. The young woman may report to her parents or to her friends on her latest date or shopping trip, indicating the type of furniture looked at and priced and the supposed terms of payment. She continues to have hope, which he supports by "going" with her, letting her and others know that she is his "steady," although in order for him to maintain a certain status within his peer group, she should not be his only known girl.

Such actions indicate a certain level of involvement on the part of the couple, particularly the young man. For him, the making of plans and the successive shopping trips may simply be elements of his game and often nothing more than a stalling device he uses to keep the girl hanging on so that he may continue to have the benefit of her sexual favors.

In many cases the more he seems to exploit the young woman, the higher his status within the peer group. But to consolidate this status, he feels moved at times to show others that he is in control. There may be a contest of wills between the two, with arguments and fights developing in public places over what may appear to be the most trivial of issues. In order to prove his dominance in the relationship unequivocally, he may "break her down" in front of her friends and his, "showing the world who is boss." If the young woman wants him badly enough, she will meekly go along with the performance for the implicit promise of his continued attentions, if not love. Again, a more permanent relationship approximating the woman's dream of matrimony and domestic tranquility is often what is at stake in her mind.

As the contest continues, and the girl hangs on, she may be believed to have been taken in by the boy's game but particularly by his convincing rap, his claims of commitment to her and her well-being. In this contest anything is fair. The girl may become manipulative and aggressive, or the boy may lie, cheat, or otherwise misrepresent himself to obtain or retain the sexual favors of the girl. In many of the sexual encounters related by informants one person is seen as a winner, the other as a loser. As one informant said:

> They trickin' them good. Either the woman is trickin' the man, or the man is trickin' the woman. Good! They got a trick. She's thinkin' it's [the relationship is] one thing, he playing another game, you know. He thinkin' she all right, and she doing something else.

In the social atmosphere of the peer group the quality of the boy's game tends to emerge as a central issue. In addition, whatever lingering ambivalence he has about his commitment to the role of husband and provider may be resolved in favor of peer-group status, which becomes more clearly at stake in his mind.

In pursuing his game, the young man often uses a supporting cast of other women, at times playing one off against the other. For example, he may orchestrate a situation in which he is seen with another woman. Alternatively, secure in the knowledge that he has other women to fall back on, he might start a fight with his steady in order to upset her sense of complacency, thus creating a certain amount of dynamic tension within the relationship, which he tries to use for his own advantage. The result is that the young woman can begin to doubt her hold on the man, which can in turn bring about a precipitous drop in her self-esteem.

In these circumstances the boy may take pride in the fool he thinks he is making of the girl, and when he is confident of his dominance, he may work to "play" the young woman, "running his game," making her "love" him. Some young men, in such instances, will brag that they are "playing her like a fiddle," meaning that they are in full control of the situation. The object here, for the young man, is to prove he "has the girl's nose open," that she is sick with love for him. His goal is to maneuver her into a state of blissful emotionality with regard to himself, showing that she, and not he, is clearly the "weak" member in the relationship.

Strikingly, it is in these circumstances that the young girl may well become careless about birth control, which is seen by the community, especially the males, as being her responsibility. Depending upon the effectiveness of the boy's game, she may believe his rap, becoming convinced that he means what he has said about taking care of her, that her welfare is his primary concern. Moreover, she wants desperately to believe that if she becomes pregnant, he will marry her or at least be obligated to her in a way he is not to others he has been "messing with." Perhaps all he needs is a little nudge.

In these circumstances, however, the girl thinks little of the job market and job prospects for the boy. She underestimates peer-group influences and the effect of other "ladies" she knows or at least strongly suspects are in his life. She is in love, and she is sure that a child and the profound obligation a child implies will make such a strong bond that all the other issues will go away. Her thinking is clouded by the prospect of winning at the game of love. Becoming pregnant can be a way to fulfill an old but persistent dream of happiness and bliss. Moreover, for numerous women, when the man is determined to be unobtainable, just having his baby is enough. Often a popular and "fine," or physically attractive, young man is sought out by a woman in hopes that his physical attractiveness will grace her child, resulting in a "prize," or a beautiful baby.

Moreover, for the young woman, becoming pregnant can become an important part of the competition for the attentions or even delayed affection of a young man, a profound if socially shortsighted way of making claim on him.

The Issue of Pregnancy

Up to the point of pregnancy, given the norms of his peer group with regard to male and female relations, the young man could be characterized as simply messing around. The fact of pregnancy brings a sudden sense of realism to the relationship between the young man and the young woman. Life-altering events have occurred. The situation is usually perceived as utterly serious. She is pregnant, and he could be held legally responsible for the long-term financial support of the child. In addition, if the young couple were unclear about their intentions before, things now may crystallize. She may now consider him seriously as a mate. Priorities may now begin to emerge in the boy's mind. He has to make a decision whether to claim the child as his or to shun the woman who for so long has been the object of his affections, often for reasons of peer-group concerns.

To own up to such a pregnancy is to go against the peer-group ethic of "hit and run." Other values at risk of being flouted by such an action include the subordination of women and freedom from formal conjugal ties, and in this environment, where hard economic times are a fact of daily life for many, some young men are not interested in "taking care of somebody else," when to do so means having less. In this social context of persistent poverty young men have come to devalue the conventional marital relationship, easily viewing women as a burden and children as even more so. Moreover, with regard to such relationships a young man wants "to come as I want and go as I please," thus meeting important peer-group values of freedom and independence. Accordingly, from the perspective of the peer group any such male-female relationship should be on the man's terms. Thus, in coming to an understanding of the boy's relationship with the girl, his attitudes toward his limited financial ability and his need for personal independence and freedom should not be underestimated.

Another important attitude of the male peer group is that most girls are whores: "If she was fucking you, then she was fucking everybody else." Whether there is truth to this with respect to a particular case, a common working conception says it is true about young women in general. It is a view with which so many young men approach females, relegating them to a situation of social and moral deficit. The proverbial double standard is at work, and for any amount of sexual activity, the women are more easily discredited than the men.

To be sure, among the young men and women there is a fair amount of sexual activity. In this social atmosphere ambiguity of paternity complicates many pregnancies. Moreover, in self-defense the young man often chooses to deny fatherhood; few are willing to "own up" to a pregnancy they can reasonably question. Among their peers the young men gain ready support. Peer-group norms say that a man who is "tagged" with fatherhood has been caught up in the "trick bag." The boy's first desire, although he may know better, is often to attribute the pregnancy to someone else.

In these general circumstances the boy may be genuinely confused and uncertain about his role in the pregnancy, feeling a great deal of ambivalence and apprehension over his impending fatherhood. If he admits paternity and "does right" by the girl, his peer group likely will label him a chump, a square, or a fool. If he does not, however, there are few social sanctions applied, and he may even be given points for his stand, with his peers viewing him as fooling the mother and "getting over," or avoiding the trick bag. But here there may also be some ambivalence, for there is a certain regard to be obtained by those of the group who father children out of wedlock, as long as they are not "caught" and made financially responsible to support a family on something other than their own terms. Hence, the boy in these circumstances may give, and benefit socially from, mixed messages: one to the girl and perhaps the authorities, and another to his peer group. Generally, to resolve his ambivalence and apprehension, the boy might at this point attempt to discontinue his relationship with the expectant mother, particularly as she begins to show clear physical signs of pregnancy.

Upon giving birth, the young woman wants badly to identify the father of her child, if primarily at the insistence of her family and for her own peace of mind. When the baby is born, she may, out of desperation, arbitrarily designate a likely young man as the father. As mentioned, there may be genuine ambiguity surrounding the identity of the father. In this atmosphere there are often charges and countercharges, with the appointed young man usually easing himself from the picture over time. There is at times an incentive for the young woman not to identify the father, even though she and the local community know whose baby it is. Given that job prospects for young black men are so limited as to be effectively nil, the woman may be better off denying that she knows the father, for a check from the welfare office is much more dependable than the irregular support payments of a sporadically employed youth.

To be sure, there are many young men who are determined to do right by the young woman, to try out the role of husband and father, often acceding to the woman's view of the matter and working to establish a family. Such young men tend to be those who are only marginally related to their peer groups. They tend to emerge from nurturing families, and religious observance plays an important role in their lives. Strikingly, these men are usually gainfully employed and tend to enjoy a deep and abiding relationship with the young woman that is able to withstand the trauma of youthful pregnancy.

Barring such a resolution, a young man may rationalize his marital situation as something of a "trap" into which the woman tricked him. This viewpoint may be seen as his attempt to make simultaneous claims on values of the peer group as well as those of the more conventional society. As another young man said in an interview:

> My wife done that to me. Before we got married, when we had our first baby, she thought, well, hey, if she had the baby, then she got me, you know. And that's the way she done me. [She] thought that's gon' trap me. That I'm all hers after she done have this baby. So, a lot of women, they think like that. Now, I was the type of guy, if I know it was my baby, I'm taking care of my baby. My o'lady [wife], she knowed that. She knowed that anything that was mine, I'm taking care of mine. This is why she probably wouldn't mess around or nothing, 'cause she wanted to lock me up.

In general, however, persuading the youth to become "an honest man" is not at all simple. It is often a very complicated social affair involving cajoling, social pressure, and at times physical threats.

An important factor in determining whether the boy does right by the girl is the presence of the girl's father in the home (Williams and Kornblum 1985). When a couple first begins to date, some fathers will "sit the boy down" and have a ritual talk; some single mothers will play this role as well, at times more aggressively than fathers. Certain males with domineering dispositions will, "as a man," make unmistakable territorial claims on the dwelling, informing or reminding the boy that "this is my house, I pay the bills here," and that all activities occurring under its roof are his singular business. In such a household the home has a certain defense. At issue here essentially are male turf rights, a principle intuitively understood by the young suitor and the father of the girl. The boy may feel a certain frustration due to a felt need to balance his desire to run his game against his fear of the girl's father. Yet the boy is often able to identify respectfully with the father, thinking of how he himself might behave if the shoe were on the other foot.

Upon encountering each other, both "know something," that is, they know that each has a position to defend. The young boy knows in advance of a pregnancy that he will have to answer to the girl's father and the family unit more generally. If the girl becomes pregnant, the boy will be less likely to treat the situation summarily and leave her. Further, if the girl has brothers at home who are her approximate age or older, they, too, may serve to influence the behavior of the boy effectively. Such men, as well as uncles and male cousins, possess not only a certain degree of moral authority in these circumstances but often the believable threat of violence and mayhem in many cases. As one boy said in an interview:

> The boys kinda watch theyself more [when a father is present]. Yeah, there's a lot of that going on. The daddy, they'll clown [act out violence] about them young girls. They'll hurt somebody about they daughters. Other relatives, too. They'll all get into it. The boy know they don't want him messing over they sister. That guy will probably take care of that girl better than the average one out there in the street.

In such circumstances not only does the boy think twice about running his game, but the girl often thinks twice about allowing him to do so.

A related important defense against youthful pregnancy is the conventional inner-city family unit. Two parents, together with the extended network of cousins, aunts, uncles, grandparents, nieces, and nephews, can form a durable team, a viable supportive unit engaged to fight in a most committed manner the various problems confronting so many inner-city teenagers, including drugs, crime, pregnancy, and social mobility (Schultz 1969; Willie and Weinancy 1970; Perkins 1975). This unit, when it does survive, tends to be equipped with a survivor's mentality. It has weathered a good many storms, which have given it wisdom and a certain strength. The parents are known in the community as "strict" with their children; they impose curfews and tight supervision, demanding to know their children's whereabouts at all times. Determined that their children not become casualties of the inner-city environment, these parents scrutinize their children's friends and associates carefully, rejecting those who seem to be "no good" and encouraging others who seem to be on their way to "amount to something."

In contrast, in those domestic situations in which there is but one adult—say, a woman with two or three teenage daughters and with no male presence—the dwelling may be viewed by young boys, superficially at least, as essentially an unprotected nest. The local boys will sometimes become attracted to the home as a challenge, just to test it out, to see if they can "get over," or be successful in charming or seducing the women who reside there. In such settings a man, the figure the boys are prepared to respect, is not there to keep them in line. The girls residing in these unprotected situations may become pregnant more quickly than those living in situations more closely resembling nuclear families. A young male informant had the following comment:

> I done seen where four girls grow up under their mama. The mama turn around and she got a job between 3 p.m. and 11 p.m. These little kids, now they grow up like this. Mama working 3 to 11 o'clock at night. They kinda raise theyself. What they know? By the time they get 13 or 14, they trying everything under the sun. And they ain't got nobody to stop 'em. Mama gone. Can't nobody else tell 'em what to do. Hey, all of 'em pregnant by age 16. And they do it 'cause they wanta get out on they own. They then can get their own baby, they get their own [welfare] check, they get their own apartment. They want to get away from mama. They really want to be grown.

As indicated in the foregoing statement, a woman may have an overwhelming desire to grow up, a passage best expressed by her ability to "get out on her own." In terms of traditional inner-city poverty experience this means setting up one's own household, preferably with a "good man" through marriage and family. A single young woman may attempt to accomplish this by purposely becoming pregnant, perhaps hoping the baby's father will marry her and help to realize her dream of domestic respectability. At the same time, there are an undetermined number of young women, unimpressed with the lot of young single men, who wish to establish their households on their own, without the help or the burden of a man (see the discussion of the male marriageable pool in Wilson 1987). It has become increasingly socially acceptable for a young woman to have children out of wedlock—significantly, with the help of a regular welfare check.

Because the woman emerges from such poor financial circumstances, the prospect of a regular welfare check can seem like an improvement. In this way the social situation of persistent poverty affects norms of the ghetto culture such as the high value placed on children, thus having a significant impact on decisions to bear children (Lewis 1975, 221–237; Tenhouten 1970, 145–173). Hence, among many young poor ghetto women, babies have become a sought-after symbol of status, of passage to adulthood, of being a "grown" woman. In such circumstances, babies can become valued emblems of womanhood. Moreover, it is not always a question of whether the young girl is going to have children, but when. Thus, given the young woman's limited social and financial outlook, she may see herself as having little to lose by becoming pregnant and, coinciding with the culturally reinforced perception, as having something to gain.

The reality of pregnancy, however, is often a bitter pill. As the girl begins to show signs of pregnancy, becoming physically bigger, she often loses the connection with her mate, although she may gain the affirmation and support of other women who have followed the same path as she.

In their small, intimate social groups, women discuss their afternoon stories, or soap operas, men, children, and social life, and they welcome prospective members to their generally supportive gatherings. Interestingly, although the women tend to deride the men for their behavior, especially their lack of commitment to their girlfriends, at the same time they may accommodate such behavior, viewing it as characteristic of men in their environment. Yet in their conversations the women may draw distinctions between the "nothin'" and the "good man." The nothin' is "a man who is out to use every woman he can for himself. He's somethin' like a pimp. Don't care 'bout nobody but himself." As one older single mother, who now considers herself wiser, said in an interview:

> I know the difference now between a nothin' and a good man. I can see. I can smell him. I can tell nothin's from the real thing. I can just look at a guy sometimes, you know, the way he dresses, you know. The way he carries himself. The way he acts, the way he talks. I can tell the bullshitter. Like, you know, "What's up, baby?" You know. "What's you want to do?" A nice guy wouldn't say, "What's up, baby? What's goin' on?" Actin' all familiar, tryin' to give me that line. Saying, "You wanna joint? You wan' some blow? You wan' some 'caine?" Hollerin' in the street, you know. I can tell 'em. I can just smell 'em.

The good man is one who is considerate of his mate and provides for her and her children, but at the same time he may run the risk of being seen as a pussy in the eyes of the women as well as his peer group. This inversion in the idea of the good man underscores the ambivalent position of the girls squeezed between their middle-class dreams and the ghetto reality. As one woman said with a laugh, "There are so many sides to the bad man. We see that, especially in this community. We see more bad men than we do good. I see them [inner-city black girls] running over that man if he's a wimp, ha-ha."

Family support is often available for the young pregnant woman, although members of her family are likely to remind her from time to time that she is "messed up." She looks forward to the day when she is "straight" again, meaning the time when she has given birth to the baby and has regained her figure. Her comments to others who are not pregnant tend to center wistfully on better days when she was not messed up. As her boyfriend stops seeing her so regularly, she may readily attribute this to the family's negative comments about the boy, but also to her pregnant state, saying time and again that when "I get straight, he'll be sorry; he'll be jealous then." She knows in a sense that her pregnant status is devalued by her family as well as her single peers, who have the freedom to date and otherwise consort with men. She may long for the day when she will be able to do that again.

When the baby arrives, however, the girl finds that her social activities continue to be significantly curtailed. She is often surprised by how much time being a mother actually takes. In realizing her new identity, she may very consciously assume the demeanor and manner of a grown woman, emphasizing her freedom in social relations, her independence. At times, during what is really a period of adjustment to a new status, she has to set her mother straight about "telling me what to do." This is usually a time when other family members go through a learning process as they become used to the young woman's new status, which she tries on with a variety of stops and starts. In fact, she really is involved in the process of growing up.

Frustrated by the continued curtailment of her social activities, especially as she becomes physically straight again, the girl may develop an intense desire to get back into the dating game. Accordingly, she may foist her child-care responsibilities onto her mother and female siblings, people who initially are eager to take on such roles. In time, however, they tire, and otherwise extremely supportive relations can become strained. In an effort to see her daughter get straight again, the young woman's mother, often in her mid-thirties or early forties, may simply informally adopt the baby as another one of her own, in some cases completely usurping the role of mother from her daughter. In this way the young parent's mother may attempt to minimize the deviance the girl displayed by getting pregnant while simultaneously taking genuine pride in her new grandchild.

Of Men and Women, Mothers and Sons

The relationship between the young man and woman undergoes a basic change during pregnancy; once the baby is born, he or she draws in other social forces, most notably the families of the couple. The role of the girl's family has been discussed. The role of the boy's family is also important, but in a different way. There is often a special bond between a mother and her grown son in the community that effectively competes with the claims of his girlfriend. The way in which this situation is resolved has important consequences for the family and its relationship to the social structure of the community.

In numerous cases of teenage pregnancy among the poor the mother of the boy plays a significant role, while the role of the father, if he is present at all, is often understated. Depending on the personality of the woman, her practical experience in such matters, and the girl's family situation, the mother's role may be understated or explicit. At times she becomes quite involved with the young woman, forming a female bond that becomes truly motherly, involving guidance, protection, and control of the young woman.

From the moment the mother finds out that the young woman is pregnant, an important issue is whether she knows the girl or not. If the young woman "means something" to her son, she is likely to know her or at least know about her; her son has spoken of the girl. On hearing the news of the pregnancy, the mother's reaction might be anything from disbelief that her son could be responsible to certainty, even before seeing the child, that her son is the father. If she knows something about the girl's character, she is in a position to make a judgment for herself. Here her relationship with the girl before "all this" happened comes into play, for if she liked her, there is a great chance the boy's mother will side with her. The mother may even go so far as to engage in playful collusion against her son, a man, to get him to do right by the girl. Here it must be remembered that in this economically circumscribed social context, particularly from a woman's point of view, many men are known not to do right by their women and children. To visit such inner-city settings is to observe what appears to be a proliferation of small children and women, with fathers and husbands largely absent or playing their roles part-time. These considerations help to place in some context the significance of the mother's role in determining how successful the girl will be in having the boy claim and take some responsibility for her child.

For in this role the mother is usually constrained, at least initially, because she is often unsure whether her son has actually fathered the child. She may, however, be careful about showing her doubt, thinking that when the baby arrives, she will be able to tell "in a minute" whether her son is the father. Thus, during the pregnancy the mother of the young man nervously waits, wondering whether her son will be blamed for a pregnancy not of his doing or whether she will really be a grandmother. In fact, the whole family, both the boy's and the girl's, is often an extended family-in-waiting, socially organized around the idea that the "truth" will be told when the baby arrives. Unless the parties are very sure, marriage, if agreed to at all, may be held off until after the birth of the baby.

When the baby arrives, real plans may be carried out, but often on the condition that the child passes familial inspection. The young man himself, the presumed father, generally lays low in the weeks after the baby's birth. He usually does not visit the baby's mother in the hospital on a regular basis; he may come only once, if at all. In an effort to make a paternal connection between the child and father, some mothers name the baby after the father, but, by itself, this strategy is seldom effective.

In a number of cases of doubtful paternity, the boy's mother, sister, aunt, or other female relatives or close family friends may form informal visiting committees, charged with going to see the baby, although sometimes the baby is brought to them. This kind of familial inspection is often surreptitious and usually takes place without the acknowledgment of the girl or her own family. The visiting committee may even go by the girl's house in shifts, with a sister going now, the mother another time, and a friend still another. Social pleasantries notwithstanding, the object is always the same: to see if the baby "belongs" to the boy it is said to. Typically, after such visits, these women will compare notes, commenting on the baby's features, saying whom the baby favors. Some will blurt right out, "Ain't no way that's John's baby." People may disagree, and a dispute may ensue. In the community the identity of the baby's father becomes a hot topic of conversation. The viewpoints have much to do with who the girl is, whether she is a "good girl" or "bad girl" or whether she has been accepted and taken in by the boy's family. If the girl is well integrated into the family, doubts about paternity may even be slowly put to rest, with nothing more being said about it.

As previously indicated, the word carrying the most weight in this situation, however, is often that of the boy's mother. The following account of a young man is relevant:

> I had a lady telling me that she had to check out a baby that was supposed to be her grandbaby. She said she had a young girl that was trying to put a baby on her son, so she said she fixing to take the baby and see what blood type the baby is to match it with her son to see if he the daddy. 'Cause she said she *know* he wasn't the daddy. And she told the girl that, but the girl was steady trying to stick the baby on her son. She had checked out the baby's features and everything. She knowed that the blood type wasn't gon' match or nothing. So the young girl just left 'em alone.

If the child very clearly physically favors the alleged father, there may be strong pressure for the boy to claim the child and approach the attendant responsibilities. This may take a year or more, as the resemblance may not be initially so apparent. But when others begin to make comments such as "Lil' Tommy look like Maurice just spit him out [is his spitting image]," the boy's mother may informally adopt the child into her extended family and signal for all other family members to do the same. She may see the child on a regular basis and develop a special relationship with the child's mother. Because of the social acknowledgment by the boy's mother of her son's paternity, the boy himself is bound to accept the child as his own. Even if he does not claim the child legally, in the face of the evidence he will often claim the child in the sense of "having something to do with him." As one informant said:

> If the baby look just like him, he should admit to hisself that that's his. Some guys have to wait 'til the baby grow up a little to see if the baby gon' look like him 'fore they finally realize that was his's. Because yours should look like you, you know, should have your features and image.

Here the young man informally acknowledging paternity may feel that pressure to "take care of his own."

But due to his limited employment and general lack of money, he "can only do what he can" for his child. In such circumstances, many young men will enact the role of the part-time father. In self-consciously attempting to fulfill this role, the young man may be spied on streets of the inner-city community with a box of "Pampers," the name used as a generic term to refer to all disposable diapers, or cans of Similac, liquid baby formula, in his arms, on his way to see his child and its mother. As the child ages, a bond may develop; the young man may take the child, if it is a boy, for a haircut or shopping for shoes or clothes. He may give the woman token amounts of money. Such support symbolizes a father providing for his child. In fact, however, the support often comes only sporadically and, importantly, in exchange for the woman's favors, be they social or sexual. The woman's support may thus depend upon the largess of the young man and may function as a means of her control.

When and if the woman "gets papers" on the man, or legalizes his relationship to the child, she may sue for regular support, what people of the community call "going downtown on him." If her case is successful, the young man's personal involvement in the making of support payments to the child may be eliminated: his child support payments may be simply deducted from his salary, if he has one. Sometimes the incentive for getting papers may emerge in the young woman's mind when and if the young man obtains a "good job," particularly one with a major institution that includes family benefits. While sporadically employed, the youth may have had no problem with papers, but when he obtains a good job, he may be served with a summons. In some cases, particularly if the young man has two or three children out of wedlock by two or three different women, young men lose the incentive to work at such good jobs when to do so only ensures that much of their pay will go to someone else. In the case of one of my informants, after the mothers of his four children got papers on him and he began to see less and less of his money, he quit his job and returned to the street corner.

There are conditions under which the male peer group will exert pressure on one of its members to admit paternity. Most important is that there be no ambiguity in the group members' own minds as to the baby's father. This is established on the basis of the baby's features. When it is clear that the baby resembles a peer-group member, the others may strongly urge him to claim it and go on to help the mother financially. If the young man fails to claim the baby, group members may do it themselves by publicly associating him with the child, at times teasing him about his connection with the mother and his failure "to take care of what is his." As one informant said:

> My partner's [friend's] girlfriend came up pregnant. And she say it's his, but he not sure. He waitin' on the baby, waitin' to see if the baby look like him. I tell him, "Man, if that baby look just like you, then it was yours! Ha-ha." He just kinda like just waitin'. He ain't claimin' naw, saying the baby ain't his. I keep tellin' him, "If that baby come out looking just like you, then it gon be yours, partner." And there [on the corner] all of 'em will tell him, "Man that's yo' baby." They'll tell him.

While the peer group may urge its members to take care of their babies, they stop short of urging them to marry the mothers. In general, young men are assumed not to care about raising a family or being a part of one. Some of this lack of support for marriage is due to the poor employment prospects, but it also may have to do with the general distrust they have of women. As my informant continued:

> They don't even trust her that they were the only one she was dealing with. That's a lot of it. But the boys just be gettin' away from it [the value of a family] a whole lot. They don't want to get tied down by talkin' about playing house, ha-ha, what they call it nowadays, ha-ha. Yeah, ha-ha, they saying they ain't playing house.

In a great number of cases, peer group or no, the boy will send the girl on her way even if she is carrying a baby he knows is his own. The young man very often lacks a deep feeling for a female and children as a family unit. He often does not want to put up with married life, which he sees as life with a woman who will have something to say about how he spends his time. This emphasis on "freedom" is generated and supported in large part by the peer group itself. Even if a man agrees to marriage, it is usually considered to be only a trial. After a few months many young husbands have had enough.

This desire for freedom, which the peer group so successfully nurtures, is deeply rooted in the boys. It is, in fact, often nothing less than the desire to perpetuate the situation they had in their mothers' homes. A son is generally well bonded to his mother, something the mother tends to encourage from birth. It may be that sons, particularly the eldest, are groomed in this way to function as surrogate husbands because of the commonly high rate of family dissolution among poor blacks (Schultz 1969; Heiss 1975; Perkins 1975; Magnum and Seninger 1978).

With respect to family life so many young boys really want what they consider an optimal social situation. In the words of peer-group members, they want it all: they want a "main squeeze," or a steady and reliable female partner who mimics the role played by their mothers in their original families, a woman who will cook, clean, and generally serve them with few questions about the "ladies" they may be seeing, and even less to say about their male friends. The young man has grown accustomed to the good home-cooked meals, the secure company of his family, in which his father was largely absent and thus unable to tell him what to do. He was his own boss, essentially raising himself, with the help of his peer group and perhaps any adult who would listen but not interfere. Many of the young men have very fond memories of the situation in which they grew up. For an undetermined number, such a life is too much to give up in exchange for the "problems of being tied down to one lady, kids, bills, and all that." In this sense the young man's home situation with his mother competes quite effectively with the household he envisions with a woman whom he does not fully trust and whom his peer group is fully prepared to discredit.

Now that he is grown, the young man wants what he had growing up, plus a number of ladies on the side. At the same time he wants his male friends, whom he is required to impress in ways that may be inconsistent with being a good family man. As the young men from the start have little faith in marriage, little things can inspire them to retreat to their mothers or other families they may have left behind. Some men spend their time going back and forth between two families; if their marriage seems not to be working, they may easily ditch it and their wife, although perhaps keeping up with the children. At all times they must show others that they run the family, that they "wear the pants." This is the cause of many of the domestic fights in the ghetto. When there is a question of authority, the domestic situation may run into serious trouble, often resulting in the young man's abandoning the idea of marriage or of "dealing" with only one woman. To "hook up" with a woman, to marry her, is to give her license to have something to say about what "you're doing, or where you're going, or where you been." For many young men, such involvement on the woman's part is simply unacceptable.

In endeavoring to have it all, many men become, in effect, part-time fathers and part-time husbands, seeing women and children on their own terms, when they have the time, and making symbolic purchases for the children. In theory, the part-time father is able to retain his freedom while having limited commitment to the woman and the little ones "calling me daddy." In many instances the man does not mind putting up with the children, given his generally limited role in child rearing, but he does mind putting up with the woman, who is seen as a significant threat to his freedom, as someone with a say in how he runs his life. As one informant commented about marriage:

> Naw, they [young men] getting away from that. They ain't going in for that 'cause they want to be free. Now, see, I ended up getting married. I got a whole lot of boys ducking that. Unless this is managed, it ain't no good. My wife cleans, takes care o' the house. You got a lot of guys, they don't want to be cleanin' no house, and do the things you got to do in the house. You need a girl there to do it. If you get one, she'll slow you down. The guys don't want it.

Unless a man would be able to handle his wife so that she would put few constraints on him, he may reason that he had better stay away from marriage. But as indicated earlier, with a generalized sense of increasing independence from men, financial and other, there may be fewer women who allow themselves to be so handled.

As jobs become increasingly scarce for young black men, their roles as breadwinners and traditional husbands decline. The notion is that with money comes a certain control and say in the domestic situation. Without money or jobs many men are increasingly unable to "play house" to their own satisfaction. It is much earlier and more fun, some say, to stay home and "take care of mama," when taking care consists of "giving her some change for room and board," eating good food when possible, and being able "to come as I want to and to go as I please." Given the present state of the economy and the way in which the economy affects the employment situation of young black men, such an assessment of their domestic outlook appears in many respects adaptive. The peer group, largely with poor employment prospects, has nurtured and supported the idea of freedom and independence from family life, in which one would have to face bills and a woman having a say in one's affairs. From an economic and social standpoint it seems very attractive for the young man to stay home with mama, to maintain his freedom, and to have a string of ladies, some of whom contribute to his financial support.

Conclusion: Sex, Poverty, and Family Life

In conclusion, the basic factors at work here are youth, ignorance, the receptivity of the culture to babies, and the young male's resort to proving his manhood through sexual conquests that often result in pregnancies. These factors are exacerbated by the impact of present economic conditions and persistent poverty on the inner-city community.

In the present hard economic times a primary concern of many inner-city residents is to get along financially as best they can. In the poorest communities the primary sources of money include low-paying jobs, crime, including drugs, and public assistance. Some of the most desperate people devise a variety of confidence games, the object of which is to separate others from their money. A number of men, married and single, incorporate their sexual lives into their more generalized efforts at economic survival. Many will seek to "pull" a woman with children on welfare mainly because she usually has a special need for male company, time on her hands, and a steady income. As they work to establish their relationships, they play roles not unlike the roles played in the young male's game to get over sexually with a female. There is simply a clearer economic nexus in many of these cases, for when the woman receives her check from the welfare department or money from other sources, she may find herself giving up a part of it just to obtain or retain male company and interest.

The economic noose constricting so much of ghetto life encourages both men and women to attempt to extract maximum personal benefit from sexual relationships. The dreams of the middle-class life-style nurtured by young inner-city women become thwarted in the face of the harsh socioeconomic realities of the ghetto. Young men without job prospects cling to the support offered by their peer groups and their mothers and shy away from lasting relationships with girlfriends. In this situation girls and boys alike scramble to take what they can from each other, trusting not in each other but often in their own ability to trick the other into giving them something that will establish or perpetuate their version of the good life, the best life they feel they can put together for themselves in the inner-city social environment.

It is important to remember the age of the people we are talking about; these are kids—mainly 15, 16, and 17 years old. Their bodies are mature, but they are emotionally immature. These girls and boys often do not have a very clear notion of the long-term consequences of their behavior, and they have few trustworthy role models who might instruct them.

The basic sexual codes of inner-city youths may not differ fundamentally from those expressed by young people of other social settings. But the social, economic, and personal consequences of adolescent sexual conduct vary profoundly for different social classes. Like adolescents of all classes, inner-city youths are subject to intense, hard-to-control urges and impulsiveness. Sexual relations, exploitative and otherwise, are common among middle-class teenagers as well, but middle-class youths take a strong interest in their future, and know what a pregnancy can do to derail that future. In contrast, the ghetto adolescent sees no future to derail, no hope for a tomorrow very different from today, hence, little to lose by having an out-of-wedlock child.

Another difference between middle-class and poor youths is their level of practical education. The ignorance of inner-city girls about their bodies is startling to the middle-class observer. Many have only an abstract notion of where babies come from and generally know nothing about birth control until after the birth of their first child, and sometimes not even then. Parents in this culture are extremely reticent about discussing sex and birth control with their children. Many mothers are ashamed to "talk about it" or feel they are in no position to do so, as they behaved like their daughters when they were young. Education thus becomes a community health problem, but most girls come in contact with community health services only when they become pregnant, sometimes many months into their pregnancies.

Many women in the underclass black culture emerge from a fundamentalist religious orientation and practice a prolife philosophy. Abortion is therefore usually not an option (Gibson 1980b, 41–54; Gibson 1980a, 55–73; Pope 1969, 756–764). New life is sometimes characterized as a "heavenly gift," an infant is very sacred to the young women, and the extended inner-city family appears always able to make do somehow with another baby. In the community a birth is usually met with great praise, regardless of its circumstances, and the child is genuinely valued. Such ready social approval works against many efforts to avoid an out-of-wedlock birth.

In fact, in cold economic terms, a baby can be an asset. The severe economic situation in the inner city is, without a doubt, the single most important factor behind exploitative sex and out-of-wedlock babies. With the dearth of well-paying jobs, public assistance is one of the few reliable sources of money in the community, and, for many, drugs is another. The most desperate people thus feed on one another. In these circumstances babies and sex are used by some for income; women receive money from welfare for having babies, and men sometimes act as prostitutes to pry the money from the women. The community seems to feed on itself.

The lack of gainful employment opportunities not only keeps the entire community in a pit of poverty, but it also deprives young men of the traditional American way of proving their manhood, namely, supporting a family. They must thus prove their manhood in other ways. Casual sex with as many women as possible, impregnating one or more and getting them to "have your baby" brings a boy the ultimate in esteem from his peers and makes him a "man." Casual sex is therefore not so casual, but is fraught with social significance for the boy who has little or no hope of achieving financial stability, and so can have no sense of himself as caring for a family.

The meshing of these forces can be clearly seen. Adolescents, trapped in poverty, ignorant of the long-term consequences of their behavior, but aware of the immediate benefits, engage in a mating game. The girl has her dream of a family and a home, of a good man who will provide for her and her future children. The boy, knowing he cannot be that family man because he has no job and no prospects, yet needing to have sex with the girl in order to achieve manhood in the eyes of his peer group, pretends to be the good man and convinces her to give him sex and perhaps a baby. He may then abandon her, and she realizes that he was not the good man after all, but a nothin' out to exploit her. The boy has received what he wanted, but the girl learns that she has received something, too. The baby may enable her to receive a certain amount of praise, a steady welfare check, and a measure of independence. Her family often helps out as best they can. As she becomes older and wiser, she can use her income to turn the tables, attracting the interest of her original man or other men.

In this inner-city culture people generally get married for "love" and "to have something." This mind-set presupposes a job, the work ethic, and, perhaps most of all, a persistent sense of hope for, if not a modicum of belief in, an economic future. When these social factors are present, the more wretched elements of the portrait presented here begin to lose their force, slowly becoming neutralized. But for so many of those who are caught up in the web of persistent urban poverty and become unwed mothers and fathers, there is little hope for a good job and even less for a future of conventional family life.

References

Anderson, B., and I. V. Sawhill, eds. 1980. *Youth employment and public policy*. Englewood Cliffs, N.J.: Prentice-Hall.

Anderson, E. 1978. *A place on the corner*. Chicago: University of Chicago Press.

———. 1980. Some observations of black youth employment. In *Youth employment and public policy*. Englewood Cliffs, N.J.: Prentice-Hall.

Arensberg, C. M. 1937. *The Irish countryman*. New York: Macmillan.

Edelman, M. W. 1987. *Families in peril: An agenda for social change*. Cambridge: Harvard University Press.

Furstenberg, F. 1976. *Unplanned parenthood*. New York: Free Press.

Gibson, W. 1980a. The alleged weakness in the black family structure. In *Family life and morality*, 55–73. Lanham, Md.: University Press of America.

————. 1980b. The question of legitimacy. In *Family life and morality*, 41–54. Lanham, Md.: University Press of America.

Green, A. W. 1941. The cult of personality and sexual relations. *Psychiatry* 4: 343–348.

Hammond, B. E., and J. A. Ladner. 1969. Socialization into sexual behavior in a Negro slum ghetto. In *Individual, sex, and society*. Ed. C. B. Broderick and J. Bernard. Baltimore: Johns Hopkins Press.

Hannerz, U. 1969. *Soulside*. New York: Columbia University Press.

Heiss, J. 1975. *The case of the black family*. New York: Columbia University Press.

Horowitz, R. 1983. *Honor and the American dream*. New Brunswick, N.J.: Rutgers University Press.

Ladner, J. 1973. *Tomorrow's tomorrow*. New York: Doubleday.

Lewis, D. K. 1975. The black family: Socialization and sex roles. *Phylon* 36: 221–237.

Liebow, E. 1967. *Tally's corner: A study of Negro streetcorner men*. Boston: Little, Brown.

Magnum, G., and S. F. Seninger. 1978. Ghetto life styles and youth employment. In *Coming of age in the ghetto*. Baltimore, Md.: Johns Hopkins University Press.

Perkins, E. 1975. *Home is a dirty street*. Chicago: Third World Press.

Pope, H. 1969. Negro-white differences in decisions regarding illegitimate children. *Journal of Marriage and the Family* 31:756–764.

Rainwater, L. 1960. *And the poor get children*. Chicago: Quadrangle Books.

————. 1966. Crucible of identity: The lower class Negro family. *Daedalus* 45:172–216.

————. 1969. Sex in the culture of poverty. In *The individual, sex and society*. Ed. C. B. Broderick and J. Bernard. Baltimore, Md.: Johns Hopkins University Press.

————. 1970. *Behind ghetto walls*. Chicago: Aldine de Gruyter.

Schultz, D. A. 1969. *Coming up black: Patterns of ghetto socialization*. Englewood Cliffs, N.J.: Prentice-Hall.

Stack, C. B. 1974. *All our kin*. New York: Harper & Row.

Staples, R., ed. 1971. *The black family*. Belmont, Calif.: Wadsworth.

————. 1973. *The black woman in America*. Chicago: Nelson Hall.

Tenhouten, W. 1970. The black family: Myth and reality. *Psychiatry* 2:145–173.

Walter, A. R. 1978. The search for applicable theories of black family life. *Journal of Marriage and the Family* 40:117–129.

Whyte, W. F. 1943. A slum sex code. *American Journal of Sociology* 49:24–31.

Williams, T. A., and W. Kornblum. 1985. *Growing up poor*. Lexington, Mass.: D. C. Heath.

Willie, C. V., and J. Weinancy. 1970. The structure and composition of "problem" and "stable" families in a low-income population. In *The family life of black people*. Ed. C. V. Willie. Columbus, Ohio: Charles E. Merrill.

Wilson, W. J. 1978. *The declining significance of race*. Chicago: University of Chicago Press.

————. 1987. *The truly disadvantaged: The inner city, the underclass, and public policy*. Chicago: University of Chicago Press.

5   Paternity Risk among Adolescent Males

FREYA L. SONENSTEIN, JOSEPH H. PLECK,
AND LEIGHTON C. KU

Even though there is little supportive evidence, teenage males in the United States are typically stereotyped as being sexually very active and irresponsible. Terms such as "sexual adventurer" or "roving inseminator" have been used to describe a prototypical young male who pursues sexual conquests to demonstrate his virility and prowess (Sorensen 1973; Wattenberg 1990).[1] Although some young men undoubtedly fit this mold, a critical question is, How widespread is this behavior? This chapter looks at what is actually known about the sexual behavior of young men in the United States. Presenting information from a nationally representative survey of males ages 15–19 years of age about their levels of sexual activity, contraceptive use, and experience with pregnancies, it examines trends over time and factors associated with paternity risk.

Since sexual intercourse is a necessary precursor to pregnancy and paternity, the characteristics of young men engaging in early sexual activity without contraceptives are important in identifying adolescents at risk of becoming fathers. Until recently, however, little information was available (Sonenstein 1986; Study Group on the Male Role in Teenage Pregnancy and Parenting 1990). Almost two decades of research on the causes and consequences of pregnancy among adolescents had primarily focused on females (Chilman 1983; Hayes 1987; Miller and Moore 1990; Moore and Burt 1982).

Service and policy interventions had also largely ignored the obvious contribution of males to the scope of the adolescent pregnancy problem. Recently, however, several program and policy initiatives have explicitly

99

targeted young men. Youth agencies like the Urban League and the Boys Clubs have initiated programs promoting responsible sexual behavior among adolescent males (Dryfoos 1990). The Family Support Act of 1988 has made paternity establishment to obtain financial support for children born out of wedlock a key piece of welfare reform. Finally, the recognition that AIDS poses a major risk for sexually active teenagers has led schools and health agencies to educate *both* young men and young women about safer sexual practices including condom use.

Unfortunately, the knowledge base which should underlie these recent policy and program initiatives has not been developed. Since 1971 the periodic collection of nationally representative data from young women has documented a dramatic increase in sexual activity and pregnancies.[2] Although no one disputes that teenage males have contributed to this trend, only two studies, one in 1979 (Zelnik and Kantner 1980) and one in 1988 (Sonenstein, Pleck, and Ku 1989), can be used to assess changes over time in male sexual behavior. At the national level, other surveys have collected information about fertility behavior of young men and women,[3] but because of methodological differences, their results cannot be used comparatively to track trends across time.

Several excellent ethnographic and clinical studies have also examined aspects of fertility behavior among groups of young men living in particular neighborhoods or communities (Anderson 1989; Hendricks and Montgomery 1983; Sullivan 1989; and Wattenberg, Brewer, and Resnik 1991).[4] Such studies provide an in-depth understanding of how these particular young men view sex, pregnancy, and fatherhood; but it is potentially misleading to attribute their attitudes and behaviors to American young men in general.[5] Data from representative samples are needed to test whether these attitudes and behaviors are prevalent among a wider group of young men.

Data Sources

The 1988 National Survey of Adolescent Males (NSAM) was designed to gather information that would address some of the major gaps in our knowledge about patterns of sexual activity and contraception among U.S. teenage males. In this survey 1,880 never-married males, ages 15–19, were interviewed between April and November 1988. The sample is representative of noninstitutionalized never-married males, ages 15–19, living in households in the contiguous United States. Young men were not sampled if they were living in college dormitories, military barracks, prisons, or other group quarters at the time of the interview. About 10 percent of 15–19-year-old males live in these kinds of situations. The sample was stratified to overrepresent black and Hispanic young men. The response rate was 73.9 percent. Throughout this chapter percentages are calculated using weighted data that adjust for sampling stratification, nonresponse and poststratification alignment with the March 1987 Current Population Survey.

The 1988 survey repeated many questions covered in the 1979 National Survey of Young Men (Zelnik and Kantner 1980).[6] The sample used in the 1979 survey was limited to young men, ages 17–21, living in households in metropolitan areas. Given the differences in sampling frames between the 1988 and 1979 surveys, comparisons between the two data sets can only be made for a restricted portion of each data set, never-married males, ages 17–19, living in metropolitan areas (609 respondents in 1979; 742 respondents in 1988).

Sexual Experience

In 1988 three-fifths of never-married young men, ages 15–19, were potentially at risk of contributing to a pregnancy because they reported having had heterosexual intercourse at least once. Table 5-1 shows the distribution of young men by age and racial/ethnic group. As expected, older males were significantly more likely to be sexually experienced than younger ones. While 86 percent of 19-year-olds had had intercourse, 33 percent of 15-year-olds had. There were also distinct differences by race and ethnicity. Whereas over two-thirds of black 15-year-olds were sexually experienced, only one-third of Hispanic and one-quarter of white males of the same age had had intercourse.

Levels of sexual experience among teenagers appear to have risen during the 1980s. Proportionately more young men reported that they were sexually experienced in 1988 than in 1979. While two-thirds of 17–19-year-old males living in metropolitan areas were sexually experienced in 1979, three-quarters of those interviewed in 1988 reported that they had had intercourse. The rise was evident among both black and nonblack young men, from 71 percent to 88 percent for black males, and from 65 percent to 73 percent for nonblack males. (Sonenstein, Pleck, and Ku 1989). A similar rise in levels of sexual experience has been observed among young women. In 1982 the National Survey of Family Growth found that 47 percent of 15–19-year-old females reported having had intercourse, compared to 53 percent in 1988 (Forrest and Singh 1990).

Although the proportion of young men who are sexually experienced has risen since 1979, the evidence suggests that the amount of sexual activity among the sexually experienced has not increased at a corresponding rate. This is an important point, since exposure to the risk of

TABLE 5-1 Never-Married U.S. Males, Ages 15–19, Who Have Had Sexual Intercourse, 1988, by Racial/Ethnic Group and Age (percentages)

Age	All races	Black non-Hispanic	White non-Hispanic	Hispanic
15 to 19 years	60.4	80.6	56.8	59.7
15 years	32.6	68.6	25.6	32.8
16 years	49.9	70.1	46.7	47.2
17 years	65.6	89.6	59.1	87.6
18 years	71.6	82.5	71.4	52.8
19 years	85.7	95.9	84.5	82.2
Unweighted N	1880	676	752	385

Note: All percentages are weighted. "All Races" includes American Indians, Asians, and Pacific Islanders. For each age except 19 years, racial differences were significant, $p <$ .001. For "All Races," differences by age were significant, $p < .001$ (chi-square).

pregnancy is a function of the frequency of intercourse and number of partners, as well as contraceptive practices. Although three-fifths of teenage men have had intercourse, they face widely varying levels of risk of paternity. Some young men have infrequent intercourse and use contraception consistently—with little risk of impregnation. Others have a high level of sexual activity and rarely use contraception—their risk is obviously higher.

While more teenagers were sexually experienced in 1988, there were actually some signs of delays in very early sexual initiation. Significantly fewer young men in metropolitan areas had initiated intercourse before the age of 15 in 1988 than in 1979, 19 percent compared to 26 percent. However, by age 17 the young men in 1988 had surpassed their earlier counterparts in sexual experience, 61 percent compared to 51 percent.

Consistent with their reports of initiating sex at slightly later ages, young men in 1988 also reported accumulating fewer sexual partners than in 1979, a mean of 6.0 versus 7.34; fewer partners in the last 4 weeks, a mean of .72 versus .96; and fewer episodes of intercourse in the last 4 weeks, a mean of 3.0 versus 4.6 (Sonenstein, Pleck, and Ku 1991). Thus although the proportion of young men who are sexually experienced appears to have risen, the level of sexual activity among the experienced may actually have dropped since 1979, reducing the opportunities for the creation of a pregnancy.

Contrary to stereotyped expectations that young American males have high levels of sexual activity with multiple partners, the data show relatively modest levels of activity among those who are sexually experienced. In 1988 the experienced 15–19-year-olds reported a mean of 1.9 partners in the past year. Table 5-2 shows the distribution of sexually

TABLE 5-2 Number of Partners in Last Year among Sexually Experienced U.S. Males, Ages 15–19, 1988, by Race/Ethnic Group (percentages)

Partners	All races	Black non-Hispanic	White non-Hispanic	Hispanic
0	9.0	9.8	8.1	14.5
1	45.3	33.7	49.4	39.4
2	25.0	27.4	23.2	33.2
3–4	12.9	18.3	11.9	9.2
5+	7.5	10.5	7.2	3.5
Unweighted N	1231	559	444	228

Partners	Age 15	Age 16	Age 17	Age 18	Age 19
0	14.2	8.0	11.1	6.7	7.8
1	33.3	50.6	44.7	48.9	43.4
2	28.9	21.7	26.9	23.4	25.4
3–4	15.4	13.6	11.8	13.0	12.5
5+	7.9	5.8	5.3	7.7	10.7
Unweighted N	161	242	313	291	224

Note: All percentages are weighted. "All Races" includes American Indians, Asians, and Pacific Islanders. Racial/ethnic differences in numbers of partners were significant at $p <$ .01. No significant differences in number of partners by age were detected (chi-square).

experienced males reporting 0 to 5 or more partners in the last 12 months by race and age. Almost one-tenth (9%) of these respondents had not had a sexual partner in the last year, and an additional 45 percent had only had one partner. Thus more than half of sexually experienced young men had no more than one partner in the last year. Only one-fifth of the experienced reported three or more partners in the last year. Black young men reported significantly more partners in the past year than did white or Hispanic respondents, but older males did not report more partners than younger ones. Other analyses indicate that sexual relationships reported by adolescent males are generally monogamous and episodic. The average sexually experienced respondent reported spending six months of the past year without a sexual partner. Only 20 percent of the sexually experienced males reported that during the past year they had had more than one partner in the same month (Sonenstein, Pleck, and Ku 1991).[7]

These data indicate that most sexually experienced adolescent males engage in low levels of sexual activity. Over half had one partner at the most in the previous year. When there was more than one partner, relationships were typically sequential and separated by months of abstinence. Nonetheless, approximately one-fifth of sexually experienced adolescent males (one-eighth of all adolescent males) reported three or more partners in the last twelve months. It is this small group of males that more closely fits the stereotype of high levels of sexual activity.

Contraceptive Use

Effective contraception is crucial to pregnancy prevention among the sexually active. In 1988 close to one-quarter (23%) of sexually experienced young men were at risk of paternity the last time they had intercourse because they reported using no contraception or an ineffective method of contraception, like withdrawal or rhythm. Over half (57%) reported that they had used a condom, either by itself or in combination with another method of contraception. One-fifth said that their partner had used an effective female method of contraception like the pill, diaphragm, IUD, sponge, foam, jelly, or suppository. Table 5-3 shows the distribution of contraceptive use at last intercourse among the sexually experienced by age and racial/ethnic group. Hispanic respondents reported the highest exposure to unplanned pregnancy. Almost one-third (31%) of the Hispanic males used no method or an ineffective method, compared to one-fifth of black respondents and almost one-quarter (23%) of white respondents. Condom use was significantly higher among the black respondents (66%) than among white or Hispanic respondents (54% and 53%). The use of effective female methods of contraception was higher among white males (22%) compared to black or Hispanic respondents (15% and 16%, respectively). There were also significant differences by age. The youngest respondents were the most likely to have used no method or an ineffective method of contraception at last intercourse. The oldest respondents were much more likely to have used an effective female method. Condom use was high at all ages, decreasing slightly for older respondents.

Comparisons with earlier data suggest a precipitous decline in the proportion of young men reporting unprotected sexual intercourse. In 1979 half of metropolitan males, ages 17–19, reported that they had used no method or an ineffective method the last time they had intercourse. In 1988 the proportion had shrunk to 21 percent. This change was accompanied by a doubling of the rates of reported condom use, from 21 percent to 58 percent. The proportions using effective female methods appeared slightly lower in 1988 compared to 1979 (22% compared to 28%). These data indicate that the acceptability and use of condoms has probably increased since 1979, and further analyses of condom use at first intercourse by the year respondents began to have intercourse indicate that most of the rise probably occurred after 1985 when AIDS became a major public health issue (Sonenstein, Pleck, and Ku 1989). Reports of condom use among young women, ages 15–19, have also risen. At first intercourse, condoms were used twice as much in 1988 as in 1982 (Forrest and Singh 1990).

TABLE 5-3 Never-Married Sexually Active U.S. Males, Ages 15–19, Using Contraception at Last Intercourse, by Method, Racial/Ethnic Group, and Age, 1988 (percentages)

	All races	Black non-Hispanic	White non-Hispanic	Hispanic
Percent using condom				
15 to 19 years	56.9	65.5	54.4	53.0
15 years	59.5	70.0	50.9	59.6
16 years	62.3	63.8	64.4	44.3
17 years	57.8	68.4	54.4	64.9
18 years	53.5	64.3	50.0	43.3
19 years	55.2	60.7	54.6	46.1
Percent using effective female method without condom				
15 to 19 years	19.7	14.5	22.2	15.6
15 years	4.9	8.6	3.2	6.1
16 years	8.2	11.1	7.4	7.2
17 years	20.6	15.9	23.7	12.5
18 years	28.6	16.3	34.1	14.5
19 years	23.0	19.7	22.6	32.3
Percent using ineffective or no contraceptive method				
15 to 19 years	23.4	20.0	23.4	31.3
15 years	35.6	21.5	45.9	34.3
16 years	29.5	25.1	28.1	48.5
17 years	21.5	15.7	22.0	22.6
18 years	17.9	19.4	15.8	42.2
19 years	21.8	19.7	22.8	21.5
Unweighted N	1244	540	437	222

Note: All percentages are weighted. "All Races" includes American Indians, Asians, and Pacific Islanders. "Using Condom" includes using condoms alone or with other methods, such as oral contraceptives. "Effective Female Methods" includes oral contraceptives, diaphragm, IUD, Today Sponge, foam, jelly, or suppository, alone or in combination with other methods, but does not include condoms. "Ineffective or No Contraceptive Method" includes withdrawal, douching, and rhythm or calendar methods, but does not include condoms or "Effective Female Methods." These three groups are mutually exclusive and sum to 100 percent. For "15 to 19 years," differences by race were significant, $p < .01$. For "All Races," differences by age were significant at $p < .001$ (chi-square).

Although a higher proportion of adolescent males was sexually experienced in 1988 compared to 1979, the risk of pregnancy for young men as a whole may have decreased because of higher rates of reported condom use among the sexually active. In 1979, 33 percent of 17–19-year-old males could be designated at high risk for paternity because they were sexually experienced and did not use an effective method of contraception at last intercourse. In 1988 the proportion at risk had dropped to 16 percent.

It is important to observe that the level of contraception at last intercourse is much higher than the share of youth who always use contraception during intercourse, that is, the level of consistent contraceptive use. Only one-third of the sexually experienced respondents said that they had used a condom 100 percent of the time with every partner in the past year. Twelve percent said that their partners had used the pill 100 percent of the time. When responses to these two questions are combined, 41 percent of the sexually experienced young men reported that they had either used a condom or the pill 100 percent of the time with all the partners they had had in the past year. The remaining 59 percent of the sexually experienced respondents were potentially without contraceptive protection at some time during the previous year.[8] Indeed, 10 percent of the sexually experienced young men reported that they had never used condoms or pills in the last twelve months.

Pregnancy Experience

Although the paternity risk appears to be lower among young men in 1988 compared to 1979, more than half of the sexually experienced in 1988 continued to have had unprotected sexual intercourse at some time in the last year. Table 5-4 shows the distribution of sexually experienced respondents in 1988 who reported that they had ever had some experience with partners' pregnancies, by racial/ethnic group and age. Over one-quarter (27%) of the sexually experienced young men responded affirmatively to the question: "Have you ever been told that you have made someone pregnant?" The proportion was lowest for white males (24%), highest for black males (35%) and Hispanic males fell in between (30%). As expected, older teens also reported a significantly higher incidence of being told about pregnancies than younger ones.

A follow-up question was asked: "Have you ever actually made someone pregnant?" The proportion of young men reporting actual pregnancies was lower. Among the sexually experienced, 8 percent reported that they had made someone pregnant. Black young men were significantly more likely to say they had made a partner pregnant than white and Hispanic men (12% compared to 7% for both whites and Hispanics). Older teenagers also reported more pregnancies than younger ones. Among 19-year-old males, 14 percent of the sexually experienced reported an actual pregnancy compared to 0.2 percent of 15-year-olds.

We can only speculate about the reasons why respondents report fewer actual pregnancies than incidents of being told that they had made someone pregnant. Some of the respondents may have had pregnancy scares that did not turn out to be real. Some may have heard secondhand about pregnancies that they could not verify. Some may doubt that they were the impregnators for pregnancies that were attributed to them. Unfor-

TABLE 5-4 Pregnancy Experience among Never-Married, Sexually Experienced U.S. Males, Ages 15–19, by Race/Ethnic Group and Age, 1988 (percentages)

Pregnancy experience	All races	Black non-Hispanic	White non-Hispanic	Hispanic
No pregnancy	73.0	65.3	76.3	69.8
Told about pregnancy	27.0	34.7	23.7	30.2
Actual pregnancy	7.8	11.6	6.5	7.3
Live birth	2.3	4.8	1.7	1.6
Unweighted N	1263	560	444	228

Pregnancy experience	Age 15	Age 16	Age 17	Age 18	Age 19
No pregnancy	82.1	76.0	78.2	69.1	65.4
Told about pregnancy	17.9	24.0	21.8	30.9	34.6
Actual pregnancy	0.2	5.1	5.4	9.2	14.4
Live birth	0.2	2.9	1.4	3.9	1.9
Unweighted N	163	248	319	300	233

Note: All percentages are weighted. "All Races" includes American Indians, Asians, and Pacific Islanders. Racial/ethnic differences in being told about pregnancy experience were significant at $p < .01$ and in actual pregnancy and birth experience at $p < .05$. Age differences in being told about pregnancy and actual pregnancy were significant at $p < .01$ (chi-square).

tunately, the questionnaire did not ask for explanations of this reporting pattern.

For each actual pregnancy, the respondents were also asked about the outcome of the pregnancy. Only 1.9 percent of all the sexually experienced respondents indicated that they had experienced a live birth.[9] The proportion, however, was higher for black young men at 4.8 percent compared to 1.7 percent for white males and 1.6 percent for Hispanic males. Thus the reported incidence of adolescent fatherhood among the sexually experienced in this sample was very low, 42 respondents (unweighted) in all. As a proportion of all 15–19-year-old never-married young men, only 1.4 percent reported that they had fathered a child. Among the black respondents the rate was 3.9 percent.

The incidence of births in the National Survey of Adolescent Males (NSAM) sample appears somewhat low compared to other available data. Estimates based on 1988 birth certificate information gathered by the National Center for Health Statistics (1990) set the birthrate for all 15–19-year-old males at 2.0 percent and at 4.8 percent for black teen males. Since the birthrate estimates from birth certificates are for a single-year, whereas the NSAM birthrates are cumulative lifetime rates, one would expect the NSAM rates to be higher, not lower. The NSAM sample was limited to never-married respondents, even though birth records include births to married teens, but it is unlikely that the absence of married respondents in NSAM fully accounts for the apparently lower rate of reported births. In 1988 only 1.8 percent of 15–19-year-old males were married (U.S. Bureau of the Census 1988), although many of these marriages were probably associated with pregnancies.

The observation that NSAM respondents may underreport births is similar to the findings of other studies that have noted inconsistencies in fertility histories provided by male respondents. Mott (1983), for example, reported that almost half the fathers in the National Longitudinal Survey of Youth had at least one discrepancy in their retrospective birth histories, and the reported cumulative birthrates for males were substantially lower than those of young women in the sample. Cherlin, Griffith, and McCarthy (1983) found in the 1980 Current Population Survey that men appeared to underreport children from previous marriages who were living with their mothers.

Male respondents may not be good informants about pregnancies and births resulting from their sexual behavior. They are, after all, reporting secondhand on conditions experienced by their partners. Some young men may have made someone pregnant or fathered a baby, but not know at all because their partner never told them. Some females may not wish to involve the father in raising the baby, having an abortion, or placing the child up for adoption. This may particularly be true if the relationship has already ended. Second, some young men may have been told they made a partner pregnant, but not believe it. They may deny their role because they feel their partner is trying to "trap" them into marriage or child support. Third, some young men may know they made someone pregnant, but not tell an interviewer, due to concerns about privacy or legal consequences. Finally, in addition to underreporting, some young men may overreport births or pregnancies, claiming they made someone pregnant or fathered a baby, when they did not. If impregnation is a sign of virility or status, some males may boast about nonexistent accomplishments. Given these potential problems with the young men's reports and the low numbers of births in the sample, our analyses focus on their levels of sexual activity and contraceptive use as measures of their paternity risk. Young men can report these behaviors based on firsthand experience and therefore, analyzing characteristics associated with risk taking may provide a more accurate picture of population at risk of producing pregnancies and births than analyzing that portion of the sample reporting pregnancies and births.

Levels of Paternity Risk

Our index of paternity risk ranks all the respondents in the sample according to their levels of unprotected sexual intercourse. Forty-two percent of the sample were considered to be at no risk for paternity because they reported no sexual intercourse in the past year. They were scored at 0. Twenty-four percent were considered to be at low risk because they had intercourse, but used condoms or pills 100 percent of the time during the past year. They were scored at 2. Combining these two categories, we see that two-thirds of U.S. male teenagers in 1988 reported behavior that put them at very low risk of contributing to a pregnancy.

The remaining respondents were grouped into four higher-risk categories based on the estimated number of times they had had intercourse without using a pill or condom during the past year. Nine percent reported one unprotected incident and were scored at 2; 15 percent reported 2–10 acts and were scored at 3; 5 percent reported 11–25 acts and were scored at 4; and 4 percent reported more than 25 incidents and were scored at 5.[10]

To identify factors associated with greater risk taking, we then used an ordered logistic regression model to regress the risk index on a set of variables describing the young men's demographic, family and personal characteristics (Maddala 1983). In ordered logit a positive coefficient means that a factor increases the likelihood of being higher in the ordered sequence, that is, increases the level of unprotected sex. A negative coefficient is associated with reduced risk.

As shown in Table 5-5, two of the most important factors associated with unprotected intercourse were race and age. Consistent with the previously reported bivariate findings, being black and being older were associated with significantly higher levels of risk taking ($p < .001$). The independent effect of race on paternity risk remained even after the effects of the generally lower socioeconomic status of blacks was controlled by including measures of family economic status in the model along with other variables. Indeed, we found that higher family income was associated with higher levels of unprotected intercourse ($p < .001$), but living in a census tract with higher poverty was marginally associated with higher levels of risk ($p < .07$). On the face of it these are inconsistent findings. However, although there is a correlation between low family income and neighborhood poverty level, these variables can and apparently do have different effects at the level of individual behavior. One interpretation, supported by other analyses we have conducted, is that when young men have access to greater economic resources through higher family income, they are able to go out more frequently with more

TABLE 5-5 Odds Ratios for Ordered Logistic Regression of
Variables Associated with Level of Unprotected Intercourse in
Last Year Among Never-Married U.S. Males,
Ages 15–19

Variable	Odds ratio	t
Black	2.046	5.861[a]
Hispanic	1.206	1.396
Other	0.748	−1.065
Family income	1.093	2.982[a]
Income missing	0.966	−0.173
Proportion of area in poverty	2.071	1.845
Living in a tract	0.914	−0.792
Age 16	2.123	5.297[a]
Age 17	2.746	7.217[a]
Age 18	3.014	7.496[a]
Age 19	4.179	8.591[a]
Lived w/ mom only at age 14	1.175	1.418
Lived w/ mom & other at age 14	1.077	0.263
Lived in other arrangement	1.239	1.100
Behind in school	1.092	0.724
Self-esteem index	1.059	0.628
Locus of control index	0.755	−4.269[a]
Mother a teenage mother	1.614	5.092[a]
Mother's age missing	1.292	1.130
Maternal employment level[b]	1.272	4.183[a]
Importance of religion	0.792	−4.230[a]
Hours worked in last year	1.000	6.582[a]
Strictness of family rules	0.811	−3.200[a]

Notes:
$N = 1849$
Model chi-square $= 403.55$
[a]$p < .001$
[b]between ages 5 and 15

young women, controlling for the effects of neighborhood poverty level.
Young men living in neighborhoods with higher poverty levels, on the
other hand, exhibit more paternity risk taking, controlling for the effects
of family income, possibly because of neighborhood norms reinforcing
high levels of unprotected sexual activity in poorer neighborhoods (Anderson 1989; Sullivan 1989), and because young men in poorer neighborhoods perceive lower opportunity costs associated with pregnancy
(Lundberg and Plotnick 1990).

Higher levels of unprotected intercourse were also significantly associated with other family characteristics. Respondents whose mothers were
teenagers when they first gave birth had higher levels of paternity risk (*p*

< .001). Respondents whose mothers worked during the respondents' developmental years also exhibited higher risk ($p < .001$). Respondents who reported that family rules about staying out late, dating, or alcohol were strict had lower levels of pregnancy risk ($p < .001$), as did respondents who reported that religion was very important to them ($p < .001$). These findings suggest that family norms, as measured by the mother's fertility history and the importance of religion, and parental supervision as measured by family rules and the mother's employment, may be key factors affecting young men's risk taking. Interestingly, family structure measured by whether the respondent lived in a two-parent household (the residual category), a single-parent household, a household composed of a mother and another adult, or another type of household did not have an independent effect on pregnancy risk. Living in a single-parent family has been found to be associated with increased rates of sexual activity among young women (Hofferth and Hayes 1987).

Finally, some of the personal characteristics of the respondents themselves were also significantly associated with higher levels of unprotected intercourse. When the respondents had worked more hours during the past year, they were more likely to have a higher level of paternity risk ($p < .001$). These respondents may also have had greater access to money, which facilitates going out with young women, an argument we made earlier about the positive association between family income and risk status. Also, young men scoring lower on an abbreviated measure of locus of control (Pleck, Sonenstein, and Ku 1991) had higher levels of risk taking ($p <.001$). Neither the abridged measure of self-esteem (Pleck, Sonenstein, and Ku 1991) nor the measure of the respondents' being behind in school showed a significant independent association with paternity risk.

Conclusions

Our analyses of data from the National Survey of Adolescent Males indicate that although three-fifths of 15–19-year-olds have experienced sexual intercourse, very few report the high levels of sexual activity that are believed to be common among young men. Most often, the young men reported a single partner in the previous year, and on average they spent six months out of the last year with no partners. A small proportion of young men, one-fifth of the sexually experienced and one-eighth of all teenage males, could conservatively be characterized as promiscuous because they had three or more partners in the previous year.

Comparisons with 1979 data indicate that more young men are sexually experienced, but the proportion of young men at risk of paternity has gone down substantially because condom use is more than twice as high as 1979 levels. In 1979 one-third of all 17–19-year-old males could be designated as potential impregnators because they had had intercourse and the last time they failed to use an effective means of contraception. In 1988 only 16 percent of 17–19-year-olds fitted this same risk criterion. However, if lack of consistent pill or condom use over the previous twelve months is used to identify paternity risk, one-third of all adolescent males would then be categorized as risk takers in 1988. There are no comparable data to assess what this statistic would have been in 1979, but it was undoubtedly higher.

Our analyses of factors associated with paternity risk taking in the 1988 sample indicate that being black and being older significantly raise the odds of a young man's exposure to risk, primarily because of the longer periods and higher levels of sexual activity among these groups. Residence in a poor neighborhood is also associated with higher levels of risk taking, a findings that corroborates ethnographic accounts of the higher acceptability of sexual activity without responsibility for contraception or potential progeny among young men in some inner-city neighborhoods (Anderson 1989; Sullivan 1989). However, the higher a young man's family income, the more likely he was to have elevated levels of paternity risk. We hypothesize that young men need money to go out with young women, and that family income and their own employment—also positively associated with risk level—are both sources for these funds. Family expectations and rules also appear to be related to risk taking, as shown by the higher levels of risk among young men whose mothers were teenagers when they had their first birth, and by lower levels of risk among males whose families had strict rules about going out and who thought that religion was important. When a young man's mother worked while he was growing up, the odds of higher risk taking increased. We could argue that children of employed mothers have lower levels of supervision than other children, providing more opportunities for sexual experimentation. Alternatively, we could argue that these children may become independent earlier than other children, leading them to try adult behaviors sooner. Finally, young men with low scores on the locus of control personality measure also showed higher levels of risk taking.

Most of the findings discussed above are consistent with the literature on fertility behavior of adolescent females, with two noteworthy exceptions. We are not aware of any study that has found that family income is related to elevated levels of sexual risk taking among females. However, we note that few studies have been able to differentiate between the effects of neighborhood income levels and family income levels. There is intuitive face validity in the notion that higher family income facilitates higher levels of sexual activity for young men; it is not clear, however, why contraceptive use does not rise accordingly. Among young women higher family socioeconomic status (measured by parents' education levels) is associated with lower levels of sexual experience and higher levels of contraceptive responsibility among the sexually experienced (Hofferth and Hayes 1987).

Furthermore, the mother's employment has not been found to be a significant independent predictor of sexual behavior among adolescent women. It is difficult to explain why young men may be more vulnerable to this factor than young women, although research in other areas of child development has uncovered a similar pattern (Desai, Chase-Lansdale, and Michael 1989).

Comparisons with the literature on female adolescents lead finally to a discussion of why, given these data about declining risk rates among adolescent males over the last decade, the estimated pregnancy rates and STD transmission rates among female adolescents have been rising. It is critical to remember that the partners of adolescent females are often not adolescent males. Among teenage women giving birth to babies in 1988, 41 percent reported that the father was over the age of 19 (National Center for Health Statistics 1990). However, the partners of adolescent males are most often the same age as the males. In NSAM a comparison of the male's age to his last partner's age revealed no statistically significant difference. Thus pregnancy and STD rates among adolescent females are partially driven by the behavior of partners who are no longer teenagers. Other analyses that we have conducted indicate that those most likely to have adopted higher levels of condom use are those who became sexually experienced in 1986 or later, the period when AIDS became the focus of public health campaigns (Sonenstein, Pleck, and Ku 1989). Thus some of the female's partners may belong to an older generation who developed their contraceptive habits before the condom campaigns.

National survey data indicate that the majority of teenage males report behavior suggesting low levels of paternity risk. In 1988 two-thirds of 15–19-year-old males had not engaged in unprotected sexual intercourse in the last year, just under one-tenth reported a single incident, and just under one-fourth reported multiple incidents. While low levels of paternity risk appear to be the norm, there is a small group of young men (9%) who report more than 10 episodes of unprotected intercourse in the past year. It is clear that preventive interventions need to target this group of high-risk males and their partners so that their exposure to the unintended consequences of pregnancy and birth are reduced.

Notes

1. See also Chapters 3 and 4 by Sullivan and Anderson in this volume.

2. The National Surveys of Young Women in 1971, 1976, and 1979, and the National Survey of Family Growth, Cycle III in 1982 and Cycle IV in 1988, have routinely collected information about sexual activity, contraceptive use, pregnancy, and its resolution for young women ages 15–19.

3. These include the 1981 and 1987 follow-up waves of the National Survey of Children, the National Longitudinal Survey of Youth begun in 1979 (used by Lerman in this volume), the Planned Parenthood Poll in 1986, the High School and Beyond Survey begun in 1980 with a cohort of high school sophomores, and the 1988 General Social Survey.

4. See also Sonenstein 1986 for a review of earlier work and Chapters 3, 4, and 10 by Sullivan, Anderson, and Wattenberg in this volume.

5. The authors of these studies are generally careful to point out the generalizations to wider populations are inappropriate.

6. See Sonenstein, Pleck, and Ku 1989 for a more detailed comparison of the two data sets.

7. Respondents were asked to provide the start and stop dates of their sexual relationships with their six most recent partners in the previous twelve months. These data were used to calculate the number of months in the last year in which there were no partners, one partner, and more than one partner. For the forty-five cases with more than six partners in the last twelve months, estimates were imputed, based on patterns observed for the third through sixth last partners.

8. Some additional proportion of the sexually experienced may have consistently been protected by using pills some of the time and condoms the rest of the time, or by 100-percent use of another effective method. At last intercourse, less than 1 percent used effective methods other than condoms or pills.

9. An additional .7 percent reported that their partner was currently pregnant.

10. The respondents reported separately the proportions of times they had used a condom and the pill for each partner. These reports were transformed into annual estimates of the proportion of times a condom was used and the proportion of times a pill was used. To calculate the number of acts of intercourse where neither method was used, we first calculated the proportion of times either a pill or condom was used. To do this, we chose the midpoint between the highest proportion of coverage reported (either pills or condoms) and the sum of both pill and condom coverage, capped at 100 percent. This midpoint percentage of coverage was subtracted from 1 to obtain a percentage estimate of no coverage, which was multiplied by the estimated number of acts of intercourse in the last year.

References

Anderson, E. 1989. "Sex Codes and Family Life Among Poor Inner-City Youth." *Annals of the American Academy of Political and Social Science* 501:59–78.

Cherlin, A., J. Griffith, and J. McCarthy. 1983. "A Note on Maritally Disrupted

Men's Reports of Child Support in the June 1980 Current Population Survey." *Demography* 20(3): 385–389.

Chilman, C. S. 1983. *Adolescent Sexuality in a Changing American Society*. 2d ed. New York: John Wiley.

Desai, S., P. L. Chase-Lansdale, and R. T. Michael. 1989. "Mother or Market? Effects of Maternal Employment on the Intellectual Ability of 4-Year-Old Children." *Demography* 26(4): 545–562.

Dryfoos, J. G. 1990. *Adolescents At Risk*. New York: Oxford University Press.

Forrest, J., and S. Singh. 1990. "The Sexual and Reproductive Behavior of American Women, 1982–1988." *Family Planning Perspectives* 22:5.

Greeley, A., R. Michael, and T. Smith. 1990. "Americans and Their Sexual Partners." *Society* 27:27.

Hayes, C. 1987. *Risking the Future: Adolescent Sexuality, Pregnancy, and Childbearing*. Vol. 1. Washington, D.C.: National Academy Press.

Hendricks, L., and T. Montgomery. 1983. "A Limited Population of Unmarried Adolescent Fathers: A Preliminary Report of Their Views on Fatherhood and the Relationship with the Mothers of Their Children." *Adolescence* 18:201–210.

Hofferth, S., and C. Hayes. 1987. *Risking the Future: Adolescent Sexuality, Pregnancy, and Childbearing*. Vol. 2. Washington, D.C.: National Academy Press.

Louis Harris and Associates, Inc. 1986. "American Teens Speak: Sex, Myths, TV, and Birth Control." New York.

Lundberg, S., and R. Plotnick. 1990. "Testing the Opportunity-Cost Hypothesis of Adolescent Premarital Childbearing." Working Paper No. 8. New York: Russell Sage Foundation.

Maddala, G. S. 1983. *Limited Dependent and Qualitative Variables in Econometrics*. Cambridge: Cambridge University Press.

Miller, B., and K. Moore. 1990. "Adolescent Sexual Behavior, Pregnancy, and Parenting: Research through the 1980s." *Journal of Marriage and the Family* 52:1025–1044.

Moore, K., and M. Burt. 1982. *Private Crisis, Public Cost: Policy Perspectives on Teenage Childbearing*. Washington, D.C.: Urban Institute Press.

Moore, K., and J. Peterson. 1989. "Wave III National Survey of Children: A Description of Data, Consequences of Teenage Pregnancy." Report. Washington, D.C.: Child Trends.

Mott, F. L. 1983. "Fertility-Related Data in the 1982 National Longitudinal Survey of Work Experience of Youth: An Evaluation of Data Quality and Some Preliminary Analytical Results." Report. Columbus: Ohio State University.

National Center for Health Statistics. 1990. "Advance Report of Final Natality Statistics." *Mon. Vit. Stat. Rept.* 39(4): 26–27. Tables 13 and 14.

Pleck, J., F. Sonenstein, and L. Ku. 1991. "Adolescent Males' Condom Use: Relationships Between Perceived Costs-Benefits and Consistency." *Journal of Marriage and Family* 53(4): 733–745.

Sonenstein, F. 1986. "Risking Paternity: Sex and Contraception among Adolescent Males." In *Adolescent Fatherhood*, edited by A. Elster and M. Lamb. Hillsdale, N.J.: Lawrence Erlbaum.

Sonenstein, F., J. H. Pleck, and L. Ku. 1989. "Sexual Activity, Condom Use and AIDS Awareness Among Adolescent Males." *Family Planning Perspectives*, 21:4, 162–167.

Sonenstein, F., J. Pleck, L. Ku, and C. Calhoun. 1991. *Determinants of Contraceptive Use by Adolescent Males*. Final Report to National Institute of Child Health and Human Development. Washington, D.C.: Urban Institute.

Sorensen, R. 1973. *Adolescent Sexuality in Contemporary America: Personal Values and Sexual Behavior, Ages 13–19*. New York: World Publishing.

Study Group on the Male Role in Teenage Pregnancy and Parenting. 1990. *The Male Role in Teenage Pregnancy and Parenting: New Directions for Public Policy*. New York: Vera Institute of Justice.

Sullivan, M. 1989. "Absent Fathers in the Inner City." *Annals* 501:48–58.

U.S. Bureau of the Census. 1989. *Marital Status and Living Arrangements: March 1988* Current Population Reports. Series p-20, no. 433, pp. 9 and 29.

Walker, S. H., and D. B. Duncan. 1967. "Estimation of the Probability of an Event as a Function of Several Independent Variables." *Biometrica* 54:167–179.

Wattenberg, E. 1990. "Evidence about Paternity Decisions: Perspectives from Young Mothers and Young Fathers." Presentation at the Annual Conference of the Association of Public Policy and Management. San Francisco, October.

Wattenberg, E., R. Brewer, and M. Resnick. 1991. "A Study of Paternity Decisions: Perspectives from Young Mothers and Young Fathers." Report submitted to the Ford Foundation. Minneapolis–St. Paul: University of Minnesota.

Zelnick, M., and J. Kantner. 1980. "Sexual Activity, Contraceptive Use, and Pregnancy among Metropolitan-Area Teenagers: 1971–1979." *Family Planning Perspectives* 12:230.

6   When and Why Fathers Matter: Impacts of Father Involvement on the Children of Adolescent Mothers

FRANK F. FURSTENBERG, JR., AND
KATHLEEN MULLAN HARRIS

After a long period of scholarly neglect, social scientists are finally beginning to pay attention to the influence of fathers on children. This new tide of interest in the role of fathers has been so strong that the standard cliché that fathers have been slighted in studies of family behavior hardly applies any longer. Recent research on teenage parenthood represents a particularly good example of the growing interest in the extent and consequences of male involvement.

Years ago Clark Vincent (1961), in a classic study of unmarried mothers, took note of the social invisibility of unmarried fathers. Vincent traced the inattention to the fathers to a number of different sources. The principal one, he claimed, could be traced to the patriarchal assumption in American culture that females must be held primarily accountable for sexual transgressions:

> The lack of research on unmarried fathers may be very inconsistent with the fact that they represent one-half the illicit-conception equation, but is quite consistent with, and can be understood within the context of, other social practices and attitudes (p. 5).

For nearly a quarter of a century Vincent's observation was occasionally registered, but left unchallenged. Not until the late 1970s did researchers begin to take full cognizance of the missing male partner of teenage parents. In the past five years a veritable outpouring of studies

The authors are grateful for support from the Ford Foundation, Hewlett Foundation, Robert Wood Johnson Foundation, and the Rockefeller Foundation.

117

has appeared on teenage fatherhood and the male partners of teenage mothers. Several recent books on this topic have culled the diverse and scattered literature on this subject (see Elster and Lamb 1986; Robinson 1988). And an excellent review by Parke and Neville (1987), commissioned by the Panel on Adolescent Pregnancy and Childbearing, has organized and synthesized the burgeoning research on teenage fatherhood.

Not surprisingly, large gaps remain in our understanding of how males contribute to the process of early family formation and of the consequences of young fathers' involvement for the economic and psychological well-being of their offspring. As Parke and Neville note, almost all research on these critical issues is confined to the transition to parenthood and the period immediately following childbirth. Next to nothing is known about patterns of support and participation by fathers beyond infancy into later childhood and adolescence. This void in our information about the continuing role of fathers means that we are largely ignorant of the long-term consequences of paternal involvement for the development of children and young adults.

There are, however, studies on the effect of fathers' participation after marital disruption has occurred. Many researchers have assumed that greater support from nonresidential fathers would reduce the ill effects of divorce (Chase-Lansdale and Hetherington 1989; Emery 1988; Weiss 1975). A few small-scale studies have produced findings that are consistent with that assumption (Hetherington, Cox, and Cox 1978; Hess and Camara 1979; Wallerstein and Kelly 1980). However, results obtained from a nationally representative sample of children in maritally disrupted families found that nonresidential fathers' involvement was unrelated to a variety of child outcomes (Furstenberg, Morgan, and Allison 1987). Children who had more frequent contact with their fathers and had closer relations were not performing better socially or emotionally in mid-adolescence.

What might explain the perplexing finding that fathers' involvement does not matter more to the well-being of children? First, the level of paternal involvement by fathers living outside the home could be too low to have much impact on the child. Even children with relatively regular relations might experience relative deprivation and be sensitive to what is lacking in their relationship with their fathers. Second, the effects of participation might vary widely, depending on the way that the fathers' attention was received by the residential parents. If mothers were unwelcoming or hostile to high levels of involvement, any positive impact might be negated. More involved fathers could pose a threat to the authority of residential parent surrogates (i.e., stepparents, boyfriends, uncles, and the like), precipitating conflict and competition. Finally, it is conceivable that fathers generally matter less than we might imagine. If relations with mothers (or mother surrogates) are positive, the added benefit of a good relationship with a father may not be very significant.

It is difficult to ascertain whether these possibilities apply more broadly to the situation of adolescent parents and their partners. We set them forth only as a reminder that the seemingly obvious benefits for children of paternal participation in disrupted (or even intact) families cannot be assumed without stronger evidence than has been produced to date. This chapter examines the consequences of paternal involvement for children's well-being in families formed by adolescent blacks in an effort to advance our knowledge about the impact of fathers' involvement on children's well-being in a population at great risk of long-term disadvantage. This research is one of the few to consider the effects of paternal involvement on children in later adolescence and early adulthood. Through the use of a unique longitudinal data set, we were able to examine the extent and quality of male involvement in the lives of children of teenage mothers for 20 years and to analyze the effect of that involvement on children's development and well-being as they became young adults. Can we demonstrate that participation by nonresidential fathers (both in and outside the home) affects the well-being of children in later life?

The Baltimore Study

The data are drawn from a study that began in Baltimore during the mid-1960s, as part of an evaluation of this country's first comprehensive care programs for teenage mothers. Some 400 teenage parents were followed from pregnancy until their children were preschoolers in 1972. The participants were all 18 or younger when their first child was born. Most were black and all came from families that were poor or had only modest means. (For a full description of the origins of the study, see Furstenberg 1976.) The first phase of the Baltimore study traced the consequences of early childbearing for the mother and, to a lesser extent, the child. A portion of the analysis dealt with the participation of the males in accounting for the success of the young mother's adaptation to premature parenthood and the early development of their children.

The early findings on paternal involvement revealed a great deal of diversity. About half of the fathers married the adolescent mother either before or shortly after childbirth. Most of these marriages were short-lived. The continued involvement of formerly married males was only slightly greater than the participation of never-married men at the time of the five-year follow-up (Furstenberg and Talvitie 1979; Mott 1990). Children sometimes benefited from the involvement of males outside the

TABLE 6-1 Number of Years Spent with Fathers during Childhood, Ages 1–18

Number of years	Biological father		Stepfather		All fathers	
	%	Cum. %	%	Cum. %	%	Cum. %
0	53.1	53.1	52.6	52.6	7.5	7.5
1	2.6	55.7	0.9	53.5	0.4	7.9
2	7.9	63.6	6.1	59.6	3.5	11.4
3	6.1	69.7	4.4	64.0	3.9	15.4
4	5.3	75.0	5.7	69.7	2.6	18.0
5	1.8	76.8	4.8	74.6	4.4	22.4
6	0.9	77.6	3.9	78.5	4.8	27.2
7	2.2	79.8	1.8	80.3	5.7	32.9
8	1.8	81.6	1.3	81.6	3.5	36.4
9	0.9	82.5	4.4	86.0	9.6	46.1
10	0.4	82.9	1.8	87.7	5.7	51.8
11	1.8	84.6	3.1	90.8	7.5	59.2
12	—	—	0.9	91.7	3.5	62.7
13	0.9	85.5	3.1	94.7	4.4	67.1
14	—	—	2.2	96.9	5.3	72.4
15	1.8	87.3	0.9	97.8	5.7	78.1
16	2.2	89.5	1.3	99.1	5.7	83.8
17	1.8	91.2	0.9	100.0	4.8	88.6
18	8.8	100.0	—	—	11.4	100.0

home, but the payoff for children was modest because so few nonresidential fathers were participating actively in the support and care of their offspring. By contrast, children of fathers living in the home were doing distinctly better. Whether this was because of the greater paternal attention received or because they enjoyed greater economic security, or because the parents were different even prior to family formation could not be discerned from the data.

A seventeen-year follow-up was conducted in 1984 to examine the situation of the adolescent mothers and their offspring in later life. Approximately 80 percent of the original sample were reinterviewed and data were collected on 296 of the children between the ages of 15 and 17.[1] (For further details about the sample and study design see Furstenberg, Brooks-Gunn, and Morgan 1987.)

Less than a sixth of the fathers were still living in the home at the seventeen-year follow-up despite the fact that nearly half of the males had resided with their children for some time. Sustained contact with biological fathers living outside the home occurred in a minority of families. About a fifth of the children had seen their nonresidential fathers at least once a week at the five-year follow-up, and a sixth of the children had regular contact at the seventeen-year follow-up. Attrition in contact occurred over time, even though more fathers were living outside the home in 1984 than in 1972. Patterns of contact were quite variable. Some fathers' increased or resumed contact as their children reached adolescence while others diminished their involvement (for a general discussion of this process see Furstenberg and Harris 1990).

Three years later a twenty-year follow-up of the children was undertaken to determine how the next generation was doing as they moved from their teen years into their early twenties. Completed interviews were obtained from 253 youths, 85 percent of the participants seen three years earlier, and about two-thirds of all eligible youth in the original sample. Attrition occurred mainly among white families, where the mother was apt to marry or move away from Baltimore during the early years of the study. With very few whites remaining in the 1987 sample, our findings are, at most, generalizable only to blacks living in urban areas.

In the following section we briefly update the patterns of paternal involvement throughout the course of the study. We then turn to the central question addressed in this paper: How does contact and closeness with biological fathers affect the well-being of the youth in early adulthood? The concluding section considers the implications of our results for public policy.

Patterns of Paternal Involvement

The children of the teen mothers were between the ages of 18 and 21 at the 1987 interview. We therefore summarize the experiences of all the children with their fathers over the first 18 years of their lives—covering the full duration of childhood. Table 6-1 shows that just under half of the youth had lived with their biological father at some time during their first 18 years. Only 9 percent, however, resided with him during this entire period. On average, children who ever lived with their father spent about a third of their childhood living with him. Typically these years were early in life, although a small number of children had only recently moved in with their father. As we have already reported, the proportion of children living with their father declined significantly from early childhood until the seventeen-year follow-up, when they were between the ages of 15 to 17. By mid-adolescence only 16 percent of the children were still living with their biological father. At the final follow-up this number slipped to 14 percent.

Besides the biological father, however, other males were present in the children's family lives. Three out of five children who never resided with their biological father lived with a stepfather or father surrogate before reaching the age of 18. Even among the children who did live with their biological father at some point, one-third also lived with a step- or surrogate father at another time. Half of these children spent at least 6 years living with a stepfather—just about the same amount of time that was spent with biological fathers. As is shown in Table 6-1, only 8 percent of the Baltimore youth never resided with any father; and at the other extreme, 11 percent lived with a father throughout their entire childhood. On average, the children in this sample spent about half of their early years living with a father of some type.

A quarter of the youth reported at the seventeen-year follow-up that some other male (usually living outside the home) was like a father to them. Often these father figures were kin who had helped raise them. In some cases these males supplemented fathers inside the home, but usually they were mentioned by children who were not living with a father at the time of the interview.

As mentioned earlier, stepfathers and father surrogates could be viewed as replacements for the biological fathers, as complementary relationships, or as competitors. In the analysis which follows, we shall look at the role of different father figures, contrasting their influence to the influence of biological fathers. Can these other males fill the void created by the disappearance of the biological father?

Contact with the Biological Father

Early in the study, contact and support from biological fathers living outside the home was relatively high. By mid-adolescence many of these males had drifted away. Figure 6-1 provides a cross-sectional view of diminishing contact among biological fathers who were not living with their children. Detailed information was not collected on the amount of interaction with these fathers early in the study, but it is likely that almost all children saw their father at least occasionally and most had regular contact with him during infancy. When the children were still preschoolers, nearly half were either living with him or saw him on a weekly basis. By the end of their teens 14 percent were living with him; only 15 percent were seeing him as often as once a week; 25 percent were not seeing him regularly but had visited with him occasionally in the preceding year; and 46 percent had not had any contact with him at all.

Figure 6-1 also traces the patterns of child support provided by nonresidential fathers during the study. A year after delivery 80 percent of the children were receiving some amount of child support. Four years later, the level of support plummeted—just one in three received financial assistance from the nonresidential father. By mid-adolescence the number of children receiving support dropped to one in six.

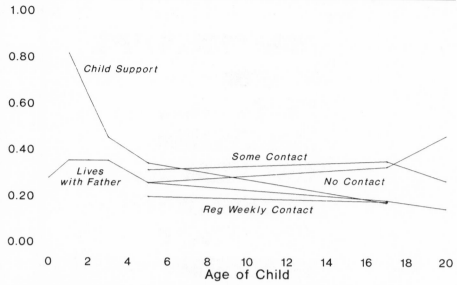

1.00

0.80

0.60

0.40

0.20

0.00

Child Support

Some Contact

Lives
with Father

No Contact

Reg Weekly Contact

0   2   4   6   8   10   12   14   16   18   20

Age of Child

FIGURE 6-1 Child Support and Amount of Contact with Biological Father by Age of Child

Early in the study never-married fathers were just as likely as previously married males to support their children, but over the long-term the fathers who had been married to the child's mother were far more likely to continue to support their children. Of those who were supplying child support in 1972, just one in nine of the never-married men continued to do so in 1984 compared to one in three of the ever-married men. These figures suggest that marriage serves to reinforce paternal obligations. In part, the marriage effect reflects the greater investment of males in the relationship to the child. Fifty-five percent of men who lived with their children for six or more years were providing child support to their adolescent children, compared to just 17 percent of those who had lived with their children for under three years, and 9 percent of those who had never lived with them at all.

Despite some indications early in the Baltimore study that men might take a greater interest in supporting their male than their female offspring, the child's gender was unrelated to the persistence of child support or visitation. However, as we shall see, male children did develop closer bonds to their fathers, even though they did not see them more regularly or were not given any greater financial assistance.

The Quality of Father-Child Relations

Unfortunately, little information on the father was collected until the five-year follow-up; therefore, we do not know much about the strength of ties

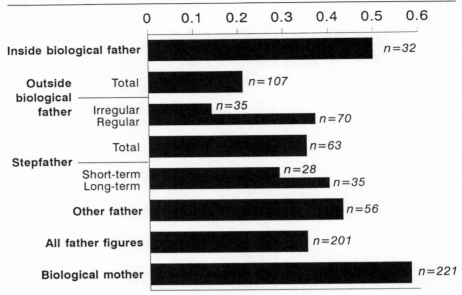

FIGURE 6-2 Proportion of Children Strongly Attached to Father by Type of Father Figure

between children and their fathers early in life. At the five-year follow-up we did learn from the mothers that 65 percent of their children who had contact with their fathers "enjoyed" the relationship very much; according to the mothers, 35 percent enjoyed it only some or not at all.

The 1984 interview, conducted when the children were between the ages of 15 and 17, permitted us to measure the quality of father-child relations more systematically. Children were asked to evaluate *the degree of closeness* and *the extent to which children identified* with their biological father (if they had any contact with him) as well as other father figures living both inside and outside the home. Their responses to the measure of closeness and identification were combined to form an index of attachment.[2]

Figure 6-2 shows the proportion of children strongly bonded to different father figures. Not surprisingly, children report the highest level of attachment to biological fathers living in the home. Still, only 50 percent are strongly attached to him according to our measure. (By comparison, a similar measure on attachment to mothers revealed that 58 percent were strongly bonded.) Both these figures are somewhat below the proportions for all blacks of similar age in the National Survey of Children, which contained an almost identical measure (Harris and Furstenberg 1990).

The index of attachment nicely captures the drop-off that occurs in the strength of ties with the biological father when he lives outside the home. Overall, just 13 percent (not shown) report a strong bond with their biological father when they are living apart from him. This figure, however, conceals an important distinction. Included in this figure are nearly two-fifths (38%) of the adolescents in 1984 who had not seen their fathers in the past year. By contrast, of those who had at least some contact with their biological father, 21 percent indicated that they had a strong bond. This figure rises to 37 percent among those who saw their fathers once a week or more on average. Thus the gap in bonding narrows substantially when we compare fathers living at home and fathers who have regular contact with their children.

Early contact between fathers and their children had no lasting effect on the level of closeness in their relationship unless it was sustained throughout the study. Although ever-married fathers have invested more in their children than never-married men, they do not necessarily develop closer relations with their offspring when they continue to see them. Even those fathers who were in the home for six or more years do not experience a stronger bond with their adolescent children than fathers who were present less than six years or who were never in the home.

In recent qualitative interviews with a subsample of the adolescent children, we learned that many of those most bitterly disappointed with their father's efforts had enjoyed a closer relationship earlier in childhood. This may help to explain why so few nonresidential fathers are regarded as important role models by their offspring even when they *continue* to see them on a regular basis and provide child support. These children are experiencing a sense of "relative deprivation" in their relations with their biological fathers. Here is one account from one of the Baltimore youths talking about important figures in his life.

Q. But your father has not played a big role in your life?

A. No. He hasn't. My father moved away. . . . Then he moved back here when I was in high school. We are able to talk. I don't respect him. I don't have anything against him, when he first came back, he was pretty much in my life.

A sizable minority (28%) of the children were living with a stepfather or a live-in father figure (mother's boyfriend) in 1984. We refer to all residential fathers other than biological fathers as "stepfathers," regardless of whether they were actually married to the youth's mother. More than a third of children living with a stepfather were highly attached to him. To examine only the more stable stepfather relationships, we defined those residential fathers who had lived in the household for six years or more as long-term stepfathers. Long-term relationships occurred in more than half of the children living in stepfamilies and 40 percent of them developed a close bond with him. In contrast, of the approximately half who had a short-term stepfather in the home (less than six years), 29 percent were highly attached to him. Evidently, the steady presence of a stepfather is often conducive to developing a strong paternal attachment, just as happens when the biological parent resides in the house.

About a fourth of the children mentioned that they had someone other than a biological father or residential stepfather who was "like a father to them." About 43 percent of these children reported having a high-quality relationship with the surrogate figure. Overall, 11 percent of the sample had a strong tie to a male who was neither a biological father nor a stepfather.

Taking all these father figures into account, just 1 percent of the children had a strong relationship with two or more fathers; 30 percent reported a strong tie to at least one; and 69 percent had no father figure to whom they were highly attached. While we have not carried out an extensive analysis of the antecedents of these attachments, we did examine whether children were more likely to form a strong attachment with a father of any type if their mothers had ever married. In fact, adolescents whose mothers ever married were twice as likely to have a close relationship with a father figure than those whose mothers never married. When the mother married the biological father, the probability of a strong father-child bond forming was especially pronounced.

Although boys were not more likely than girls to have contact with a father figure, they did establish closer bonds to their fathers when there was contact. Among those who had contact with any type of father, 44 percent of the boys versus 27 percent of the girls were strongly attached to him. Regardless of the type of father figure, boys consistently report closer relations than girls.

In summary, only a small minority of the children of teen mothers form close bonds to their biological father (who may or may not live in the home); a somewhat greater number (but still a small fraction of the total sample) develop strong ties with another father figure, either a stepfather in the home or a relative or former stepfather outside the home. This brings us to the central questions of whether relations with these different father figures affect how well the adolescent children are doing in early adulthood.

Paternal Involvement and the Well-Being of Children

In addressing these questions, we examine the impact of paternal involvement (of both biological fathers and father surrogates) in 1984 on various outcomes measured in 1987. The measures in 1984 summarize a history of relations between children and their fathers. Although a great number of children saw relations with their biological fathers deteriorate at some point in their childhood, only a handful experienced the opposite situation—a strengthening of ties after early childhood. Consequently, we cannot say a great deal about how changing patterns of paternal involvement affect the development of children. But at least we can be reasonably certain about the direction of causality. We will investigate whether greater involvement of fathers and the establishment of a strong bond with their children before or by mid-adolescence lead to better outcomes in early adulthood.

Measures of Youth Well-Being in Early Adulthood

The twenty-year follow-up provides a wide range of measures of successful adjustment in early adulthood. We have selected four different indicators of well-being: (1) socioeconomic achievement measured by an index of educational and employment attainment; (2) whether or not the adolescent had a child before age 19; (3) whether or not the child had spent time in jail; and (4) a subset of items from the Beck Depression Inventory. The construction of these measures is described in greater detail in Appendix 6-A.

In order to determine the representatives of the youths in our study, we compared the Baltimore children of teen mothers with a comparison group matched by race, locality, and the age of the mother at first birth drawn from the 1987 National Survey of Children (NSC), a nationally representative study of youths between the ages of 17 and 22. Among blacks the Baltimore sample and the comparison group reported similar behavioral patterns and similar characteristics. The patterns of educational attainment and early fertility among children of teen mothers in the two samples were almost identical. Imprisonment was far higher in the Baltimore sample, but we believe that the disparity is the result of the failure of the NSC (a telephone survey) to obtain accurate reports and to locate youths who were in jail in their teen years. The NSC did not contain the Beck Depression Inventory, but other measures of emotional well-being yielded comparable results. The offspring of adolescent mothers did not perform as well as the children of later childbearers, but the differences were modest.

Nonetheless, a number of youths in the Baltimore study were displaying serious problems by their late teens and early twenties. About a quarter dropped out of high school and did not show any immediate prospect of graduating or obtaining a GED; almost a quarter (a third of the girls and 15% of the boys) had a birth by age 19; 16 percent of the youth (3% of the girls and 29% of the boys) had been or were in jail; and 31 percent showed a strong indication of depressive affect.

The Presence of Fathers and Adolescent Children's Well-Being

How much of the variability in the four outcomes can be traced to the presence or absence of father figures in the lives of the adolescent children we studied? We first examined a series of bivariate comparisons that tested the overall effect of the presence of four different types of father figures on each outcome measure: whether or not a biological father was present in the home; whether or not the child had contact with the non-residential biological father; whether or not a stepfather was present in the home; and whether or not the child mentioned an adult male (inside or outside the home) who was like a father.

Figure 6-3 displays the results of these bivariate comparisons in a series of bar graphs. The results compare the magnitude of difference on any of the four outcome measures for the presence (or absence) of different father figures. Take, for example, the initial comparison examining the outcomes for children who were or were not living with a biological father in 1984. The results are surprising, for they show a relatively modest effect of having a biological father in the home for the different outcomes three-and-a-half years later. While in all cases the relationship was in the predicted direction, it did not reach statistical significance for three out of the four outcome measures, imprisonment being the exception.

Turning next to the influence of the biological father outside the home, we find the overall effect of having contact with him is even less apparent. Children who had contact with nonresidential fathers were not doing better than children who had not seen their father in the past year on all measures of outcomes. Even when we confined our comparisons to fathers whom children saw regularly, no consistent effects were detected on the outcome measures.

Similar results emerge when we examine the bivariate effect of other father figures living either inside or outside the home. Children in step-parent households at the time of the 1984 interview were not doing better on the various outcome measures three-and-a-half years later. When we confined our contrasts to children who were in stable stepparent families (where they had resided with their stepfather for at least six years), we detected a modest but not statistically significant effect. Like the children of biological fathers in the home, children with long-term stepfathers did not seem to be doing a great deal better in early adulthood than all children in the study.

Finally, we examined children living in single-parent households who identified a person who was like a father to them. Compared to their peers who mentioned no such person, these children fared no better at the twenty-year follow-up, although they were less likely to be high on the

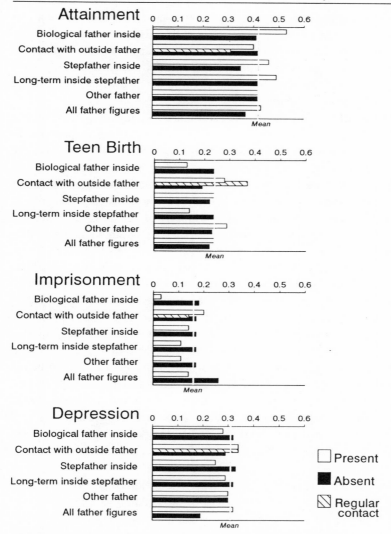

FIGURE 6-3 Outcomes for Adolescent Children, by Presence of Father Figures

depression measure. In sum, the presence of fathers at most appears to have only a weak effect on key outcomes in early adulthood.

There are several possible explanations for the limited impact that a father's presence has on his child's well-being. The protective benefits of living with the father may not be very conspicuous among the tiny group of children who lived in stably married families because many of these children often do not have very close relations with their fathers. It is also possible that children not living in two-parent families do as well because other father figures assume an important role in their life, although our bivariate comparisons seem not to support this explanation. Alternatively, we might find that involvement with fathers of any type may confer only modest advantages to the children in our study. Perhaps, as we pointed out in the introductory section, relations with the mother may override the effect of paternal involvement.

These different interpretations can be partially tested with the data at hand. Figure 6-4 examines the same four constellations of paternal involvement subdivided according to the quality of the relationship between adolescent children and their fathers. Adding the information on the strength of the ties between fathers and their children brings the results into sharp focus. Children are doing far better at the twenty-year follow-up if they have a close relationship with any of the different father figures. But close ties count for more when they are living with a father than when they are not.

Look first at the children who were living with their biological fathers. Recall that these children were split evenly into those who were close to their fathers and those who were not. Between these two groupings a huge difference occurs on three out of four outcomes. Among those who had a close bond with their fathers, more than two-thirds were high on the measure of attainment, having entered college or found stable employment after graduating from high school; none had had a child before age 19; and only a fifth were high on the depression index. (The incidence of serious problems with the law was also low, but not different from youth who were not close to their residential biological fathers.) By contrast, the youth living with their biological fathers who were not as close actually were doing worse on average than all children in the sample.

The identical pattern recurred when we examined the children who were living in stepfamilies. The third of the children who had close ties with their stepfathers were performing extremely well in early adulthood, especially if we consider the children who had longstanding and stable relationships with their stepfathers. The children in these families were doing as well as those who grew up with their biological father. It appears that the conjunction of stable *and* close relations with a male figure in the home produces high rates of successful adjustment in early adulthood.

This finding is echoed among the adolescent children who were not living with a father but were strongly attached to him at the time of the seventeen-year follow-up. Although they were not doing as well as the young adults who had the benefit of growing up with a father in the home throughout early adolescence, they were performing significantly better

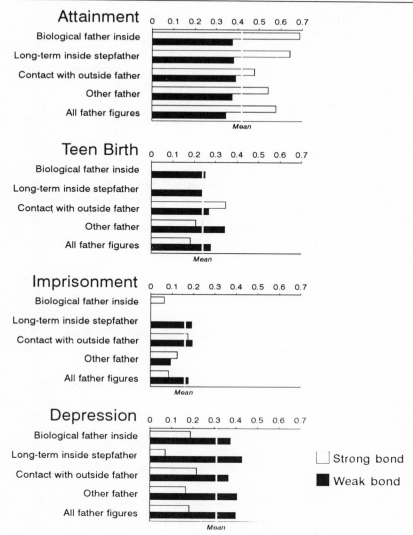

FIGURE 6-4 Outcomes for Adolescent Children, by Level of Attachment to Father Figures

than youth who had not established a close tie with a father figure on three of the outcome measures. The exception is the measure of teen childbearing, where closer ties are predictive of higher rates of teen parenthood. We shall have more to say later about this anomalous result.

Finally, in Figure 6-4 we can also see that children who had a close relationship with a male who was like a father to them also did better than average on the different outcome measures. Again, anything less than a close tie to a father surrogate does not improve adolescent children's chances of doing well on the four outcome measures.

TABLE 6-2 Independent Effects of Attachment to Father Figures on Educational
Attainment, Teen Births, Imprisonment, and Depression

	Educational attainment	Teen birth	Imprisonment	Depression
Female	1.10	0.29**	18.40**	0.58
Close to inside father	2.15*	0.26*	0.21*	0.37*
Close to outside biological father	1.25	3.00*	0.74	0.71
Close to other father	1.69	0.92	0.89	0.33
Close to mother	0.74	1.11	0.49	0.73
Number of cases	221	221	221	221

Note: The numbers come from logistic regressions and reflect the effect of each status on
the odds of each behavior. Thus, being female increased the odds of college attainment by
10 percent, but decreased the odds of a teen birth by 71 percent (1 − .29). Inside fathers
include biological fathers and stepfathers. The asterisks denote the impacts measured with
the most statistical reliability, either at the 5-percent (*) level or the 1-percent (**) level of
significance.

Using a multivariate statistical analysis, we reexamined the independent impacts of the presence of, and the child's attachment to, different
types of fathers. We also measured the possible independent effects of the
level of attachment to mothers. Finally, we examined the possibility that
these father and mother effects differed for boys and girls.

Our results confirmed the findings shown in Figures 6-3 and 6-4. The
effect of the father's presence, by itself, had relatively little impact on
outcomes for adolescent children. When we measured the father's presence, while holding constant the degree of attachment, the effect of the
father's presence virtually disappears. At the same time a strong bond
with a father who lives with the child promotes a variety of positive
outcomes.

Table 6-2 presents a selected set of impacts, including the effects of
attachment to inside fathers (biological fathers or stepfathers), to nonresidential biological fathers with whom the children have contact, and to
"other" (surrogate) fathers. Also shown are the effects of attachment to
mothers and of the gender of the child. The columns reveal the odds ratio
for each effect; an odds ratio of 2 implies a doubling of the odds, while a
ratio of .5 means a 50-percent reduction in the odds of an event.

The results indicate that attachment to a father figure has beneficial
effects on all outcome measures as the children enter adulthood. Again,
the only exception is the impact of a close tie with the nonresidential
biological father on teenage childbearing. Children who live with their
biological father or with a stepfather in a long-term relationship benefit
the most from a strong bond with their inside father. Children who were

strongly attached to a residential father were twice as likely to have entered college or to have found stable employment after high school; 75 percent less likely to have had a teen birth, 80 percent less likely to have been in jail, and half as likely to have experienced multiple depression symptoms. The positive effects of a close bond with an inside father are significant for all of the outcomes measuring a successful transition to adulthood.

A strong attachment to another father figure is also important in improving children's chances of high attainment and in reducing depression symptoms, although the effects are not statistically significant. The probability of a teen birth and imprisonment is also reduced if children have a close bond with another male who is like a father to them; however these effects are weak.

A close bond with the outside biological father has the least impact on outcomes for adolescent children. Although the children who had contact and were strongly attached to their nonresidential biological father were more likely to have high measures of attainment and to avoid imprisonment and depression, the advantage of the attachment was only marginally beneficial.

In fact, a perverse effect is evident for the teen birth outcome. Children who were strongly attached to their nonresidential father were more likely to experience early childbearing than those who were not attached to their outside biological father or who had no contact with him. Our exploration of gender interactions revealed why this result occurs. Boys who had contact and were strongly attached to their nonresidential fathers were more likely to report a teen birth than girls who had a close tie with their outside father. Since boys are overrepresented among children with a strong bond to their outside father, this interaction increases the overall chances of teenage childbearing for children attached to their outside father.[3]

Oddly, the level of attachment to the biological mother has very little impact on the well-being of children as they enter adulthood. A close tie with the mother does not mediate the effects of attachment to a father figure, nor does it improve the chances of educational or economic attainment, or lower the probability of teenage childbearing. Closeness to the mother does reduce the likelihood of imprisonment and depression, but not significantly. We were surprised to find that those children who had a close bond with their mother were not doing significantly better on the measures of well-being in 1987 than the children who were not close to their mother. Perhaps this is because the variability in maternal closeness was low, but it may suggest that this measure takes on different meaning when it is applied to mothers than fathers.

Conclusions

These results refine our understanding of the psychological impact of fathers in the lives of disadvantaged children. They also help to explain the frequently contradictory findings of prior research attempting to establish the psychological benefits for children of paternal involvement. Do fathers contribute to the child's psychological well-being, apart from the economic assistance that they provide? The answer appears not to be a straightforward yes or no.

When we examined four varied measures of children's well-being, we found that the presence of a father inside the home confers only a modest advantage; contact, even regular contact, with fathers outside the home had little effect on positive outcomes for adolescent children. Children only benefit from a close paternal relationship. Unfortunately, more often than not, the ties that they develop with fathers are neither continuous nor close.

Public policy cannot regulate family intimacy, but it may be able to foster conditions that promote stronger bonds between children and their fathers. The Baltimore study furnishes evidence that marriage, especially a marriage that survives, indirectly increases the likelihood of successful adjustment in early adulthood by boosting the odds of a strong paternal bond. Unfortunately, we know little about the conditions that produce stable marriages.

It is believed that economic security, especially for males, may contribute to the desirability of marriage and its durability. While such a belief seems plausible enough, it is not buttressed by a great deal of data. There is no simple correlation between economic cycles and separation statistics, but there is some support for the proposition that marriages falter or never occur when expectations of male contributions are low. We need to look more carefully at ways of increasing the economic payoff of marriage in hopes that it may indirectly lead to a greater sense of children's well-being.

Clearly, marriage is not always in a woman's best interest or the best interest of the child. Unstable marriages and conflictual relationships within marriage elevate the chances of a poor relationship with a father outside the home. And our data show that a poor relationship is worse than no relationship at all. It may interfere with the child's developing a bond with another father figure, disturb his/her relationship with the mother, or directly undercut the child's ability to function as an adult. Consequently, we walk a thin line when we attempt to promote matrimony as a public good if many or most marriages turn out to be unstable or conflict-ridden.

The same logic applies to our efforts to maintain ties between fathers and children. Obviously, insisting that fathers maintain economic obligations to their children has economic benefits. The maintenance of contact may also have social and psychological advantages for children. Again, however, our evidence suggests a qualified response. Only a third of the males who had regular contact and fewer than a third of those who were providing child support had developed a strong bond with their offspring. If our results are any indication, the claim of psychological benefits for children is dubious. We must remind the reader, however, that our findings, if they can be generalized at all, apply only to blacks who began families at an early age.

No one knows how to foster stronger and more lasting attachments between children and their fathers, whether the father is the biological parent or a surrogate. Establishing support groups for prospective fathers represents a constructive step, but these services probably do too little for too few fathers over too brief a time to make much difference in children's later lives. The successful design of more lasting programs remains a high priority. This may involve the location of male support figures in the child's social network who may fill in for absent fathers. Whether we can engineer a strong paternal bond by cultivating such ties is very much a question open to further exploration.

It is also clear from our data that some children do well despite the lack of a paternal presence. Can we assume that one parent is sufficient so long as that parent is a skillful and loving figure? Perhaps other figures enter the child's life who may not be father surrogates, but who provide additional guidance, support, and material assistance. We need to know more about how and why children manage successfully in single-parent families.

The general rediscovery of the importance of fathers in the children's lives is a salutary development in social science research. The restoration of the father's place in the family undoubtedly has important implications for public policy. Our greatest fear, however, is that we may leap to action before we learn what those implications are.

Appendix 6-A Description of Outcome Measures of Adolescent's Well-Being.

Teen Birth: This measure indicates whether the adolescent had mothered or fathered a child before age 19. Direct questions about childbearing and fertility histories provided the information. All adolescents had reached the age of 19 (with the exception of a small number who were a few months from their nineteenth birthday) by the 1987 interview, so that exposure was not an issue. Among the adolescents in the Baltimore Study, 24 percent had experienced a teen birth (33% of the girls and 15% of the boys).

Attainment: This measure is based on an intricate coding scheme regarding academic achievement and subsequent work history. Briefly, our method first considered the adolescent's educational achievement and then adjusted the score by the employment record. Adolescents who had graduated from high school and were attending college or graduate school were coded at the high end of the attainment scale. Also, high school graduates in steady employment were scored high on attainment. Those coded in the middle range were high school graduates who were unemployed but looking for work or in a training school, and those adolescents still in high school and at grade level. Adolescents who were still in high school but had failed one or more grades fell at the low end of the attainment scale. And finally, high school dropouts were also at the bottom of the attainment scale, unless they had accumulated substantial work experience (which moved them up the index slightly). Represented as a three-category index (collapsed from a five-category index), 42 percent were high on attainment, 24 percent fell in the middle range, and 34 percent scored low on attainment.

Depression: This indicator is an additive scale based on a subset of twelve items from the Beck Depression Inventory measuring emotional well-being. Various statements were read to the adolescent concerning his/her emotional state, to which the adolescent responded that he/she felt that way most of the time, some of the time, only a little of the time, or none of the time during the previous four weeks. Examples of the items include: "I felt sad." "I was bothered by things that usually don't bother me." "I did not feel like eating, my appetite was poor." "I felt that I could not shake off the blues, even with help from my family or friends." "I had trouble keeping by mind on what I was doing." "During the past four weeks, I felt depressed; I felt fearful; my sleep was restless; I felt lonely."

Responses for each item ranged from 0, indicating no incidence, to 3, indicating frequent occurrence of the adverse emotional state. An additive index was constructed from these twelve items by summing their responses. The index was then dichotomized by selecting the proportion of respondents who fell above one-half of a standard deviation above the mean, indicating excessive symptoms of depression. For the sample as a whole, 31 percent fell in this tail of the distribution.

Imprisonment: This outcome measure indicates whether the adolescent had ever spent any time in jail, prison, or a correctional facility. Delinquent behavior among the Baltimore children displayed the typical gender pattern, with 3 percent of the girls and 29 percent of the boys spending some time in jail, or 16 percent overall of adolescents who had ever been in jail.

Notes

1. Almost all of the children lost to follow-up had left the study in the first phase. Some, especially the small number of whites in the sample, moved out of the Baltimore area and were excluded; about 10 percent of the children were put up for adoption or had died.

2. The index of attachment was constructed using children's responses from the following two items measuring closeness and identification in the father-child relation:

How close do you feel to your father?
  1. extremely close
  2. quite close
  3. fairly close, or
  4. not very close.

How much do you want to be like the kind of person he is when you're an adult?
  1. a lot
  2. quite a bit
  3. just a little, or
  4. not at all.

The response distributions were standardized by categorizing the top two responses as high, and the bottom two as low. An additive index was then formed by summing the high responses so that a 2 on the index indicated that the father-child bond was very strong ("high" on both measures of attachment). Levels of strong attachment shown in subsequent tables and figures thus refer to this high score on the index, where attachment in the father-child relation is the greatest.

3. When we explored the possibility that attachment to a father figure may result in different outcomes for boys and girls, no significant interactions were found—with the exception that boys who were highly attached to their outside father were more likely to report a teen birth than girls who had a close bond with their outside father. However, the effects of the interactions between gender and attachment revealed an interesting pattern with regard to the outcomes. Girls who were strongly attached to a father figure experienced greater success in the outcome measures than the boys who were attached to a father.

This result explains why we observed no gender differences on the four outcomes. Boys more often enjoy a close relationship with their father than girls, and thus the steady presence of a father may increase their chances of doing well, if only because it provides the arena for forming a close bond with a father figure. However, even though girls are less likely to become strongly attached to a father figure, they apparently derive greater benefits from that attachment. In other words, controlling for all other effects, when a girl forms a close bond with a father, her chances of favorable outcomes are better than when a boy is highly attached to a father. However, since more boys develop close ties with a father figure, the interactive effect balances the compositional effect, resulting in similar probabilities of a successful transition to adulthood by gender.

References

Chase-Lansdale, P. L., and M. Hetherington. 1989. The impact of divorce on life-span development: Short and long-term effects. In *Life-span development and behavior*, edited by P. B. Baltes, D. L. Heatherman, and R. Lerner, 10:105–150. Hillsdale, N.J.: Lawrence Erlbaum.

Elster, A., and M. E. Lamb. 1986. *Adolescent fatherhood*. Hillsdale, N.J.: Lawrence Erlbaum.

Emery, R. E. 1988. *Marriage, divorce, and children's adjustment*. Beverly Hills, Calif.: Sage Publications.

Furstenberg, F. F., Jr. 1976. *Unplanned parenthood*. New York: Free Press.

Furstenberg, F. F., Jr., J. Brooks-Gunn, and S. P. Morgan. 1987. *Adolescent mothers in later life*. New York: Cambridge University Press.

Furstenberg, F. F., Jr., and K. M. Harris. 1990. The disappearing American father? Divorce and the waning significance of biological parenthood. In *The Changing American Family: Sociological and Demographic Perspectives*, edited by S. J. Scott and S. E. Tolnny. Boulder: Westview Press, 1992. April.

Furstenberg, F. F., S. P. Morgan, and P. A. Allison. 1987. Paternal participation and children's well-being after marital dissolution. *American Sociological Review* 52:695–701.

Furstenberg, F. F. and K. Talvitie. 1979. Children's names and paternal claims: Bonds between unmarried fathers and their children. *Journal of Family Issues* 1(1): 31–57.

Harris, K. M., and F. F. Furstenberg, Jr. 1990. Affective mobility: The course of parent-child relations in adolescence. Paper presented at the annual meetings of the American Sociological Association, Washington, D.C. August.

Hess, R. D., and K. A. Camara. 1979. Post-divorce family relationships as mediating factors in the consequences of divorce for children. *Journal of Social Issues* 35:79–98.

Hetherington, E. M., M. Cox, and R. Cox. 1978. The aftermath of divorce. In *Mother-child, father-child relations*, edited by J. H. Stevens, Jr., and M. Mathews, 149–176. Washington, D.C.: National Association for the Education of Young Children.

Mott, F. 1990. When is a father really gone? Paternal-child contact in father-absent homes. *Demography* 27(4): 499–517.

Parke, R. D., and B. Neville. 1987. Teenage fatherhood. In *Risking the future*, edited by S. L. Hofferth and C. D. Hayes, 2:145–173. Washington, D.C.: National Academy Press.

Robinson, B. 1988. *Teenage fathers*. Lexington, Mass.: Lexington Books.

Vincent, C. E. 1961. *Unmarried mothers*. New York: Free Press.

Wallerstein, J. S., and J. B. Kelly. 1980. *Surviving the breakup*. New York: Basic Books.

Weiss, R. 1975. *Marital separation*. New York: Basic Books.

II

Rights and Obligations

7   Legal Rights and Obligations:

An Uneven Evolution .

RUTH-ARLENE W. HOWE

While much data on child bearing trends and the characteristics of young unwed mothers exists, very little is known about young unwed fathers (Smollar and Ooms 1987). In the decades since 1960, out-of-wedlock births have increased dramatically. According to the U.S. Bureau of the Census,[1] illegitimate births in 1960 were just 5.3 percent of all births. By 1987 the proportion had risen to 24.5 percent of the 3.8 million reported live births—nearly every fourth child was being born to unmarried parents. About one-third of these 933,000 babies had teenage mothers. And since the average male sexual partner is at least two years older than his female partner, about 70 percent of the fathers of children born to teen mothers were young men, many black and Hispanic, ages 19 to 25 (Ooms and Herendeen 1988).

The incidence of out-of-wedlock births is likely to increase, especially given the rapidly growing population of unmarried cohabitants. Of significance is the fact that in 1988 about 31 percent of unmarried cohabitants, or 802,000, had children under 15 in their households. This was more than a fourfold increase over the 196,000 cohabitants counted in the 1970 census.[2] Thus, as stated in the 1988 prefatory note to the new Uniform Putative and Unknown Fathers Act (UPUFA) of the National Conference of Commissioners on Uniform State Laws (NCCUSL), "unmarried fathers are not simply ones who can be categorized as absent or uncaring

The author both gratefully acknowledges the research assistance of Scott Brody, Ronald Gonzalez, Rex A. Guinn, Richard Husband, and Kenneth Whitted, and expresses her thanks to Daniel R. Coquillette for research grants received from the Dean's Fund.

fathers. There is an expanding population of unwed men who wish to play a role in the upbringing of their children."

During the 1980s federal legislation such as the Family Support Act of 1988 and numerous state enactments declared early establishment of paternity and rigorous enforcement of child support obligations to be public policy priorities. Today, the societal preference is to hold parents financially responsible for the care of their dependent children rather than to have such costs totally assumed by the public.

Some believe that this shift in policy holds promise for furthering the best interests of out-of-wedlock children. In the past, the majority of out-of-wedlock children never had paternity adjudicated. Consequently, they were not eligible for various benefits under social security, workmen's compensation, or inheritance laws. Child welfare advocates assert that "identification of the father may have more than financial importance for out-of-wedlock children. It provides them with a sense of identity and knowledge of their biological heritage" which may be very crucial for healthy growth and development (Nichols-Casebolt 1988).

Clearly, the winds of change are blowing. Parental support obligations are not modified or excused because of a parent's age or marital status. As the law moves to enforce support, a logical inquiry concerning young unwed fathers is whether they enjoy the same legal rights with respect to their children as other parents. Generally, a parent, unless proven to be unfit, is deemed to have a legal right to the custody of his or her child. This custodial right includes the right to give or withhold any required consents to adoption, marriage, or enlistment in military service, to name the child, and to make decisions covering all aspects of a child's upbringing—all routine daily care and supervision, education, medical care, and religious training (Sussman and Guggenheim 1980).

Succeeding sections of this chapter shall (1) review the status accorded unwed fathers in the past and the differing statuses recognized today in the United States; (2) discuss the constitutional guarantees that protect a legal parent-child relationship; (3) trace the uneven evolution of the unwed father's constitutional rights as articulated by the United States Supreme Court in cases decided since 1972; (4) discuss and contrast the rights and obligations of unwed fathers as currently defined by certain federal and state laws with the approach taken in the new UPUFA; (5) speculate how scientific advances in paternity testing may impact upon young unwed fathers; and (6) conclude with a short summary and plea for social interventions other than legal reforms.

Status of Unwed Fathers: Historical Overview

Black's Law Dictionary defines *parent* as "[o]ne who procreates, begets, or brings forth offspring," without reference to marital status or age. But every male parent has not been a father to whom the law accords legal rights or imposes legal obligations.

Under English Common Law

Historically, a child born out of wedlock was *filius nullius*—"the son of no one." This doctrine concerned matters of inheritance and treated the child as having no ancestor from whom "inheritable blood" could be derived. It should be carefully distinguished from the custodial concept of *filius populi*—"son of the people." Under the *filius populi* doctrine an illegitimate child was considered to be in the custody of the local church or parish. Neither parent, mother or father, was deemed to have any custodial rights to the child (Comment 1985). Around the end of the eighteenth century the doctrine of *filius populi* was modified to exclude only the unwed father from having any custodial rights and to recognize an exclusive right to custody in the unwed mother.

In the United States similar common-law rules for many years denied the unwed father legal parental status. On occasion, state courts might accord an unwed father custodial rights superior to all but the mother;[3] courts in other jurisdictions might grant custody to an unwed father if the mother was either dead or disinterested.[4] Courts like Utah were completely hostile to granting any custodial rights to an unwed father.[5] Most states denied the unwed father opportunity to be heard in matters pertaining to his child's adoption, generally requiring only the consent of the illegitimate child's mother.

United States Law Today

Three categories of unwed fathers are recognized: legal (adjudicated or presumed), putative, and unknown.

LEGAL FATHERS. The *adjudicated* father is one who has been judicially determined to be the biological father of a particular child as the outcome of either a paternity suit brought against the man by the mother, the child, or the state, or an action initiated by the man himself to have his parenthood established. Formerly, most paternity suits were quasi-criminal and required proof "beyond a reasonable doubt" (Nichols-Casebolt 1988). Today, in most states, the paternity suit is a civil action in which the plaintiff, to prevail, must present sufficient evidence to support a finding of paternity under the lower civil standard of "by a preponderance of the evidence." A man's name or signature on a birth certificate, the prior filing of an affidavit of intention to claim paternity, a course of conduct such as living together or sexual intimacy with the mother, either with or without the introduction of blood or genetic test results, if not refuted by a male defendant, may be deemed sufficient evidence to satisfy the "preponderance of the evidence" standard.

Under some state statutes an unwed father who shuns marrying his child's mother, without any formal court proceedings, may still be considered a particular child's "presumed" legal father if he does certain things. For example, under Section 4, Presumption of Paternity, of the Uniform Parentage Act (UPA; 9B Unif. L. Ann. 298, West Supp. 1990), promulgated by NCCUSL in 1973 and presently enacted in whole or in part by nineteen states,[6] a man is "presumed" to be the natural father of a child if:

> (4) while the child is under the age of majority, he receives the child into his home and openly holds out the child as his natural child; or
> (5) he acknowledges his paternity of the child in a writing filed with the [appropriate court or Vital Statistics Bureau], which shall promptly inform the mother of the filing of the acknowledgement, and she does not dispute the acknowledgement within a reasonable time after being informed thereof, in a writing filed with the [appropriate court or Vital Statistics Bureau] (Brackets in original text).

The presumptions can be rebutted in a court action, but only by clear and convincing evidence. A court decree establishing paternity of the child by another man rebuts the presumption (Kohn 1987).

PUTATIVE FATHER.   Section 1 of NCCUSL's 1988 UPUFA defines a *putative* father as "a man who claims to be, or is named as, the biological father or a possible biological father of a child, and whose paternity of the child has not been judicially determined." Review of statistical data on young unwed fathers, generally men in their mid-twenties or younger, indicates that most of them fall into this category (Smollar and Ooms 1987). Judicial establishment of paternity and obtaining court support orders against young unwed fathers were not major public policy priorities until the mid-1980s.

UNKNOWN FATHERS.   The third legally recognized category of unwed fathers are the *unknown* fathers. The UPUFA defines the *unknown* father as "a child's biological father whose identity is unascertained." The Act expressly denies any legal status to "a donor of semen used in artificial insemination or in vitro fertilization whose identity is not known to the mother or whose semen was donated under circumstances indicating that the donor did not anticipate having any interest in the resulting child." Except for such situations of assisted conception, this writer suspects that, given the changing social and sexual patterns of interaction and the new, more definitive methods of paternity testing, there will be fewer "unknown" or "unascertainable" biological fathers in the future. Of course, there still may be situations where a mother or her family may be reluctant to reveal the identity of the father.

Fourteenth Amendment Guarantees for Legal Parents

In this section the constitutional protections generally accorded "legal" parents (all married or divorced parents, unwed mothers, and unwed males considered to be legal fathers as defined above), are described in order to provide a benchmark standard against which to assess the evolving legal rights and obligations of all young unwed fathers (as presented below). Thus, "[w]hile the U.S. Constitution makes no mention whatsoever of either parents or families . . . the legal rights of parents to bear children, raise their offspring, and guide their family according to their own beliefs are firmly rooted in the first ten amendments to the Constitution (otherwise known as the Bill of Rights)" (Sussman and Guggenheim 1980, 1). Section 1 of the Fourteenth Amendment, in pertinent part, declares:

> [N]or shall any State deprive any person of life, liberty, or property, without due process of law; nor deny to any person within its jurisdiction the equal protection of the laws.

The first quoted clause is popularly known as the Due Process Clause; the second, as the Equal Protection Clause.

The Due Process Clause

Two distinct rights are recognized to flow from the Due Process Clause: a *substantive* right protecting an individual's liberty or property interests and a *procedural* right requiring that notice and a hearing be held before a protected interest can be taken away by the government (Comment 1984).

For more than sixty years the Supreme Court has defined "liberty" to include the right "to marry, establish a home and bring up children" (*Meyer v. Nebraska*, 1923). The Court has described the custody rights of parents to be "far more precious . . . than property rights" (*May v. Anderson*, 1953). And, in its 1972 landmark *Stanley* decision (concerning a putative father and discussed below), the Court said:

> It is plain that the interest of a parent in the companionship, care, custody, and management of his or her children comes to this Court with a momentum for

respect lacking when appeal is made to liberties which derive merely from shifting economic arrangements. (*Kovacs v. Cooper* 336 U.S. 77.95 (1949), (Frankfurter, Jr., concurring), 405 U.S. 645, at 651 1971)

Nevertheless, parents' substantive rights to the custody and control of their child may be subordinated to the state's interest in the child's welfare, under the concept of *parens patriae*. In resolving conflicts between parental rights and the state's interest in the welfare of a child, courts today apply a "best interest of the child" standard. As previously noted, early common law just assumed that the nonmarital child's interests were best served first by vesting custody in the local church or parish and later by giving exclusive custody to the mother.

With respect to proceedings concerning the creation, maintenance, or termination of the parent-child relationship, the Due Process Clause of the Fourteenth Amendment, at a bare minimum, has been held to prohibit a state from denying notice and an opportunity to be heard to one deemed to have a liberty interest in the relationship. To determine what procedural due process is required in a particular case, the Supreme Court, since its *Mathews v. Eldridge* (1976) decision, has weighed and considered three distinct factors:

> First, the *private interest* that will be affected by the official action; second, the *risk of erroneous deprivation of such interest* through the procedures used, and the *public value*, if any, of *additional or substitute safeguards*; and finally, *government's interest*, including the function involved and the fiscal and administrative burdens that the additional or substitute procedural requirement entail (424 U.S. 319 at 355; emphasis added).

The Supreme Court, depending on the time, place, and circumstances of the particular case before it, has reached seemingly conflicting conclusions with respect to procedural matters in applying the *Eldridge* balancing approach. Several important decisions from the 1980s can be noted to illustrate this.

In *Little v. Streater* (1981) the Court held that denial of free blood tests to indigent defendants in paternity actions would be a denial of due process. The Court stated that "the private interests implicated here are substantial [for] . . . at issue is the creation of a parent-child relationship" (452 U.S. 1 at 13). Yet in *Lassiter v. Department of Social Services of Durham County*, also decided in 1981, the Court employed its *Eldridge* analysis to conclude that lack of appointed counsel for an incarcerated mother during a proceeding to terminate her parental rights did not render the proceedings fundamentally unfair.

A year later, in *Santosky v. Kramer* (1982), the Court applied its *El-*

dridge analysis to conclude that an established legal parent-child relationship was entitled to the due process protection, requiring the State of New York, which sought to terminate John and Annie Santosky's parental rights, to show "by clear and convincing evidence" (the highest civil standard of proof) that grounds existed to justify terminating their parent-child relationships.

Yet, five years later, in *Rivera v. Minnich* (1987), when a putative father-defendant argued in a paternity proceeding that the fourteenth Amendment Due Process Clause was violated by a Pennsylvania statute that allowed a paternity adjudication to rest on the lower "preponderance of the evidence" civil standard, the Court simply said that the case was not controlled by *Santosky*. Affirming the Supreme Court of Pennsylvania's ruling that the preponderance standard was constitutionally permissible, the Court bluntly stated that the higher evidentiary standard is not required in paternity proceedings because "the putative father has no legitimate right and certainly no liberty interest in avoiding financial obligations . . . validly imposed by state law." Further, the Court said that finding a "causal connection between an alleged physical act of a putative father and the subsequent birth of the plaintiff's child sufficient to impose financial liability on the father will not trammel any pre-existing rights" (483 U.S. 574, at 579–580).

The Equal Protection Clause

For family law the mandate of the Equal Protection Clause of the Fourteenth Amendment can be summarized as requiring "that legislation must operate equally upon all members of a group that is defined reasonably and in terms of a proper legislative purpose. The Clause . . . does not forbid 'unequal laws' and does not require every law to be equally applicable to all individuals. Of necessity, classification must be permitted, otherwise there could be no meaningful legislation" (Krause 1986, 18–19). A law, to withstand constitutional challenge, must be equally applicable to everyone similarly situated.

Under early English common law, the married father had a nearly absolute right to the custody of his child. He could be deprived of custody only where danger to the child or corruption of the father was proved (Clark 1988). This rule received little support in this country and has been abolished now in England as well.

Today in the United States, when living together, neither parent has any greater legal standing than the other to determine issues concerning their children (Sussman and Guggenheim 1980). Nevertheless, until well after the middle of the twentieth century, courts accepted and followed the maternal preference presumption rule that, upon the parents' separation or divorce, the welfare of a child of "tender years" was best served by giving custody to the mother (Clark 1988).

When considering either the rights accorded legal parents under the Equal Protection Clause or the emerging recognition of rights to be accorded young unwed fathers, the 1966 comments of Justice Douglas in *Harper v. Virginia Board of Education* are instructive.

> In determining what [is] unconstitutionally discriminatory, we have never been confined to historic notions of equality any more than we have restricted due process to a fixed catalogue of what was at a given time deemed to be the limits of fundamental rights. . . . *Notions of what constitutes equal treatment for purposes of the Equal Protection Clause do change.* . . . We have long been mindful that where fundamental rights and liberties are asserted under the Equal Protection Clause, classifications which might invade or restrain them must be closely scrutinized and carefully confined (383 U.S. 663 at 669–670; emphasis added).

Indeed, over time the Supreme Court has shifted the standards for testing constitutional challenges under the Equal Protection Clause. To survive review, a legislative classification once merely had to be reasonable, not arbitrary, and to rest on some ground of difference having a fair relationship to a permissible state purpose. Today if challenged legislation involves a suspect class (such as race) or impinges upon a fundamental right (such as to vote, travel or procreate), it will be scrutinized to determine whether (1) the classification is necessary to promote a compelling state interest, (2) the state interest is clearly articulated, and (3) the classification demonstrably promotes that interest.

Since gender is not a suspect class, gender-based distinctions once passed muster under traditional equal protection review because of the relative ease of showing some relationship to a permissible state purpose. But starting with *Reed v. Reed* (1971) (invalidating Idaho's statutory preference for males in estate administration) the Supreme Court has displayed sensitivity to some issues of gender involving married or once married persons. Hence, the law now requires gender equality in a variety of contexts. Either spouse can be ordered to pay alimony to the other, or any noncustodial parent can be ordered to pay child support. As more fathers, upon divorce, have begun to seek custody of their children, the "tender years" doctrine has lost much of its significance. In many states it has been abolished by statute;[7] in others it has been eliminated by judicial decision.[8] Many of the states which have adopted Equal Rights Amendments to their state constitutions have found their "tender years" doctrine to be a violation of those amendments.

In contrast, the unwed father, with respect to his child, is just not deemed to be "similarly situated" as the child's mother. Therefore, he may be deemed not to have equal rights with her. For example, the unwed prospective father, just as a married or divorced male, cannot veto the decision of a woman to have an abortion.[9] He enjoys no legal right to prior notice of an abortion. (See Chapter 14, "The Role of Unwed Fathers in the Abortion Decision," by Arthur Shostak.)

Significant Supreme Court Decisions about Unwed Fathers

Historically, in the United States, an identified putative father could always be required to support his offspring (Clark 1988; Comment 1985), although in practice this was seldom done. However, neither imposition nor fulfillment of this obligation automatically guaranteed that an unwed father's relationship with his child would be considered a "liberty" interest, entitled to the constitutional protections accorded other parents.

Four major U.S. Supreme Court cases concerning unwed fathers and decided between 1972 and 1983 are next reviewed, and two California cases heard by the Court during its 1988–89 term (one of which was dismissed for lack of a federal question). While some of these cases involved men who were not young, nevertheless, these are the significant cases for determining the constitutional law of paternal rights of young unwed fathers.

Stanley v. Illinois *(1972)*
Peter Stanley had lived with his children and their mother as a de facto family for over eighteen years. Yet, upon the mother's death, Illinois took custody of the Stanley children in a simple "dependency proceeding" because they had no living mother or adoptive parent. Under state law, an unwed father such as Stanley was irrebuttably presumed to be unfit, although all other parents, including unwed mothers, could only lose custody of their children via a "neglect proceeding" in which their unfitness was established.

The Supreme Court, after reviewing the Illinois statute, held that "Illinois was barred, as a matter of both due process and equal protection, from taking custody of the children of an unwed father, absent a hearing and a particularized finding that the father was an unfit parent" (Comment 1989). Justice White, writing for the majority, declared that the private interest "of a man in the children he has sired and raised, undeniably warrants deference and, absent a powerful countervailing interest, protection." In what later became known as "infamous Footnote 9," Justice White accorded all unwed fathers the right to be heard prior to deprivation of their parental status, stating that the incremental cost of offering unwed fathers an opportunity for individualized hearing on fitness appears to be minimal. If unwed fathers, in the main, do not care about the disposition of their children, they will not appear to demand hearings. Extending opportunity for hearings to unwed fathers who desire and claim competence to care for their children creates no constitutional or procedural obstacle to foreclosing those unwed fathers who are not so inclined (405 U.S. 645 at 657).

While *Stanley* was a landmark case that recognized the unwed father's interest in maintaining a relationship with his illegitimate children, it was not a unanimous decision. Chief Justice Burger, with Justice Blackmun concurring, wrote a strong dissent, expressing the view that the state had constitutionally legitimate reasons (like the maternal presumption) for distinguishing between unwed fathers and unwed mothers.

On the same day the Court decided *Stanley* it also remanded two adoption cases[10] for further state court proceedings consistent with its *Stanley* holding. But was *Stanley* to be read as requiring advance notice of any adoption or termination proceeding to all unwed fathers? Such a requirement could seriously impede adoptions. Or, under *Stanley*, was notice required only to legal and putative unwed fathers, with merely a good-faith effort required to notify an unknown father? Some states interpreted *Stanley* broadly to mandate advance notice to *all* unwed fathers, and rewrote their adoption laws to require the unwed father's preadoptive consent. Other states interpreted *Stanley* more narrowly to require only the latter (Redden 1982; Barron 1975).

Quilloin v. Walcott *(1978)*

Six years passed before the Supreme Court next had an opportunity to clarify the rights of unwed fathers. Leon Quilloin, an unwed father, challenged the constitutionality of Georgia's adoption law after he was denied veto power over his eleven-year-old son's adoption by Randall Walcott, mother's husband of nine years. Georgia adoption law only required the consent of an illegitimate child's mother if the father had not legitimated his child either by marrying the mother and acknowledging the child as his own (Ga. Code § 74-101) or by obtaining a court order declaring the child legitimate and capable of inheriting from him (Ga. Code § 74-103). For a decade Quilloin had done neither, nor had he sought visitation rights or custody. He simply never acquired the status of a "presumed" father. And even in opposing the adoption, he did not seek custody or actively object to the child living with the mother.

At a parental fitness hearing the Georgia trial court determined Quilloin to be fit, but deemed it to be in the child's best interest to allow the adoption. Important factors considered by the lower court were that: (1)

the mother found the child's visits with the biological father to have a disruptive effect upon the boy; (2) the father provided support payments on an irregular basis; and (3) the child expressed a desire to be adopted by the mother's husband. The Georgia Supreme Court affirmed.

In a unanimous opinion the U.S. Supreme Court held that Quilloin was not "entitled as a matter of due process or equal protection to an absolute veto over adoption of his child, absent a finding of his unfitness as a parent." The Court balanced the state's interest in "rearing children in a family setting" against Quilloin's due process and equal protection interest in absolute veto power over his son's adoption. As to due process, the Court stated that the Georgia court only had to make findings of what was in the child's best interests. As to the equal protection claims, the Court held that although Quilloin for years had been subject to the same child support obligation as a married or divorced father, because he never sought nor had legal custody nor full control and responsibility for his child, the state permissibly could draw a distinction and give him less veto authority than it granted a married or divorced father.

Unlike Peter Stanley, Leon Quilloin failed to exert any significant control over his child for eleven years. The Court simply could not find that he had developed any substantial parental relationship or that he had any liberty interest in that relationship deserving protection. Thus *Quilloin* narrowed the scope of *Stanley* and clarified some of the uncertainty raised by "infamous Footnote 9." The Court also laid a foundation for its *Lehr v. Robertson* (1983) decision by inferring that if a putative father does not employ those specific methods provided by state law to acknowledge paternity or to legitimate his out-of-wedlock child, then he cannot complain of denial of substantive rights that are nonexistent.

Caban v. Mohammed *(1979)*

Almost one year after Quilloin the Supreme Court heard *Caban v. Mohammed*, a challenge to a New York statute very similar to the Georgia law unsuccessfully challenged by Leon Quilloin. New York Domestic Relations Law Section 111, for adoption of a child born out of wedlock, required only the consent "of the mother, whether adult or infant."

The *Caban* scenario, unlike *Quilloin* but like *Stanley*, involved unwed parents who lived together as a de facto family. For five years Abdiel Caban and Maria Mohammed shared a home; Maria gave birth to two children, and Abdiel was listed as the father on each child's birth certificate. He contributed to the support of the family. Even after the parents separated and each married another, Caban continued to see and interact with his children on a weekly basis.

When the children's mother and her husband petitioned to adopt the children in 1976, Caban and his wife cross-petitioned to adopt. The adoption petition of the mother and her husband was granted; Caban appealed. Both the New York Supreme Court, Appellate Division, and the Court of Appeals affirmed the adoptions, basing their rulings on the New York statute and the fact that the adoptions could be denied only if Caban could show that they were not in the children's best interests.

Before the Supreme Court, Caban asserted two claims—that the adoptions violated his right to equal protection and that he possessed a due process right to maintain a parental relationship with his children under *Quilloin*. In a close, 5-to-4 decision, the Court accepted his first claim without ever addressing his second; Justice Powell, writing for the Court's majority, found the New York statute to be overbroad and "to discriminate against unwed fathers even when their identity is known and they have manifested a significant paternal interest in their child." He found the statute both "excluded some loving fathers from full participation in the decision whether their children will be adopted and at the same time, enabled some alienated mothers arbitrarily to cut off the paternal rights of fathers." The Court set the adoptions aside.

Justice Powell stressed that when a father fails to come forward to participate in the rearing of his child, nothing in the Equal Protection Clause will preclude the state from denying him the privilege of veto power over his child's adoption. But since Caban was identified as the children's father, had established a close relationship with them, and had a history of day-to-day involvement in their care, he should have a say in adoption proceedings. The *Caban* opinion, however, carefully limited the right to fathers in situations similar to Caban's. In this respect, the holding is consistent with the underlying rationales of both *Quilloin* and the portion of *Stanley* that extended protection to those fathers who had shown interest in their children's welfare.

Four dissenters, Justices Stewart and Stevens, joined by Chief Justice Burger and Justice Rehnquist, viewed unwed mothers and unwed fathers as not similarly situated. Justice Stewart wrote that the common-law custodial preference given to mothers should carry "with it a correlative power . . . to place her child for adoption or not to do so." So, after *Caban*, the question is left open whether a gender-based distinction involving adoption of newborns might be upheld as not violating the Equal Protection Clause.

Lehr v. Robertson *(1983)*

If the 1972 *Stanley* decision raised the curtain on a stage upon which an unwed father's relationship with his child could receive constitutional protection, then the 1983 *Lehr* decision dropped the curtain on a decade of wrestling with the confusion spawned by *Stanley's* imprecise language. *Stanley* suggested two distinct approaches: extend procedural due process protection to all unwed fathers or extend protection only to those fathers who show an interest in their children's welfare and have a relationship with them.

Jonathan Lehr and Lorraine Martz cohabited for approximately two years prior to Jessica's birth in 1976. Lehr visited Lorraine in the hospital during her confinement, but his name did not appear on Jessica's birth certificate. After Lorraine's discharge from the hospital, Jonathan and Lorraine did not live together or marry. Lorraine kept her whereabouts from Lehr until, with the help of a detective agency, he found her in August 1978 and discovered that she had married Richard Robertson when Jessica was eight months old.

On 21 December 1978, when Jessica was past two years old, the Robertsons filed an adoption petition in Ulster County. The Ulster Court checked the New York putative father registry and, finding no registration, gave Lehr no notice of the pending adoption.

On 30 January 1979, at his own initiative and unaware of the pending adoption, Lehr filed a petition in Westchester County Family Court seeking a determination of paternity, an order of support, and reasonable visitation with Jessica. Notice of this proceeding was served upon the Robertsons, whose attorney informed the Ulster County Court. The Ulster Court took no steps to inform Lehr of the pending adoption, although the judge did enter an order staying Lehr's paternity proceeding until he could rule on a change of venue.

Finally, on 3 March 1979, Lehr learned of Jessica's pending adoption when he received notice of the change of venue motion. Four days later Lehr's attorney called the Ulster County judge to inform him that he would seek a stay of the adoption proceeding and learned that the judge had signed the adoption order that morning. Lehr filed a motion to vacate the adoption on the grounds that it was obtained by fraud and in violation of his constitutional rights to prior notice and to equal protection. The New York courts rejected his arguments.

The Supreme Court found that the New York statutory scheme sufficiently protected the unwed father's interest in assuming a responsible role in his child's life. If the child's mother refused formal marriage within six months after the child's birth, there were six categories into which a father might fall which would make him a presumed or adjudicated legal father or a putative father entitled to notice of an adoption. Moreover, the Court held that the right to receive notice was completely within Lehr's individual control. If he had filed with the state putative father registry an intent to claim paternity, his interest would have been protected and he would have been notified of the adoption.

Lehr decisively "rejected the tacit assumption of *Stanley* that a biological relationship in itself might warrant some constitutional protection" (Raab 1984). The *Lehr* majority described the significance of a mere biological link as

> offer[ing] the natural father an opportunity that no other male possesses to develop a relationship with his offspring. If he grasps the opportunity and accepts some measure of responsibility for the child's future, he may enjoy the blessings of the parent-child relationship and make uniquely valuable contributions to the child's development (463 U.S. 248 at 262).

Thus, instead of viewing the "nature" of the parent-child relationship as creating a protected liberty interest, *Lehr* focused first on the "weight" to be given to the relationship in order to determine if Lehr had any liberty interest. If a putative father has not sufficiently exercised those rights and duties legally imposed on the father of a legitimate child, no liberty interest will be recognized. The *Lehr* majority, by placing more significance on the psychological and social nature of the parent-child relationship than on any biological link, shifted the full onus of responsibility to the putative father to take advantage of "the opportunity" he is offered.

The Court also rejected Lehr's claim of denial of equal protection. Since he never established a substantial relationship with Jessica, he was not one of the class of parents (mothers and fathers) in fact similarly situated with regard to their relationship with their child. The Court ruled that nothing in the Equal Protection Clause prevents a state from according such parents different legal rights.

Post-Lehr *Decisions*

Following *Lehr*, the class of putative fathers accorded constitutional protections is open only to those who actively seek *and* assume parental responsibility and can show a substantial relationship with their child. *Lehr* opened the way, also, for upholding "gender-based" distinctions in state adoption statutes. If one parent, a father, abandons or never establishes a custodial relationship, even if due in part or whole to a mother's concealment of her pregnancy, a state may treat these parents differently as regards their rights to consent to or veto an adoption. Rulings in two cases reviewed by the Supreme Court during its 1988–89 term dramatize the Court's present unwillingness to enlarge the class or to accord any new rights to unwed fathers generally.

MCNAMARA V. SAN DIEGO COUNTY DEPARTMENT OF SOCIAL SERVICES (1988). Known as *In re Baby Girl M* during lengthy California state court proceedings, this case raised the issue whether an unwed father has a right to the custody of his child if the mother, immediately after birth, relinquishes the newborn to an agency.

Ed McNamara did not learn of the 18 July 1981 birth of his daughter until 1 August 1981, after the mother had placed her in foster care with the county agency. Although the agency knew of the father's existence, on August 24th it placed the baby in an adoptive home with a couple chosen by the mother. Agency personnel first had contact with McNamara on August 5th. He declared his interest in keeping his child on August 17th, an entire week before the child's placement in the adoptive home, but one week after the agency had petitioned to terminate his rights on August 10th. On 2 November 1981, the father reaffirmed his desire for custody and announced his intent to fight the adoption.

In December 1981 the California trial court terminated McNamara's rights. Although finding him to be "fit," adoption was determined to be in the "best interests" of the child. Under California law, a "natural (biological) father" had limited rights. To be a "presumed father" and enjoy rights generally equal to those of the mother, a man had to meet the statutory requirements of California's Parentage Act (Comment 1989). Because McNamara was not a presumed father, his consent to adoption was not required. Of course, as noted by the court, the chronology of events gave McNamara no "reasonable opportunity to establish himself as a presumed natural father."

Citing California's "parental preference" (Calif. Civ. Code § 4600(c)), McNamara argued on appeal that physical custody of a minor should go to a parent, if fit, as against a stranger. He also argued that the trial court should have made dual findings: whether an award of custody to him as a parent would be detrimental to the child, and whether adoption was required to serve the best interests of the child. In March 1983, when the child was not yet two, the state appellate court agreed with McNamara, reversed the termination, and remanded the case. It seemed that McNamara had established his rights.

But alas, on remand, McNamara's rights were terminated for a second time. He again appealed, and in October 1984 the California Supreme Court reversed the termination and remanded the case in favor of the father. Now the child was over three years old. On remand, the trial court terminated McNamara's rights for the third time. When McNamara's appeal was acted upon in 1987, his daughter was nearly six years old and had been in the same "preadoptive home" since she was five weeks old. The California Court of Appeals concluded that the "best interests" of the child mandated that McNamara, concededly a "fit" parent, be denied her custody.

Yet McNamara pressed on. He asked the U.S. Supreme Court to consider whether it is a denial of equal protection to terminate an unwed father's rights (1) solely on the best interests standard when the father has promptly manifested a significant parental interest and would be a good parent; and (2) without an adverse finding on the father's fitness when other parents and unwed mothers do not lose their rights under similar conditions. The Court accepted the case for review on 18 April 1988.

However, on 6 December 1988, just a few days after hearing oral arguments, the Court dismissed the matter, concluding that it lacked jurisdiction for want of a properly presented federal question. McNamara's constitutional claims, in fact, had not been addressed in the California state court ruling from which he appealed. Rather, the California Appeals Court had concentrated on construing the California statutory "detriment" standard.

MICHAEL H. AND VICTORIA D. V. GERALD D. (1989).   In May 1981 Victoria D. was born to Carole D., wife of Gerald D., in California. Gerald was listed as father on the birth certificate and claimed Victoria as his daughter, but blood tests showed a 98.07-percent probability that Michael H. was Victoria's father. During Victoria's first three years she and her mother resided at times with Michael, who held her out as his child, at times with another man, and at times with Gerald, with whom they have lived since June 1984.

When Victoria was one-and-a-half years old, Michael petitioned the California Superior Court to establish his paternity and right to visitation. His biological relationship was undisputed. He had developed a substantial relationship with Victoria; had lived with her and contributed to her financial support. The court, however, granted Gerald summary judgement on the ground that California Evidence Code Section 621 provides that a child born to a married woman whose husband is neither impotent nor sterile is the child of that marriage. The California Court of Appeals affirmed, rejecting Michael's procedural and substantive due process challenges to Section 621, as well as Victoria's due process and equal protection claims brought by a court-appointed guardian. Victoria's assertion of a right to continued visitation with Michael was rejected because California law denied visitation to a putative father who had been prevented from establishing his paternity. Michael appealed to the Supreme Court.

On 15 June 1989, eight months after hearing oral arguments, Justice Antonin Scalia, writing for a plurality of the Court, declared that California's statutory preclusion from establishing a legal parent relationship did not violate the substantive or procedural due process rights of a biological father of a child born to a woman married to another man. Justice Scalia's lead opinion was only signed by three justices—Chief Justice Rehnquist, who endorsed it fully, and Justices O'Connor and Kennedy, who each expressly opted out of an extensive footnote. Justice Stevens concurred separately. Justice Brennan's sharp dissent was joined by Justices Marshall and Blackmun; Justice White, joined by Justice Brennan, wrote a separate dissent. While an opinion from such a divided court will be narrowly construed and limited to similar factual circumstances, it nevertheless sends a chilling message to those who may father a child of a married woman that, even if they "act like a father" and "develop a relationship with their offspring," the sanctity of the "unitary marital family" will be upheld.

Impact of Legislation and Certain State Judicial Decisions

To understand fully the current legal status of unwed fathers in the United States, one must consider more than the several Supreme Court cases just reviewed. Certain federal and state laws, including several uniform state laws promulgated by the National Conference of Commissioners on Uniform State Laws (NCCUSL)[11] must be noted, as well as several state supreme court decisions.

Federal Laws

Federal legislation, instead of defining the legal rights of unwed fathers, rather consistently has imposed a support obligation upon them and prodded the individual states to increase the effectiveness of their support enforcement programs. As a corollary to the increasing incidence of out-of-wedlock births and a rise in the cost of the federal Aid to Families of Dependent Children (AFDC) welfare program, Congress was forced to enter the field of child support enforcement in 1974.

SOCIAL SERVICE AMENDMENT OF 1974 (P.L. 93-647). This amendment added Title IV-D to the Social Security Act (42 U.S.C. §§ 651–662, 1982 and Supp. 1986). It mandated establishment and enforcement of child support orders under the auspices of the federal Office of Child Support Enforcement (OCSE). When an unwed mother applies for AFDC, as a condition of eligibility, she must cooperate with the child support enforcement office in identifying and seeking child support from the child's father, unless she has good cause to be exempted (e.g., incest, rape, or danger of harm to her or her child). Additionally, she must assign her support right to the AFDC agency, making the father's debt due directly to the state (Ellman, Kurtz, and Stanton 1986; Krause 1981).

CHILD SUPPORT ENFORCEMENT AMENDMENT OF 1984 (P.L. 98-378). When Congress reviewed the ten-year performance of the federal OCSE, it discovered that many children were the victims of economic abuse. Congressional response was passage of the Child Support Enforcement Amendments (CSEA) of 1984 (98 Stat. 1305),[12] which mandated states to improve their child support enforcement programs by enacting a number of specific remedies and procedures, including established guidelines for support orders, expedited processes for enforcing orders, wage withholding, imposition of liens upon both real and personal property, and interception of federal and state tax refunds (Howe 1988). The goal was to increase the amount of money paid by noncustodial parents for child support, thereby reducing the burden on taxpayer-subsidized public assistance programs (Ellman, Kurtz, and Stanton 1986). By 1988 all but a handful of states had adopted child support guidelines—most specifying a minimum payment of approximately $50 per month to establish a parent's obligation and to set the basis for increasing support when the parent's income increased.

The 1984 CSEA effectively eliminated all statutes of limitation in paternity actions by requiring every state "to have procedures which permit the establishment of the paternity of any child at any time prior to such child's eighteenth birthday" (42 U.S.C. § 666(a)(5)). In spite of this, in 1987 the average paternity establishment rate (as a proportion of all out-of-wedlock births) was only 31 percent. (The rates varied from a high of 87% to a low of 1.4%). And thirty states failed a federal audit of their efforts to establish paternity (Ooms and Herendeen 1988).

FAMILY SUPPORT ACT OF 1988 (P.L. 100-485). Signed into law on 13 October 1988, Title I of this Act, Child Support and Establishment of Paternity, promises to greatly increase the numbers of paternity determinations. In the words of the Act's principal author, Senator Patrick Moynihan, its central features stress family responsibility and community obligation in the context of the vastly changed family arrangements of the last fifty years, (e.g., the prevalence of unwed parenthood, along with the rise in divorce and the increase in maternal labor force participation). One of the Act's basic moral signals is that no one escapes (economic) responsibility for parenthood (Ooms and Herendeen 1988).

Certain provisions of the Family Support Act may impact greatly upon young unwed fathers. Henceforth, (1) state guidelines for setting child support awards can no longer be merely advisory, but must be used as a rebuttable presumption; (2) immediate automatic withholding of child support payments from the noncustodial parent's paycheck will occur regardless of whether there has been any default of payment; (3) to combat past reluctance to pursue paternity, states must meet new, tougher standards for improving paternity determinations; (4) there will be federal matching of 90 percent of the cost of blood and other tests to establish paternity; (5) states must institute simpler, civil procedures for establishing paternity and settling paternity disputes; and (6) states must collect Social Security numbers from both parents at the time of the child's birth, although the numbers will not be recorded on the birth certificate.

Relevant Uniform State Acts

UNIFORM ACT ON PATERNITY (UAP). Promulgated in 1960 by NCCUSL, the UAP was partially or fully adopted in six states (Kentucky, Maine, Mississippi, New Hampshire, Rhode Island, and Utah) and continues to be the law in those states, although NCCUSL has withdrawn it. In the same vein as the cited federal legislation, the express language of Section 1 of the UAP stressed obligations, not rights. The unwed father is "liable to the same extent as the father of a child born in wedlock . . . , for the reasonable expenses of the mother's pregnancy and confinement and for the education, necessary support and funeral expenses of the child." This support obligation attaches to the father of the child even if the mother is married to another man.

UNIFORM PARENTAGE ACT (UPA). This Act, promulgated by NCCUSL in 1973 following the U.S. Supreme Court's *Stanley* decision, has been enacted in whole or in part by nineteen states. The UPA addresses major issues such as establishing or terminating a legal parent-child relationship and certain presumptions of paternity. Since the major thrust of the UPA concerns the status of children born out of wedlock, the Act does not per se delineate specific legal rights of putative fathers. Rather, Section 4 of the UPA (Presumptions of Paternity) accords protected or preferred status—at least an assurance of receiving notice of court proceedings—to "presumed" fathers.

California is one state, however, that has amended its UPA provision regarding a natural (biological) father who is not a presumed father (Calif. Civ. Code § 7017(d)(2)). In 1986 an amendment mandated a broad-ranging parental preference in custody matters for a putative father who promptly seeks to shoulder the burdens of paternity.

Ironically, on 15 May 1989, just five months after the Supreme Court dismissed *McNamara*, the California Court of Appeals, Third District, in *Jermstad v. McNelis* (No. C003203), on facts very similar to those in *McNamara* but occurring after the 1986 amendment, ruled that "an unwed father who has diligently pursued the opportunity to establish a legally recognized custodial relationship with his child is entitled to the parental preference to custody in proceedings under the California paternity statute, read in light of federal constitutional law (as enunciated in *Stanley, Quilloin, Caban,* and *Lehr*)." The court concluded that the parental preference under the paternity act precludes measuring the best interests of the child by comparing the father's circumstances with those of the prospective adoptive parents.

UNIFORM PUTATIVE AND UNKNOWN FATHERS ACT (UPUFA).
First approved by the Conference at its August 1988 Annual Meeting, after a three-year drafting effort under the chairmanship of Arthur H. Peterson, Assistant Attorney General for Alaska, this Act won the approval of the American Bar Association's House of Delegates on 7 February 1989. It is now available for enactment by the individual states. Its purpose is both to codify U.S. Supreme Court decisions and to provide answers to some questions left open by certain decisions (UPUFA Prefatory Note).

The clear post-*Lehr* challenge has been to balance the clashing rights and interests of the unwed father against those of the unwed mother, while still furthering and protecting the best interests of the child. One writer in the *Harvard Women's Law Journal* has commented:

> Of course, it would not be an easy legislative task to draft a notice statute that attributes appropriate weight to father's due process rights, mother's and children's privacy interests, timing considerations and administrative efficiency. For example, delicate balancing and careful language would be necessary to implement the *Lehr* dissent's standard of "reasonable effort" that does not require notification of every putative father nor an "exhaustive search" in every circumstance (Raab 1984, 286, n.96).

The UPUFA is an appropriate response to the challenge. It attempts to protect the legitimate interests of the unwed father who wants to maintain or establish and develop a parental relationship with his child. It addresses both procedural and substantive due process considerations with respect to a variety of possible court proceedings—adoption, custody other than in the context of divorce, paternity, and termination of parental rights.

First, Section 2(a) affirmatively declares that every putative father has a right to bring "an action to determine whether he is the biological father of a particular child, in accordance with [applicable state law] at any time, unless his paternity or possible parental rights already have been determined or are in issue in pending litigation" (brackets in original text).

Sections 3 and 4 contain the substantive due process protections to be accorded putative and unknown fathers. Notice must be given to every known putative father by the person seeking to free the child for an adoption. If it appears to the court, at any time, that a putative father may not have been given notice, the specific steps that the court must take in making an "inquiry of appropriate persons in an effort to identify him" are laid out in Section 3(e). Any putative father who responds to notice or voluntarily comes forward may participate as a party in a Section 3 adoption or termination proceeding, or in a Section 4 proceeding, to change or establish legal or physical custody or visitation rights with respect to his child.

While *Lehr* and the 1988 cases, *McNamara* and *Michael H.*, have narrowed the class of putative fathers to be accorded constitutional protection, *Lehr* did mandate states to protect the putative father's "opportunity" to form a relationship and once formed to fully protect it, unless foreclosed by a state statutory conclusive presumption of fatherhood in another man, as in *Michael H.* What *Lehr* did not do was to specify the factors for determining when a sufficient father-child relationship is established. UPUFA Section 5 fills this gap.

Fourteen factors are listed in Section 5 that, when applied, can cover a wide spectrum of fathers from the "casual progenitor" to the one who lives with the mother in a stable relationship. The factors also refer to various types of conduct, such as paying support, exercising visitation rights, and trying to "grasp the opportunity" to act as a parent. Finally, they cover various descriptions of factual circumstances, such as the age of the child (objective) and the existence of a parent-child relationship (subjective). The court may take note of a father's written acknowledgment of paternity, filed with the appropriate agency, or a state putative father registry. While its probative value might be slight, such a filing could be some evidence of intent to assume responsibility for the child and of an interest in having a parental relationship with the child. Careful application of these fourteen factors should provide sound judicial decision making on behalf of both parents and their children.

For example, had California had a statute similar to the UPUFA in November 1981, when Ed McNamara first opposed the adoption of his daughter, the trial court would have had both to determine both his paternity and, applying the fourteen factors, to rule on his fitness to parent. Given the mother's relinquishment of the child for adoption by unrelated third parties, once Mr. McNamara's paternity had been adjudicated, he would have benefited from the traditional parental preference applied in custody contests between natural parents and unrelated third parties.

State Putative Father Registry Acts

During the 1980s some twelve states (Idaho, Michigan, Missouri, Montana, Nebraska, New York, North Carolina, Oklahoma, Tennessee, Texas, Utah, and Wisconsin) established putative father registries. Two of these (Missouri and Montana) have the UPA, and another state (Utah) has the UAP. Young men residing in one of these states, to protect their interests, should know the particulars about their state law and carefully comply.

While each state statute is different, seven states seem to share three types of statutes. These groupings are New York/Oklahoma/Tennessee; Michigan/Montana; and Utah/Idaho. In addition to putative fathers filing an intent to claim paternity, in- and out-of-state adjudicated fathers and those having acknowledged paternity are in the New York/Oklahoma/Tennessee registries. All states except Missouri require identifying data on the mother, as well as the child's name and date and place of birth. A notarized filing or witnessed signing is required in all but Utah, which merely accepts a registrant's signature. Some states permit filing until relinquishment by the mother for adoption or commencement of a proceeding to terminate parental rights. Michigan and Montana permit filing only before a child's birth; New York/Oklahoma/Tennessee allow filing for any reasonable time before or after a child's birth.

The most obvious reason for an unwed father to file is to gain notice of an adoption or termination of parental rights proceeding. In Idaho and Utah failure to file can be treated as an abandonment: as grounds for termination of parental rights in Idaho, and as a waiver of notice of adoption in Utah. Additionally, Utah forbids a nonfiler from initiating an action to establish paternity.

The Comment to UPUFA Section 3 notes that in 1987 two paternity registry laws were held unconstitutional as they applied to two fathers. In *Application of S.R.S.* the Nebraska Supreme Court held a statute requiring the father to file within five days after birth of his child inapplicable to a father who lived with the mother before and after the child's birth and who never had occasion to formally claim paternity until after the mother left him and placed the child for adoption. In *Matter of K.B.E.* the Utah Court of Appeals found that, even though a father who filed his claim on the day his child was born failed to file timely enough under the statute (the mother and her grandfather had filed an adoptive petition just hours before), nevertheless, to apply the statute in such circumstances would violate the father's constitutional rights.

Although some feminists strongly support limiting notice of proceedings solely to those filing in putative father registries (Erikson 1984), drafters of the UPUFA refused to take such a hard-nosed approach, but, under the UPUFA, registration by itself does not elevate one to the status of being a "presumed" father.

Impact of Scientific Advances in Paternity Testing

Blood-test evidence has been offered in paternity actions since the 1930s. Tests based on the ABO blood-typing system and the later-developed Human Leukocyte Antigen (HLA) tissue-tying tests can only definitively exclude an alleged male from being a particular child's father. For a male not so excluded, test results have to be interpreted to estimate the percentage probability of paternity. A newly developed identification technique known as "DNA fingerprinting" can now, with certainty, determine whether a particular person is a particular child's father (14 Family Law Reporter 1504).

DNA is an abbreviation for deoxyribonucleic acid, the chemical structure of a molecule that carries the body's genetic information and is found in every living cell with a nucleus (over 99% of the cells of the human body). "When a person is conceived, his or her DNA is formed by the combination of the chromosomes in the father's sperm and the mother's ovum. . . . Since a person's DNA is derived half from [each parent] the question of whether a man is the father of a particular child can be resolved by comparing the "bar codes" of the man, the child, and the child's mother" (Jackson 1989).

One of the first courts to accept DNA fingerprinting to determine paternity in a civil proceeding is the New York Surrogate's Court for New York County. (*In re Baby Girl S.*, 5 August 1988). Many cases are reportedly being resolved without trial on the basis of DNA-fingerprinting tests. The technique should rapidly become the established primary method of paternity testing. Unwed fathers who wish to overcome outmoded presumptions that have survived largely because of the inaccuracy of previous paternity testing methods will be helped greatly.

Although DNA analysis is slightly more expensive than some other forms of paternity testing, it is anticipated that the cost will not limit its utilization. Hence more young unwed men should expect that they will be required to submit to such testing. If paternity is established, they will be subject to having all federal enforcement remedies applied to them. Youth will not be a shield. A 1988 West Virginia Supreme Court of Appeals case, *Kathy L.B. v. Patrick J.B.* (1 July 1988), interpreting the state's 1986 paternity statutes as a case of first impression, sounds a sobering note. The defendant father, after establishment of paternity, was ordered to make retroactive child support payments to the plaintiff-mother, as well as to pay for her birth expenses, her child's health care insurance premiums, and her attorney fees and court costs. Other courts in Florida, Massachusetts, Mississippi, Texas, and Washington have made similar rulings.

Conclusion

Thus it might be said that all three categories of unwed fathers recognized in the United States today—legal, putative, and unknown—have moved up the legal status ladder from the bottom rung they once occupied under English common law. But young unwed fathers as a rule do not yet enjoy all the constitutional protections accorded married or divorced parents. Many courts also continue to find rational reasons for not treating unwed fathers and unwed mothers as "similarly situated."

In this writer's opinion, the legal rights and obligations of all unwed fathers have evolved unevenly. Because of the public policy shift to hold parents financially responsible for their offspring, as reflected in federal and state legislation, and because of the new technology (DNA finger-printing) that enables definitive establishment of paternity, *most* unwed fathers can expect to have the full financial obligations of parenthood imposed upon them. In contrast, their legal rights as parents may be heavily circumscribed or completely thwarted by the actions of the mother of their child. For the most part, the obligations imposed outstrip the legal rights accorded.

The controlling Supreme Court cases discussed above may have re-quired states to protect the putative father's "opportunity" to form a rela-tionship, and once formed to protect it fully, but they have also down-played the import of a mere biological link without any showing of a substantial father-child relationship. A young man may not have the re-sources to maintain a separate household into which he could accept his child, and thereby establish a significant relationship with the child. If indigent, he may not be able to retain legal counsel to advocate in his behalf. And he may reside in a state that does not make appointed coun-sel available. In sum, there is a basic contradiction between basing a father's financial obligations entirely on an alleged biological tie with no assessment of parental interest but according him rights to seek custody or veto an adoption only upon demonstrated parental interest or relation-ship.

Clearly, a continuing open question is how best to balance the some-times clashing interests of the unwed father and mother in ways that further and protect the best interests of the child. If states begin to enact UPUFA or laws essentially modeled after it, state courts will have the criteria to determine better when a sufficient father-child relationship ex-

ists and warrants protections. In time, more states may abolish their conclusive presumptions that deem a woman's husband at the time of conception or birth to be a child's presumed legal father. This would enable
more men to have standing to immediately seek to have their paternity of
a child judicially decreed. But these anticipated legal developments will
not address or resolve the most pressing issues faced by young unwed
fathers individually or by society at large.

Young men who father children before concluding their education or
acquiring the requisite skills to be gainfully employed, self-supporting
individuals, capable of earning average incomes, may find themselves so
saddled with financial obligations that all their other life choices—with
respect to education, career, marriage, housing—are dramatically limited. When the obligations of parenthood are thrust upon one too soon,
lifelong poverty and low achievement can be the result. Tragically, the
current social attitudes and behaviors of many low-income ethnic minority males guarantee them such assigned roles. Ultimately, society must
come to grips with the internal structural flaws that perpetuate the poverty
and racism which deny full and equal participation in the fruits of our
capitalist system to many of these young men.

To stem the debilitating, increasing incidence of children fathered out
of wedlock, more is needed than legal reforms. A range of social utilities
other than law—educational programs, motivational supports, and outreach services—is desperately needed to reduce the incidence of early
fatherhood, as well as to help those young men who become fathers acquire the requisite job and fathering skills.

Notes

1. See U.S. Bureau of the Census 1989, *Statistical Abstract of the U.S.*
(108th ed.), p. 62, table 87, Births to unmarried women, by race and age of
mother, and ibid. 1991, *Statistical Abstract* (110th ed.), p. 66, table 87, Live
births by race and type of Hispanic origin—Selected characteristics, 1985 and
1987, and p. 67, table 90, Births to unmarried women, by race of child and age
of mother: 1970 to 1987.

2. See U.S. Bureau of the Census 1988, *Households, family, marital status
and living arrangements: March 1988*, Current Population Report, Series P-20,
·no. 437, p. 7, table 5. Unmarried couple household, by presence of children:
1970 to 1988.

3. Comment, Delineation of the Boundaries of Putative Fathers' Rights: A
Psychological Parenthood Perspective, 15 *Seton Hall L. Rev.* 290, 296, n.40
(1985), citing cases from California, Michigan, Minnesota and Missouri.

4. See ibid., n.41, citing *In re Guardianship of Smith*, 42 Cal. 2d 91, 265
P.2d 888 (1954).

5. See ibid., n.43, citing *Thomas v. Children's Aid Society*, 12 Utah 2d 234, 239, 364 P.2d 1029, 1031 (1961): "The putative father occupies no recognized paternal status at common law or under [Utah] statutes . . . except that it will make him pay for the child's maintenance if it can find out who he is."

6. Alabama, California, Colorado, Delaware, Hawaii, Illinois, Kansas, Minnesota, Missouri, Montana, Nevada, New Jersey, New Mexico, North Dakota, Ohio, Rhode Island, Texas, Washington, Wyoming.

7. See Clark 1988, 799, n.20, for listing of statutes in sixteen states, including among others, Arizona, California, Colorado, New York, Virginia, and Wisconsin.

8. Ibid., 800, n.21, for cases from eight jurisdictions: Alaska, Illinois, Iowa, Kentucky, Maryland, Nevada, Pennsylvania, and the District of Columbia.

9. The U.S. Supreme Court in *Planned Parenthood of Central Missouri v. Danforth*, 428 U.S. 52 (1976) invalidated both Missouri's spousal consent to abortion law and its parental consent requirement for abortion of an unmarried minor. The Court reasoned that if a state could not veto a women's decision to have an abortion (*Roe v. Wade*, 410 U.S. 113 (1973)), it could not give that power to a third person, be it a spouse or a parent. Yet because of the tension surrounding the rights of minors and the permissible limits on those rights, and the rights of parents to control the conduct of their children, the Court in subsequent cases has "said that [a] statute may not require the minor to obtain her parents' consent in all cases, but must provide an alternative procedure, here obtaining a court's approval, obviating parental consent" (*Bellotti v. Baird*, 1979) and "held that the requirement of parental notification was constitutional as applied to the immature dependent minor" (*H.L. v. Matheson*, 1981, as discussed in Clark 1988, 232).

10. *Rothstein v. Lutheran Social Services of Wisconsin & Upper Michigan*, 405 U.S. 1051 (1972; an unmarried father's challenge to a completed adoption) and *Vanderlaan v. Vanderlaan*, 405 U.S. 1051 (1972; unmarried father's claim to visitation rights remanded to an Illinois appellate court).

11. The purpose of the National Conference of Commissioners is to promote uniformity in state law on all subjects where uniformity is desirable and practicable. One of the oldest of state organizations designed to encourage interstate cooperation, the conference, since its founding in 1892, has drafted over 200 uniform laws on numerous subjects in various fields of law, many of which have been widely enacted like the Uniform Commercial Code (UCC) and Uniform Child Custody Jurisdiction Act (UCCJA). The conference is composed of commissioners from each state, the District of Columbia, and Puerto Rico, usually four in number. State governors appoint lawyers, judges, legislators, and law professors. All commissioners are members of the bar. See National Conference of Commissioners on Uniform State Laws 1990, 2–3.

12. Current version codified in scattered sections of 42 U.S.C. (Supp. IV 1986).

References

ABA adopts Uniform Putative and Unknown Fathers Act. *ABA Juvenile & Child Welfare Law Reporter* 8(2):31–32. April.

Barron, J. 1975. Notice to the unwed father and termination of parental rights: Implementing *Stanley v. Illinois*. *Family Law Quarterly* 9:521–546.

Clark, H., Jr. 1988. *The law of domestic relations in the United States*. 2d ed. St. Paul: West Publishing.

Comment. 1984. *Lehr v. Robertson*: Procedural due process and putative fathers' rights. *DePaul Law Review* 33:393–410.

———. 1985. Delineation of the boundaries of putative father's rights: A psychological parenthood perspective, *Seton Hall Law Review* 15:290–322.

———. 1989. A modern-day Solomon's dilemma: What of the unwed father's rights? *University of Detroit Law Review* 66:267–296.

Deeply divided Supreme Court upholds paternity-presumption law. 1989. *Family Law Reporter* 15(33):1391. 20 June.

Ellman, I. M., P. M. Kurtz, and A. M. Stanton. 1986. *Family law: Cases, text, problems*. Charlottesville, Va.: Michie.

Erikson, N. 1984. The feminist dilemma over unwed parents' custody rights: The mother's rights must take priority. *Law and Inequality* 2:447–472.

Howe, R.-A. W. 1988. Who speaketh for the child? *New England Law Review* 23:421–435.

Jackson, D. 1989. DNA fingerprinting and proof of paternity. *Family Law Reporter* 15(28):3007–3013. 16 May.

Kohn, M. 1987. *Child support enforcement and young unwed fathers*. Paper commissioned by Family Impact Seminar for H.H.S.-sponsored October 1986 conference. Available from Project SHARE, P.O. Box 2309, Rockville, MD 20852.

Krause, H. 1981. *Child support in America*, Charlottesville, Va.: Michie.

———. 1986. *Family law in a nutshell*. 2d ed. St. Paul: West Publishing.

National Conference of Commissioners on Uniform State Laws (NCCUSL). 1990. *1990–91 Reference Book*. Chicago, Ill. Available from NCCUSL, 676 North St. Clair Street, Suite 1700, Chicago, IL 60611.

Nichols-Casebolt, A. 1988. Paternity adjudication: In the best interest of the out-of-wedlock child. *Child Welfare* 67(3):245–254.

Ooms, T., and L. Herendeen. 1988. *Young unwed fathers and welfare reform*. Meeting highlights and background briefing report. Washington, D.C.: American Association for Marriage and Family Therapy Foundation. 18 November.

Raab, J. 1984. *Lehr v. Robertson*: Unwed fathers and adoption—how much process is due? *Harvard Women's Law Journal* 7:265–286.

Redden, K. 1982. *Federal regulation of family law*. Charlottesville, Va.: Michie.

Smollar, J., and T. Ooms. 1987. *Young unwed fathers: Research, review, policy dilemmas, and options*. Washington, D.C.: U.S. Department of Health and Human Services. Available from: Project SHARE, P.O. Box 2309, Rockville, MD 20852.

Sussman, A., and M. Guggenheim. 1980. *The rights of parents*. New York: Avon.

Title 1 of the Family Support Act of 1988. 1988. *Family Law Reporter* 15 (4):2001–2008. 22 November.

Uniform Putative and Unknown Fathers Act. 1988. *Family Law Reporter* 15 (17):2017–2024. 28 February.

U.S. Bureau of the Census. 1988. *Households, family, marital status, and living arrangements: March 1988*. Current Population Reports. Series p-20, no. 432. (Advance report, issued September.) Washington, D.C.: Government Printing Office.

———. 1989. *Statistical abstract of the United States: 1988*. Washington, D.C.: Government Printing Office.

———. 1991. *Statistical abstract of the United States: 1990*. Washington, D.C.: Government Printing Office.

U.S. Supreme Court Cases

Bellotti v. Baird, 443 U.S. 622 (1979).

Caban v. Mohammed, 441 U.S. 380 (1979).

Harper v. Virginia Board of Education, 383 U.S. 663 (1966).

H.L. v. Matheson, 450 U.S. 398 (1981).

Lassiter v. Department of Social Services of Durham County, 452 U.S. 734 (1981).

Lehr v. Robertson, 463 U.S. 248 (1983).

Little v. Streater, 452 U.S. 1 (1981).

Mathews v. Eldridge, 424 U.S. 319 (1976).

May v. Anderson, 345 U.S. 528 (1953).

McNamara v. San Diego County Department of Social Services, 109 S.Ct. 546 (1988).

Meyer v. Nebraska, 262 U.S. 390 (1923).

Michael H. and Victoria D. v. Gerald D., 109 S.Ct. 2333 (1989).

Planned Parenthood of Central Missouri v. Danforth, 428 U.S. 52 (1976).

Quilloin v. Walcott, 434 U.S. 246 (1978).

Reed v. Reed, 404 U.S. 71 (1971).

Rivera v. Minnich, 483 U.S. 574.

Roe v. Wade, 410 U.S. 113 (1973).

Rothstein v. Lutheran Social Services of Wisconsin & Upper Michigan, 405 U.S. 1051 (1972).

Santosky v. Kramer, 455 U.S. 734 (1982).

Stanley v. Illinois, 405 U.S. 645 (1972).

Vanderlaan v. Vanderlaan, 405 U.S. 1051 (1972).

State Court Cases

Application of S.R.S., 408 N.W.2d 272 (Neb. 1987).

In re Baby Girl M., 141 Cal. App. 3d 432, 191 Cal. Rptr. 339 (App. 1982); *In re*

Baby Girl M., 207 Cal. Rptr. 309, 688 P.2d 918 (Cal. 1984); and *In re Baby Girl M.*, 191 Cal. App. 3d 786, 236 Cal. Rptr. 660 (Cal. App. 4th Dist. 1987).

In re Baby Girl S., (N.Y. Surrogate Ct., N.Y.C., 5 August 1988) 14 FLR 1504.

Jermstad v. McNelis, 258 Cal. Rptr. 519 (Cal. App. 3d Dist. 1989) 15 FLR 1381.

Kathy L.B. v. Patrick J.B., (W. Va. Sup. Ct. App. No. 18201, 1 July 1988) 14 FLR 1509.

Matter of K.B.E., 740 P.2d 292 (Utah App. 1987).

8 Ethical Dimensions of Young Unwed Fatherhood

GEORGE W. HARRIS

The common stereotype of the young unwed father envisions him as a somewhat shiftless, sexually irresponsible, uncaring individual with little concern for the difficulties he has created for the lives of those around him. Like all stereotypes, however, this is misleading. It is misleading not only because it is empirically false in vast numbers of cases, but also because it distorts the moral terms in which society as a community addresses the problems that accompany young unwed parenthood.

The moral distortion arises from the exclusive focus on the young unwed father's responsibilities. If we view a person as recklessly causing harm to others in the insensitive pursuit of his own narrowly defined interests—whatever those interests might be—we are likely to think of what his *responsibilities* are to those whom he has harmed as a result of his irresponsible behavior. We are not likely to think very much in terms of his *rights*. And even if we do, we are likely to consider those rights diminished due to his irresponsible behavior. Here our decreased concern for his rights and our increased concern for the rights of those he has harmed are the result of our perception of him as needlessly bringing harm to others. And as our concern for the rights of his victims increases, so does our concern that he shoulder an increased burden of responsibilities.

So far, there is nothing distorted about this way of thinking. It is as it

The author wishes to express his appreciation to Theodora Ooms for her helpful editorial suggestions.

should be. For example, a man who has raped a woman has forfeited some, if not all, of his rights to our concern for his sexual interests and he has increased his responsibilities to the woman he has harmed. Central to our moral focus in such contexts are the victim's rights and the transgressor's responsibilities.

But we should not begin our moral deliberations about how to treat a young unwed father with a predetermined moral focus of the sort that minimizes any significant emphasis on his rights. If in any particular case the facts lead us to think of him as a transgressor who has forfeited some of his rights, then our moral focus should certainly reflect this. But we should begin our moral deliberations with a clear idea about what a father's legitimate interests are and what his normal responsibilities are in his pursuit of those interests. Only when there is clarity in regard to the normal case can we see how he might forfeit the right to pursue some of his interests, and inherit the burden of additional responsibilities, if he is guilty of some moral transgression in pursuing his interests. Thus any balanced inquiry into the ethical dimensions of young unwed fatherhood will begin with just as much concern for the legitimate interests of the young unwed father and his right to pursue those interests as with his responsibilities towards those affected by his actions.

Talk of moral rights, however, already presupposes to some degree a situation of moral conflict, a situation where the different parties are in dispute about whose interests are to be given priority in the resolution of moral claims of some sort. Ordinarily, disputes of the sort involved in parenthood take place within the context of marriage and the family. But the moral concepts that provide guidance within the context of marriage and the family are generally not expressed in terms of rights and corresponding responsibilities. Personal relationships that depend heavily upon talk about rights are already on their way to becoming depersonalized. For example, a family that can get along without the need for making rights claims on each other is likely to be stronger than one that keeps a constant eye on assuring the rights of its members. This is especially true when the regulation of these rights comes at the cost of the personal aspects of family relationships like love, spontaneity, commitment, and accommodation.

Here, however, the focus will be on a context in which the parents are not only young, but both unmarried and irreconcilably alienated.[1] This creates a conflict in which rights claims do make sense and where the moral concepts internal to ordinary family relationships cannot provide sufficient guidance. To insist upon the full normal use of marriage and family concepts here and to avoid the use of rights concepts is to fail to recognize that the moral situation is an unusual one.

What then are the moral rights and responsibilities of young unwed fathers? More specifically, what are these rights and responsibilities in regard to issues of paternity, custody, support, visitation, and adoption for those young unwed fathers for whom marriage to the mother, for whatever reasons, is not an option?

Rights and Responsibilities: A Balanced Perspective

Discussion of unwed fathers, of whatever age, usually begins with their responsibilities, primarily in terms of child support. This is somewhat understandable given the crucial needs of the child, but, as I have suggested, it can lead to a distorted perspective on the father's moral status and of the moral situation in general. The distortion results from narrowing the focus on the rights of the child and the mother to the point of obscuring any vision of the father's rights at all. It would be odd if the father were the bearer of responsibilities but not the beneficiary of any rights. This is not true of other persons in general. Why should it be true of unwed fathers?

A more balanced perspective on the conflicts involved in young unwed fatherhood places the rights and the responsibilities of the unwed father in the context of the rights and responsibilities of the other parties involved. From such a perspective, we can distinguish the following sets of rights:

1. the rights of the unwed father,
2. the rights of the child,
3. the rights of the unwed mother,
4. the rights of related third parties (e.g., grandparents), and
5. the rights of unrelated third parties (the public).

A clear understanding of the nature of the conflicts in which these various rights are involved requires us also to distinguish among the different types of young unwed fathers. First, there are differences in age and maturity. Next, there are differences in mental competence. And finally, there are differences in economic status. These differences are certainly relevant to what the young unwed father's rights and responsibilities are.

One further preliminary distinction is required to understand the nature of these conflict situations. It is that between *prima facie* rights and responsibilities and *actual* rights and responsibilities. Here the term *prima facie* is used to indicate a very commonsense idea and should not arouse suspicions of an arcane legal or philosophical vocabulary. To say that someone has a prima facie right or a prima facie responsibility is to say that, everything else being equal, he or she has that right or responsibility. But, of course, sometimes there are relevant complicating factors which make the situation one where everything else is not equal, and where the prima facie right fails to be an actual right. The only cases, therefore, in which a prima facie right or responsibility is an actual one are those in which there are no relevant complicating factors to prevent what is prima facie from being actual.

For example, a child has a prima facie right to support from its parents. But suppose for some reason beyond their control it is physically impossible for the parents to provide the support. The child's prima facie right, in this case, cannot be an actual right, because it is absurd to say that someone has an obligation to do something impossible for that person. A prima facie right might also fail to become an actual right by being overridden by a stronger, more fundamental right. For example, a young male might have a prima facie right to a sexual interest in a young female, but his prima facie right fails to become an actual right when his exercise of that right threatens her stronger right not to be sexually interested in him. Similarly, a young unwed father might have a prima facie responsibility to support the mother, but if it is impossible for him to do so, or if doing so conflicts with his ability to support the child—in some contexts, a stronger responsibility—his prima facie responsibility fails to become an actual one. Thus if we are to understand the competing concerns in the conflicts of unwed fatherhood, we must see that it is not actual rights and responsibilities that conflict but prima facie rights and responsibilities that compete with each other for the status of being actual rights and responsibilities.

Finally, for the sake of the current discussion, let us say that a person has a prima facie right to pursue an interest if that interest is morally legitimate, and to the extent it can be pursued in a morally legitimate way. To respect such rights is to respect a person's *autonomy*. Let us also say that a person has a prima facie responsibility to respect the autonomy of others, that is, to respect their rights to pursue their morally legitimate interest to the extent these can be pursued in morally legitimate ways.

The Rights of the Unwed Father

With these distinctions in mind, we can turn to a more concrete discussion of the young unwed father's moral rights and responsibilities. What I hope to construct is a conception of his rights and responsibilities that is *nonpatriarchal*. Women have correctly objected to certain forms of gender bias in various conceptions of morality and personal relationships. One form of gender bias can be called *patriarchy*. And for present purposes, to say that a conception of sex and gender roles is patriarchal is to

say that it systematically conceives of the interests of women as subordi-
nate to those of men. That society has been greatly influenced by such
patriarchal concepts is, I believe, undeniable. I take it as a restriction on
the arguments I will give on behalf of the rights of young unwed fathers
that they do *not* depend on patriarchal conceptions of sex and gender
roles. If this is true, then the rights I argue for are those that would be
held by such young men in a nonpatriarchal, sexually egalitarian society.
As a second restriction on the adequacy of any conception of the *actual
rights* of young unwed fathers, I accept the following requirement: no
right that would be an actual right in a sexually egalitarian society should
be *enforced* in our society by legal sanction if the practice of doing so
would reinforce a current system of patriarchal subordination.

The Right to Procreate

One of the most important rights at issue here is the right to procreate,
and not all young males have this right, not even as a prima facie right.
Others have the right to procreate as a prima facie right but not as an
actual right.

It is more plausible that some mentally retarded persons have a prima
facie right to procreate than it is that some young males or females at
certain levels of immaturity do. A person has only those rights consistent
with whatever responsibilities he or she has, and in many cases young
males and females, especially those of minority age, are simply too immature to shoulder the responsibilities of parenthood. The dependent
child, it must be remembered, has many welfare interests, all of which
are morally legitimate and all of which the parent has a prima facie responsibility to provide for. Given this fact, procreational interests are not
morally legitimate interests for these immature youths to pursue, and consequently they do not have even a prima facie right to procreate. Some
mentally retarded persons, on the other hand, are capable of the responsibilities of parenthood and hence are less suspect as potential parents.

An objection might be made here that I have implied that the prima
facie right to procreate entails at least some prima facie parental responsibilities and that this is false. A donor to a sperm bank, it might be
argued, does not have a prima facie parental responsibility to the potentially resulting child, and neither does a surrogate mother. There might
also be social practices that break the connection between procreation and
parental responsibility. For example, parental responsibilities may be
taken over collectively by other designated members of the community in
order to free the natural parents to provide needed services in times of
extreme economic stress.

In our society, however, the absence of any standing social practice that displaces the parental responsibility of those who conceive children leaves intact their prima facie responsibility to provide their children with parental care. To the extent to which this is true, then, those who are incapable of parental responsibility are not eligible for the right to procreate. To say otherwise is to say that procreational interests can be legitimately pursued without any parental regard for the future welfare of the child.

It does not follow from this, of course, that we are morally justified in disregarding the immature youth's interest in the fetus or the child once a pregnancy occurs. But we should not *begin* our moral deliberations with the view that these youths have a prima facie right to procreate that we must honor unless we can somehow counter it with a stronger, more fundamental right. Immature youths do not have such a right, and it is important to note that this is just as true for immature females as it is for immature males.

The same reasoning might be thought to apply to indigent youths as well, since they too might be unable to carry out the responsibilities of parenthood. But I think this would be a mistake. It may very well be that in some circumstances indigence removes the *actual* right to procreate, but it removes it in a different way than does immaturity. It is one thing to be incapable of the responsibilities of parenthood because of one's circumstances; it is another to be incapable because of one's immaturity. The indigent has the prima facie right to procreate because he is personally capable of parenthood. The immature youth, however, is incapable of parenthood because of his person. He is simply not yet—perhaps through no fault of his own—the kind of person that can have the prima facie right to procreate because he is not yet the kind of person capable of taking on the responsibilities that accompany that right.[2]

Indigent, sufficiently mature youths, then, do have the prima facie right to procreate. Thus if their indigence is an impediment to fulfilling their parental responsibilities, if it cannot be removed by their own efforts, or if it is due to unjust social practices that are inconsistent with respecting their rights to pursue their morally legitimate interests in morally legitimate ways, then it seems plausible to say that society has the prima facie obligation to aid these indigent males in gaining access to the means of fulfilling parental responsibility and to procreational autonomy. Thus their prima facie right to procreate includes the prima facie right to education and employment opportunities. This is to ensure that their indigence, when it is no fault of their own, does not remove their actual right to pursue their legitimate interest in procreation.

This is no small point in regard to what the moral responsibilities of the community are to indigent, but mature youths. And if it is true that unemployment and lack of education play a leading role in the rate of young unwed pregnancy, these elements play an even larger role for young indigents as obstacles to being responsible parents. This compounds the importance of society's role in the education and employment of these individuals. Furthermore, the emphasis here is on these youths as having a legitimate moral interest in being responsible parents, rather than on their merely being the source of support for children who would otherwise be a burden to the state or to the mother. This point is often missed by some feminists, whose concern for the young unwed father's responsibilities often seems totally detached from any concern for his rights or for him as a victim of circumstances similar to those of the young unwed mother.[3]

The Rights to Paternity, Custody, and Visitation

To determine when the biological father has the right to custody or visitation, we must first examine the conditions under which he has the right to be the social father to the child, and therefore the right to paternity. The issues, then, are these: (1) when does the biological father have the right to paternity, (2) when does his right to paternity include the right to custody, and (3) when does his right to paternity include the right to visitation?

I have argued elsewhere (Harris 1986) that the fetus of a pregnant woman should be considered the father's as well as the mother's if the fetus is the result of the father pursuing a morally legitimate interest in sex and procreation in a morally legitimate way. To pursue these interests in a morally legitimate way, the father must pursue them without violating the legitimate interests of the woman with whom he has had sex; he must respect her autonomy. Moreover, he must pursue these interests in a way that is consistent with and productive of moral harmony. That is, he must be attentive to how his pursuit of these interests will affect and make possible or impossible the pursuit by others of their morally legitimate interests; he must respect the autonomy of all parties involved.

Where these conditions are satisfied, the fetus is the father's as well as the mother's, and everyone—including the mother—has a prima facie obligation to the father not to harm the fetus. Moreover, if the young unwed male has become a biological father as the result of a morally legitimate sexual and procreational practice that respects the legitimate interests of all parties involved, he has at least a prima facie right to paternity.

It can be concluded from what we have said about the right to procreate that those young males who do not have the right to procreate do not have the right to paternity, although there might be good moral reasons for granting some of them limited privileges of paternity. Also excluded from the right to paternity are those mature young males whose biological fatherhood is the result of morally illegitimate sexual and procreational practices. For example, a man who becomes a biological father as the result of rape does not have the right to paternity, since he has violated the sexual and procreational autonomy of the mother. Nor does a man who has become a biological father as the result of casual sex that completely ignores the procreational consequences of his behavior, that fails to respect the legitimate interests and the autonomy of others, including the interests and autonomy of the resulting child. And although there are many other ways in which a biological father might fail to have the right to paternity by engaging in sexual and procreational practices that fail to respect the autonomy of others, it does not seem to me that a young male forfeits the right to paternity merely by the fact that he is unmarried.

To argue, in the present context, that young unmarried males forfeit the right to paternity by virtue of the fact that they are unmarried would be to argue that the only morally legitimate sexual and procreational practices are those that take place inside marriage. And to argue this would be to argue that marriage is a necessary condition for respecting the sexual and procreational autonomy of others. It is difficult to see how such an argument could be successful.[4] Moreover, even if one thinks that procreation and sex outside marriage is morally illegitimate, it does not follow that morally illegitimate behavior *always* results in the loss of a right. For example, a person does not sacrifice the right to a fair trial by virtue of the fact that he has been unfair in his dealing with others.

Therefore, those young unwed males who have the right to procreate and who have pursued their interests in sex and procreation in ways that respect the autonomy of others have the prima facie right to paternity. The issue now concerns the conditions under which the right to paternity includes the right to custody and when it includes the right to visitation.

Here the rights of the child play a major role in determining the unwed father's right to custody. If we assume that the father has the right to paternity, we can conclude that he recognizes the importance of the child's welfare, that is, the child's right to the conditions under which its welfare and autonomy are possible. If the father cannot provide these conditions sufficiently as a custodian, then he does not have the right to custody. If he can provide sufficiently for these conditions, then he has a prima facie right to custody which competes with that of anyone else who has a prima facie right to custody. The same is true of the mother.

The problematic cases, of course, are those where both the father and the mother have a prima facie right to custody. Who should have custody? It is plausible to say that this should be determined by the best interests of the child in terms of the child's autonomy and welfare. Where both the father and the mother are equally well qualified parents who equally have the right to be social parents, the issue must be decided in some other way—either by joint custody (where this will not cause undue harm to the child), by an arbitrary procedure that recognizes the equality of the parents, or by appeal to other moral criteria.

If the father has the right to paternity but does not have the right to custody, it is difficult to imagine that he does not have at least some visitation rights. What would the right to paternity come to if a father did not at least have the right to visit with his child to the extent that would allow him to play some parental role in the child's life? Moreover, the visitation rights of the father should be as extensive as possible, consistent with the rightful interests of the child and other related parties. Otherwise, the restriction of the father's visitation rights is a violation of his legitimate interest in being a parent.

Generally, then, a young biological father has the prima facie right to paternity if he has pursued his interest in sex and procreation in a morally legitimate way. He has the prima facie right to custody with full parental rights if he is capable of providing for the conditions for the child's welfare and autonomy. In the case of alienation from the mother, the father has the actual right to custody with full parental rights if he can provide better for the welfare and autonomy of the child than anyone else who has the prima facie right to custody. He has the right to visitation if he has the right to paternity but does not have the actual right to custody. Moreover, his visitation rights should provide for the most extensive contact possible with the child consistent both with his capacity and desire for parenthood and with the rightful interests of the child and others involved.

The Right to Paternity Determination

Paternity determination is usually done at the request of the mother in response to child support requirements. This practice understandably reflects society's interest in the rights of the child and the mother and the father's responsibilities to them. Nevertheless, some argue that requiring paternity determination *at birth* is cumbersome and unjustified as a *general* policy because there are many cases where the mother—for whatever reasons—does not desire that a paternity determination be made. If the mother can provide for the child and does not desire contact with the father, why require determination of paternity at birth?

There are, however, moral reasons for determining paternity other than those connected with the interests of the mother and the child. The father has parental rights as well. And if my reasoning is correct, society has the prima facie responsibility to protect at least some young unwed fathers' parental rights.

Suppose a young male fathers a child, but the pregnancy and birth of the child are concealed from him by the mother. She could achieve this either by relocating or by lying about the real father, or it could be the result of ignorance. In any case, the young male can hardly be a good father if he has no way of knowing whether he is a father in the first place. A policy that required paternity determination at birth would eliminate this. Moreover, I cannot see that there is any other policy that would be procedurally adequate to satisfy a sufficient notice requirement. If there is no other such policy, the policy of paternity determination at birth is necessary to respect the right of an unwed father to a hearing to determine what his paternal rights are. Of course, society's legitimate interest in the married family unit puts restrictions on just how much the state can do for unwed parents, but this is as true for unwed mothers as it is for unwed fathers. And if society—given the burdens of its other commitments—cannot afford to determine paternity at birth for the sake of the father, this should only be after taking the young unwed father's legitimate interests into account, rather than dismissing them as superfluous to the issue. Continued treatment of men—regardless of age—as the bearers of parental responsibility but not the beneficiaries of familial relations will result in the unbalanced attitudes that create and sustain many of the current problems of young unwed parenthood.[5]

The Right to Abortion Notification

It does not follow from any of the previous claims about young unwed fathers that they have any prima facie legal right that gives them a veto power over an abortion decision by the mother. Legal *consent* requirements on a woman's abortion decision are, I believe, impossible to justify. The practice of forcing women to give birth once pregnant could not be less than an extensive restriction on how women in general are to live.

Notification requirements, however, have a different standing, especially regarding the mother's moral responsibility to notify the father in some circumstances. In some cases, a young unwed father in his sexual and personal relations with the mother has let his procreational and parental interests be known in advance of such relations. Moreover, in some such cases, such a father has respected the autonomy and legitimate interests of the mother. In such cases, he has a legitimate moral interest in the fetus. This is enough for him also to have the prima facie right to notification by the mother of an abortion decision on her part. To say that he has no such prima facie right in such cases and yet to affirm the rights previously mentioned is to reach an odd conclusion. It is tantamount to saying that the parental rights of a male can begin only with the birth of a child but that his parental responsibilities begin with conception.

The point of such notification is simply to inform him that the mother intends to terminate the fetus, in which the father has a morally legitimate interest. This might affect his future relationship with the mother. It might affect his future sexual and procreational practices. He might attempt to convince her without coercion to continue with the pregnancy. but in any event, it is difficult to see that such a decision on the mother's part would be irrelevant to his life.

Of course, this prima facie right is held only by those fathers who respect the autonomy of the women with whom they have been involved. Sexual practices on the part of males who do not respect the autonomy of women do not generate even a prima facie right to such notification. This applies to rapists, manipulators, abusers, many who practice casual sex, and males who do not have the prima facie right to procreate. Nor does a male with the prima facie right to such notification have the actual right to such notification where notifying him would de facto abridge the woman's legitimate autonomy. No woman has any responsibility to any man in regard to his parental and procreational interests if that man constitutes an undue threat to her welfare.

Furthermore, even when the prima facie moral right to abortion notification is in place, it does not follow that this *moral* right translates unproblematically into a *legal* right to such notification. When enforced in the context of the influences of patriarchy, a practice of legally coercing such notification could have the effect of reinforcing patriarchal subordination of the legitimate interests of women. This, I believe, is a sufficient reason for requiring a reasonable assurance that such reinforcement of patriarchal bias will not result before implementing any such legal practice. Moreover, I do not believe that there is such a reasonable assurance in the present social context.

Now let us see what some of the young father's responsibilities are in terms of the responsibility to honor the rights of other parties involved in the conflict situations of young unwed parenthood.

The Rights of the Child

The rights of the child are difficult to overemphasize. Without support, the child is unable to care for its own basic physical and emotional needs. Without love and affection, it becomes jaded and dejected. Without guidance, it becomes delinquent and its life prospects severely truncated. And since the child is helpless through no fault of its own and is brought into the world as a result of the choices of others, it definitely has a right that someone provide an acceptable level of parental support.

There are, however, two important questions that are crucial to determining *paternal* responsibility: (1) what level of support is required by the child's rights, and (2) under what conditions does the burden of this support fall on the father rather than someone else?

In answering the first question, one standard often referred to by the courts and mentioned in the United Nations Declaration on the Rights of the Child (O'Neill and Ruddick 1979) is the standard of the best interests of the child. The use of such a standard for determining what the child's rights are must be distinguished from its use in determining custody decisions or the rights of the parents to custody. As a standard for determining the rights of the child, and thus the responsibilities of the parents, it has resulted in a great deal of rhetorical overkill about children's rights. Every right from the right to adequate prenatal care to the right to the best level of economic support that can be provided by the best efforts of both parents has been claimed for children (Krause 1977, 258–260). But the best interest standard employed in this context flies in the face of other relevant moral considerations.

Parents also have rights. They too are members of the community; their legitimate interests and autonomy are of intrinsic importance and are due respect and consideration. Not only are parents people who have nonparental prima facie rights that might compete with the prima facie rights of the child, they also have parental rights that preclude the best interest standard of determining the child's rights. If a parent has any rights of parental authority that are not determined solely by the interests of the child, the child cannot have even a prima facie right to have what is in its best interests. To say that it does is to rule out in advance that a prima facie parental right could ever defeat the child's prima facie right in the competition for being an actual right. This would be tantamount to depriving the parental right of any power at all, actual or prima facie. Any doubts about the advisability of the best interest standard in this context should dissipate upon the realization that it would impose on any parent the responsibility to surrender his or her children to the custody of others the moment someone else could provide a better life for them. Parental responsibility isn't that stringent, and children's rights aren't that compelling.

Nonetheless, children's rights are compelling, especially in the younger, less autonomous years of the child, the years of most relevance to young parents, for few children of very young parents will be much more than infants. In considering the rights of the child, then, I will restrict the discussion to the rights of the early years.

Among the rights of the child are the right to an adequate level of prenatal and postnatal care, the right to an adequate level of personal nurturing, the right to an adequate level of the amenities of life, and the right to adequate custodial arrangements. Included within the right to adequate custodial arrangements is the child's right to be in an environment free from unnecessary tensions that unduly threaten prospects for an acceptable and meaningful life and for substantive expression of his or her autonomy. All of these rights—it is safe to say—are at least prima facie rights that compete with the prima facie rights of others in any conflict situation.

But to establish that the child has these prima facie rights is not yet to establish who has the responsibility to honor them. Our concern, of course, is to determine the conditions under which it is the biological father who has this responsibility.

Some of the factors determining responsibility here have to do with the standing of the father independent of his relationship to the mother, and others are determined by his relationship to her. Our earlier distinctions concerning fathers are relevant here. Whether the father is of majority of minority age, mature or immature, mentally competent or not, and whether he is indigent or not—all are factors potentially relevant to what his prima facie and actual responsibilities are.

There are also issues concerning his relationship to the mother. We have already stipulated that we are interested only in cases where marriage to the mother is not an option. But why marriage is not an option may make a difference. Marriage may not be an option for a variety of reasons, not all of which are due to the father's choice. In the case of an unemancipated minority female, it may be due to the choice of her parents. It may be due to the choice of the parents of an unemancipated minority male. And in some cases, it may not be legally possible due to age requirements set by the state not subject to parental consent exceptions.

Apart from matters of choice as to marital status are the age and maturity relationships between the father and mother and the relative differences in their economic status. One notable case, *Michael U. v. Jamie B.*, Cal. Rptr. 39 (Sup. Ct. 1985), involved a sixteen-year-old male and a twelve-year-old female. This case is certainly different from that of two nineteen-year-olds, or a twenty-year-old female and a fifteen-year-old male. There is also a potentially relevant difference in whether the mother is indigent and the father is not, or vice versa.

The circumstances under which the pregnancy occurred may also make a difference. For example, what if the male is a minority male, age fifteen or sixteen, of normal maturity, and has been seduced by a majority female? If the sexual manipulation of a minor female by a majority male is to be thought of as an unwarranted assault on her sexual and procreational autonomy, why should things be thought otherwise when the manipulation is reversed? And if the sexually manipulated minority female has no responsibility to the majority male who has wrongfully violated her autonomy, why does a minority male have responsibilities to a majority female who has wrongfully invaded his autonomy? And what if the father has been deceived into thinking that the sexual act is part of a long-standing relationship but, in fact, this has never been the mother's intention? Does such deceit not violate his autonomy and constitute an abridgment of his autonomous procreational choice? Certainly these circumstances serve to distinguish relevantly different situations in which a young unwed father might find himself.

Generally, I think the guiding thought here should be this: where a person who has the right to procreate has had sexual intercourse that results in pregnancy and the birth of a child, that person has a prima facie responsibility to honor the rights of the child previously enumerated to a degree proportional to both parents' responsibility and culpability. (I have purposefully stated this without reference to gender, since it has ramifications for the responsibilities of the mother as well.) This would mean that indigence does not, in itself, remove the prima facie responsibility of support. The responsibility of support is removed then only in cases involving mental incompetence or inculpable immaturity, and in cases where the actions of someone else have shifted the burden of support. All of these are exceptions, where the imposition of the responsibility of support upon the young unwed father would ignore the fact that the sexual and procreational practices that led to pregnancy involved violations of *his* sexual and procreational autonomy by the morally illegitimate behavior of others. And we must keep in mind that violations of autonomy admit of degrees, and thus the shift of responsibility admits of degrees.

The Rights of the Unwed Mother

Some may object to treating the unwed father and mother as moral equals. Usually an unwed pregnancy imposes the greatest burden on the pregnant woman. It certainly restricts her sexual and procreational autonomy more than it does the man's, at least in typical cases. When combined with indigence and moral and religious beliefs that preclude abortion, it restricts her autonomy in almost every dimension of her life. Of course, when pregnancy is the result of unencumbered choice, what are otherwise restrictions on autonomy become the substance of autonomous expression. Sometimes this expression is a mutual expression of the autonomous sexual and procreational choices of both the mother and the father. Sometimes it is not. The responsibilities of the father to provide financial support for the child and the mother will depend, in part at least, on the sexual and procreational practices that led to the pregnancy in the first place.

We must be careful here to distinguish between child support and support for the mother. But this is not always easy. Relief for food expenses for a two-year-old is child support. But is relief for medical expenses during childbirth support for the child or for the mother? Clearly it can be construed as both. Yet there may be costs to the mother due to pregnancy, childbirth, and her parental responsibilities that she would not have had, except for the pregnancy and subsequent birth, but relief for which cannot be exhaustively accounted for in terms of support for the child. Some losses due to pregnancy and childbirth will be losses incurred by the mother independent of her parental role and might be recoverable only with support—lost educational opportunities, for example. In some cases, then, the mother has a right to support where the support is indistinguishable from support for the child, and in other cases, she has a right to support that is distinctively hers.

Here we must also be careful not to oversimplify the classification of young unwed females. Again, not only are their age, maturity, and mental competence important, but also economic status—whether they are indigent or not. Also relevant are whether the option of marriage was ruled out by the mother's choice, the father's, or someone else's; whether the pregnancy was due to a real or rationally assumed continuing relationship; and whether the mother or the father acted with culpable deceit, negligence, coercion, or in some other way that might have wrongfully violated the legitimate sexual and procreational interests of the other party.

At one end of the spectrum is an indigent minority-age female whose pregnancy and childbirth were due to her being raped, coerced, or deceitfully seduced by a prosperous majority-age male. At the other end is a prosperous majority-age mother, the father of whose child is a fifteen-year-old indigent male who was coerced or deceitfully seduced by her. In the former case, the mother not only has a prima facie right to support related to the child but to independent support as well. In the latter case, it is not clear that the mother merits either. There might also be cases in which the mother has the right to support for the child, but none for herself. And, of course, we must remember that these factors admit of degrees, as does the notion of contributory culpability.

It will be helpful, then, in determining the father's responsibility of support for the mother to keep in mind the following kinds of cases: (1) cases where the pregnancy and childbirth are the result of mutual and autonomous sexual and procreational choices of both the mother and father, (2) cases where pregnancy and childbirth are the result of the father's autonomous choice but not the mother's, (3) cases where pregnancy and childbirth are the result of the mother's autonomous choice but not the father's, and (4) cases where pregnancy is not the result of the procreational choice of either the mother or the father. Since we are interested only in cases where the parents are alienated, we must keep in mind whether the alienation is the result of mutual choice or, if not, which party decides for separation and why.

The father's burden of support is going to be greatest in (1), (2), and (4), where the alienation is the result of his choice and where the mother cannot support herself. It will be least in (3), where the alienation is the result of the mother's choice, where she is able to support herself, and where the father is indigent. The guiding thought should be that where a young mother cannot support herself—and even in some cases where she can—she has a prima facie right of support related to the child, the support coming either from the father, his parents, her parents, or the state. Here we may say that where a young male who has the right to procreate has had sexual intercourse that results in pregnancy and the birth of a child, he has the prima facie responsibility to provide the mother support of the child to a degree proportional to the culpability of the mother and the father. The father also has the responsibility of independent support of the mother for relief of losses or of harms incurred by her due to pregnancy and childbirth to a degree that reflects proportional culpability.

The Rights of the Grandparents

One of the rights that the grandparents—that is, the parents of the young unwed father and mother—have is that their children act responsibly in regard to sex and procreation, because in ordinary circumstances the irresponsibilities of the child devolve to the parents as responsibilities. Sometimes the sexual and procreational practices of a minor who is not yet mature enough to be held fully accountable for his or her actions result in invasions of the legitimate interests and autonomy of others. If this result is due to irresponsible child-rearing practices on the part of the grandparents, then it is plausible to say that the grandparents share in the liability for the harms caused, at least to some degree. Yet where sex is concerned, the best efforts at responsible parenthood do not always result in responsible children. At any rate, although they are not by any means the only rights grandparents might plausibly claim, I restrict my comments here to rights that accrue to the grandparents as a result of the inherited responsibility of child support, especially the rights to custody or visitation.

In some cases, the inherited responsibility of child support will not result in either the right to custody or visitation. For example, suppose the grandparents have been so remiss in their child-rearing practices that their dependent child has—as a result of their influence—deceived someone into a procreational act just in order to have sex with that person. It is plausible to say that if their child has not reached the age at which it is reasonable to hold him responsible for his actions, then, everything else being equal, the grandparents have the responsibility to support the offspring of such behavior, but not the right to either custody or visitation. The same may be said in the case of force. Suppose that the parents of an immature minor male had taught their son that when girls say no to offers of sex they really mean yes and that they secretly long to be raped. Liability for the consequences of such attitudes certainly does not entail any right of access to a resulting child, child support requirements notwithstanding. Child-rearing practices like these, then, create responsibilities for the parents who practice them, but no corresponding parental rights.

In the more common case, however, inherited responsibility of child support will result in either a right to custody or a right to visitation. Seldom do the irresponsibilities of minors devolve *completely* to their parents as responsibilities, especially in regard to sex. Moreover, it is seldom that only one set of grandparents is to blame for the situation, just as it is seldom that only the father or the mother has been sexually irresponsible.

It seems plausible to say that the grandparents have a prima facie right to custody only when the parents do not have the actual right. And the parents might not have the actual right to custody for a number of reasons. They might not have the right to procreate; they might not have access to the means of providing custodial care; or they might have lost the right to custody because of culpable behavior. In cases such as these, where the grandparents inherit the responsibility for child support, but where their child-rearing practices have not rendered them unfit parents, the burden of child support gives them *some* parental rights to the grandchild. If neither parent has the right to custody but both sets of grandparents have prima facie parental rights, it is plausible to determine custody between the grandparents on the best interest standard. This assumes, of course, that the state is a parent of last resort. Should it not be in the best interest of the child to be put into the custody of grandparents who are fit and who have parental rights, it is plausible to say that the grandparents should be granted the most extensive visitation rights possible consistent with the best interests of the child and the legitimate interests and autonomy of others.

The Rights of the Public

The permissible sexual and procreational practices of young unwed fathers are restricted not only by the rights of family members but also by the rights of unrelated members of the public. The rights of the public tend to fall under two general classifications: (1) the right to be free of unnecessary welfare burdens and (2) the right to be free of undue threats from delinquent children of irresponsible parents, married or unmarried. The first right is derived from the assumption that the state is to be a parent of last resort and from the responsibilities the state has in protecting the rights of the child and other members of the family. If the state has to shoulder the burdens rightfully belonging to the young unwed father in regard to other family members, then the cost of that burden will come at the expense of the legitimate interests and autonomy of unrelated members of the public. For example, the cost may be in terms of other very important welfare needs of the general public. In this sense, then, the public has an interest in the sexual and procreational practices of young unwed fathers.

The second right is derived from the various rights against harm and interference that any ordinary citizen has and that are vulnerable to the consequences of family practices. The breakdown of the family can and sometimes does lead to the most vicious of crimes against unrelated parties, especially where the children from such backgrounds are left to roam the streets with the worst possible role models. Delinquent parenting often produces delinquent children. To be sure, such children are not always from unwed parents. I would not even say that there is more delinquency among the children of unwed parents than among those of married parents, although there might be. But the lack of adequate parenting is sometimes attributable to the lack of a commitment between the parents to each other. Sometimes the lack of marital ties reflects this lack of commitment, and the lack of such a commitment sometimes results in delinquent children. When it does, delinquency can pose a threat of harm to others. Protection against these harms, then, is a legitimate public interest.

It must be emphasized, however, that the welfare consideration regarding policy decisions is more basic than the delinquency consideration for two reasons: (1) it is founded in the pubic's interest in avoiding unnecessary welfare burdens and (2) it is founded in the public's interest in the rights of the child. Moreover, when the welfare interests of the child are the concern expressed in parental decisions, the probabilities of delinquent influence by the parents are diminished. When the child's welfare interests are not given due concern by the parents, the rights of the child already give the public sufficient reason for the removal of custody. It is unlikely, then, that there would be any policies restricting parental rights that would be justified on the delinquency issue alone or that would be more extensive than is justified on the welfare criterion.

Nonetheless, the public's right to preserve the married family might put some limitations on how extensive a set of parental rights a young unwed parent—whether male or female—can have. The more difficult task, of course, is deciding what policies the state is justified in enforcing against the irresponsible sexual, procreational, and family practices of young unwed parents—especially fathers—in the name of protecting these rights. Here the issue is the parental rights of the young father versus the public's right to the means necessary to its protection.

In this regard, it is often in the interests of the state to facilitate and encourage the adoption of children of unwed parents by others who are both desirous of and fit for parenthood. When such adoption can be effected without the wrongful interference in anyone's autonomy and legitimate interests, the dual purpose of avoiding unnecessary welfare burdens and protection against delinquent influence can be permissibly achieved. The difficulty is determining when the father has a right to paternity determination, custody, or visitation such that the adoption of his child by another would constitute a wrongful violation of his autonomy and his legitimate interests. What should be clear by now, however, is that the fact that a father is young, unwed, and alienated from the mother does not, in itself, render considerations of his interests in paternity morally superfluous to the adoption issue. Thus, for the state to pursue the legitimate public interests referred to above without due consideration to the father's interests would be for the state to pursue morally legitimate interests in a morally illegitimate way. This would be wrong.

Conclusion

I have tried to address the topic of young unwed fatherhood in a way that is designed to sensitize us, especially policymakers, to the complexities of the issue. I have suggested a balanced conceptual framework that takes into account the young unwed father's legitimate interests and rights without relieving him of his rightful responsibilities, which are extensive. In asserting that some young unwed fathers have a right to procreation, to custody, to visitation, to paternity determination, to notification of abortion, and to consent to adoption, I have not denied that the unwed father has correlative obligations. Nor have I suggested that concern for his interests should in any way support or promote a system of sex and gender roles that systematically subordinates the interests of women to the interests of men. Indeed, the kinds of rights I emphasize put a premium on male parenthood that is inconsistent with the old patriarchal view of fatherhood. Fathers are not simply providers of secondary care. Their legitimate interests include an interest in primary care roles, not simply as a responsibility but also as a right. Policy should reflect this.

Notes

1. Certainly not all young unwed couples are irreconcilably alienated. But many are, and these are the focus of attention in what follows.

2. By parity of reasoning, such young men do not have even the prima facie right to sexual intercourse, unless there is no risk that intercourse will result in procreation.

3. Here the concern for the father's rights is not a concern for a system of "patriarchy" that systematically subordinates the rights and interests of women to those of men. Feminists are correct to insist on a society in which such a system of subordination of one gender by another is eliminated. But it is totally implausible to think that in a nonpatriarchal society young unwed fathers will not have any rights but only responsibilities.

4. There are, of course, many people who believe in the exclusivity of sex and procreation within marriage. It is unclear, however, that the prevalence of such a belief is due to rational reflection. It is even less clear that there is a tradition of such exclusivity that is based on some rationale other than the authority of tradition. From this it does not follow that there cannot be a rationale for such exclusivity, but I cannot think of what it could be.

5. New federal legislation, the Family Support Act, 1988, requires that both parents' social security numbers be collected by the state at the time of birth. This is essentially a legal requirement for paternity determination.

References

Ellman, Ira Mark. 1986. "Nontraditional Families." In *Family Law*, edited by Ira Mark Ellman, Paul Kurtz, and Ann M. Stanton, 781–928. Charlottesville, Va.: Michie.

Harris, George W. 1986. "Fathers and Fetuses." *Ethics* 96(3): 594–603.

Krause, Harry D. 1977. *Family Law*. St. Paul: West Publishing.

O'Neill, Onora, and William Ruddick, eds. 1979. *Having Children*, 111–114. New York: Oxford University Press.

Reeves, Benjamin G. 1974. "Protecting the Putative Father's Rights after *Stanley v. Illinois*: Problems in Implementation." *Journal of Family Law* 13: 115–147.

III

Policies and Programs

9 Creating Federal Leadership in Research and Policy Development

LINDA M. MELLGREN

One million teen pregnancies a year. Sixty-four percent of teen births are out-of-wedlock births. Two million teenage parents. Special school programs for parenting teens. What are the images that these phrases bring to mind? Is there a single male face—a concerned young father—among them? If not, then teenage pregnancy and parenting still remains a woman's problem.

During the 1970s and 1980s government agencies at all levels spent hundreds of millions of dollars providing services to pregnant and parenting teenage mothers. Millions of research dollars have been spent on trying to understand how to prevent pregnancies and deliver pregnancy and parenting services. Arguably, these efforts may not have been sufficient to address the need. But it is clear that they have focused on only half of the teenage pregnancy problem—the female half. Young fathers, and especially young unwed fathers, have remained persistently absent. This chapter relates the story of one effort to change the federal policy perspective regarding the interests, rights, and responsibilities of young unwed fathers.

Origin of Emerging Federal Interest

One of the institutional roles of the Office of the Assistant Secretary for Planning and Evaluation (ASPE) within the Department of Health and Human Services (DHHS) is to explore the possible connections among issues that are usually narrowly focused within specific program legisla-

193

tive authority. This role has encouraged ASPE staff to think about issues and policy from a broad perspective. The Young Unwed Fathers Project began in 1985 with staff conversations about the issues of male responsibility, pregnancy prevention, parenting, paternity establishment, and child support.[1] Informal discussions led to a more systematic review of the research and of the department's efforts to assist young fathers. What we found was that the intense research and program development activities focusing on adolescent mothers since the middle of the 1970s had for the most part neglected any examination of adolescent and young adult fathers.

Who were the young men 50-percent responsible for the epidemic of out-of-wedlock births to teenage women? Were they all deadbeats, walking out when told about the pregnancy? Or did they care about their children, spend time with them, and provide them financial or other support? Were programs available to help these men become better parents, or were all efforts concentrated on making them financially responsible? It did not take much investigation to realize that there was a huge gap in the department's policy consciousness. By oversight or design a whole class of persons, young unwed fathers, was not considered in deliberations about DHHS responsibilities for children and families. Information about unwed mothers was available on numbers and rates of birth, onset and frequency of sexual activity, educational attainment, life histories, general demographics, program interventions, and availability of services. But there were no comparable program or research data on the young fathers.

It became apparent that young fathers were not the primary concern of any program, and that no program had a legislative mandate broad enough to address the full range of young fathers' needs. Rather, there would have to be interaction among programs and new ways to coordinate. But before coordination and interaction could occur, there had to be a broadening of consciousness, a recognition that ignoring young fathers was not in the interest of program clientele, the program, or the public as a whole.

Young Unwed Father's Project

The vehicle we chose to raise consciousness about issues affecting young unwed fathers was an intermural conference at which researchers and program people could share with each other their diverse perspectives on the role of young fathers and their experiences in working with them. The conference's findings and deliberations would then be shared with a wider audience across the country.

After gaining the support and commitment of Arnold Tompkins and David Rust, then Deputy Directors for Social Services Policy and for Income Security Policy, respectively, and of Robert Helms, then Assistant Secretary for Planning and Evaluation, support and additional funding was solicited from other agencies. In the end, five additional offices within the Department of Health and Human Services and the Departments of Labor and Commerce agreed to provide financial or analytical support for the project.[2] While no agency saw young fathers as a mandatory target of its programs, there was sufficient interest in the population to get the project off the ground.

The research reflected in the commissioned papers and the discussions at the symposium held in October 1986, confirmed the assumption that there was no place that young unwed fathers fit into the current bureaucratic scheme (Smollar and Ooms 1987). There were few linkages among programs that provided employment, child support enforcement, and welfare and support services for either young unmarried mothers or fathers. Most adolescent pregnancy programs tried to integrate education, employment, health care, access to welfare, and parenting services for young mothers, but few programs took such a comprehensive view towards services for young unwed fathers. Most providers of services to young mothers or to young males that might be fathers had no knowledge of the issues surrounding paternity establishment or child support. Child support enforcement agencies were less than aggressive in establishing paternity, unless the father had sufficient income for child support.

The research and staff discussions also indicated that there was some validity to the stereotype of the "bad" young men who knowingly, even purposefully, father a child and then refuse to take any responsibility for the child's financial and social support. But it also became clear that the lives of many unwed fathers reflect the same pathos, confusion, and "trying to do the right thing" seen in the lives of many young unwed mothers. The Young Unwed Fathers Project found that many young men don't just walk away; some are pushed away, some are never asked to be involved, and some are not given the help they need to become responsible parents. These are the stories that must also be told. These are the dilemmas that our policies have not addressed.

Tales of Four Young Men

Being a responsible parent has never been easy. But if it is not easy for a mature adult with a good marriage and a comfortable income, consider what it means to be an unwed parent when you are young, poor, and without good job prospects. How can you be a responsible parent, when society provides so few supports to help in doing so? How can you be a father when so little is done to protect your rights to be legally recognized as a father? To help describe the population and set the stage for the policy discussion that follows, four typical scenarios about young unwed fathers, representing four different dilemmas for public policy, have been developed—those of Julio, Chaz, Robert, and Mac.

Julio

Julio lives in a major urban area in the western part of the United States. His parents both work in the service industries, but they have higher expectations for their children. Julio was not an exceptional student but did graduate from high school. He is now working as a garage mechanic but does not know what he wants to do for the long term. His parents dream of a college education and a professional career for him.

Julio and Maria had met at school and dated for over a year. They had had sex irregularly for some months, occasionally using a condom or withdrawal as a means of birth control. They had gone to a family planning clinic together for birth control pills, but never got the prescription filled. Julio and Maria had talked about getting married, but neither felt ready to make a long-term commitment. They never talked about what they would do if Maria got pregnant.

Maria told Julio she was pregnant and did not know what to do. They told their families right away, and both families immediately blamed the pregnancy on the other partner. Maria's parents forbade her to see Julio; for a while she resisted, talked to him on the phone, and met him secretly after school.

Her parents had her transferred to a high school for pregnant girls. The teachers there encouraged her to involve her family in the program, but there was very little encouragement to include Julio or to talk about his responsibilities. Julio's parents were plainly relieved when Julio stopped talking about Maria and the coming baby, but were concerned that he was quiet and withdrawn.

After the baby was born, Julio went to see Maria and his child. Julio asked if the baby was given his name, but Maria said the hospital staff wouldn't put his name down on the birth certificate because they were not married. Maria's mother made it clear he was not welcome and his help not wanted. Julio tried to find out how he could be named the child's father. His parents were very angry that he wanted to do this; his friends told him he was crazy; the hospital staff told him he would have to hire a lawyer and go to court. He knew he couldn't afford a lawyer, so he stopped asking questions. But Julio feels bad; every child needs a father, he says.

Should the government help young men like Julio? Does every child have the right to have two legal parents? Should paternity establishment be a universal requirement? Should help in establishing paternity be as readily available to young fathers as it is to young mothers? Should a young man be assisted in acknowledging and supporting his child over the objections of the child's mother or her family?

Chaz

Chaz is 25; he married Tika, the mother of his two-year-old son Ali, six months ago. Chaz and Tika had waited to get married until Chaz could find stable employment at a decent salary. They now are doubly excited because Chaz has just gotten a promotion, and because Tika is expecting a second child. They don't have a lot of money; Tika will probably have to go back to work after the new baby is born. They hope that between Tika's mom and his, they won't have to pay for child care.

One day Chaz answers the door to be served a court summons. He has been named the putative father in a paternity action brought by the state on behalf of another mother and child. The mother's name on the summons looks familiar, but it takes a while for him to place it.

He had dated Shanta when he was 19, introduced by mutual friends. Shanta had been only 15, boy-crazy, and more than willing to have sex with him. After they broke up, he had heard that she was pregnant. Some friends had said that the baby was his, and for a while he had bragged about fathering the child to his friends. But he was never sure it was his child. Shanta had started dating someone else right after they broke up; she never told Chaz that he was the father.

Chaz was scared; he and Tika were just making it. They didn't have any money to hire a lawyer, and they certainly didn't have money to pay child support. Tika was going to be very angry.

Should the government help young men like Chaz? Should his "first" child have primary claim on his support? Should his new family be taken into account in the determination of any child support amount? Should the government have the right to hold him responsible for retroactive support, even if he was never told of his child or asked for monetary support?

Robert

Robert grabbed the umbrella stroller, picked up his two-year-old daughter April, and ran to catch the bus. He was late for work again. He had already been reprimanded once for being late; if it happened too many times, he knew he might lose his job and then he might lose April, too. Her mother, Chari, had come by last week, wanting money. He thought she was high; she acted very strange. Chari had said she wanted to take April home with her to spend some time with April's grandmother. But when he had given her money, she had left. April hardly knew her mother anymore.

Robert had never intended to become a single parent. He had had a lot of girl friends when he had been a teenager and had slept with most of them. But Chari had been different; he had been in love. When she got pregnant, he had talked her out of having an abortion. He had wanted to marry her. But Chari hadn't been interested in marriage; she wanted to have fun.

At first Chari and April had lived with Chari's mother. Robert stopped by frequently to play with the baby, to bring over diapers or toys or clothes. He tried to give Chari a little money each week. As Robert fell out of love with Chari, he fell in love with his daughter. When he got laid off, he started taking care of April while Chari went to work. Sometimes he would stay at Chari's, but over time he began taking April back to the apartment he shared with several friends. Chari moved in with her new boyfriend; she didn't seem to want April around very much. When he got called back to work, he found a day care center that would take toddlers and filled out the application.

He had called the city agency listed under paternity establishment to find out how he could get paternity established and legal custody for April. They told him they did not get involved in custody cases, and if the child's mother wanted paternity established, she should come in and file an application. No one seemed interested in helping him establish his rights as April's father.

Should the government help young men like Robert? An unmarried mother's right to custody is presumed but a father's must be established—should government help be available to help him get custody? Should there be parenting programs available to young fathers? Who should help him find out about the programs and services that might be available to him as the custodial parent?

Mac

Mac lived in the sprawling inner city of a large metropolitan area. His mother worked hard trying to keep the family together, holding down two low-paying jobs just to make ends meet. She was proud she had never been on welfare. She had gotten her first job when Mac was a baby and his father was killed in Vietnam; she had taken a second job when Mac's stepfather walked out, leaving her with Mac and three half sisters all under age ten. Mac knew his mother loved them all very much; but she was always at work or too tired to pay much attention to her son.

Mac met Jayna when they were both 14. They were inseparable from the start, providing each other with the unconditional support that had not been available from their own families. Even when Mac dropped out of school, Jayna was on his side, telling everyone it was his life, and he had to decide what was right for him. Mac encouraged Jayna to graduate; he knew she was smart and that it mattered to her. It mattered to Mac, too, but he felt he had no choice. Mac couldn't read and it made him feel stupid. It was his secret; even Jayna did not know.

Mac was always looking for work and occasionally managed to get a job, but no job seemed to last. Usually he and Jayna went out on Jayna's money. Jayna was doing fine working in a downtown department store; she had gotten two promotions in the last year. Mac was proud, but it sometimes made him mad—he wanted to be able to show his woman a good time on his money, not hers.

Then Jayna got moody, felt sick, complained about getting fat, and was always chiding Mac about not having a job. Finally one night she told Mac that she was going to have his baby. Mac was devastated and delighted. He wanted to get married right away. Jayna said she wasn't about to marry a man who couldn't take care of her, much less a family. Jayna said she would be better off going on welfare than marrying him. Welfare might not be much, but at least it was secure. But if Mac could get a job and keep it, perhaps she would reconsider. She said she still loved him, but with a baby on the way she needed a man, not a boyfriend.

Should the government help young men like Mac? Would his new role as father help motivate him to participate in a basic education program so he could learn to read, maybe even get his GED? Should job training programs give priority to fathers? Should unemployed parent benefits under the AFDC program be available to young parents who don't meet the eligibility requirements of having held a job in three of the last six months? Would such changes increase the likelihood of marriage?

Is There Anyone Out There to Help?

There are few advocates for young men like Julio, Chaz, Robert, and Mac. Nor are there more then a handful of programs in the country that focus on providing support for young fathers. Federal policies and programs give little encouragement to young unwed fathers for any aspect of parenting except to require the provision of financial support. What support can these young fathers expect? What federal programs are involved with this population?

Aid to Families with Dependent Children

The Aid to Families with Dependent Children (AFDC) program provides cash assistance to poor families who are deprived of support because of the death, incapacity, unemployment, or absence of a parent, or the unemployment of the primary wage earner. The program is administered by the Office of Family Assistance within the Administration for Children and Families in DHHS. While there are some federal requirements, many of the specific eligibility criteria and the benefit levels are set by states. In fiscal year 1990 the total cost of the program was just over $21 billion, of which 54 percent was paid for by the federal government (Committee on Ways and Means 1991). AFDC recipients are categorically eligible for Medicaid, the federal-state-funded health care program, and in most cases eligible to receive food assistance coupons under the Department of Agriculture's Food Stamp Program. Several important changes were made to the program in the Family Support Act of 1988. These include requiring that all adult recipients with children over three years of age participate in work and/or training programs (the JOBS program), providing child care and Medicaid benefits for up to one year when a recipient leaves AFDC with earnings, and requiring all states to establish an unemployed parent program.

The AFDC program is primarily designed to provide benefits to families whose income has been determined by the state to be insufficient to provide for themselves and their children. Most AFDC families are single parent families, headed by women. Young women with a child in their care, like Shanta, represent about 16 percent of the adult female AFDC recipient population. In 1989 there were 519,000 adult women, ages 11 to 21, receiving AFDC benefits out of a total adult female recipient population of 3.3 million (Office of Family Assistance 1989). A woman under age 18 is defined as an adult if she had a child in the unit receiving AFDC benefits. Young adult males under age 22 represent a much smaller part of the AFDC adult recipient population, not quite 34,300 or 9.4 percent of the adult male recipient population (Office of Family Assistance 1989).

Through the AFDC–Unemployed Parent (AFDC–UP) program a young unwed father may get benefits if he is living with his child and the child's mother and he or the child's mother is incapacitated, or if he (or the mother) is currently unemployed and meets the work experience requirements for eligibility in the unemployed parent program. To be considered unemployed, the family's principal earner must be employed for fewer than 100 hours a month (or employed 100 hours or more when the work is intermittent and the excess hours temporary). The principal earner must also have been unemployed for at least 30 days prior to receiving benefits and must have worked for at least 6 quarters over a period of 13 prior quarters, been involved in a work or training program, or have been eligible to receive unemployment compensation. Income eligibility requirements are set by the states and are the same as for the basic AFDC program. However, many young men and women do not meet the employment criteria that make them eligible for the AFDC–UP program.

Until the passage of the Family Support Act in 1988, state participation in the AFDC–Unemployed Parent program was optional; 27 of 50 states and the District of Columbia had such a program. Since October 1, 1990, all states have had to provide unemployed parent benefits to eligible families at least six out of twelve months in each year. Because Jayna could qualify as the principal earner, Mac and Jayna might be able to receive benefits under the AFDC–UP program if they married or decided to live together after she had the baby. When neither parent's attachment to the labor force is sufficient to make him or her eligible for the unemployed parent program, the presence of the father in the home, if paternity was acknowledged, could make the mother and the child ineligible for AFDC. In many states a family of three, trying to live on the minimum wage income of $6,968 per year, would be worse off than a family of two receiving only AFDC benefits, especially if the minimum wage job does not provide for private health insurance coverage.

A young unwed father (not living with his child's mother) with custody of his child could file for basic AFDC benefits on behalf of himself and his child. If a young custodial father like Robert were to lose his job, he would be eligible to apply for AFDC benefits. Under the JOBS requirements in the Family Support Act, he might also be required to participate in employment activities to locate a new job or to receive additional training to upgrade his employment prospects. He would have access to child care and Medicaid for 12 months if he left AFDC because of employment. Young men like Robert might be concerned, however, about getting involved with the system. Even though paternity was not in doubt, Robert could not afford to hire a lawyer to fight for legal custody of April. Federal law would require that the state pursue child support from Chari as the noncustodial parent, but no federal reimbursement would be available for the state to help Robert establish legal custody if Chari attempted to reclaim custody of her child. Robert might be justified in his concern that the courts would not consider a young unwed father who is unemployed as a suitable parent for a toddler.

Child Support Enforcement Services

Child Support Enforcement provides assistance in establishing paternity and in establishing and enforcing child support awards. The program is administered by the Office of Child Support Enforcement (OCSE), the Administration for Children and Families in DHHS. In 1989 the total cost of the program was $1.4 billion, of which 71 percent was paid for by the federal government. Collections resulting from program activities amounted to $5.3 billion, of which 75 percent was passed through to families. The remaining 25 percent was retained by the federal and state governments to offset the cost of AFDC benefits and to provide incentive payments to states (Office of Child Support Enforcement 1990). In 1990 total child support collected through the CSE program increased to $6 billion, an increase of 15 percent over 1989. Program expenditures were $1.6 billion, an increase of 18 percent over 1989 (Committee on Ways and Means 1991).

There are no national or state requirements that all children have paternity established or have financial and social support from both parents. Public child support enforcement activities are undertaken when a woman seeks benefits under the AFDC or Medicaid programs or when a referral is made on the child's behalf from a foster care agency. Cooperation with the Child Support Enforcement agency is a condition of eligibility for these programs and women are exempted from cooperation only for good cause, such as rape, incest, or threats of physical violence against the mother or child. Under new requirements in the Omnibus Budget Reconciliation Act of 1990 (P.L. 101-508), pregnant women receiving Medicaid, but not AFDC, are also exempted from the cooperation requirements. All other women may apply for child support enforcement services under Title IV-D of the Social Security Act.

In several states all women seeking child support establishment (divorced, separated, or never married) are required to apply for IV-D services as a part of the state's child support adjudication process. However, as long as a woman does not receive welfare for herself or her child or request child support enforcement services, men like Julio and Chaz are ignored. Once public help is sought, the circumstances surrounding the birth are mostly irrelevant. A father like Julio, who was chased away, or a father like Chaz, who was never told, is as responsible for the economic support of his child as the father who walks out on a wife, three "planned" kids, a dog, a station wagon, and a house in the suburbs. Although it is good public policy to expect all fathers to be responsible for their children, men like Julio and Chaz may with justification view the child support enforcement system as punitive and unjust.

Child support enforcement agencies are required to establish paternity and child support awards on the request of either parent, but the putative father's access to services is neither well publicized nor encouraged. Until very recently, there have been few materials published by the federal Office of Child Support Enforcement that explain child support issues from the noncustodial father's point of view. Some local child support enforcement offices may not even know they are required to provide services at the request of noncustodial fathers, and the availability of such services is not widely publicized. Young men who try to establish paternity over the objections of the mother might be required to pay the cost of the genetic testing required to prove paternity. Currently, the most reliable test in widespread use is the human leucocyte antigen (HLA) test, which confirms the identity of the father, or excludes him, with over 95-percent probability. Its cost ranges from $200 to $500, depending on the laboratory.

Neither establishment of paternity nor of a child support award is required if it is determined not to be in the best interest of the child to do so and if the mother has filed and received a good-cause exemption from the AFDC program, unless the child support agency can proceed without the direct involvement of the mother. The number of cases where good cause is claimed is very small—in 1989 only about 8,300 cases out of a total caseload of almost 6 million. A finding of good cause is made in about 60 percent of cases in which a good-cause exception is claimed by an AFDC recipient (Office of Child Support Enforcement 1990). If good cause is denied, the custodial parent may be removed from the AFDC grant. The children's portion of the grant is unaffected by her removal, but an alternative payee may be sought for the children's grant. There is no information available on whether the frequency of applications for or approval of good cause exceptions for young unmarried mothers differs from those of older mothers.

Job Training Partnership Act

The Job Training Partnership Act (JTPA) provides year-round training and employment programs for economically disadvantaged youths and adults and a summer youth employment and training program. JTPA programs are administered by the Employment and Training Administration of the Department of Labor. States and local governments, however, have primary responsibility for the management of these training programs. At the local level, the program is administered by private councils and local governments. In fiscal year 1991, the total JTPA appropriation was $1.8 billion for year-round programs for disadvantaged adults and youths and $683 million for the summer youth program. Forty percent of local program funds for the year-round programs are targeted to youth, although no funds are specifically targeted to young parents. It is fairly certain that some of the young men served each year are fathers, but there is no process to identify them as fathers nor to provide any special support services (just as there are few services provided to mothers, as such).

Since the prime mission of the program is to deal with employment and training service needs, local entities that run JTPA programs can provide special support services for young fathers but only to enable them to participate in program activities and to assist them in retaining employment. Young men like Mac, whose problems are not limited to employment or training but include readiness employment, have more limited options. With encouragement from his girlfriend and the "system" he would be willing to be a father to his child. Mac's problems are multiple, however, and while interest in work-readiness programs such as literacy training is increasing, these programs are not yet widely available as an integral part of JTPA youth services.

The Adolescent Family Life Program

The Adolescent Family Life (AFL) program is the only federal program solely focused on the complex issues and problems of early adolescent sexuality and adolescent pregnancy and parenting. The program is administered by the Office of Population Affairs, within the Office of the Assistant Secretary for Health, DHHS. The demonstration activities of the federal AFL program emphasize parental involvement, postponement of sexual activity, comprehensive care for pregnant teens, and adoption as a positive alternative to abortion or early parenting.

Through its model demonstration grant program the AFDC supports (1) "care" projects that develop and test family-centered approaches for comprehensive health, education, and social services designed to help teenage mothers have healthy babies and to improve subsequent life prospects for both infants and mothers, and (2) "prevention" projects focused on primary prevention of sexual activity, mainly through educational activities targeted on teen girls as well as teen boys. The third component of the AFL program supports research grants that are contributing to the understanding of the broad issue of adolescent pregnancy. In 1991 AFL provided a total of $7.8 million in funding for 51 demonstration projects and 5 research grants. Since 1982 AFL has funded approximately 160 demonstration projects and 55 research projects. Almost half of the demonstration projects focused on primary prevention activities.

In 1986 through 1989 AFL and the Department of Labor undertook a collaborative effort to add employment and training components of six competitively selected "care" programs. These projects, located in Tucson, Arizona; San Francisco, California; Savannah, Georgia; Camden, New Jersey; Salem, Oregon; and Dallas, Texas were designed to increase coordination at the local level between the health and job training systems in providing services to adolescent parents. One of these programs was designed to serve adolescent fathers and others have also made some effort to serve this target group. The Urban Institute was awarded funds to evaluate the process by which job services for adolescent parents could be linked to the health delivery system.

In fiscal 1990 AFL funded their first project designed expressly to provide comprehensive services for young fathers. The project, called DADS (Diapers, Autos, Daughters, and Sons), is an expansion of an existing family support and education project funded by AFL in the early eighties. The project provides all the required educational, health, and social services to pregnant and parenting adolescents, their infants, and the extended families of both fathers and mothers (Office of Adolescent Parenting Programs 1990).

AFL is not the only, or even the primary, funding source for teenage parenting programs. Other federal programs—Medicaid, Maternal and Child Health Services, AFDC, Title XX Family Planning, Special Supplemental Food Program for Women, Infants, and Children (WIC)—may be used to support "care" and pregnancy prevention services; however, none are solely directed towards teenage pregnancy prevention. In addition to the pregnancy care and parenting projects funded by AFL, there are hundreds of teen pregnancy and parenting programs in the country. These are funded by state and local governments and a variety of charitable and other private sources, often with linkages to federal programs (Congressional Budget Office 1990). Young men like Julio would not, however, always be welcome at these programs because the primary goal and resource commitment for these programs is to provide care for the pregnant adolescent and/or the young mother and her infant. A few of these teenage parenting programs have succeeded in involving young fathers; other programs have found it difficult to attract and keep them involved. Perhaps this is because young men are often perceived as an appendage to the mother and child, and not as clients in their own right. While the AFL, the National Urban League, Planned Parenthood, and other organizations have made efforts to develop pregnancy prevention programs specifically targeted on males, very little research and demonstration funds have been aimed explicitly at services for young fathers. One notable exception is the Teen Father Collaboration, directed by the Bank Street College of Education and funded by the Ford Foundation and eight community foundations across the country (see Chapter 14).

When the Young Unwed Fathers Project examined programmatic efforts in 1986, approaches that treated both young parents as legally, financially, and emotionally responsible for the well-being of the child were not evident at the federal or community level. Based on the papers and discussions at the symposium, a number of suggestions were made to help federal and state governments and local communities adopt a more inclusive policy approach to young unwed fathers. Among the more prominent suggestions were the need to explore issues surrounding paternity establishment, the need to develop cross-program and cross-discipline training and information dissemination strategies, and the need to examine funding mechanisms to encourage inclusion of services targeted at young unwed fathers. To continue the policy and program dialogue, some 20,000 copies of the Young Unwed Fathers Project final report (Smollar and Ooms 1987) were distributed throughout the country, primarily to local and state programs that provide a variety of services to teenagers and young adults. The Administration for Children and Families and the Office of Maternal and Child Health in the Public Health Service at DHHS, and the Employment and Training Administration at the Department of Labor took the lead in ensuring this broad distribution of the report.

In addition to the dissemination efforts discussed above and research activities conducted by the Office of the Assistant Secretary for Planning and Evaluation (OASPE),[3] some of the suggestions outlined in the report have been pursued at the federal level. The Office of Child Support Enforcement within the Administration for Children and Families (DHHS) released a report in December of 1990 entitled *The Changing Face of Child Support Enforcement: Incentives to Work with Young Parents* (Center for the Support of Children 1990). This report discusses the issue of child support from the perspective of both young mothers and young fathers and provides an overview of social, legal, and administrative issues that must be understood if child support services to young parents are to be successful. Additionally, it includes innovative program approaches that have shown promise in working with this population. In early 1991 a compendium entitled *Adolescent Fathers: Directory of Services* was published by the National Center for Education in Maternal and Child Health (Association of Maternal and Child Health Programs 1991). Sponsored by the Maternal and Child Health Bureau (DHHS), this document provides information on programs throughout the country which primarily serve adolescent fathers or which have a service component for adolescent fathers as part of a broader target population. This compendium should be very useful in providing direction for communities and organizations interested in developing programs for young fathers and in facilitating the exchange of information among such programs. The Department of Labor's Job Corps program will be instituting a parenting curriculum in its residential training program and all enrollees (parents and nonparents) will be required to participate. Regulations were published on 6 April 1990, and the curriculum will be implemented in September 1991. Since passage of the Family Support Act, additional activities have been undertaken which affect young unwed fathers. These will be discussed later in this chapter.

Although federal efforts have not been extensive, a number of important nonfederal projects have been initiated or completed subsequent to the Young Unwed Fathers Project. In 1987 the Center for the Support of Children held a two-day forum on the issues affecting child support services for young families and issued the proceedings from that meeting (Kastner et al. 1988). In 1988 the Children's Defense Fund issued a report entitled *Adolescent and Young Adult Fathers: Problems and Solutions*, drawing on much of the research and discussion from the Young Unwed Fathers Symposium (Adams and Pittman 1988). The Advocacy Center for Child Support published a book entitled *The Teenage Parents' Child Support Guide* that provides information relevant to both teenage mothers and fathers on their rights and responsibilities (Schnell 1988). Most recently, Public/Private Ventures, a private foundation in Philadelphia, has funded a multisite demonstration to determine effective strategies for working with young unwed fathers around issues such as parenting, paternity establishment, employment, and child support (see Chapter 16). These and other projects have helped keep the attention of policymakers and program operators at all levels on the continuing need to address the complex issues of young unwed fatherhood.

Implementation of the Family Support Act—A Congressional Nudge in the Right Direction

In the Family Support Act of 1988 Congress expressed concern about the growing number of out-of-wedlock births and the apparent lack of vigorous efforts at paternity establishment by state child support enforcement programs. While the Family Support Act did not specifically address the issue of young unwed fathers, a number of provisions in Title I: Child Support Enforcement, Title II: JOBS, Title IV: Related Amendments and Title V: Demonstrations may have an effect on this population.

The Child Support Enforcement Amendments in Title I of the Family Support Act provide for several changes in the area of paternity establishment: they require states to improve their performance in establishing paternity; they require states to conduct genetic testing in contested paternity cases; they allow states to charge non–AFDC clients for genetic tests; and they increase the federal matching rate to 90 percent of the costs of genetic tests needed to establish paternity. Although these provisions do not require states to target young unwed fathers, as states work to improve their performance, they may find that paternity is easier to establish while children are young and there is still a positive relationship between the unwed parents. As 33 percent of out-of-wedlock births are to young women under age 20 and an additional 36 percent are to women, ages 20 to 24, young men will most likely be affected by this increased effort (U.S. Bureau of the Census 1990). The increase in the federal matching rate for genetic testing may also affect states' willingness to pursue paternity in cases where support payments may be very small or not even possible because the young father is currently unemployed.

Title I also encourages states to institute a simple civil process for voluntarily acknowledging paternity and civil procedures for establishing paternity in contested cases. It also requires states to collect Social Security numbers from both parents at the time a child's birth certificate is issued. The effect of these provisions is not clear, since these provisions are essentially voluntary and unenforceable.

The JOBS program in Title II focuses on education, employment, and training for AFDC caretaker recipients, about 50 percent of whom are never-married mothers. The original Senate bill included fathers as eligible for JOBS services, but the Act as finally passed only provided for up to five state demonstrations under which noncustodial parents of AFDC children could participate in state JOBS programs to acquire the skills needed to be capable of providing financial support. This demonstration authority has attracted considerable attention as an innovative approach to the nonsupport problem. Secretary Sullivan has included this demonstration as one facet of an initiative to help minority males. While the demonstration authority does not explicitly target young unwed fathers, such targeting is encouraged by the design of the demonstration. The application materials request that states consider both early- and late-intervention models. Early intervention designs focus on noncustodial parents who have not yet established paternity or support awards for their children. It is anticipated that young fathers would be a significant proportion of those parents targeted for early intervention services. The Department of Labor, the PEW and Ford Foundations, and the Manpower Demonstration Research Corporation (MDRC) have joined with the Department of Health and Human Services to make the funding and design of this demonstration a collaborative effort. Solicitation for applications for the demonstration were initiated in 1991 and participating states were selected by spring 1992 (see Chapter 16).

Section 401 of the Family Support Act made the AFDC unemployed parents program mandatory for all states as of 1 October 1990. States are required to have a program which provides benefits for at least six out of the last twelve months when parents are unemployed or underemployed. The program is to emphasize training, education, and employment services. Although families where neither parent has had previous attachment to the work force are still excluded, some additional young family units, married or not, might receive assistance through this expansion.

More significantly, perhaps, for young unwed fathers, new demonstration authority in Section 503 allows for testing of alternative definitions of unemployment. Three states have been selected for demonstration sites—California, Utah, and Wisconsin. These demonstrations will test the effects of modifying or eliminating the 100-hour rule and other durational requirements. These requirements are thought to possibly discourage family formation, since many young men do not have a strong attachment to the work force and their presence in the home with their children could adversely affect their families' eligibility for AFDC.

Section 504 authorizes demonstration projects to address child access problems. Three states have been selected to participate in the demonstration—Florida, Idaho, and Indiana. These projects will evaluate the effect of mediating visitation disputes on the payment of child support and the duration and frequency of litigation. In fiscal year 1990 FSA committed $1.4 million for the demonstration and evaluation. While there were no requirements to include unwed fathers in the project, at least one of the three sites has included in its client population cases which involve paternity adjudication. Additional funding of up to $1.9 million for more sites and related evaluation activities was appropriated in fiscal year 1991. Four additional sites were added to the demonstrations as a result of increased funding.

Two additional demonstrations in Title V could be used to target young unwed fathers: Section 505 Demonstration Projects to Expand the Number of Job Opportunities to Certain Low Income Individuals, and Section 506 Demonstration Projects to Provide Counseling and Services to High-Risk Teenagers. Congress appropriated $4.5 million dollars for the job opportunities demonstration. Ten sites were selected in fiscal year 1990, five to ten additional sites will be selected in fiscal year 1991. However, none of the selected sites has identified young unwed fathers as a priority group. As of the end of fiscal year 1990, no funds had been requested or appropriated for the demonstration for high-risk teenagers.

Lacking a Male Perspective

Until recently, government policies relating to out-of-wedlock births have rarely been examined from the perspective of the young father. This lack of male perspective is reflected in the often disparaging language used to describe the behavior of young men who have fathered children outside of marriage. The position taken by the federal government and by many of the "helping" agencies in our society is adversarial as well. Such negative attitudes and behaviors are likely to exacerbate the persistent lack of support for the establishment of paternity and child support in some communities and subcultures.

Young unwed fathers, like young unwed mothers, are characterized by emotional ambivalence and immaturity as they assess what it means to take on the role of parent. Some walk away from those responsibilities, others are driven away, but many participate in the parenting process as best they can.

Julio, Chaz, Robert, and Mac are not real unwed fathers, but their stories are real. Most of us have heard these stories before—less sympathetically—from the viewpoint of the young mother, or her family, or the government. These stories neither affirm nor negate the appropriateness of current government policies for the Aid to Families with Dependent Children, the Child Support Enforcement, the Adolescent Family Life, or the Job Training Partnership programs. They do, however, make us stop and think about how these and other programs and policies might be reviewed and modified to better support the parenting efforts of young fathers. It is hoped that the Young Unwed Father Project will stimulate communities and government policymakers to incorporate the male perspective into research and program initiatives.

Notes

1. The author, Linda Mellgren, and her co–project officer for the Young Unwed Father Project, Jerry Silverman, are policy analysts in the Office of the Assistant Secretary for Planning and Evaluation in the Department of Health and Human Services. The views and opinions expressed in this paper are the author's and do not necessarily reflect the views and opinions of the Department of Health and Human Services.

2. The federal agencies collaborating with the Office of the Assistant Secretary for Planning and Evaluation in the funding of the project included, at the Department of Labor, the Employment and Training Administration; at the Department of Health and Human Services (DHHS), the Office of Child Support Enforcement and the Office of Family Assistance, both within the Administration for Children and Families, and the Office of Population Affairs of the Public Health Service. Three other agencies provided planning and analytical support—the Bureau of the Census in the Department of Commerce and, at DHHS, the Office of Human Development Services and the National Institute for Child and Human Development of the National Institutes of Health. The project was completed under a contract with MAXIMUS, Inc. and its subcontractor, the Family Impact Seminar, then located at Catholic University of America.

3. The Office of the Assistant Secretary for Planning and Evaluation has funded four projects related to the issues of young unwed fathers and paternity

establishment. One project has been completed and three are still underway. The completed project included a report on paternity establishment among never-marrieds and a one-day conference on improvements to the Alimony and Child Support Supplement of the Current Population Survey that would aid in research about paternity establishment and its relationship to child support awards and payments (Aron, Barnow, and McNaught 1989). Freya Sonenstein of the Urban Institute received funding to conduct a nationally representative survey of paternity establishment practices at the community level. Charles Adams at Ohio State University received funds to investigate the organizational dynamics of the paternity establishment process and in particular, the relationship between the courts and child support enforcement agencies. Robert Lerman (American University) and Arthur Lewbel (Brandeis University) have a grant to study the relationship between child support, work, and family outcomes for young men and young women, based on data from the National Longitudinal Survey on Youth (NLSY).

References

Adams, Gina, and Karen Pittman. 1988. *Adolescent and Young Adult Fathers: Problems and Solutions.* Washington, D.C.: Children's Defense Fund.

Aron, L. Y., B. S. Barnow, and W. McNaught, 1989. *Paternity Establishment Among Never-Married Mothers: Estimates from the 1986 Current Population Survey Alimony and Child Support Supplement.* Report prepared for the Office of the Assistant Secretary for Planning and Evaluation, Department of Health and Human Services, 1989. Washington, D.C.

Association of Maternal and Child Health Programs. 1991. *Adolescent Fathers: Directory of Services.* Washington, D.C.: National Center for Education in Maternal and Child Health.

Center for the Support of Children. 1990. *The Changing Face of Child Support Enforcement: Incentives to Work with Young Parents.* Washington, D.C.: Office of Child Support Enforcement, U.S. Department of Health and Human Services.

Committee on Ways and Means. See U.S. Congress. House.

Congressional Budget Office. See U.S. Congress.

Kastner, C., et al. 1988. *Child Support Services for Young Families: Current Issues and Future Directions.* Proceedings of Forum on Child Support Services for Young Families. Washington, D.C.: Center for the Support of Children.

Office of Adolescent Parenting Programs. See U.S. Department of Health and Human Services.

Office of Child Support Enforcement. See U.S. Department of Health and Human Services.

Office of Family Assistance. See U.S. Department of Health and Human Services.

Schnell, Barry T. 1988. *The Teenage Parents' Child Support Guide.* Yorklyn, Del.: Advocacy Center for Child Support.

Smollar, Jacqueline, and Theodora Ooms. 1987. *Young Unwed Fathers: Research Review, Policy Dilemmas, and Options*. Report prepared for the Office of the Assistant Secretary for Planning and Evaluation, Department of Health and Human Services. Washington, D.C.: Government Printing Office.

U.S. Bureau of the Census. 1991. *Statistical Abstract of the United States: 1990*. Washington, D.C.: Government Printing Office.

U.S. Congress. Congressional Budget Office. 1990. *Sources of Support for Adolescent Mothers*. Washington, D.C.: Government Printing Office.

U.S. Congress. House. Committee on Ways and Means. 1992. *Green Book: 1991*. Washington, D.C.: Government Printing Office.

U.S. Department of Health and Human Services. Office of Child Support Enforcement. 1990. *Fourteenth Annual Report to Congress for Period Ending September 30, 1989*. Washington, D.C.: Government Printing Office.

U.S. Department of Health and Human Services. Office of Family Assistance. 1989. *Characteristics of AFDC Recipients, FY 1989*. Washington, D.C.

U.S. Department of Health and Human Services. Office of Population Affairs. Office of Adolescent Pregnancy Programs. 1990. *The Adolescent Family Life Demonstration Projects: Program and Evaluation Summaries*. Washington, D.C.

10   Paternity Actions and Young Fathers

ESTHER WATTENBERG

For more than a decade, legislation[1] and legal[2] decisions have asserted a public ethos: the legal rights of children must be protected regardless of the marital status of their parents. Despite this assertion the number of nonmarital children legally linked to their fathers is still inadequate, frustrating equal protection efforts to safeguard the interests of these children.

Why have conclusive paternity actions, the key to child support and other benefits, remained at a number inadequate to serve the interests of a growing generation of out-of-wedlock children? A search for answers to this perplexing question takes on a sense of urgency when one observes the ever-increasing rise of births to young parents occurring outside of marriage and the failure of these parents to establish paternity to safeguard the rights of their children.

It is worth noting that while children of unmarried parents bear the unmistakable burden of economic inequality when paternity is not legally determined, the social stigma has lessened. This has been reflected in the semantic search for a nonjudgmental designation, which went from "bastard" to "out-of-wedlock," and then to "nonmarital." In this paper "out-of-wedlock" and "nonmarital" are used interchangeably.

This chapter explores the issues that surround paternity determination through analysis of the findings of a study of the institutional and professional barriers (Wattenberg 1988) and of the issue as seen from the perspective of young, unmarried parents (Wattenberg, Brewer, and Resnick 1991). But first let us examine how serious the problem is.

213

Dimensions of the Problem: Lagging Paternity Actions

Teenage out-of-wedlock births (births to women aged 19 and under) have more than doubled between 1970 and 1989 (Moore 1992). In 1989, 67 percent of all teen births occurred outside of marriage compared with 30 percent in 1970. The racial factor is significant: in 1989, 92 percent of births to black, young mothers aged 15–19 were nonmarital, 55 percent for white. Among Hispanics (who may be black or white) the rate was 54 percent (Moore 1992). Nonmarital births are now at the highest fraction of all births ever recorded in the history of the nation, representing more than a fivefold increase since 1970. While the demographic facts are continuously reported, explanations of the high level of births to adolescent parents are a subject of debate (see Abrahamse, Morrison, and Waite 1988).

Although there has been a concentration of attention on the rates of out-of-wedlock births to school-age adolescents, the disproportionate increase among young, adult women should not escape notice. The age distribution of unmarried mothers has recently shifted upward. The highest rates of births to unmarried mothers are now concentrated among women aged 18–19 and 20–24. In 1987 more than two-thirds of out-of-wedlock births were to women aged 18–29 years, and more than 50 percent to women aged 20–29 years (*Monthly Vital Statistics* 1991). This phenomenon reflects, to some extent, the postponement of marriage and the rise in numbers of childbearing women in this age group.

In striking contrast to the surge of out-of-wedlock births the lagging rates of paternity adjudication persist, both in size and consequences. Despite the fact that the legal link of the child to the father is a vehicle for a range of entitlements, secured by statute and judicial decisions, conclusive paternity actions are not evenly pursued by the states and wide disparities exist.

State data on paternities recorded 1985 to 1988, indicate that thirteen states actually diminished their efforts (Committee on Ways and Means 1992). The remaining states show remarkable variations in their efforts to improve paternity adjudication. Among large states, the 1988 rates vary from a high of 67 percent in Michigan to a low of 14 percent in Louisiana and 20 percent in New York. The explanation probably lies in variations on priority setting, caseload sizes, simplified procedural steps, and administrative leadership.

Overall, the rates of paternity adjudication to out-of-wedlock births remain disappointingly low, as we see from Table 10-1.

Looking at the years 1983 through 1989, we see that the proportion of

TABLE 10-1 Total Number of U.S. Out-of-Wedlock Births and
Paternity Adjudications, 1983 through 1986

	Out-of-wedlock births	Paternity adjudications	Percent adjudicated
1983	737,900	208,270	28.2
1984	770,400	219,360	28.5
1985	828,200	231,838	28.0
1986	878,477	244,996	27.9
1988	1,005,299	306,513	30.5
1989	1,094,169	339,243	31.0

Note: The data must be treated cautiously. States use various definitions for paternity adjudications, and local reporting to state offices lacks reliability checks. Ratios of paternities established to
out-of-wedlock births are somewhat misleading since paternities
may be established for older children and out-of-state children in
any given year. A few research projects are underway to develop
more accurate results.
Source: Office of Child Support Enforcement 1987; *Monthly Vital
Statistics Report* 1988; U.S. Bureau of the Census 1989; Committee on Ways and Means 1992.

adjudicated births has never surpassed 31 percent of the total out-of-wedlock births and has shown only a slight increase since 1983.

Accurate data on the number of paternities in process, partially completed, and fully acknowledged are not readily available.[3] However, it is
conservatively estimated that, overall, only one of three out-of-wedlock
births is followed by paternity adjudication. Illustratively, in Hennepin
County, Minnesota (a large, urbanized county), from 1982 to 1985, with
9,501 referrals for paternity action that came to the county attorney's
attention, only 3,763 paternities were established, leaving 5,738 children
without a legal father within that three-year period.

While paternity actions appeared to receive only fitful attention by a
significant portion of states, a growing number of studies and reports
(see, for example, Ellwood 1988; Hayes 1987) linked the origin of long-
term welfare dependency to the entry into the AFDC system of teen
mothers and their out-of-wedlock children. Further, the composition of
AFDC had changed dramatically over the years: the largest component of
the welfare population was now unmarried parents and their children. As
national attention was directed to the increasing poverty of children, out-
of-wedlock children were identified as the poorest of all poor children.[4]

An unmarried young mother and her child are most likely compelled
to rely on AFDC for meeting basic human needs of food and shelter.

Three-quarters of unmarried teens seek public assistance at some time within four years following the birth of their child. Black teens are twice as likely as white teens to receive AFDC in any given year (Moore 1987). The long-term welfare dependency of unmarried mothers is reflected in the fact that 62 percent of all AFDC mothers under the age of thirty started their welfare history as teen mothers.[5]

In the complicated chain of associations between early childbearing, out-of-wedlock births, and subsequent long-term reliance on public assistance, an unarguable reality is revealed: poverty rates are strikingly high for out-of-wedlock children living in families where the mother is 15–24 years of age. Of these female-headed families, 69 percent of white families and 78 percent of black families were trapped under the poverty level in 1989 (U.S. Bureau of the Census 1991a, 111).

In sum, for a child being born out of wedlock to a poor mother the likelihood of enduring a long spell of poverty over a lifetime is a grim reality. Precocious parenthood tends to produce poor outcomes in health, education, economics, and personal life choices for the young mother, with related effects for her child.

Benefits of Paternity Determination for the Child

It is a basic assumption of this chapter that it is nearly always in the best interest of the child to have paternity determined legally. Paternity determination for a child born out of wedlock brings a number of benefits directly to the child, and indirectly to the mother.

- Social Security Benefits: The child may be eligible for certain benefits through the Social Security system. In cases where the father has been employed and has contributed to Social Security, if the father becomes disabled or dies, the child is entitled to receive a benefit until the age of eighteen.
- Armed Services Benefits: The father may draw an extra allowance to provide a household for his dependents who do not have to be living with him. For enlisted personnel this allowance may range from $289.90 to $528.90 per month. The child is also eligible for commissary and post exchange privileges. If the father incurs a service-connected disability, the child is eligible for an educational benefit (which can be as much as $404 per month for a full-time student).[6]

  The importance of recognizing the resources available to an unmarried father in the armed services is underlined with data provided by Lerman (1985). Almost half of the black fathers in the armed services between the ages of 18 and 21 make a child support payment of a significant amount—a mean yearly payment of $919. Significantly, older black fathers, ages 22–26, are an even more important resource for an out-of-wedlock child; their mean yearly payment, $1,767, is larger than the child support payment from a civilian employed, unmarried father, which is $1,272. Interestingly, the data on white, unmarried fathers are incomplete for those aged 18–21, but significant for older fathers, ages 22–26, more than half of whom make payment of a substantial sum per year—$2,086. This is considerably higher than the child support payment from a father in civilian employment—$1,462.

- Health Care Benefits: If a father's employer-provided health care plan covers a marital child, then plan benefits also must be available to the nonmarital child.
- Worker's Compensation: Nonmarital children are eligible for dependent's benefits under Worker's Compensation.
- Child Support: Establishment and enforcement of a child support court order depend on paternity adjudication.

When paternity is established, other nonmonetary benefits follow as well. The child may use the father's name. When the identity of the father is proven, a child gains access to important genetic information and medical history. In addition, increasing evidence from adoption studies indicates that the child may derive intangible benefits from knowledge of his or her biological heritage. Paternity identification may, thus, be a factor in strengthening emotional growth and development in the child.

The Policy Context

For policy purposes, an important consideration, then, is the critical step of legally linking an out-of-wedlock child to the father. The life chances of that child can be enhanced by the benefits that flow from the legal paternity connection.

The first federal act in 1975, the Child Support Enforcement Act, P.L. 94-88, addressed paternity actions and child support enforcement by directing states to develop programs and procedures in compliance with federal mandates.[7] In effect, this legislation established an *entitlement* to paternity services for nonmarital children. Originally, the main impetus for federal tightening of the child support system was to reimburse the government for some of its welfare outlays by capturing child support payments. The child's interest was not the major concern. In the case of AFDC, the child support is claimed by the government, except for $50, which is assigned to the mother. Nevertheless, the 1975 act established the principle that encouraging paternal financial responsibility towards all children was good public policy. Of remarkable interest is that the services in IV-D programs for establishing paternity were made universal, to be available to all unmarried mothers, whether receiving AFDC or not.

The Child Support Enforcement Amendments of 1984, P.L. 98-378, reinforced the policy importance of paternity (see Office of Child Support Enforcement 1984). States were mandated to simplify procedures through "expedited processes" for establishing and enforcing child support orders. Paternity establishment could also be included in this directive to "expedite processes" in order to improve timeliness and effectiveness. Further, states were required to extend statutes of limitations for establishing paternity at least until the child's eighteenth birthday. This was a significant policy decision. Statutes of limitation were so sharply drawn in some states (e.g., within a child's third birthday) that they effectively denied nonmarital children equal protection.

Later, in 1988, vigorous paternity determinations and child support efforts were emphasized as indispensable components of welfare reform in the Family Support Act, P.L. 100-485.[8] Standards for improving paternity adjudications were outlined; a provision for federal matching of 90 percent of the cost of blood and other tests to establish paternity was enacted; states were encouraged to institute civil procedures; and Social Security numbers for both parents at the time of the child's birth were to be secured to improve locating the absent father. These new provisions and services were also made available to non–AFDC families. In a somewhat reluctant step, the Secretary of Health and Human Services was granted the power to grant waivers to five states to pursue demonstration programs that would enlist unmarried fathers in work and training programs to enable them to meet their financial obligations to their children (see Chapter 16).

Along with these policy initiatives, a surge of interest in young, unmarried fathers emerged (see, for example, Parke and Neville 1987; Smollar and Ooms 1988). The conspicuous neglect of these young males was previously identified as a peculiar phenomenon of the nation's concerns with the problems of adolescent pregnancy and childbearing. Teenage pregnancy and parenting had been overwhelmingly characterized solely as a problem concerning teenage females. Only when researchers finally turned their attention to young fathers did bits and pieces of knowledge about their role in providing financial and parenting support to their nonmarital children begin to emerge. Studies on their decision making in paternity actions remained sparse, however.

Establishing Paternity for Nonmarital Children: 1983–84 Study Exploring the Arena of Contending Interests

An intriguing paradox was taking shape: a heightened interest in the role of unmarried fathers and the presence of a legislative and judicial framework to assure the rights of the nonmarital child, uncompromised by parental status, were not matched by energetic advocacy for rights and needs of the child. The pivotal importance of paternity establishment, which could provide a base of support for a child through eighteen years of the child's dependent status, remained, curiously, without articulate support.

To explore this paradox, a study was initiated in 1983–84 in Minnesota (Wattenberg 1988), which noted that paternity cases involve a web of varied and often conflicting interests—the mother, the father, the grandparents, the social service professionals, the child support enforcement system, and the courts. In the complex interplay of all these elements, an inescapable conclusion was reached: the paramount interests of the child had slipped out of focus.

The study used structured interview schedules to derive data from seventy-eight Minnesota community social service agencies, hospitals, and school-based social workers, and eighty-seven county IV-D offices; it also surveyed a sample of twenty-five young unmarried mothers. A special study of young, black, unmarried fathers was also commissioned (Battle 1984). The Minnesota study revealed the complex interplay of factors that shape paternity decisions. Discretionary judgments, guided somewhat loosely by broad policies, pervaded the AFDC/IV-D connection; the court system could be arbitrary; the social service and health agencies were largely inattentive to paternity issues.

Perhaps the most striking finding of this exploratory study was the lack of information on the benefits of paternity adjudication for the child that threaded through the complicated maze enmeshing young parents and their out-of-wedlock child. The young unmarried parents had incomplete, often distorted, and sometimes factually incorrect information. The health personnel in maternal and child health clinics and at the hospital routinely did not present the information to the young parents and were not, themselves, thoroughly familiar with the benefits. The social service personnel knew even less than their young clients about the advantages to the nonmarital child of a paternity determination. Yet the benefits, both financial and psychological, could, over an eighteen-year period, potentially enhance the life chances of this growing and disadvantaged cohort of children.

Agency and Program Barriers

At the time of the study the benefits of paternity adjudication were not routinely discussed with the young mother or the father of the baby in any of the community agencies or county offices administering the AFDC grant. Written materials were available only in isolated cases. Rights generally went unexplained. Even such basic issues as the right to an attorney and a court-appointed guardian and the availability of blood tests were rarely discussed.

The observation that social service workers in community-based programs and in health and school settings serving teen parents paid little attention to paternity issues was perhaps the most provocative finding in the study. In fact, the study showed that the basic information that social service workers had on paternity establishment procedures was often factually incorrect, vague, or rumor-laden. Only two of the seventy-eight responding agencies indicated that they held staff-training workshops on these issues.

Methods of introducing putative fathers to their role in paternity proceedings varied widely among the eighty-seven counties surveyed. Telephone messages and formal letters were often the first contact. Not infrequently, fathers were either entirely ignored or confronted, abruptly, by a sheriff serving papers.

For AFDC and IV-D offices, paternity determination for the child of young, unmarried parents is not a high priority. The reasons lie in the incentive formula for funding which is based on recovering child support monies.

The following quotes from survey respondents clearly express the problem:

> There is little or no financial incentive in teenage paternity adjudications; and when caseloads become heavy, there is an acknowledgment that little attention can be paid to paternity of teenage parents because [the chance of] the recovery of child support is dim.

> Often cases are prioritized [after initial interview] not by the child's right to have paternity established, but by [the] potential payer's ability to pay, including ease of collection.

The Teen Mother: Additional Barriers

A sizable portion of teen mothers believe that paternity and child support enforcement procedures are enmeshed in a system that is capricious, arbitrary, and punitive. Indeed, they are hesitant to discuss paternity since the process of its establishment is shrouded in uncertainty and complexities that are not easily explained or understood. Consequences, both intended and unintended, lead them to a strategy of avoidance. Although most mothers in the survey were not in a stable relationship with the father of their child at the time of the survey, they indicated they would not pursue paternity in order to protect him from the negative consequences that a court enmeshment might bring: financial harassment, medical expenses, imprisonment on statutory rape charges. Street knowledge tends to sway many decisions, even though such knowledge may be highly inaccurate. In many communities rumors persist that paternity adjudication can lead to criminal prosecution.

According to agency personnel, many teen mothers strongly object to any agency efforts to establish paternity. They believe that visitation rights, which are granted to a legally determined father, might hamper future or current relationships with other partners. For these and other reasons, many mothers seek a "good cause exception" from paternity adjudication. Moreover, grandparents on both the paternal and maternal sides exhibit a broad range of behaviors regarding the establishment of paternity, behavior that has a significant impact on the welfare of the child. Consistent outreach to grandparents was reported by only a very few social service respondents.

Community-based agencies deal chiefly with services related to parenting, employment and training, child welfare, and crisis intervention. The programs are aimed at helping mothers grapple with basic survival needs. Agency respondents noted that establishment of paternity seemed almost irrelevant, given the inevitable problems that arise when immaturity collides with parenthood. When the focus is on immediate and pressing issues such as food and shelter, and troubling relationships with the father of the child and their own parents, it is difficult to ask teen mothers to shift their attention to nebulous, long-term benefits for the child. Further, a sizable portion of agency social service workers noted that the decision to pursue or not pursue paternity was the mother's decision, and they had no inclination to "interfere" with that decision. This position was reinforced by the agency workers' perception that, even if child support could be obtained, it would be of little benefit if the mother received AFDC. (AFDC requires that recipients assign the child support payment to the state to offset the public cost of AFDC; a 1984 amendment allows $50 per month to go directly to the mother as a passthrough.)

In the judgment of a significant number of personnel in both social services and health settings, the small economic benefits derived from establishing paternity are considered a poor trade-off when weighed against problems that might arise over the visitation rights normally accorded a legally established father. The long-term interests of the child thus became subordinated to the more immediate need to ameliorate the crisis-ridden life situation of the minor mother. The commitment to pursue paternity was neither shared by social services personnel nor by teen mothers.

The uses of the "good cause exception" clause, as incorporated in the 1975 Child Support Enforcement Act (P.L. 94-88), are not well known and have not been systematically studied. This clause was designed to allow for those conditions (rape, physical and emotional harm to a child) in which it is not in the child's best interest to legitimize a family formation that includes a biological father with destructive propensities. Wide disparities among the states are noted in the use of this clause, which mandates an investigation when "good cause" is claimed. In 1987, out of 268,766 reported paternities established (Office of Child Support Enforcement 1987), 7,812 "good cause" claims were requested, but almost half were refused. There are no reliable data on the extent to which mothers use the clause to avoid a paternity action in order to avoid being penalized (loss of her grant amount) for failure to cooperate with AFDC regulations.

Despite this pattern of resistance, caseworkers reported that reluctance to pursue paternity often changes when the child reaches two or three years of age. At that time the mother often receives news of the father's increased financial capability or of his relationship to another woman, just as her own financial hardship is increasing. Indeed, there were observations that tied the act of initiating a paternity action, at this stage, to empowerment: mothers "felt good" about taking an action for their child in an otherwise "helpless" situation.

The Unmarried Father and Paternity

After a long period of disregard a wave of attention has focused on the role of the young father in the expanding cohort of unmarried parents. At least three national conferences have been held (see City University of New York 1987; Smollar and Ooms 1988; and Kastner et al. 1988) and, by the late eighties, books and journal articles were being published in a small but steady stream (Smollar and Ooms 1988). These efforts have contributed findings that are beginning to shape a deeper understanding of young, unmarried fathers and their various relationships to their family of origin, their partners, and their out-of-wedlock children.

What is known about young unmarried fathers must still be considered tentative, however, and subject to critical scrutiny. Although a number of researchers have turned their attention to the role of young unmarried fathers in providing financial and parenting support to their children, studies on paternity establishment are still sparse and those which derive information on paternity decisions directly from unmarried fathers, as opposed to young unmarried mothers, are sparser still. What is known about the unwed fathers' attitudes, influences, and family decision making is derived from fragmented studies, impressionistic case descriptions, and indirect information from adolescent mothers. Contradictory interpretations abound, especially about the strength of fathers' involvement with their children. An understanding of the factors that encourage or discourage paternity actions is relatively unknown territory, despite the fact that paternity adjudication is a pivotal link in the matrix of relationships of this young family formation. Almost all studies issue a cautionary note on the reliability of their data for the purposes of generalizing. Various profiles are drawn, ranging from the "predatory inseminator" to the nurturing, caring partner and father. One is led to the conclusion that, based on our current knowledge, there is no modal pattern of family formation of young, unmarried parents. Rather, we are introduced by these fragmented studies to a range of possible relationships and a variety of family configurations.

One of the few studies (Battle 1984) specifically exploring paternity decisions was based on data derived from forty-six young male volunteers recruited from neighborhood contacts. This study noted that more than half of its sample came from large poor families headed by single parents. More than half had not completed high school. The incomplete nature of schooling was noted in the fact that 25 percent of the sample had difficulty in reading the self-report portion of the questionnaire. Thirty-seven percent were unemployed and only 20 percent worked full-time. Only 15 percent were working at jobs that secured more than $3,000 per year. The competition for the scarce earned dollar among the respondents was intense. Many respondents reported that they were expected and did, in fact, try to contribute to family income to help their siblings. Their contributions to their child were necessarily sporadic and sparse. Eighty percent provided money for food, and a small number contributed toward medical care and clothes. The money amounts ranged from $5 to $25 per month, although there was no consistent pattern. Twenty-six percent would give money to the mother only when she asked, and about one-third would give money on special occasions only.

In the self-report, fathers portrayed their relationships with mother and children as compassionate and caring. The majority stated they provided baby-sitting and some physical care for their infants, although only a small segment actually lived with the young mothers, and more than half did not see the mother on a regular basis. Respondents in Battle's study were asked a series of questions designed to determine their level of understanding and knowledge of paternity issues. Fathers clearly demonstrated that the linkage between legal paternity acknowledgment and benefits to their children was unknown to them. Information on this issue appeared not to have been transmitted in their formal or informal associations. In the course of the interview, fathers were made aware that, once paternity was legally established, a range of benefits could flow. The benefits they valued most for their children were Social Security and health insurance. The psychological security of their child's knowing his or her father's identity was given a low rating.

Specific information on the legal requirements of paternity establishment was uneven, often incorrect, with a high number of "don't know" responses. Respondents disclosed a general concern about the complexity of AFDC rules and regulations. They expressed fear that their admission of paternity would jeopardize this essential stream of income for their partner and their child. Further, they expressed hesitation in acknowledging paternity to "officials." When respondents were asked, "Why would the partner of a teen mother not admit to being the father of the child?" one father answered: "The father will admit it to everyone but not to official sources such as welfare authorities, schools, and agencies . . . afraid of child support enforcement, or maybe he doesn't believe the child is his. . . ." Another replied: ". . . signing any papers scares people away. Any time legal papers are mentioned to someone who isn't knowledgeable, it will cause the person to evade the situation."

Paternal grandparents, according to the respondents in Battle's study, play a mixed role in paternity decisions. More than half of the grandparents were not consulted in the paternity decision. However, 54 percent of the grandparents did help their sons financially; and 89 percent wanted their sons to keep the babies. On the other hand, 70 percent of the grandparents did not want their sons to marry the mothers. One should not go overboard in interpreting this slim data base, but the role of paternal grandparents should also not be overlooked. In a suggestive clue the finding that an overwhelming number of grandparents did not want their sons to marry the mothers of their grandchildren parallels the finding that a comparable number of maternal grandparents did not want the fathers of *their* grandchildren to marry their daughters.

Sorting through the sparse studies on fathers of out-of-wedlock children, recurrent themes emerge, dominated by a need to explode the myths of the sexual "hit artist" who abandons partners and children to the welfare system. New stereotypes emerge: the caring, earnest father whose economic inadequacy has reduced his contributions to a box of pampers now and then; or the socialized victim of the underclass, a child of the ghetto who is an unemployed dropout; the "cowboy" or "street dude" who will provide for his child when he can, but only on *his* terms, not according to the official mandates of the law. In truth, the dearth of empirical knowledge about unmarried fathers stands in marked contrast to the abundance of hypotheses about their roles.

Paternity Decisions of Young Unmarried Parents: 1989–90 Study of Unwed Couples

In 1989, with funding from the Ford Foundation, the author and her colleagues set out to learn more about the factors that encourage or discourage young unmarried parents in their decision to establish paternity for their out-of-wedlock child (see Wattenberg, Brewer, and Resnick 1991). The study also sought to discover the differential profiles of those who legally admitted paternity—the "avowers"—and those who did not—the "disavowers." The two distinctive features of the study were that interviews were with matched pairs of parents—both the mother and the father of the child—and that the sample was mixed racially.

The study was conducted in Hennepin County, Minnesota, in cooperation with the county AFDC and IV-D offices. The sample was drawn from the AFDC files of unmarried mothers aged 21 years and younger who had a child 12 months of age or younger. The mothers' ages ranged from 14 to 21. Fathers' names, linked to the mothers' names, were obtained from the paternity unit of the IV-D offices. The fathers' ages ranged from 15 to 36. For a small part of the sample, fathers who were not listed in the IV-D Office files were voluntarily identified through the mothers. The sample was judged to be a representative sample in terms of racial distribution of the county AFDC population, although the younger ages were somewhat oversampled. Black couples were distinctly younger than their white counterparts both at the birth of their first child and at the time of interview. A total of 334 in-depth interviews were conducted by same race, same gender graduate students with 126 matched pairs of parents and with 82 single parents (67 female and 15 male). Each interview was conducted in a place of the young parents choosing. Each participant received a payment of $25 for the interview. In a one-year attempt at follow-up only 22 percent of the original sample could be reached for interview.

Only 18 percent of the children in this sample were living with both biological parents at the time of the interview when the child was under one year of age. Repeat pregnancies were common. At the time of the first interview 32 percent of white women and 48 percent of black women had had two or more children. In general this was a very low income group, more than half had dropped out of school, were heavily reliant on public assistance programs, were highly mobile in their living arrangements and had very tenuous attachments to the labor market. Under 10 percent of those interviewed had lived at their current address for a year or more. A high proportion had a troubled family history, had experienced abuse, and reported having run away or wanted to run away from home.

Several distinct, but interrelated, findings are of particular significance for understanding the paternity decisions of this group of young parents:

1. The birth of an out-of-wedlock child is not the result of a casual encounter. A sizable proportion—almost half—across racial lines reported living together with the mother of their child in varying lengths of time from a few months to more than two years before the birth of their child. The large majority of fathers reported that they were present at the birth of their baby (67% of white fathers and 61% of black). While the father's relationship to the mother becomes increasingly ambivalent in the year after the birth of the child, 25 percent of fathers were still living with the mother and their child at the time of the interview, when the child was one year old or younger. The data on "living together" relationships should be treated with caution, inasmuch as fathers generally inflated their commitment to the relationship, according to the mothers of their children. On the other hand, there was reluctance in reporting this arrangement because of fear of jeopardizing the mother's AFDC eligibility.

2. The vast majority of male respondents (78%) reported that marriage was not even discussed as an option upon learning of the pregnancy, whereas 51 percent of white females and 31 percent of black females reported that it was. However, marriage as a future possibility also revealed some gender and racial differences: 29 percent of white men and 42 percent of white women, but only 15 percent of black women and 20 percent of black men, were confident that marriage was in their future.

3. The father's attachment to the child persists, even when his relationship to the mother is in transition or dissolved. To begin, only a small percentage of respondents across gender and racial lines reported that the father did not acknowledge biological paternity. According to self-reports, only 17 percent of white males and 15 percent of black males disavowed their putative fatherhood.

   Although the birth of the child was not a signal for forming a residential family unit of both parents with the child, since mothers and fathers established or maintained living arrangements with separate kin and friendship networks, many fathers continued a relationship with their child. The attachment was more marked among black males than among their white counterparts. Only 16 percent of black mothers and 22 percent of white mothers reported that the fathers no longer see their children. More than two-thirds of the fathers across racial lines indicated that they visited their child and made contributions toward the child's care. The amount of visitation and the kinds of assistance given to their child, both financially and other, varied widely, and no distinct profiles of fathers' attachment to the child could be derived from the wide variations.

4. The most valued aspect of acknowledging paternity across race and gender groups was the importance of the father's name on the birth certificate. Over 80 percent of all groups asserted that this was an undeniable obligation that parents owed to a child. However, in actual behavior, only a little more than half of the unmarried fathers had actually signed a declaration of parentage, the vehicle for placing the child's name on the birth certificate (62% of black respondents versus 52% of white respondents). A striking majority across race and gender lines again demonstrated the value of ensuring the father's connection to the child by stating that legal paternity, through court adjudication, was important. Again, the discrepancy between belief and behavior was evident. Slightly over one in four white unmarried parents was engaged in the lengthy process of a court adjudication, and only one in six black unmarried parents.

5. The responses suggested that hospitals were neglectful and possibly discriminatory in the way they provided information to the young unwed fathers about paternity establishment. Among the 60 percent of fathers present at their child's birth, 62 percent of white fathers and 41 percent of black fathers reported that although the declaration of parentage form had been presented to them they were given no explanations about it. In addition the respondents clearly perceived the criminalized procedures associated with adjudicated paternity and child support as a major barrier to their establishing paternity. However, 76 percent identified the quality of the relationship between the young parents as the pivotal circumstance for the decision to pursue legal paternity.

Clearly, policies and programs will have to be redesigned to meet the realities of life circumstances of young unmarried parents in order to enable them to fulfill their role as responsible parents.

Ambivalence on Paternity Issues

From the responses on the survey sent to social services personnel and from the Battle and Ford Foundation studies, we identify an ambivalence among the population of young low-income unmarried parents toward vigorous paternity adjudication efforts as they presently exist. An unmistakable reluctance to proceed with vigorous paternity adjudication efforts characterizes the contemporary milieu, at all levels. Consequently, the child's long-term interests remain silent, unexpressed, and neglected.

Judicial philosophies among local jurisdictions, and even between individual judges, cause uncertainty in initiating changes. Differences on the role of civil procedures and the use of alternative administrative routes to paternity determination prevail. The assignment of child support obligations to teen fathers and the "male responsibility" ethic have varying interpretations. For some courtrooms, the punitive tone toward fathers is considered important for "prevention" purposes. For others, local anecdotes of female entrapment of unsuspecting males determine a dismissive attitude toward an action. In sum, personal philosophies of judges, along with discretionary judgment in judicial procedures, cast an enigmatic light on approaches to paternity action.

State legislatures are also divided on the issue, as we observe that thirty states are out of compliance with the federal mandates on paternity adjudication and state agencies continue to lag in their paternity efforts (U.S. General Accounting Office 1987). The community itself is in doubt. No sharp signals have been received that provide a "get tough" stance on unmarried fathers and their responsibilities toward their children. Equality in bearing the consequences of out-of-wedlock births has not received serious consideration. The federal level has sent the clearest signal of expectation of the father's responsibility. But here one notes that the child support law is basically designed for the divorced and separated. Only erratic attention has been paid to the children of the "never-married."

Less well understood, however, is the disregard of the paternity issue by health and social services personnel for whom the welfare of children is a core ethic. The sentiments around unmarried fathers and their responsibilities toward their children are divided (Barrett and Robinson 1982). The "self-determination" of the young mother in eliminating the presence of the father may be reinforced by social service agencies whose goals for the mother are immediate stabilization. In addition, however, there is a lingering notion that the AFDC bureaucracy and the judicial procedures will enmesh these young unmarried parents in harmful ways. Paternity adjudication and child support enforcement are perceived as the pursuit of the father for his money, alone, to repay the state, without regard for improving the economic status of the mother and child.

Our interviews revealed that for social workers, attuned to short-term, tangible, everyday pressures in the lives of women and children, the value of linking the child to the father is nebulous. First of all, the father is perceived as not having a financial future worth protecting for the child; second, if adoption is the plan, the father's legal presence is an unwelcome complication. It is the teenage mother who is involved with the community agencies and the services they offer, either voluntarily or involuntarily. To work with her, alone, to plan for her future is an absorbing task. The parallel development of community services for unmarried fathers has not yet appeared, except in isolated circumstances.

The more probing response, namely, to examine the role of the unmarried father and the rights of the nonmarital child has, in fact, only just begun. Turning social work's full attention to the child's best interests, as reflected in paternity establishment and child support enforcement, is yet to be accomplished.

Current Status of Paternity Issues for Young Unmarried Parents

A traditional assumption that there is an irrevocable obligation of the father toward his child is receiving mixed responses in the current environment. The dismal economic outlook of the unmarried father encourages kin and family to disconnect him from the child. Complicating the picture are the fiscal interests of the state, which are perceived as punitive by young unmarried parents, and the perception of caseworkers that child support enforcement has little or no benefit for their clients. Child support awards, in the view of social service personnel, are nearly always inadequate and uncertain, with little promise of improving the standard of living for mothers and their children. The principle upholding paternity as a fundamental right owed every child is undermined by these negative connotations. Finally, there is no widely held agreement on what kind of family formation provides continuity and permanence for a child. Public policy that might force the linkage of a "miserable father" with an "unwilling mother" cannot be sustained.

The barriers are formidable: a significant proportion of unmarried mothers, as AFDC recipients, are in overwhelming life circumstances. Poverty, the drug scene, and a deteriorating sense of life's options pervade their lives. Marriage is rarely ever mentioned as an option.[9] The fathers of their children are increasingly perceived as economically and socially without value.

Despite these perceptions, three distinct but interrelated movements are beginning to change attitudes toward paternity establishment so as to appreciate its benefits for the nonmarital child.

1. The application of the concept of gender equality leads to the expectation that young males should share the consequences of an out-of-wedlock birth. This awareness has alerted social service providers to the role that can be played by young, unmarried fathers. The widely held belief that the father's exclusive role is one of financial responsibility is broadening to see his role in sharing the parenting tasks. In addition, the equity argument that *he* should be a participant in the work and training mandates of welfare reform is gaining ground.
2. The general tendency to think only of short-range goals in which the father is defined as a noncontributing person is changing. Several programs around the country are linking unmarried fathers to work opportunities to enhance their future capacity for child support.
3. As the role of unmarried fathers gains visibility and his rights begin to be protected, his responsibilities are stressed and the perception that he has a future worth protecting for his child gains ground.

In spite of these welcome trends, it is tempting to conclude that current national and state paternity policy for young parents is in a state of confusion, partly due to the lack of definition of "responsibility," and little consensus on what kind of family formation provides stability and continuity for the child. Moreover, there is a growing awareness emerging in judicial arrangements for paternity determinations which are, in sizable number, voluntary. Nevertheless, cumulative information and insights reinforce a policy that articulates a fundamental right: every child is owed the identity and recognition of two parents.

Conclusion

Until we know more about the attitudes and influences affecting paternity decisions, we may not be able to design policies and programs that will enable fathers to fulfill a responsible role toward their children. To this end, we propose the following recommendations.

Research Recommendations
- Create a framework for defining a father's responsibility in financial and nonfinancial terms.
- Assess demonstration programs that provide simplified procedures and expeditious means of securing voluntary adjudications.

- Explore the "good cause exception" circumstances and specify what parental bonds are *not* in the child's best interest.
- Explore the characteristics and social situations of young unmarried women who are "disavowers," i.e., who reject their partners as plausible candidates for the fathering role, and of young unmarried fathers who evade and avoid the paternity connection.
- Identify the patterns of cohabitation that discourage paternity decisions.
- Determine the differences between AFDC and non–AFDC unmarried mothers in their patterns of avowing or disavowing paternity.
- Learn how the community culture encourages or discourages paternity.
- Learn why fathers play a dwindling role in the lives of their nonmarital children.

Program and Policy Recommendations

- Simplify and decriminalize paternity establishment. The father's identity should be known to all nonmarital children, so that all may receive financial and other benefits that are their legal right. In order to facilitate this a simple declaration of parentage form should be offered at birth and separated from the legal adjudication and procedures involved in child support. The whole process of establishing paternity should be decriminalized, and there should be careful monitoring to assure that all unwed parents are provided accurate information about paternity and given a chance to sign the declaration of parentage.
- Reach out to young unwed fathers. Effective outreach strategies for unmarried fathers need to be developed that will: woo them into the social service system; introduce them to education, training, and job opportunities; provide them a "safe" environment to receive information on paternity adjudication and to understand the consequences; and publicize the legal services available to protect their rights.
- Reform child support guidelines. Rescind or repeal state guidelines that mandate a support order when there is no income; where appropriate, assign a token child support payment; recognize the unwed father's nonfinancial contributions, such as child care; and improve follow-up.
- Market the message. Develop a community strategy to provide information to various networks on the benefits of paternity to a nonmarital child. Provide outreach to young, unmarried parents who are not in school and not on AFDC—a particularly underserved population.

- Increase funding. Increase incentive payments to IV-D offices to raise the priority of paternity actions; increase resources for over-burdened and understaffed IV-D offices with heavy caseloads. It is time-consuming to deal with the hesitancies and confusions of young, unmarried parents. State interests in conserving judicial and fiscal resources may postpone or ignore procedures. These items need legislative attention.

An enormous and increasing number of children are growing up with the severe disadvantage of no legally established father. While we have, to some extent, uncovered the complex influences that surround the decision to establish paternity for an out-of-wedlock child, a wholehearted national commitment to ensure a better future for the child has not yet evolved. Finding realistic ways for fathers to meet their obligations should be a prominent agenda item for the nineties.

Notes

1. For a legislative history of child support enforcement, see Office of Child Support Enforcement 1984.

2. For a complete review of legal decisions, see Krause 1981.

Note also that state statutes that have discriminated against out-of-wedlock children have been consistently struck down as unconstitutional. Decisions based chiefly on the constitutional equal protection clause have established the principle of equity between marital and nonmarital children. Among the important decisions affecting this constitutional protection, note the following: *Levy v. Louisiana*, 391 U.S. 681 (1968), established the right of out-of-wedlock children to recover compensation for the wrongful death of their mothers; *Wever v. Aetna Casualty and Surety Co.*, 406 U.S. 164 (1972), established their right to collect benefits under the state's workers' compensation program; the right to support was established by *Gomez v. Perez*, 409 U.S. 535 (1973); and their right to public assistance was established in New Jersey, *Welfare Rights v. Cahill*, 411 U.S. 619 (1973).

3. Information gathered from a telephone communication with B. Galloway, Office of Management and Budget, Washington, D.C., March, 1989. See also U.S. Bureau of the Census 1985 and Barnow 1992.

4. See U.S. Bureau of the Census 1991b, 3, and U.S. Bureau of the Census 1991a, 15.

5. Personal communication with W. Weder, quoting Family Assistance Office 1987.

6. Information received from telephone communication with representatives from the Office of Benefits, the Air Force, and the Office of Veterans Administration Benefits, March 1989.

7. P.L. 94-88, 1975, which established the Child Support Enforcement Act, Federal/State Child Support Enforcement Program, Title IV-D of the Social Secu-

rity Act, requires the states to establish paternity as the necessary prerequisite to the collection of child support. When a needy unwed mother applies for welfare assistance, she must agree to cooperate with the state in determining paternity and establishing child support. She must name the father and help locate him, unless she has "good cause" to be exempted from the requirement (for example, incest, rape, or danger of harm to her or her child). The paternity establishment services of the child support system must be available to any custodial parent upon request. Sometimes there is a small fee.

8. See the several titles under the Family Support Act, 1988 (P.L. 100-485).

9. Several focus group discussions held in January 1989 with social services personnel working in programs serving adolescent parents made this assertion.

References

Abrahamse, Allen F., Peter A. Morrison, and Linda J. Waite. 1988. *Beyond Stereotypes: Who Becomes a Single Teenage Mother?* Santa Monica, Calif.: Rand.

Barnow, B. 1992. "Paternity Establishment among Never-Married Mothers: Estimates from the 1986 Current Population Survey, Alimony, and Child Support Supplement." Special Report no. 56B. Madison, Wis.: Institute for Research on Poverty. August.

Barrett, R., and R. Robinson. 1982. "Teenage Fathers: Neglected Too Long." *Social Work* November: 484–488.

Battle, S. 1984. *Male Responsibility: The Black Adolescent Father—An Exploratory Study.* A paper commissioned by the Ford/McKnight Project. Mimeo.

City University of New York. Graduate Center. 1987. *The Male Role in Teen Pregnancy and Parenting: New Directions in Social Policy.* Sponsored by the Ford Foundation, 1985 through 1986. New York.

Committee on Ways and Means. See U.S. Congress. House.

Ellwood, D. 1988. *Poor Support: Poverty and the American Family.* New York: Basic Books.

Hayes, C., ed. 1987. *Risking the Future: Adolescent Sexuality, Pregnancy, and Childbearing.* Vol. 1, Final Report of the National Council Panel on Adolescent Pregnancy and Childbearing, and vol. 2, Working Papers. Washington, D.C.: National Academy Press.

Kastner, C., et al. 1988. *Child Support for Young Families: Current Issues and Future Directions.* Proceedings of forum. Washington, D.C.: Center for the Support of Children.

Krause, H. 1977. *Family Law in a Nutshell.* St. Paul: West Publishing.

———. 1981. *Child Support in America: The Legal Perspective.* Charlottesville, Va.: Michie.

Lerman, R. 1985. *Family Law in a Nutshell.* St. Paul: West Publishing.

Monthly Vital Statistics Report: Final Data from the National Center for Health Statistics. 1988. Vol. 37, no. 3. Supplement. Table 16, p. 30. July.

———. 1991. Vol. 40, no. 8. Supplement. December.

Moore, K. A. 1987. *Facts at a Glance*. Washington, D.C.: Child Trends.

———. 1992. *Facts at a Glance*. Washington, D.C.: Child Trends.

Office of Child Support Enforcement. See U.S. Department of Health and Human Services.

Ooms, T., and T. Owen. 1988. *Young Unwed Fathers and Welfare Reform*. Background briefing report of seminar held on 18 November 1988. Washington, D.C.: Family Impact Seminar.

Parke, R., and B. Neville. 1987. "Teenage Parenthood." In Hayes 1987.

Smollar, J., and T. Ooms. 1988. *Young Unwed Fathers: Research Review, Policy Dilemmas, and Options*. Washington, D.C.: Government Printing Office. Available from Project SHARE Resource Center, P.O. Box 2309, Rockville, MD 20852.

U.S. Bureau of the Census. 1985. *Child Support and Alimony: 1985*. (Advance data from the March–April 1986 Current Population Surveys.) Tables B, C, and E. Washington, D.C.: Government Printing Office.

———. 1989. *Statistical Abstract of the United States: 1988*. Table 87, p. 62. Washington, D.C.: Government Printing Office.

———. 1991a. *Poverty in the United States: 1988 and 1989*. Current Population Report p-60, no. 171. Washington, D.C.: Government Printing Office.

———. 1991b. *Child Support and Alimony: 1989*. Current Population Report p-60, no. 173. Washington, D.C.: Government Printing Office.

U.S. Congress. House. Committee on Ways and Means. 1992. *Overview of Entitlement Programs*. Washington, D.C.: Government Printing Office.

U.S. Department of Health and Human Services. Office of Child Support Enforcement. 1984. *Child Support Enforcement: Ninth Annual Report to Congress for the Period Ending September 30, 1984*. Appendix A, Legislative History, 111–124. Washington, D.C.: Government Printing Office.

———. 1987. *Child Support Enforcement: Twelfth Annual Report to the Congress for the Period Ending September 30, 1987*. Vol. 2, Fiscal Year 1987 Statistics. Tables 40 and 44, pp. 49 and 54. Washington, D.C.: Government Printing Office.

U.S. Department of Health and Human Services. Office of Family Assistance. 1987. *Quality Control Review Data Report, Fiscal Year 1986*. Washington, D.C.: Government Printing Office.

U.S. General Accounting Office. 1987. *Child Support: Need to Improve Efforts to Identify Fathers and Obtain Support Orders*. Report to the Secretary of Health and Human Services. Washington, D.C.: Government Printing Office.

Wattenberg, E. 1988. "Establishing Paternity for Non-marital Children." *Public Welfare* Summer: 9–13.

Wattenberg, E., R. Brewer, and M. Resnick. 1991. *A Study of Paternity Decisions of Young Unmarried Parents*. Final report submitted to the Ford Foundation, February. New York: Ford Foundation. Available from the authors, Center for Urban and Regional Affairs, University of Minnesota.

11   The Problems and Promise of Child Support Policies

SANDRA K. DANZIGER,
CAROLYN K. KASTNER, AND
TERRI J. NICKEL

As recent studies have discovered rather high rates of young unwed fatherhood, researchers have begun to question the role of these fathers in their children's lives and the conditions that hinder versus promote father involvement. One of several critical components of fathering is the provision of financial support, or the young man's ability to perform the breadwinner role. The extent to which young unwed fathers fulfill this obligation is, by almost any available measure, far below any adequate standard.

The poor levels of economic support occur for several complex and interrelated reasons. First, these men may have few resources to share with their children and thus are blocked from becoming providers, no matter what their motivation or desires may be. Second, young unwed mothers may not want to share their parental responsibilities with the men, and may not accept an offer of involvement from the fathers. Third, the couple or their families may not want to comply with formal, legal channels for forcing the fathers to provide support. Here perhaps the obligation is being fulfilled but not officially acknowledged as such. Finally, the system designed to establish, collect, and enforce the support obligation may be ineffective and inadequate.

Given the weak performance of the system, the consensus across the nation is that reform is overdue (Garfinkel and McLanahan 1986; Ellwood 1988; Kahn and Kamerman 1988). In this paper we assess the system's response to the young unwed fathers. First, we provide estimates of participation by young unwed fathers in the child support system

235

across the nation, and we examine what happens when they are successfully processed through the courts using the example of one strong state system.

Second, we describe more general barriers in the current system that preclude participation. We classify these in three types of structural problems—(1) lack of uniformity in paternity guidelines; (2) administrative practices based on collection procedures for older fathers; (3) the federal incentive of payments for collections. Third, we assess the promise of new directions, as indicated by the reforms of the 1988 Family Support Act (P.L. 100-485) and by several local pilot programs targeted to reach young unmarried parents. Finally, we summarize the needed components of a model paternity system and the long-term benefits of promoting increased child support among this population.

Current System

Involvement

While the most recent national figure for receipt of child support among all those eligible is quite low, the figures for the never-married, the young, and the minority group members in this population are even worse. The 1986 Current Population Survey indicates that for 1985 only 18.4 percent of the never-married had court orders for support, as compared to 81.8 percent of those divorced or 43.1 percent of those separated (U.S. Bureau of the Census 1989). Similarly for eligible mothers aged 18–29, 44.6 percent had awards from the courts, compared to 70.5 percent of the women aged 30–39 and 67.7 percent for those aged 40 or more. Racial and ethnic differences in 1985 indicate that 70.6 percent of whites, 36.3 percent of blacks, and 42.1 percent of Hispanics had court orders for support.

Given a legal order, the chances of receiving some payment within each of these groups were very similar in 1985—74 percent received some amount of what they were awarded. However, the mean amounts paid in child support for the year across these categories suggest great discrepancies (U.S. Bureau of the Census 1989). The never married received only $1,147 in 1985, compared to $2,528 for the divorced and $2,082 for the separated; the younger women, ages 18–29, received $1,000 less on average than did those 30 or over. Racial differences in mean amounts paid were smaller but still indicative of disadvantage; for example, whites received $540 more than blacks in 1985.

Of all the problems these figures highlight, the largest gap appears to be the lack of awards for children born outside of marriage. If only 18 percent had awards, then 82 percent were outside the child support system. Many have probably not had paternity legally established. Some may have had paternity established without child support orders. This lack of participation is also evident in findings on the frequency of paternity establishment compared to other outcomes for children born to single adolescent mothers (Danziger and Nichols-Casebolt 1988). Of a sample of 5,724 children born in 1980–81 to single mothers aged 19 or under, only a small group, 3 percent, were adopted in marriage or had their parents marry within the first few years. Another 25 percent had paternity established via naming of the father on the birth record. This step could facilitate but not substitute for court-decreed paternity in this particular state, Wisconsin. Another 15 percent had paternity settled in the courts. This left the remaining 57 percent with no formally identified father.

Effectiveness

For those who do participate in the courts, what outcomes can currently be expected? While there are vast differences across the states, some indication of the viability of support among young fathers is illustrated from data on paternity case performance in Wisconsin. From 1980 to 1987 in selected counties over 6,100 paternities were established where the father was aged 26 or less at the time of the case opening. Of those cases 78 percent were ordered to pay support, averaging $107 per month. Of those with orders 77 percent paid some amount over the period of study. The average amount paid was $75 per month, which was about 67 percent of what these fathers were ordered to pay and about 12 percent of their average income. Enforcement measures could certainly be improved by, for example, expanding wage assignment orders from the current 50 percent of fathers with legal obligations. Such measures are likely to increase support from young noncustodial fathers.

Current Barriers

The systems of establishing paternity and obtaining child support have only in recent decades been related to one another. Historically, the child born outside of marriage was afforded very few rights regarding the legal relationship with his/her father. Until the U.S. Supreme Court intervened in a series of cases in 1968, the nonmarital child was often denied rights of paternal support, as well as inheritance, custody, name, and claims under such programs as Worker's Compensation. In addition, prior to 1968, even if the child was awarded paternal support, some states extended these rights no further than the period of time the child was likely to be unable to support itself, or to a period not exceeding a set number of years (Krause 1981).

Today the established principle is that the nonmarital child is entitled to legal equality with the child of married parents. But prior to the Child Support Enforcement Amendments of 1984, some states continued to place a statute of limitations on the establishment of paternity. As of 1984, only 23 states had statutory provisions for setting child support amounts for nonmarital children, compared to 34 states that had statutes specific to setting support in divorce or separation proceedings (Melli 1984).

While enforcement of the parental child support obligation has been a federal policy concern since 1950, it was not until 1967 that legislation was passed requiring state welfare agencies to initiate the establishment of paternity for AFDC children born out of wedlock. In all states either legitimation (i.e., marriage of the parents) or a declaration of parentage are prerequisites for child support and inheritance. Paternity can be established either through court proceedings or through written admission of paternity by the father. Where the alleged father denies paternity, the case may eventually go to trial; however, most disputes are settled in pretrial hearings or in prior administrative proceedings. The most common form of legal evidence is a blood test to compare genetic markers of both parents and the child, which usually settles disputes of paternity (Horowitz and Davidson 1984). For example, in one California county, of 2,000 paternity cases per year 1,800 were uncontested. The other 200 required blood tests, but very few of these went to trial (Kohn 1987). When a father voluntarily acknowledges paternity in writing, this affidavit and the mother's written statement can form the basis of the paternity record from which a court can establish paternity and order a support award.

The routine process of establishing paternity and support through the state child support agency generally does not address the needs of young clients, nor does it provide the services necessary to ensure support. Joyce Everett (1988) charges that many state and county practices actually create barriers. In her article, "Child Support Enforcement: Barriers in Serving Young Families," she points to (1) the absence of uniform procedures for establishing paternity, (2) the fragmentation and discontinuity of the service delivery system, (3) the low priority assigned to paternity cases, due in part to the federal reimbursement incentive structure. The legal procedures for handling paternity establishment cases vary across states, and even within states, a range of complex procedures govern paternity determinations.

Although paternity establishment is now a civil process in most jurisdictions, it began as a criminal process and still has many criminal due process elements. For example, in some states a court hearing is necessary to voluntarily acknowledge a child's parentage. A court appearance for many young fathers, whose previous experiences with the judicial system may have been unpleasant, can be frightening and intimidating. Often during such hearings, the father must publicly admit to sexual activity that resulted in the birth of a child and must be advised by a judge of his responsibility to financially support the child. Complex legal procedures for establishing paternity have two side effects. One is to inadvertently discourage voluntary acknowledgments. Many fathers will not admit paternity if a court appearance is required. Furthermore, the court costs of paternity hearings, in which the likelihood of recovering child support is slim, also discourage child support agency workers from active pursuit of contested paternity cases (Everett 1988).

Litigation of paternity cases is also problematic because there are inconsistencies in the classification of paternity actions. Some courts clarify paternity cases as civil actions, other courts make them criminal actions, and still other jurisdictions classify paternity cases as quasi-criminal actions (Browning 1987). As a result, paternity cases may be heard under criminal statutes in one county, while in others they are heard under the state's civil statutes, but the burden of proof is the criminal standard.

In some states a voluntary acknowledgment of paternity or conduct demonstrating acknowledgment is insufficient evidence for determining paternity in a court proceeding. Blood test results must augment other forms of evidence. These procedural inconsistencies can be confusing and thus restrict the degree to which community service and hospital-based programs can provide reliable information and referral sources for child support enforcement programs.

Administrative Complexities

While federal regulations require the states to designate a separate governmental unit to administer the child support enforcement program, the delivery of services is decentralized. The state child support enforcement agency supervises the program while the counties deliver the services. County enforcement programs have the formidable task of integrating the delivery of services provided by an array of agencies, both within and outside of the programs and this often results in poorly coordinated services, and/or duplication of services. Even organizational structures of county offices may vary across and within counties. For example, case management procedures that are designed to process the flow of cases through the stages of absent parent location, paternity establishment in court hearings, and enforcement and monitoring of support in the administrative agency have many different organizational arrangements, and these differences can affect system accountability and accessibility to the public (Everett 1988).

Problems in the referral and communication channels across the various interrelated agencies may result in serious gaps and/or obstacles in the enforcement process. Case flow originates with a referral from the AFDC, Title IV-A office. Paternity case intake in the child support enforcement, IV-D unit, may be held up by case backlog, by discontinuities in the pattern and flow of cases. Presumably, priority procedures permit the IV-D office to process cases selectively with those with the greatest collection potential first. Usually cases given the highest priority are the least complex—those involving divorced and employed noncustodial parents, and/or those in which the absent parent's location is less problematic.

In contrast, paternity cases are often more complex and are not a high priority, because the fathers involved in these cases tend to be young, unemployed, underemployed, in school, or perhaps entangled in illegal activities. These young men presumably lack the incomes for immediate recovery of support payments. Thus, these paternity determinations are a long-term investment that require an elaborate tracking system to assure future payments. Moreover, financial incentives paid by the federal government to the states for vigorous pursuit of paternity cases are not as high as incentives for enforcing preexisting support orders.

Delays in case referrals and follow-up, due to such problems as the absence of statewide computer systems, also create service delivery gaps and discontinuity, particularly in paternity cases. Referrals to the state's attorney's office for paternity establishment services are frequently delayed by the absence of sufficient location information, backlogs in the court docket, and shortages in trained personnel to represent the state in paternity hearings. Deficiencies in county case management systems create difficulties for the IV-D unit to monitor the progress of paternity cases in the state's attorney's office. Some cases are therefore simply lost in the process of agency referrals (Everett 1988).

Current Standards for Setting and Collecting Support

Establishing paternity and enforcing support are functions of the state child support agency and not the child welfare agency or health department. The existing federal formula for financing the child support program is based on a ratio of administrative costs to collections. Child welfare agencies or health departments are not subject to the revenue generating expectations of the child support agency. Were they the locus of decisions about paternity, the case processing would perhaps be less tied to program costs. Where short-term administrative costs are high and collections prospects are low, a decision may be made not to pursue a case in the child support agency.

The Family Support Act of 1988, P.L. 100-485, establishes standards for establishing paternity and an enhanced federal match for paternity testing, but it does not address the impact of low collection potential on administrative decision making. The current cost/collections ratio does not measure long-term costs or cost shifting. While the state child support agency avoids incurring extra administrative costs in the short term by not opening the paternity case that has a low collection potential, the family, other state agencies, and perhaps even the child support agency itself may be paying higher long-term costs.

Establishing paternity only on the basis of immediate collection potential ignores potential social and psychological benefits to children. Ignoring the long-term collection potential raises future costs by increasing the family's chance of remaining dependent on welfare. In addition, such an approach reduces fatherhood to a financial responsibility, a troubling notion to other service providers, who may be trying to encourage young fathers to take a broader view of their parenthood. What message do we give fathers when we ignore them in their youth only to pursue them later when their income has increased?

New Directions

Federal Legislation

Congress designed recent welfare reform to promote the number of paternities established, especially among younger parents. In Title I of the Family Support Act of 1988, P.L. 100-485: "Child Support and Establishment of Paternity," Congress clarified mandates on statutes of limitation, set new standards to speed case processing, encouraged simple civil processes for paternity establishment, and increased federal assistance for the costs of paternity tests. The Family Support Act also emphasizes enforcement services to custodial parents under age 24.

Beginning 1 October 1991, states were required to attain a specific rate of paternity establishment or make progress toward that goal. The relevant index is the proportion of all children in Aid to Families with Dependent Children (AFDC) cases born out of wedlock for whom paternity has been established. To be in compliance a state agency must attain a paternity establishment ratio that: equals 50 percent, meets the national average of all states, or represents an increase of 6 percent from the base year (1988), and of 3 percent for each year after 1992. The law also mandates that states require each parent to furnish his or her social security number in the process of issuing birth certificates, so as to assist in the process of locating and identifying parents.

Changes with respect to parentage testing have been adopted to facilitate paternity establishment. States will now be required to order paternity tests upon the request of any party in a contested case. And for all paternity cases the federal match for the cost of paternity tests has been increased from 66 to 90 percent.

Congress addressed the issue of standardizing and simplifying paternity establishment by adopting a new section of Title IV-D: "Encouraging states to adopt simple civil process for voluntarily acknowledging paternity and a civil procedure for establishing paternity in contested cases." The section also clarifies the intent of the Child Support Amendments of 1984, P.L. 98-378, on the issue of statutes of limitation. While all states are required to adopt a law allowing paternity establishment at any time prior to a child's eighteenth birthday, the effective date and eligibility for paternity establishment under the new law is 16 August 1984. The law applies to any child for whom paternity has not yet been established and to any child for whom a paternity action was brought but dismissed because of a particular state's statute of limitations of less than eighteen years. This clarification removes a significant barrier for nonmarital children.

In addition to these changes in paternity procedures, the Family Support Act of 1988 also set new time requirements for processing all child support cases, including paternity cases. The law requires the Secretary of Health and Human Services to establish standard time limits governing the period within which a state agency must accept and respond to requests for services. This should reduce case backlogs at the county level.

State Initiatives to Improve Paternity Establishment
Some states have gone beyond mandates in federal law and financing to create their own incentives for increasing the number of paternities established. Some states are correcting the imbalance in the incentive structures by offering cash to county agencies for establishing paternities. A recent Ohio law provides funding for incentives to local county agencies that increase the number of paternities established annually. California adopted a law in 1988 that requires the Department of Social Services to provide payments to each county at a rate of $90 per child for each paternity established. The same legislation also calls for a study to determine if other incentives should be established.

Beyond revisions in administrative and legal procedures, state child support enforcement agencies are beginning to implement novel strategies to improve paternity establishment and collections from young fathers.

Three major strategies have been used in the states of Washington, Georgia, Nebraska, and Illinois: (1) aggressive educational campaigns, (2) alleviation of cost burdens in genetic testing, and (3) adoption of a modified consent process for paternity acknowledgments.

WASHINGTON. The Department of Social and Health Services in the state of Washington has a statewide educational campaign to inform youth about the Child Support Enforcement Program, paternity services, and family responsibility. Members of the Governor's Efficiency Commission looked at these issues and initially recommended development of materials for distribution to high schools. Over 35,000 comic books, styled after similar publications in Georgia and Marion County, Indiana, have been distributed to schools. One comic book is aimed at young mothers, and another at young fathers. Yet another comic book, "Patman," specifically describes paternity establishment and the rights and responsibilities of young unwed fathers.

Educating the general public about the child support system was also one of the commission's goals. A comprehensive training workshop curriculum—including student manuals, brochures for parents of students, a board game, and a videotape—has been developed and approved as part of the public school family life curriculum for seventh, ninth, and eleventh graders in one county. A similar curriculum is now being presented as a workshop by five local employers during the workday.

NEW HAMPSHIRE. Another school-based public awareness program is being presented in high schools around New Hampshire. Entitled "Pathways," the program informs teens about the responsibilities of early parenthood, especially the legal and financial consequences, and the benefits of paternity establishment. Emphasis is placed on how decision making about sexuality can affect and limit life options. This program was developed by the New Hampshire Division of Human Services, and consists of a modular package featuring a videotape, presenter materials (statistics, presentation tips, information on public assistance programs), student materials (role-playing guide, budget worksheets), actual case histories, and evaluation forms.

GEORGIA. An innovative approach to the education of young unwed parents is underway in Georgia. *Glorious Dilemma*, a skit being performed around Muskogee County since 1984, presents real life situations that teens will face as parents. Scenes portrayed include a young father hearing from the child support enforcement program of his new financial responsibility that will last eighteen years, and a teen mother's interviews with welfare and child support workers where she is asked personal questions about her sexual activities. The presentations of *Glorious Dilemma* are given at junior high and high schools, health clinics, and other interested organizations. The skit was written by a IV-D worker and has enjoyed a concerned and emotional response from its teenage audiences.

Another educational tactic initiated by the Georgia Office of Child Support Recovery is the statewide circulation of a newspaper in comic-strip format entitled *Looking beyond Teenage Pregnancy*. In each comic frame a young parent asks a question such as "How will the state find out who the father is?" and a factual response is stated below. The last page lists the addresses and telephone numbers for all the child support offices in Georgia. Fact sheets with general information about teenage pregnancy and child support responsibilities are also distributed to junior high and high schools. For many young Georgians, these educational media offer a first introduction to the existence of young parents' rights and responsibilities and to the child support program.

NEBRASKA. *Looking beyond Teenage Pregnancy* has been adopted by the state of Nebraska. Barriers to paternity establishment are being attacked by an educational campaign aimed at young parents plus a reduction of procedural fees for unemployed fathers. Two brochures—one for young mothers and one for young fathers—have been developed and sent to schools, community action groups, social services agencies, hospitals, general practitioners, and others in a mass mailing in late 1988. Each brochure follows a question-and-answer format on issues such as the legal procedure for establishing paternity, genetic testing, medical support, adoption, custody, and interstate child support payments. A third brochure presents the overall goals of, and services provided by, the Nebraska Child Support Enforcement Program.

Genetic testing is presented as a means of clearing wrongfully accused "fathers." To lower testing costs for young fathers, all costs of genetic testing consented to by the putative father are now borne by the state agency, even if the young man is found to be the father. In addition, contracts negotiated with the biomedical laboratories performing the blood tests specify that DNA testing will be performed free of charge in cases where the certainty of blood test results fall below 95 percent.

ILLINOIS. In 1988, the state of Illinois received an award from the Federal Regional Office of Child Support Enforcement for its 100-percent increase in the number of paternity establishments over the previous five years. This increase may be attributed in part to the IV-D agency's distribution of blood testing funds at the county level, where the monies are used at the discretion of the attorney involved with paternity establishment cases. The county decided to manage paternity cases with a "consent process" that allows acknowledgment of paternity outside the courtroom, following disclosure of paternal obligations. Although courts have been reluctant to allow this practice universally, simplified paternity consent procedures have encouraged voluntary paternity acknowledgment in Pennsylvania, Indiana, Michigan, Missouri, and Oregon.

INDIANA.   The most ambitious public sector program is operated out of the Marion County Prosecutor's Office in Indianapolis, Indiana (see Pirog-Good, Chapter 12 in this volume). Fathers between ages 15 and 21 earn monetary credit towards payment of their child support orders with predetermined nonmonetary activities. Every hour spent in school, with the child, or in job/parenting training is given a dollar equivalent that the young father "earns" towards payment of his child support debt, in accordance with a predetermined schedule. Marion County is the only jurisdiction that operates such a program.

Local Social Services
More efficient procedures and greater awareness of the Child Support Enforcement Program are only some of the changes being developed. Many young fathers still remain outside the child support enforcement system, and private social services programs are finding that they sometimes provide support to their children in the form of diapers, clothing, baby-sitting care, recreation, and food. Many programs hope to advance the importance of regular and consistent *in-kind* support soon after the birth of the baby, in the hopes that it will lead to regular and consistent *cash* support later in the father's life. Because an unrealistically high financial obligation may drive the unemployed and uneducated young father further underground, some private programs do not encourage these young men to cooperate with the local child support enforcement programs. Recognition of, and credit for, noncash contributions are perhaps a more successful welcome mat for a young father's initial step through the door of the child support system.

Low levels of child support payments by noncustodial fathers may be due not only to a lack of employment or enforcement, but also to weak bonds with the child. Where is the incentive for a father to make monthly payments for a child he doesn't know and may have never seen? In-kind support is closely linked to the extent of the father's involvement with his child. Fathers who are included in prenatal and immediate postnatal parenting classes have been known to provide some form of support on a more regular basis. In a California program this had even resulted in lower medical costs to the public through improved well-being of the mother, and prevention of low birth weight children (Barth, Claycomb, and Loomis 1988).

Without further education about child support enforcement and related services, the young unwed father who is willing to provide in-kind support to his child may avoid legal, formal procedures. In many instances there is no apparent incentive for him or for the young mother to establish paternity. Even faced with a denial of AFDC eligibility for refusing to cooperate with this process, many mothers are reluctant to disclose the father's identity or whereabouts. Several programs around the nation, however, have reversed this pattern (see Brown 1990 for report on Maine). Almost all of these model social service programs

- are community-based
- pursue active outreach to young fathers
- use case management
- have linkage agreements with other service agencies
- have male mentorship and male staff
- provide concrete services, such as job placement
- provide family services, such as teaching parenting skills
- encourage paternity establishment and payment of child support in some form

Summary

Model Components
The Indianapolis TAPP Program and other programs described above have several common elements designed to overcome barriers and empower young men to become responsible parents. While the range and mix of services to young fathers vary according to the individual goals of the programs, three components are common to the more promising paternity establishment efforts: (1) public outreach and education, (2) education and job training for fathers, and (3) support and assistance for responsible parenting.

PUBLIC OUTREACH AND EDUCATION. Outreach and education to young people and the general public are a critical component to improving paternity establishment for children born to young parents. The majority of unmarried young parents are not aware of or using the child support services available to them. Child support agencies need to reach the immediate target group of young parents, as well as their parents, schools, churches, and service providers influencing their opinions. In addition, all teens would benefit from information on the legal rights and responsibilities of parenting. Increasing teens' knowledge should lead to greater paternity establishment and should have a deterrent effect on adolescent pregnancy, as teens make more informed decisions about the consequences of sexual activity.

As noted earlier, several states have developed educational materials especially for young parents about child support and paternity. In addition to materials developed by the child support agencies, Planned Parenthood in Kalamazoo, Michigan offers a brochure, *Males and Babies and Michigan Law*. The San Francisco Teenage Pregnancy and Parenting Project counsels young mothers and fathers to establish paternity, citing parental responsibility, visitation, and support as a benefit to the mother, father, and child. The Young Fathers Project in three Maine sites offers counseling on the legal responsibilities of fatherhood to the young men in their programs.

Two common elements characterize the more successful outreach efforts: active outreach at the community level and male staff. Active outreach is necessary to expand enrollment. While young fathers can be recruited to programs through their parents, few fathers walk into teen parenting programs voluntarily. They certainly cannot be expected to apply for assistance to an enforcement office. Outreach to schools, local community centers, and other agencies serving young men is necessary, as is the commitment of male staff to attract and keep fathers in parenting programs.

EDUCATION, TRAINING, AND EMPLOYMENT FOR FATHERS. Asked if his proposed crackdown on child support might penalize some disadvantaged young men by not addressing their poor employment prospects, Senator Daniel Patrick Moynihan answered, "It sure as hell does" (*National Journal*, 19 September 1987). Education, training, and employment for noncustodial fathers were eliminated from the Family Support Act of 1988 in the Conference Committee. Congress made it clear that this bill was designed to assist the custodial parents of poor children. While custodial parents are participating in federally funded job training programs across the nation, assistance for noncustodial parents is limited to a small number of demonstration sites (see description of the Parents' Fair Shares Demonstration in Chapter 16 of this volume and Furstenberg, Sherwood, and Sullivan 1992). Until these programs are evaluated, assistance to young, unwed fathers will likely be limited to a handful of state and locally funded programs.

Young fathers are more likely to have dropped out of school and to have lower basic skills than fathers older at the birth of their first child, suggesting that they may be less capable of providing support (Marsiglio

1987). Assessments of their capacity to support their families suggest that it may be cost-effective over time to invest in young fathers. Organizations looking beyond welfare reform to strengthening family formation recommend child support enforcement and support services for young parents. The William T. Grant Foundation Commission on Work, Family, and Citizenship report *The Forgotten Half* recommends more vigorous implementation of the 1984 amendments to the Child Support Enforcement Act and the reevaluation of welfare policies that inadvertently discourage the establishment of legal paternity. In addition to funding demonstration projects, state programs could also recognize noncash contributions, including child care and participation in education and training programs designed to increase future earnings, as legitimate ways to meet parental obligations.

The Children's Defense Fund (CDF) has called for society to insist that young men accept personal responsibility for the children they father and, when necessary, to help these fathers fulfill their responsibility for young families. Calling attention to rising unemployment and declining earnings among young men, CDF suggests that the minimum wage be increased, that job creation efforts be mounted in low-income communities, and that basic support services be provided all families unable to earn enough to support their families (Children's Defense Fund 1988).

Addressing these needs of the fathers, the Indianapolis program and others serving young fathers offer education, training, and employment opportunities. The Maryland Child Support Administration has proposed the development of a similar program. Florida, Michigan, and Maryland provide job clubs to adjudicated noncustodial fathers in AFDC cases. These programs operate on the assumption that a short-term investment in the father will reap long-term benefits for the father, mother, and child. Increasing enforcement without building capacity among young fathers is unlikely to net increases in child support payments.

IN-KIND AND FLEXIBLE LEVELS OF SUPPORT. Broadening the definition of support to include nonmonetary support allows young parents to define immediate responsible behavior within their limited and erratic income patterns, while also enhancing their long-term earnings capacity through school completion and job training. However, with one exception (in Indiana), state and federal law and regulation measure child support only in cash contributions. This narrowly defines the accepted range of responsible behavior by young fathers, who are more likely to be unemployed or underemployed, to have irregular employment, and to have lower wages than older fathers. While responsible and supportive behavior among young fathers is documented in several recent studies, it is not recognized by the courts or child support agencies unless in the form of cash payments (Danziger and Radin 1990; Sullivan, Chapter 3 in this volume). Recognizing in-kind support of food, clothes, and so on in lieu of cash payments has been widely discussed as a way of formally recognizing the informal support and participation of young fathers in the lives of their children.

Long-Run Impact

The authors of the Family Support Act and many state and local policymakers believe that a child support system that encourages the father's assumption of parental responsibility is an important profamily policy. It may discourage unwed parenthood and encourage our youth to consider more carefully the consequences of their sexual behavior before rather than after the fact. If designed to help *both* young unwed parents in fulfilling their obligations to the child, it may even promote better father-child relations. Innovations currently being tested could transform the current system into a well-designed set of services oriented to the child's welfare, rather than a complex array of quasi-criminal legal proceedings geared to collecting support payments and reimbursing public expenditures. The new federal guidelines and state and local efforts at administrative change should help this process and improve the opportunities for the children of young unwed fathers.

References

Barth, R. P., M. Claycomb, and A. Loomis. 1988. "Services to Adolescent Fathers." *Health and Social Work* 13:277–286.

Brown, S. 1990. "If the Shoes Fit: Final Program Implementation Guide of the Maine Young Fathers Project." Portland: University of Southern Maine.

Browning, C. D. 1987. "The Burden of Proof in a Paternity Action." *Journal of Family Law* 25:357–372.

Children's Defense Fund. 1988. "Adolescent and Young Adult Fathers: Problems and Solutions." Washington, D.C.: Adolescent Pregnancy Prevention Clearinghouse.

Danziger, S. K., and A. Nichols-Casebolt. 1988. "Teen Parents and Child Support: Eligibility, Participation and Payment." *Journal of Social Services Research* 11:1–20.

Danziger, S. K., and N. Radin. 1990. "Absent Does Not Equal Uninvolved: Predictors of Fathering in Teen Mother Families." *Journal of Marriage and the Family* 52:636–642.

Ellwood, D. 1988. *Poor Support: Poverty in the American Family.* New York: Basic Books.

Everett, J. E. 1988. "Child Support Enforcement: Barriers in Serving Young Families." In *Child Support Services for Young Families: Current Issues and Future Directions*, edited by C. Kastner, 63–73. Washington, D.C.: Center for the Support of Children.

Furstenberg, F. 1988. "Good Dads—Bad Dads: Two Faces of Fatherhood." In *The Changing American Family and Public Policy*, edited by A. Cherlin, 193–218. Washington, D.C.: Urban Institute Press.

Furstenberg, F., K. Sherwood, and M. Sullivan. 1992. *Caring and Paying: What Fathers and Mothers Say about Child Support*. New York: Manpower Demonstration Research Corporation.

Garfinkel, I., and S. McLanahan. 1986. *Single Mothers and Their Children: A New American Dilemma*. Washington, D.C.: Urban Institute Press.

Horowitz, R., and H. Davidson. 1984. *Legal Rights of Children*. Colorado Springs: Shepard's/McGraw Hill.

Kahn, A., and S. Kamerman. 1988. *Child Support: From Debt Collection to Social Policy*. Beverly Hills, Calif.: Sage Publications.

Kohn, M. 1987. "Child Support Enforcement and Young Unwed Fathers." Catholic University Conference Paper.

Krause, H. 1981. *Child Support in America: The Legal Perspective*. Charlottesville, Va.: Michie.

Marsiglio, W. 1987. "Adolescent Fathers in the United States: Their Initial Living Arrangements, Marital Experience, and Educational Outcomes." *Family Planning Perspectives* 19:240–251.

Melli, M. 1984. *Child Support: A Survey of the Statutes*. Special Report. Madison, Wis.: Institute for Research on Poverty.

Pirog-Good, M. 1993. "In-Kind Contributions as Child Support." Chapter 12 in current volume.

Sullivan, M. 1993. "Young Fathers and Parenting in Two Inner-City Neighborhoods." Chapter 3 in current volume.

U.S. Bureau of the Census. 1989. *Child Support and Alimony: 1985*. Current Population Reports. Series p-23, no. 154. Supplemental Report. Washington, D.C.: Government Printing Office.

William T. Grant Foundation. 1988. *The Forgotten Half: Pathways to Success for America's Youth and Families*. Commission on Work, Family and Citizenship. Washington, D.C.

12   In-Kind Contributions as Child Support:

The Teen Alternative Parenting Program

MAUREEN A. PIROG-GOOD

Defaults on child support obligations exceed \$4 billion annually (Horowitz 1985). Lack of child support by noncustodial fathers clearly contributes to the fact that nearly half of the children living in households headed by women are poor (Corbett 1986). Given that most teenage fathers are full-time students, unemployed, and come from low-income families, it is not surprising that their child support compliance is worse than average and that most of their child support is unpaid (Rivera-Casale, Klerman, and Manela 1984).

The poor support compliance of teenage fathers is not a trivial matter, given that between two and ten percent of all teenage boys will father a premarital pregnancy (Elster and Panzarine 1983; Lerman 1986). In fact, several studies have shown that the single largest source of support of teenage mothers and their children is the AFDC program (Klerman 1985). It has been estimated that more than half of all AFDC disbursements are paid to households in which the mother was a teenager when her first child was born (Wertheimer and Moore 1982).

In response to the escalating burden on poverty programs of nonsupport of children by noncustodial parents, Congress passed the 1984 Child Support Enforcement Amendments, requiring states to use proven enforcement techniques for the collection of child support. Although cost-effective (Royce 1981), child support enforcement techniques are typically punitive sanctions imposed when the obligor has defaulted on his support payments. While the severity of the sanctions imposed relate to the ability of the obligor to pay support (Turner 1985), it is not obvious how teenage fathers have fared under the 1984 amendments. Young fathers typically experience a variety of social and economic disadvantages, including less education, more limited access to prestigious jobs, and more frequent experiences of racism and poverty than their nonfather contemporaries (Chilman 1980; Card and Wise 1978).

If young fathers have too little income to pay child support, perhaps they can be encouraged to assist mothers and children with in-kind services and to invest in themselves so they can provide cash support in the future. The Marion County (Indianapolis) Child Support Enforcement Unit (CSEU) decided to test this idea, offering young fathers the chance to earn credits against their child support obligations by engaging in visitation, parenting classes, schooling, and training. This paper addresses two questions: (1) To what extent did young fathers take up the offer? and (2) Did the credits stimulate increased family involvement or education and training among youth fathers?

Traditional Child Support Enforcement

When the Social Security Act established the Aid to Dependent Children program (today's AFDC program) in 1935, most children were eligible for welfare because their fathers were deceased. In contrast, by 1982, the Department of Health and Human Services determined that 86 percent of AFDC children had parents living outside the home (U.S. Government Accounting Office 1987). Moreover, more than 10 percent of the 62 million children in the United States receive assistance from AFDC, and total disbursements in 1985 were $14 billion. Concerned with the escalating costs of the AFDC program and the social effects of the paternal abandonment of children, Congress unanimously amended title IV-D of the Social Security Act to enact the Child Support Amendments of 1984, P. L. 98-378.

The 1984 amendments contain a variety of enforcement provisions including expanded use of state and federal income tax refund interception, the use of liens and bonds, reports to consumer credit agencies when support delinquencies are in excess of $1,000, and automatic income withholding when the arrearage equals one month of support (Horowitcz 1985). Bench warrants for arrest are issued when the obligor is found in contempt of court, a situation where the errant parent willfully fails or refuses to provide court-ordered support (Turner 1985).

The Family Support Act of 1988, P. L. 100-485, strengthened enforcement efforts further by requiring mandatory wage withholding in all support cases unless good cause can be demonstrated or a written agreement is reached between both parties which provides for an alternative arrangement. In addition, this act mandated that state guidelines concerning the amount of child support awards be utilized and set targets for states in the establishment of paternity cases.

Apparently, the processing of paternity and child support cases among young unwed fathers has varied significantly across states. Prior to the 1984 amendments a study (Rivera-Casale, Klerman, and Manela 1984) of five New England states found that unwed teenage fathers are liable for child support in Connecticut and Massachusetts, but are not typically prosecuted or are not liable for support in Rhode Island, Vermont, or Maine.

Like Massachusetts, Indiana makes no distinction between minors and adults as it pertains to paternity establishment or child support enforcement. Thus, the support orders of young men are enforced with automatic income withholding, the interception of income tax refunds, liens, credit bureau reporting and, in cases of contempt of court, jail. Estimates of activity among young absent fathers in Marion County, Indiana, showed that 62 percent had child support automatically withheld from their paychecks, 53 percent were given notice that liens would be placed against their real property due to support arrearage, 35 percent were reported to the local credit bureau for arrears in excess of $1,000, 21 percent were issued bench warrants for their arrest, and 8 percent were required to give proof that they had gone on job interviews but were unable to find employment.[1] Thus, in Indiana, as elsewhere, the relationship between the Child Support Enforcement Unit (CSEU) and the noncustodial parent is adversarial.

The Teen Alternative Parenting Program

In the summer of 1986 the Marion County CSEU started the Teen Alternative Parenting Program (TAPP) to encourage participants to pay part or all of their weekly child support obligation (typically set at the minimum of $25/week) through in-kind payments or credits. Young fathers could earn credits for maintaining a regular visitation schedule with their child, continuing school or pursuing a GED, participating in parenting classes and/or job or vocational training classes. The TAPP program formalized the credit system through one or more individualized ninety-day contracts between the custodial and noncustodial parents and the CSEU. For the duration of their participation in TAPP, other actions for noncompliance with a child support order such as involuntary income withholding, reporting arrears to local credit rating bureaus, and incarceration were suspended.

The objective of TAPP is to improve child support compliance by increasing the willingness and long-run ability of young men to pay child support. To encourage the absent father's willingness to pay child support, the program provides credits for regularly visiting his child and attending child care classes. The hope is that these in-kind credits will stimulate added visitation and involvement and thus strengthen the bond between fathers and their children. Previous research has found that among divorced men, those with strong bonds to their children prior to the divorce, pay more child support (Pearson and Thonnes 1985). Similarly, there is evidence that more child support is paid by men who have regular contact with their children (Chambers 1979; Wallerstein and Huntington 1983; Furstenberg et al. 1983). Men who already have strong bonds to their children may visit more often, but frequent visitation may also serve to maintain and strengthen father-child attachments.

Because young fathers typically have unrealistically high expectations of the abilities of young children (DeLissovoy 1973; Field et al. 1980), many TAPP participants are referred to parenting classes designed to educate young men about the developmental stages of children, appropriate methods of interacting with children, and child care. Such knowledge may serve to mitigate the frustration of young fathers who interact with their child.

TAPP is also designed to improve the long-run ability of young men to pay child support by investing in their human capital. Thus, TAPP provides in-kind credit for young men who regularly attend school or GED classes. There is ample evidence that young fathers have lower educational goals and poorer educational achievement than their nonfather contemporaries (Chilman 1980; Hendricks and Montgomery 1984; Card and Wise 1978; Lerman 1986). This necessarily compromises their long-term employment and vocational opportunities and consequently their ability to adequately support their children. TAPP credits for school attendance, job training, or work towards a GED represent an effort to reduce the educational disadvantage of young fathers. TAPP schedules preemployment and vocational training whenever a young father is unemployed or underemployed. Some young men are taught how to apply for a job. This involves help with résumé preparation and advice about proper demeanor, as well as loans of professional-looking clothing, for interviews. Some fathers have participated in short training courses in fast-food industries, truck driving, and so on. Substantial research indicates that young fathers often lack marketable skills, experience prolonged periods of unemployment (Gilchrist and Schinke 1983), and have lower occupational attainment as adults (Card and Wise 1978).

Finally, the CSEU hopes to use the promotion of investments in human capital and parent involvement to reduce the adversarial nature of the agency's relationship with the absent parent. TAPP literature provided to participants describes an agency that wants to work with rather than against the absent parent. The idea is that, if participants believe that TAPP counselors are interested in their well-being, they may become more willing to pay their support obligations.

The administrative process evolved in several stages. The first was obtaining agreement from the Indiana Department of Public Welfare to accept the in-kind payments of program participants in lieu of cash. The department initially refused on grounds that TAPP credits would substitute for money owed to the state and federal governments. After several months of negotiation, approval to implement TAPP finally came from the Family Services Federal Administration in the Department of Health and Human Services. TAPP is the only program nationwide that permits the child support of AFDC recipients to be paid with in-kind contributions.

Second, an administrative change took place in the program in the first two years of TAPP's operation. Initially, only $12.50, or half of the weekly support obligation, could be paid with in-kind payments. This restriction on in-kind credit ensured that when the absent parent was in compliance with the support order, the custodial parent on welfare would benefit by $50, since AFDC recipients may keep the first $50 of child support without any reduction in their AFDC benefits. Subsequently, TAPP participants have been allowed to negotiate all of their support order with in-kind credit. However, because each TAPP contract is signed by the custodial and noncustodial parents as well as a TAPP counselor, control over the $50 disregard payment can still be exercised by the custodial parent.

Third, the CSEU decided to offer TAPP to young men regardless of whether or not their children were AFDC recipients. As of the collection of the data for this study, all non–AFDC mothers agreed to participate in TAPP despite the fact that this meant a potential loss of child support. However, only twelve of the sixty-three women who were involved with TAPP were not AFDC recipients.

Finally, GED, parenting, and job training classes are now provided by local, nonprofit agencies at no cost to program participants or the prosecutor's office. Because arrangements for services are with a number of nonprofit agencies, there is some variation in the quality of some services provided, and other services, specifically the parenting classes, have been available to participants only on an irregular basis.

The Data

The data for the sixty-three individuals offered the TAPP option and a matched comparison group of sixty-three nonparticipants were collected during January and February of 1988. Demographic and support compliance information were recorded for program and comparison group members. Additionally, TAPP participation data were recorded for the sixty-three individuals who were offered the option of participating in TAPP. In cases where a young man had support orders for more than one child, the child with the earliest support order was selected for the subsequent statistical analyses.

The comparison group members had an active child support order from the Marion County CSEU, but were not offered the option of joining TAPP. The characteristics used to match the two groups included the race of the father, the age of the father when the child support order started, and whether or not the custodial parent was an AFDC recipient. These characteristics were chosen because evidence exists to indicate that, over the relevant range, support compliance increases with age (U.S. Bureau of the Census 1987). Similarly, because minorities face greater discrimination in the labor force, a comparison group comprised of fewer minorities would have greater access to legitimate means of earning income, and hence means of paying support.

The program and comparison samples included AFDC and non–AFDC custodial parents. Because non–AFDC parents retain all support payments while AFDC parents do not, the incentives to participate in TAPP should be higher for absent fathers whose children are on welfare. Custodial mothers on welfare would be more likely to agree to the substitution of in-kind services for cash, since they would gain little money (at most $50 per month) even if the father made support payments.

The reasons why some young men were offered TAPP, while others were not, are not clear. The CSEU intended to offer TAPP to all eligible young men. However, given a caseload in excess of 65,000, limited staff, and limited access to nonprofit agency services, the enrollment of young men into TAPP was not aggressively pursued. A special computer run, generated for the purposes of this research, clearly indicated that far fewer than half of the eligible population were approached about TAPP. Statistical analyses concerning these two groups suggests only minor differences between those who were or were not offered TAPP. For these reasons the activities of the comparison group provide a good indication of what the TAPP group would have undertaken in the absence of TAPP.

Characteristics of Individuals Offered TAPP versus Comparison Group Members

Most of the young fathers in the study sample were nonwhite and had children on welfare. On average, they were only between eighteen and nineteen years of age at the time of their first child support order, about a year after they had become fathers. Some 80 percent of both groups had children on welfare and about two-thirds had voluntarily accepted paternity. Most had only one child. The only significant difference between the two groups is in the proportion who ever held a job; 81 percent of the TAPP group, but only 63 percent of the comparison group, reported holding a job. This suggests that those individuals offered TAPP may have been somewhat more employable than those in the comparison group.

Characteristics of Young Men Offered TAPP

Of the 63 young men offered the option to join TAPP, 12 refused, 17 signed at least one TAPP contract but never actually participated, 29 signed contracts and participated in the program, and 5 had just been invited to join the program but had not had the opportunity to sign a contract. Thus, as Table 12-1 shows, of the fifty-eight young men who had the option and opportunity to participate, 50 percent actually participated. Those who ultimately refused to participate (by refusing outright or by completely failing to comply with TAPP contracts) were more likely to have children who were AFDC recipients and to have held a job than those who actually participated in TAPP. This suggests that individuals who had greater employability and better means to pay child support as well as individuals whose support was used to defray AFDC expenses self-selected out of TAPP.

Participation in Specific TAPP Activities

Participation in activities that could generate in-kind child support was far less than had been anticipated. Only half of those offered TAPP engaged in any activity, and only a handful engaged in anything other than visitation. The modest to low percent of TAPP eligibles who actually undertook TAPP activities that provided in-kind credits suggests that many teen fathers do not concern themselves with the possible sanctions imposed by the CSEU for nonsupport.

To arrive at participation rates for each of the TAPP activities, the TAPP contract of each participant was examined to determine which activities were included as well as the extent to which these contractual obligations were met. Each TAPP contract was tailored to meet the needs

TABLE 12-1 Characteristics of Young Men Offered TAPP

	TAPP participants (N = 29)	Refused TAPP (N = 29)	Just started, no contract (N = 5)
Average age when support order started	18.46	18.73	17.56
Nonwhite (%)	86	90	100
Males whose children are AFDC recipients (%)	72	90	80
Average age at birth of child	17.86	18.02	17.05
Average number of children	1.17	1.34	1.0
Ever had a job (%)	69**	93**	80
Voluntary paternity (%)	69	72	80
Average number of years with a child support order	1.01	1.10	.23
Weekly support obligation	$21.55	$24.14	$22.50

*Statistically reliable at the 10-percent significance level.
**Statistically reliable at the 5-percent significance level.

of both the absent and the custodial parent, and hence not all young fathers were able to obtain in-kind credit for all TAPP activities. For example, one father was attending a college a great distance from his child and consequently, TAPP credit for visitation was not part of his contract. Similarly, credit for high school attendance or GED class participation was not offered to high school graduates.

Table 12-2 indicates the number and percentage of those signing contracts who were offered TAPP credit for visitation, job training or counseling, school or GED class attendance, and attendance at parenting classes. The activities most frequently appearing in TAPP contracts were visitation (76%) followed by parenting classes (72%), job training or counseling (50%), and school or GED class attendance (41%).

By far, the activity for which most young men received TAPP credit is visitation; 77 percent of those offered TAPP credit for regularly visiting their child received such credit. An average of $72.86 in TAPP credit was provided for those twenty-seven fathers who maintained a regular visitation schedule. Because we were unable to obtain reliable visitation data for treatment and control samples, it is difficult to determine the impact of TAPP on visitation. The best available evidence from other data sources indicates that 63.3 percent of fathers absent from AFDC households headed by adolescent mothers visit their infants at least once a week (Danziger 1988). However, this percentage diminishes monoto-

TABLE 12-2 Participation in TAPP

	Number offered TAPP credit (%)	Number who received TAPP credit (%)	Total amount of TAPP credit given (average amount)
Visitation	35	27	$1,967.25
	(76)	(77)	($72.86)
Job training/ counseling	23	5	$ 118.00
	(50)	(22)	($23.60)
School/GED	19	8	$ 402.00
	(41)	(42)	($50.25)
Parenting classes	33	3	$ 57.00
	(72)	(9)	($19.00)
Any of above	46	29	$2,544.25
	(100)	(63)	($87.73)

nically to 24.4 percent by the time the child exceeds age three. For those young men offered TAPP credit for visitation, their children were, on average, slightly over six months of age when their support orders became effective. Thus, the 77 percent of TAPP participants offered visitation credit who actually maintained a regular visitation schedule with their children compares favorably to the 44.8 percent of absent fathers who maintain regular contact with their children, six months to one year of age. Thus, it would appear that TAPP participants offered visitation credit may have more contact with their children. Nonetheless, because not all fathers absent from AFDC households are teenagers and because of differences in the definitions and duration of regular visitation, this finding should be viewed cautiously.

Approximately 40 percent of those offered TAPP were high school dropouts. Similarly, 40 percent of the young men in a national probability sample who eventually became absent parents were high school dropouts (Lerman 1986). TAPP credit for school or GED attendance was offered to 41 percent of those individuals with TAPP contracts. Of those individuals offered credit for school/GED attendance, only eight individuals (42%) accrued any such credit. An average of $50.25 was provided to those individuals who partially or completely fulfilled the school/GED component of their TAPP contracts.

Only five or 22 percent of the individuals who were offered TAPP credit for job training or counseling actually received TAPP credit for participating in these activities. Since job training courses and counseling were regularly available to TAPP participants, this low level of participation is probably best explained by a lack of interest on the part of participants.

Parenting classes attracted the lowest amount of TAPP participation. While 72 percent of those individuals signing TAPP contracts were referred to the parenting classes, only three individuals, or 9 percent, actually attended one or more parenting classes. Unlike job training and counseling, however, the parenting classes were not offered on a regular basis, and many participants complained that the location of the classes was inconvenient. Thus, the low participation rate in these classes should not necessarily be construed as reflecting a lack of interest in learning parenting skills on the part of those referred.

Teenage fathers come disproportionately from low-income, minority households. Their early school and employment experiences are considerably worse than average (Lerman 1986). Moreover, among absent teenage fathers with paternity suits, nearly 50 percent have juvenile court records for offenses unrelated to paternity (Pirog-Good 1988). Thus, these young men constitute a population which is exceptionally difficult to service. This, in conjunction with the fact that some young men self-selected out of TAPP because they were willing and able to pay their child support, helps to explain the low TAPP participation rates. Although some may express concern for this low participation, the local CSEU argues that TAPP is offered for those young men who are willing, but currently unable, to meet their fiscal responsibilities. TAPP was never designed to ameliorate the problems of recalcitrant or problem youths, but rather is offered as a nonadversarial alternative for paying child support.

Child Support Owed and Paid

Evidence on the potential impact of TAPP on child support compliance appears in Table 12-3. Comparison group members owed and paid more child support than the individuals offered TAPP. However, these differences can be attributed to a combination of two factors unrelated to TAPP. First, the weekly child support obligations of the comparison group members were 12 percent larger than the support obligations of individuals offered TAPP. Second, on average, the child support orders of the comparison group members had been effective for two months longer than those of the individuals offered TAPP. These facts also largely explain the greater amount of support paid by comparison group members ($27,508.44 versus $17,878.05).

Because of the differences in the length and size of the support orders, the more appropriate measure of a potential TAPP impact is the propor-

TABLE 12-3 Child Support Compliance

	Offered TAPP (N = 63)	Comparison group (N = 63)
Average number of years with child support order	.99	1.18
Weekly support obligation	$22.82**	$25.63**
Child support paid (%)		
Cash only	30	31
Cash and TAPP credit	34	—
Child support		
Owed	$59,710.00***	$88,538.10***
Paid-cash only	17,878.05*	27,508.44*
Paid-cash and TAPP credit	20,546.30	—

Note: The population of individuals offered TAPP was matched with a sample of young men who were not offered the option of joining TAPP, based on average age, race, and AFDC–recipiency status.
*Statistically reliable at the 10-percent significance level.
**Statistically reliable at the 5-percent significance level.
***Statistically reliable at the 1-percent significance level.

tion of child support owed that was paid. Table 12-3 shows that TAPP and comparison groups did not differ in the percentage of support paid. Further, no significant differences appeared, even when one included the credit provided for in-kind services. Thus, on the basis of outcomes for this sample, young fathers who were able to substitute in-kind activities for cash payments did not respond by increasing their overall compliance with child support obligations.

Child Support Owed and Paid to Offset AFDC Disbursement

In Table 12-4 one can examine the short-run impact of the implementation of TAPP on AFDC receipts for those men offered the program. The total amount of money owed to the AFDC program was 44 percent greater for those individuals who were not offered TAPP. This was due to the fact that those who were not offered TAPP had larger support orders that had been effective for a longer period of time than the individuals offered TAPP.

Individuals offered TAPP reimbursed the AFDC program over a full year a *total* of $107.78 in *cash*, or .004 percent of what was owed. While comparison group members had better compliance records, they were hardly exemplary. Over an average of 1.18 years, they reimbursed AFDC a total of $724.00, or .017 percent of what was owed. If those offered

TABLE 12-4 Support Owed and Paid to Offset AFDC Disbursements

	Offered TAPP (N = 51)[a]	Not offered TAPP (N = 51)
Total amount owed AFDC	$30,400.75	$43,772.63
Average amount owed AFDC	569.09	858.29
Total amount paid to AFDC[b]		
Cash	107.78	724.00
TAPP credit	2,018.75	.00
Total	2,126.53	724.00
Average amount paid to AFDC		
Cash	2.11	14.20
TAPP credit	39.58	.00
Total	41.69	14.20
Percent of AFDC obligation paid		
Cash	4	7
TAPP credit	7	0
Total	7.4	1.7

[a]Only 51 of the 63 individuals in TAPP and comparison groups had children who were AFDC recipients.

[b]The total amount paid to AFDC was estimated by assuming that the total support paid by absent fathers was made in monthly installments. Thus, because support payments are generally irregular, the amount paid AFDC is an underestimate of the true amount. For example, if a youth had a support order and had paid $100 over three months, then his average monthly payment would be $33.33, less than the $50 disregard, so that given the estimation procedure used, nothing would be paid to AFDC. If, however, the youth had only paid support in a single month, $50 would be paid to the absent parent and $50 would offset AFDC expenditures.

TAPP paid *cash* at the same rate as the comparison group members, the AFDC program would have been reimbursed an additional $395.21. Thus, the cost of TAPP in terms of lost AFDC revenues was relatively small for the eighteen months of operation covered in this study.

Table 12-4 also indicates that if TAPP credit is included in the AFDC reimbursements, then individuals who were offered TAPP reimbursed the program a total of $2,126.53, or .074 per cent of the amount due. Some of the activities for which in-kind credit was provided are designed to enhance the long-run employability and support compliance of participants. At the same time, encouraging these men to attend school and participate in job training or GED classes diminishes their short-run employability and their ability to make cash payments against child support awards. Still, when in-kind credit is included as part of support compliance, individuals offered TAPP appear to outperform comparison group members by a factor of four. However, since information on the voluntary visitation, education, and training activities of comparison group members is not available, an accurate comparison of the value of cash *and* in-kind payments for the two groups cannot be established.

In addition to the above analyses I estimated statistical models to determine the impacts of having been offered TAPP, of the level of TAPP participation, and of the type of TAPP participation on child support compliance. These models controlled for the observed differences in the TAPP and comparison groups including the weekly amount of the support obligation, the number of children with support obligations, race, AFDC–recipiency status of the custodial parent, whether or not the absent parent had ever had a job, and his age at the beginning of the support pay order. The TAPP participation variables did not show up as a significant predictor of child support compliance, partly because of the small sample size. However, two variables did have a significant impact—whether or not the absent father had ever held a job and the father's age at the beginning of the support order. As one would expect, individuals with some record of employment and older fathers at the time they were required to start paying child support showed better compliance records.

Conclusions and Program Update

TAPP has been an innovative program designed to offer an alternative mechanism for the payment of child support by young absent fathers. After the completion of this study's data collection phase in 1990, TAPP was renamed the "On Track" program but maintained the same overall structure and approach. Since 1990 the program has increased the emphasis on educating teen fathers concerning child support and the family court, eliminated the credit for parenting classes, reimplemented the requirement that teen fathers pay at least half of their child support in cash, and extended some credits for obtaining/maintaining a job.

Even with these changes, this program continues to stand in stark contrast to the often harsh and impractical traditional methods of collecting child support from young fathers (Pirog-Good and Good 1990; Good and Pirog-Good 1989). Young absent fathers typically do not own property on which liens can be placed. Automatic wage withholding is an administrative nightmare when employment is sporadic at best. It is unclear whether imprisonment is desirable or effective in eking out child support from young men who are usually in school, unemployed, and living in low-income households.

Unfortunately, the innovative effort to encourage youth fathers by providing credits for parenting, education, and training achieved meager results. Even taking account of the value of in-kind payments, the percentage of support paid by those offered TAPP and the comparison group was

remarkably similar. While this was due in part to the low levels of participation in TAPP, it is encouraging to note that those individuals who self-
selected out of TAPP appear to have proved somewhat more employable,
and hence able to pay their child support. In fact, in several instances, the
young men who chose not to take advantage of TAPP obtained jobs and
married or moved in with the custodial parent.

On the positive side, the short-run costs of operating TAPP borne by
the AFDC program were minimal, and preliminary evidence suggests that
when the value of in-kind contributions is considered, those offered
TAPP outperformed the comparison group in reimbursing AFDC.

Many government and government-sponsored agencies attempt to improve the educational achievement of teenagers, reduce school dropout
rates, reform juvenile delinquents, reduce drug dependency, and improve
the employability of our youth. These programs are often targeted specifically at low-income teenagers who are often minorities and from broken
families. Since young men who father out-of-wedlock children and who
have court-mandated support orders are drawn disproportionately from
this population, it is ironic that traditional child support enforcement tac-
tics run counter to our attempts to assist these young men. While the
importance of parental obligations should not be denied, greater inter-
governmental cooperation is required to coordinate the child support enforcement efforts for young men with the efforts of other agencies concerned with the well-being of this population. TAPP, a unique program
nationally, offers one mechanism whereby this coordination can be
achieved. Through the joint efforts of CSEU, the AFDC program, and
local nonprofit agencies, a more humane method of support collection is
offered for those individuals who choose to participate.

Finally, because TAPP is designed to improve the parenting, education, and employability of young men, not all of the potential societal
benefits of the program have been measured and included in this study.
Many of the program's components are designed to improve long- rather
than short-run support compliance. A sufficient amount of time has yet to
elapse to determine the magnitude of these long-run benefits.

Note

1. These percentages were computed from the comparison group data obtained for this study and described in the data section of this article.

References

Card, Josefina J., and Lauress L. Wise. 1978. "Teenage Mothers and Teenage Fathers: The Impact of Early Childbearing on the Parents' Personal and Professional Lives." *Family Planning Perspectives* 10:199–205.

Chambers, David. 1979. *Making Fathers Pay: The Enforcement of Child Support*. Chicago: University of Chicago Press.

Chilman, Catherine. 1980. "Social and Psychological Research Concerning Adolescent Childbearing, 1970–1980." *Journal of Marriage and the Family* 42:793–805.

Corbett, Tom. 1986. "Child Support Assurance: Wisconsin Demonstration." *Focus* 9(1):1–5.

Danziger, Sandra K. 1988. "Father Involvement in Welfare Families Headed by Adolescent Mothers." Working paper 87-88-04. School of Social Work. Ann Arbor: University of Michigan.

DeLissovoy, Vladimir. 1973. "Child Care by Adolescent Parents." *Children Today* July–August:22–25.

Elster, Arthur B., and Susan Panzarine. 1983. "Adolescent Fathers." In *Premature Adolescent Pregnancy and Parenthood*, edited by E. R. McArney. New York: Grune & Stratton.

Field, T., et al. 1980. "Teenage Lower Class Mothers and Their Preterm Infants: An Intervention and Developmental Follow-Up." *Child Development* 51:426–436.

Furstenberg, Frank F., et al. 1983. "The Life Course of Children of Divorce: Marital Disruption and Parental Contact." *American Sociological Review* 48:656–658.

Gilchrist, Lewayne D., and Paul Schinke. 1983. "Teenage Pregnancy and Public Policy." *Social Service Review* June:307–322.

Good, David H., and Maureen A. Pirog-Good. 1989. "Patterns of Heterogeneity and Their Implications for the Processes Generating Teenage Paternities and Crimes." *Sociological Methods and Research* 17(4):402–425. May.

Hendricks, Leo E., and Teresa A. Montgomery. 1984. "Educational Achievement and Locus of Control Among Black Adolescent Fathers." *Journal of Negro Research* 53:182–188.

Horowitz, Robert M. 1985. "The Child Support Amendments of 1984." *Juvenile and Family Court Journal* 36(3):5–26.

Klerman, Lorraine V. 1985. "The Economic Impact of School-Age Child Rearing." In *School-Age Pregnancy and Parenthood: Biosocial Dimensions*. New York: Aldine De Gruyter.

Lerman, Robert I. 1986. "Who Are Young Absent Parents?" *Youth and Society* 18(1):3–27.

Pearson, Jessica, and Nancy Thonnes. 1985. "Child Custody, Child Support Arrangements and Child Support Payment Patterns." *Juvenile and Family Court Journal* 36:49–56.

Pirog-Good, Maureen A. 1988. "Teenage Paternity, Child Support and Crime" *Social Science Quarterly* 69(3):527–546. September.

Pirog-Good, Maureen A., and David H. Good. 1990. "Child Support Enforcement for Teenage Fathers: Problems and Prospects." Unpublished manuscript.

Rivera-Casale, Cecilia, Lorraine V. Klerman, and Roger Manela. 1984. "The Relevance of Child-Support Enforcement to School-Age Parents." *Child Welfare* 63(6):521–532.

Royce, Carolyn K. 1981. "One Road to Welfare Reform." *State Legislatures* July–August:29–33.

Turner, Kenneth. 1985. "Contempt and Punishment for Nonsupport." *Juvenile and Family Court Journal* 36(3):87–92.

U.S. Bureau of the Census. 1987. *Child Support and Alimony: 1985.* Current Population Reports. Series p-23, no. 152. (Advance data from March–April 1986 Current Population Surveys.) Washington, D.C.: Government Printing Office.

U.S. Government Accounting Office. 1987. *Child Support: Need to Improve Efforts to Identify Fathers and Obtain Support Orders.* Report to the Secretary of Health and Human Services. Washington, D.C.: Government Printing Office.

Wallerstein, Judith, and Dorothy S. Huntington. 1983. "Bread and Roses: Nonfinancial Issues Related to Fathers' Economic Support of Their Children Following Divorce." In *The Parental Child Support Obligation: Research, Practice and Social Policy,* edited by Judith Cassetty. Lexington, Mass.: Lexington Books, D. C. Heath.

Wertheimer, R. F., and K. A. Moore. 1982. *Teenage Childbearing: Public Sector Costs.* Washington, D.C.: Urban Institute.

13   Involving Unwed Fathers in Adoption Counseling and Teen Pregnancy Programs

M. LAURIE LEITCH, ANNE M. GONZALEZ, AND THEODORA J. OOMS

Most teenage pregnancies are not a result of a casual sexual encounter but of a relationship between a man and young woman of at least a few months' duration. It is important therefore to ask to what extent do health care professionals, social workers, and others reach out to include the baby's father when they provide services to unwed pregnant teens and teen mothers? How is he involved, if at all, in decisions about the pregnancy and the care of his child? What are service providers' views of the role and responsibilities of young fathers when they are not married to the young mothers?

To address these questions, this chapter draws primarily on the findings of an exploratory study of staff attitudes, practices, and policies towards the unwed father in a sample of twelve programs for adolescent mothers. To supplement these findings, the authors turn to a somewhat larger study designed to examine the broader issue of family involvement in teen parent programs which included some questions specifically related to involving the young unwed fathers.[1] Before describing the focus and design of these studies, we provide some historical background on the development of teenage pregnancy and parenting programs in general and how an interest in the young fathers began to evolve.

Background

Since the late seventies communities throughout the United States have set up programs designed to provide a wide range of health, education, and social services to pregnant teenagers and teenage mothers and their babies.[2] This trend was fueled by the Adolescent Pregnancy Act of 1978, which gave grants to community programs to provide, either on site or by referral, ten core services. Programs were encouraged to add additional services (Weatherley et al. 1986).

Prior to the seventies, services for unmarried mothers had traditionally consisted of residential maternity homes and counseling focused on helping the young mothers place their babies for adoption. By contrast, because the majority of today's unwed mothers keep their babies, these new community-based programs' main goals are to help these mothers prepare for and adapt to the various responsibilities of parenthood, including getting the necessary health care for themselves and their babies and preventing further pregnancies. Many programs also focus on helping the young mother complete her education. In 1981 a study identified over 1,000 community-based programs; of these, 25 percent were deemed comprehensive because they provided the ten core services listed in the Adolescent Pregnancy Act (cited in Weatherley et al. 1986).

This provision of publicly and privately subsidized services to support unwed mothers reflected a reversal of the centuries-old attitude towards "illegitimacy," in which the unmarried mother was stigmatized and shunned and the man who impregnated her was generally unaffected and seldom blamed (Young 1954). Gradually, as attitudes towards young unwed mothers became more supportive, attitudes towards the unwed fathers shifted, with an increasing emphasis on his responsibilities and, more recently, on his needs.

A few isolated articles in the professional literature had challenged both the stereotyping and program neglect of the young unwed fathers, but for the most part the social work and allied professions continued to ignore them (see, for example, Pannor, Nassarik, and Evans 1971; and Hendricks 1980). In 1978 a survey of a small sample of teen parent programs reported little to no involvement of staff with either the teen mother's family or the baby's father (Forbush 1981). It is interesting to note that in a book published in 1981 which explored the family context of adolescent pregnancy and parenting, none of the eleven contributors were able to cite data, research, or program experience related to the teen mothers' male partners (Ooms 1981). The young unwed fathers remained in the shadows, essentially invisible.

In the early eighties, reflecting a growing interest in the familial and social context of adolescent pregnancy, program practice began to shift a little. Gradually, increased attention began to be paid to the role and needs of the male when a teen woman became pregnant. Growing numbers of sex education and pregnancy prevention programs aimed at young men as well as women were established in schools and communities. The National Urban League launched a national pregnancy prevention public awareness campaign entitled "Encouraging Male Responsibility." There was a short-lived experiment in the seventies to target a handful of federally funded planning programs on young men, and in the eighties the school-based health clinic movement provided sexuality-related and other health services to male and female high school students. These shifts in practice represented a positive change by acknowledging both the responsibilities and the needs of the men and by at least attempting to reduce the burden (economic, social, and psychological) carried by the young women.

Some staff working in teen parent programs acknowledged that young pregnant women were much influenced by, and dependent upon, others who were close to them including their boyfriends, parents, siblings, and friends. Teenage pregnancy, in other words, began to be viewed systemically, both in terms of its effect on the teenager's significant others and the effect of their reactions and behavior on her (see, for example, Furstenberg 1981).

Researchers noted that, not surprisingly, a teen's pregnancy and giving birth often had an effect on the baby's father and his family. In one interesting study, interviews with the pregnant teen revealed that both the young father's and her parents attitudes had an important influence on her decision about how to resolve her pregnancy (Rosen 1980). And contrary to the stereotype, several new studies found that many young unwed fathers were in regular contact with their child's mother and provided varying degrees of practical and emotional support to her and their child (Elster and Lamb 1986; Parke and Neville 1987; Robinson 1988). Other studies have shown that the attitudes of the teenage mother's parents towards the father of the baby strongly influenced the amount of contact he was able to have both with her and with his child (Furstenberg 1981; Cervera 1991).

The focus of the service providers' lens began to widen to include the pregnant teenager's family context, and her relationship with the baby's father. Several studies noted that 80 percent or more of teen mothers continued to live with their parents or other relatives after the child was born. Some programs began to work more with the teen mother's family of origin, especially her mother, the baby's grandmother. A few programs initiated efforts to reach out to the young father, although many of them found it difficult to do so and became easily discouraged (Robinson 1988, Chap. 8).

In an attempt to learn more about how to involve young fathers several research and demonstration programs were funded (see Elster and Lamb

1986). The most ambitious of the program initiatives was the Teen Father Collaboration, funded by the Ford Foundation and specifically designed to serve teenage fathers by helping them in their roles as parents. The collaboration was situated in eight urban sites (see description in Chapter 15).

Among the various types of programs serving pregnant teens, those specializing in adoption counseling and placement were much less likely than multiservice agencies to involve unwed fathers, until a series of Supreme Court decisions, beginning in 1972, accorded the fathers some rights in the adoption decision (see Chapter 7). A few studies found that there were unwed fathers who wanted to be involved in the decision about whether to have an abortion and who were emotionally affected by an abortion (see Chapter 14). One study reported on a sample of birth fathers who were searching for their children, and another examined the attitudes of members of the adoption triangle—adoptive parents, birth mothers, adoptees—and adoption personnel towards the birth fathers and opening adoption records for them (Sachdev 1991).

In 1981 the federal Adolescent Family Life (AFL) Demonstration Projects was reauthorized under Title XX of the Public Health Services Act, which amended the original 1978 law. The legislation continued the grants program but added a new emphasis on research, prevention services, family involvement, and services to promote the adoption option. There was no separate mention of working with the unwed fathers, but in subsequent years the program officers issued various program guidelines to grantees to encourage them to involve young fathers. From 1981 through 1990 the AFL Office funded about 150 programs providing both prevention and care services and serving approximately 150,000 clients. After a decade since the beginning of this initiative it is important to ask to what extent the broad national network of community-based teen parent programs was following the lead of this small number of demonstration programs, and beginning to pay some attention to the baby's father and the father's extended family.

This chapter reports on two studies intended in part to address this question.[3] The studies were designed to explore the extent to which AFL demonstration programs were serving teen mothers, broadening their focus and strategy to include members of both the unwed mother's family and the unwed father and his family—both families being part of the baby's family system.

In neither study was the sample sufficiently large or representative to generalize the findings to the universe of teen pregnancy programs across the nation. However, the visibility of these federally funded demonstration programs and the fact that the grants were awarded in a competitive process suggest that the findings probably represent some of the best practices in the field. Among specific questions relating to unwed fathers, these studies focused on the following:

- What do teen pregnancy program staff view as the principal purpose, if any, of working directly with the baby's father? What is their attitude to his role, rights, and responsibilities?
- In practice how extensively do teen pregnancy programs work with young fathers? In what ways do staff try to involve them, and what is their response? What strategies appear to be successful?
- When the pregnant teen is considering adoption as a plan for her baby, to what extent do program staff involve the baby's father?
- To what extent do program staff work with either set of grandparents—the unwed mother's and/or the unwed father's?
- Is involving the young unwed father seen as a practice designed solely to provide more support for the teen mother, or is it part of a broader strategy, reflecting a family systems view of adolescent pregnancy and parenthood that gives weight to the father's needs, rights, and responsibilities?
- What are the program factors that either hinder or encourage working with the birth father and his family?
- How can family and father involvement (FI) best be measured? What evidence do we have, if any, of the effects of FI on the teen client, her child, and her relationship with her family and with her baby's father?

Study of Paternal Involvement in Teen Pregnancy Programs, 1986

The first study reported here was a small exploratory study conducted in 1986. Its findings were presented by two of the present authors (Leitch and Gonzalez) at the conference on Young Unwed Fathers held at Catholic University in Washington, D.C., in October 1986. Twelve teen pregnancy and parenting demonstration programs funded by the federal Adolescent Family Life Office were selected for the study because they had reported having provided some services to the clients' male partners and extended family members. Thus, these programs were chosen not because they were typical of program practice towards the young fathers, but rather because in this respect they appeared to be innovators. Ten programs were situated in urban sites; two in rural sites. The programs were based in a variety of settings: three in a hospital or clinic setting; the others in school settings or community social service agencies.

Telephone interviews were conducted with the staff person designated as most knowledgeable about the services provided to young fathers. In most cases these were line workers in the agency, although four respondents also had supervisory responsibilities. The agency staff welcomed the opportunity to share their "practice wisdom," and no one refused to be interviewed. Each interview took between forty to sixty minutes and followed a structured protocol covering five domains of interest:

1. Program, philosophy, and goals with respect to the baby's father and his family.
2. Extent and forms of paternal involvement.
3. Involvement of the father in the pregnancy decision process.
4. Involvement of the paternal family.
5. Family and program factors affecting paternal and family involvement.

Findings with respect to each of these domains will be summarized below.

Program Philosophy and Goals

Program staff were asked about their goals in involving the baby's father and, in a separate question, about involving the father's family, the paternal grandparents. The large majority of respondents clearly believed that the main purpose of involving the young father was to try to increase his support of the teen mother, both during pregnancy and after delivery. The young mother or mother-to-be was their primary client, the birth father was viewed simply in relation to her. For the most part, respondents did not see it as their job to assess the unwed father's feelings, reactions, or needs for services.

Additional goals mentioned included those related to the baby's psychological well-being, such as promoting father-infant bonding, and, in adoption counseling, goals related to the future adoptive parents (for example providing the father's complete medical history).

Only three of the twelve staff interviewed (two from urban sites, one from a rural site) articulated a more comprehensive set of goals for working with the unwed father. These included providing him with information about his rights, imparting parenting knowledge, improving his self-esteem, helping him become more responsible for sexual behavior, encouraging him to join a support group with his partner, providing referrals to GED and job-training programs and to counseling and drug treatment programs. The program staff did not volunteer that they placed an emphasis on helping the fathers establish legal paternity or child support.

Respondents cited a number of goals for working with the young father's family, although clearly the majority of programs only did so in a very small proportion of cases. Indeed, one respondent said her agency would seldom if ever involve the father's parents, even if the teen mother lived with them after the baby's birth.

Only four respondents stated that their agency mission was to provide services to all persons affected by the teen's pregnancy. In these programs the primary agenda of working with extended families was to help the grandparents on both sides be supportive of their children during the decision-making process. To do this, they frequently would have to defuse the emotional atmosphere so that the adolescent could fully participate in the decision about keeping the baby or placing it for adoption.

Another cited purpose of working with the paternal grandparents was to clarify what kind of emotional and financial support they might be willing and able to provide if the pregnant teen's decision was to keep the child. Availability of family support and resources was sometimes an important consideration in the decision not to place the baby for adoption. One agency worker had noted an increase in the numbers of pregnant teens who were planning to live with the birth father's family after delivery because the mother's own parents would not support her decision to keep the baby.

With respect to the adoption-counseling aspect of their services, two reasons were mentioned for working with the birth father's parents. The first was in situations where the birth father, usually supported by his family, was resisting the teen mother's plans for adoption. In this case the counselor would try to mediate between the families. The second was to help the grandparents on both sides work through their grief at losing a grandchild. Some believed that resolution of the grandparents' as well as the young parents' feelings of loss is essential if the adoption decision is to be sustained after the child's birth. Moreover, unresolved feelings of loss were thought to be associated with repeat pregnancies, although no research, to our knowledge, has yet been done to substantiate this belief.

Extent and Forms of Paternal Involvement

Program staff were asked about the ways in which they would typically involve birth fathers, and which of these ways seemed to be the most successful. With the exception of one program, all respondents said they tried to encourage the involvement of the baby's father as early as possible in the service delivery process. Those agencies providing pregnancy testing on site, which most of these programs did not, could raise the issue of whether or not the father should be informed when the pregnancy was first confirmed by positive test results. But most program staff did not begin efforts to get the father involved until somewhat later in the process. In all programs surveyed the father's involvement was contingent on the pregnant teen's cooperation and consent.

There were some variations between rural and urban programs in the reported availability of young fathers. In the urban programs the pregnant teens were more likely to say, especially at first, that the birth father was "just not around" or "I don't know where he's from" or deny that they knew his identity. This was in stark contrast to the response of a rural program respondent who said, "It's a very family-oriented population, lots of the fathers come in with the girl for the pregnancy testing." The other rural programs reported that the pregnant teens were usually ready from the beginning to involve the birth father. One rural respondent commented on how impressed she was with the degree of interest many fathers demonstrated in many aspects of the pregnancy. By contrast, an urban respondent emphasized the instability of clients' relationships with men. The respondents mentioned no striking differences in the extent of father involvement by race.

When asked what they would do if the pregnant teen initially refused to have the baby's father involved, only two respondents said that they would from that point on drop the issue.[4] Several respondents said that they would only push for the father's involvement if and when adoption became a real possibility. The others said they would continue to raise the issue in their contacts with their client and would try different strategies.

Program staff tried to assess the type of relationship the couple had in order to decide how to reach the father and involve him. Indeed, the quality of the couple's relationship was the strongest predictor of the birth father's involvement. Two respondents noted that the younger fathers were more cooperative than older males.

Some program staff said that they found it most effective to go out to meet the young father in the community. Others would try to reach him through his peer group. Most programs in the sample were making intense efforts to broaden the type of services offered to the young fathers. Prenatal and childbirth classes were the services most commonly offered to fathers. Programs with a residential maternity component tended to use recreational and social activities to foster male involvement. Among other services offered to the fathers were peer support groups, vocational and adult educational services, home visits, and couple counseling or therapy.

A wide range of father involvement strategies was described by the twelve respondents. Listening to the fetal heartbeat was often used as the first step, before offering counseling. In one agency a "welcome letter" was sent to the baby's father (with the mother's permission), explaining the services and encouraging him to come in and ask any questions he might have. One respondent said that "we're more successful after delivery, when reality really hits." But several others noted that they found paternal involvement dropped off markedly after delivery. Among the most successful "hooks," in addition to listening to the fetal heartbeat, were recreational activities like "water babies" classes, which were a big hit.

Use of male staff and/or male volunteers was also viewed as very helpful. The successful results respondents reported when using male staff suggest that a major reason why many unwed fathers are reluctant to become involved is that program staff who are women approach the young fathers from a position of "female advocacy," oriented to helping the young father meet the teen mother's needs, whereas the male staff may address themselves more directly to his feelings and needs.

Involvement of Putative Fathers in the Pregnancy Resolution Process
All the respondents stated that the birth father had a strong influence on the pregnant teen's decision about the resolution of her pregnancy. If he wished her to keep the baby, whether he was willing or not to provide financial or emotional support, she was likely to do so. And if the pregnant teen was ambivalent about what was best for her and the baby, the male's last-minute input was often reported to dictate her final decision.

Respondents were asked if their approach to the expectant father differed according to the pregnant teen's plans for the baby. Their responses seemed to depend on the extent to which the agency itself handled the adoption, or whether the adoption component was referred to another agency. (While all the programs reported that they offered some adoption counseling, some of the programs did not have the capacity to provide actual adoption services.) Thus, those agencies in the sample that referred adoption cases out tended to leave the issue of male involvement to the adoption agency.

Several respondents stated that their strategy would depend on the pregnant teen's decision. When adoption was a serious possibility, legal requirements for paternal notification and so on compelled them to try to get him in. On the other hand, if the teenager was planning on keeping the baby, agency staff said that they "would only push for [the father's] involvement if the teen had unresolved issues with him that would get in the way." Several other respondents, however, pointed out that since a teen may change her mind about her resolution decision several times during the course of her pregnancy, their approach to the birth father was the same—that is, they would attempt to involve him in the process, no matter what the mother's initial decision was. No respondent mentioned that a reason for involving the father would be to explore and, if necessary, help with the effects that the mother's decision—either to place or to keep the child—would have on him.

Involvement of the Unwed Father's Family
All the agencies in this sample attempted in varying degrees to involve the unwed father, although few actively sought to engage his parents in the program. A notable exception was one rural program respondent who said, "It's hard to hide things here, sometimes his parents come in with their son, and the pregnant teen comes in with her parents for the first visit." Three of the twelve respondents had no services for the paternal parents, although services were available to the maternal parents. One of these programs had no services for either family. In several programs contact with the putative father's parents would be an exception and usually only at the paternal grandparents' initiative, such as in those cases in which the grandparents were actively offering support and care for their grandchild and/or were opposing an adoption plan. The extent to which this lack of outreach to paternal grandparents was due to staff attitudes or to lack of resources, such as time and sufficient staff, was not clear from these interviews.

Overall, seven of the agencies made an occasional attempt to involve the paternal family. Four agencies had a policy of working intensively with the baby's father and his parents. They were most likely to do so if the young couple were still involved with each other, or if the father came in on his own initiative. Agencies offering comprehensive services appeared to be more committed to working with all the parties affected than agencies in health settings whose primary responsibility was providing prenatal care. Certainly the availability of resources in terms of staff, funds, and training affects the extent to which agencies worked with fathers and their families, as well as differences in staff attitude and program philosophy.

In summary, the picture that emerged from these interviews regarding the programs' involvement of paternal grandparents is that outreach and involvement activities are arrayed across a continuum, with the majority of programs having low involvement and a few (especially those in rural areas) clustering around the high-involvement end. The cases in which the father's parents are most likely to be involved appear to be those in which there is disagreement between the young couple's families about whether to keep the baby or put it up for adoption. This is likely to be true for a very small number of their total teen client population, since the overwhelming majority of unwed teens do not choose adoption. In the rural programs it seemed that the teen's pregnancy often brings paternal and maternal families together to work cooperatively on behalf of the young parents and their child.

Family and Program Factors Affecting Involvement of the Unwed Father and His Family

These interviews provided some clues about the family and program factors that either impeded or facilitated the involvement of the unwed father and his parents. For example, other studies have noted that the quality and longevity of the couple's relationship were believed by the respondents to be the major factor in determining whether the young father would participate in the program (Westney, Cole, and Munford 1986), and this was confirmed by the respondents in these interviews. In some cases the teen mother did not even inform the male that she was pregnant and he was about to be a father. Program staff reported that they generally respect her decision not to inform him and often worry that if he is notified there is a risk that he will be "disruptive" in the planning process.

The pregnant teenager's parents' attitudes towards the young father may also have a strong influence on the extent of his involvement. For example, if they dislike him or blame him for the pregnancy, they will resist his being involved in the early stages of the decision-making process or in other aspects of the program. The pregnant teen may be torn between her loyalties to her parents and to her baby's father. Her parents' negative feelings can often be mediated by a skilled counselor, who can help work through their anger and disappointment and learn to understand the putative father's responsibilities, and in the case of an adoption plan, his legal rights in the process.

The extent to which the unwed father's parents become involved in the program is largely shaped by the degree to which they have a supportive relationship with their son, the extent to which he confides in them and asks for or accepts their support. An underlying paradox in these cases is that when a young father's relationships with the teen mother and/or with his parents are most destructive or dysfunctional is exactly when the program staff are least likely to help, since such situations are the most time-consuming and difficult, and require extensive clinical skills. Yet these may be the very situations where help is most needed.

In terms of program factors, agencies which refer adoptions out and those which provide only one or two services appear to be far less likely to make efforts to work with the putative fathers than comprehensive service programs.

A major barrier to broader involvement efforts is the size of the staff person's caseload. Reaching out to include the father and his family takes a lot of time. If the counselors' caseloads are high and they are given no extra or independent caseload credit for working with the father or family members, and/or inadequate supervisory or administrative support, program staff will have little incentive to carry out active outreach to the baby's father and extended family members on either side.

In one author's experience (Leitch) with teen pregnancy programs, it is not unusual to find that few staff have experience or training in conflict resolution, mediation, family counseling, or family therapy. Staff, therefore, do not feel competent to manage a complex system of interaction between families that may be conflictual. Thus, they are less likely to work with and involve the young parents' family members when they are in conflict with one another, even though these are the family situations for which help is most needed. Staff in-service training and development programs geared toward information sharing, skill building, and mutual support for working with these kinds of family situations are clearly very much needed.

Family Involvement in Adolescent Pregnancy and Parenting Programs (FIAPP) Study, 1986–88

The second study reported on here was conducted in 1986–88 by a research team at Catholic University that included two of the present authors (Leitch and Ooms) and was designed to explore ways in which federally funded teen pregnancy program staff involved the families of their clients—the pregnant teens and teen mothers. This was a topic that had hitherto largely escaped research attention. Teen pregnancy program descriptions and evaluations, such as the Urban Institute's cross-site evaluation of the programs funded by the federal Office of Adolescent Pregnancy programs (OAPP), had not asked the programs to collect data on contacts with putative fathers or family members (Burt et al. 1984).

The one pioneer effort prior to the FIAPP study, the Adolescent Family Life Collaboration (AFLC), was a demonstration project conducted at five sites and coordinated by the Bank Street College of Education. The collaboration, initiated in 1984, was designed to develop and demonstrate program models that involved family members (including the baby's father) in programs that served pregnant and parenting teens. The sites chosen were ones where programs had already proven that they were successful in bringing in the adolescent fathers.

The AFLC programs served a total of 223 pregnant and parenting teenage girls, the majority from minority backgrounds, and also a total of 90 maternal grandmothers and 55 young fathers. In-depth interviews held with the clients and family members revealed a number of the critical issues that families had to deal with during a teen's pregnancy and after she brought the baby home. Family participation was found to be strongly linked to two positive outcomes: the teenagers whose mothers were involved were more likely to remain in the program and less likely to become pregnant again than teens whose mothers were not involved. In addition, the teenagers who lived with their mothers were more likely to remain in school (Rosen, Rogers, and Cannon 1988).

The Family Involvement in Adolescent Pregnancy and Parenting study, like the Bank Street AFLC study, defined family relationships to include the putative father, and several questions asked of respondents related specifically to his involvement. In part 1 of the study, a questionnaire was mailed to all 79 demonstration programs funded by the Adolescent Family Life (AFL) Office in 1986. Questionnaires were sent to a total of 183 program administrators, supervisors, and line workers, and to 53 evaluators. Responses were received from a total of 97 administrators, supervisors, and line workers. and from 28 evaluators, representing a little over a 50-percent response rate (a considerable number of the program staff were no longer on the staff of the programs).

The development of the questionnaire was based on exploratory site visits to five programs and included both precoded and open-ended responses. Domains of interest included staff attitudes, program practices—including type of services provided to fathers and family members—and program barriers towards family involvement. Family involvement was defined as including the involvement of the young unwed father. On some questions the respondents were asked to distinguish between issues and attitudes about involving the teenage mother's family (i.e., the maternal grandparents or her other relatives) and those about involving the unwed father and his family.

Part 2 of the FIAPP study was a quantitative analysis of secondary data available from five programs that examined the effects of family involvement on a variety of teen and infant outcomes. These five programs were chosen because they were the only AFLC programs that had high-quality, longitudinally computerized data, including outcome data, available for secondary analysis.

The major findings of the overall study can be summarized as follows (see Hanson et al. 1990):

1. Teen pregnancy and parenting programs employed a variety of family/father involvement practices, yet most of these efforts were sporadic and haphazard and not part of a deliberate plan to involve family members. Most programs viewed the purpose of involving

family members (and fathers) as a way to obtain more support for their primary client, the teen mother. Only a small number viewed the family/couple as the unit of service and made systematic efforts at every stage to bring them into the program and to assess and meet their needs.

2. Most program administrators and staff were enthusiastic about family and father involvement and believed that it had positive effects on teen clients, their babies, and family relationships and support. Yet they cited a number of program and other barriers, such as: high staff caseloads, limiting the time available to work with the family; failure to give caseload credit for the contacts with the baby's father or the teens' parents; lack of specific training or program guidelines for staff, especially in how to work with couple and family conflicts; resistance on the part of the teen herself, the unwed father, and/or the family to being involved; and difficulty in maintaining the involvement beyond the initial stages of contact.

3. The FIAPP study identified a wide range of family involvement practices and services used in these programs, enabling the researchers to construct a rudimentary scale of the various components of Family Involvement (FI). It was not possible to assign weights to the various items on the scale in terms of which types of family involvement were more important (i.e., those associated with positive outcomes); moreover, no data were available about the intensity or duration of any particular component. It is hoped that future studies will be able to refine and validate the Family Involvement scale.

The FI scale was used to rate the five programs in part 2 of the study, which had adequate quantitative data, in terms of their levels of family involvement. Thus, a high score obtained on the scale reflected the number of items on the scale that were present in the program and conveyed little about the quality or intensity of commitment or effort to work with families. In the analysis, the study found an association between high family involvement as measured on the FI scale and some positive outcomes, including improved relationships, improved school attendance, and less reliance on welfare. Again the results, while encouraging, can only be viewed as suggestive due to the limitations discussed above.

4. There were a number of interesting findings in the FIAPP study that related specifically to the putative/unwed fathers. Overall, it was encouraging to learn that program directors and staff were consciously aware of the need to work with the fathers. Many were

making some efforts to do so, but they clearly thought they should do more. Only a small number of the staff felt they had about the right amount of contact with the fathers; most believed they should have more contact with them—82 percent of the directors and 95 percent of the supervisors and line workers. About 40 percent of the staff felt they had about the right amount of contact with the teen mother's family, while 60 percent believed they should have more contact.

Program staff indicated some ambivalence about involving fathers. The large majority of respondents (83%) said that the teen mother would be told in the intake interview that the father of the baby would not be involved if she did not wish; only half (50%) said that she would also be told that it was usually in her (and her baby's) best interest to have the father involved. The programs much less routinely included fathers in the service plan and the fathers' attitudes towards the pregnancy were less likely to be assessed than the attitudes of the teen mothers' parents. Nearly 80 percent of the supervisors said that the teen mother's family's attitudes were assessed in most cases, whereas only 50 percent said they assessed the father's attitudes. Because studies have found the baby's father to often be quite influential in shaping the pregnancy resolution decision and plans for care of the baby, the lack of contact with him deprives program staff of valuable information in their work with the pregnant teenager and teen mother.

With respect to the results of the quantitative analysis in part 2 of the FIAPP study, there are several interesting findings related to unwed father involvement. For example, the father's involvement in counseling was associated with improved economic outcomes for the teenage mother. Seventy-five percent of the fathers who were involved in program services contributed economically to the child's support, compared with only 39 percent of those who had not been involved. It was also found that when the father was involved, female clients were more likely to report using contraceptives, and using them more frequently. Finally, and not surprisingly, it appeared that family involvement (both of the baby's father and the paternal and maternal grandparents) was associated with improvements in the teen mother's relationship with her baby's father.

5. The major program barriers to family/father involvement identified in the FIAPP study were very similar to those identified in the earlier exploratory study focusing on father involvement. These included high staff caseloads limiting the time available to work with

the family and father; a failure to give caseload credit for the contacts with the family and father; lack of clear and strong administrative support for leadership for FI; lack of specific training for staff in how to resolve family conflict and to work with multiproblem families; and insufficient funding to develop additional services for fathers and family members.

Again it must be emphasized that, although these results are encouraging about the positive effects of family and father involvement, they must be viewed as preliminary. Moreover, correlation does not imply causality. It could well be that those cases in which the families and fathers became involved were those where it was easiest to involve them, because they already had somewhat better relationships with the teen mother/client prior to enrollment in the program than those who did not enroll or those who enrolled but whose family was not involved.

Conclusions

These two studies represent preliminary explorations on a broad topic that has received little attention. The results suggest that a number of programs designed to target the teen mother (and her child) are trying to work with the baby's father, and some are finding ways of doing so successfully with quite a number of young fathers. Unwed fathers are a heterogeneous group with many different needs, and some are much easier to involve than others. Programs need to be flexible, to adapt their approach to different situations. In some situations the fathers themselves will be very resistant; in others the unwed mothers or their families will resist involving the fathers; and in some situations the program staff will be resistant. Resistance, however, does not imply a lack of need.

Some involvement strategies seem more successful than others. Involving fathers and their families as early as possible in the process seems most effective. In rural communities it seems to be easier to involve young fathers than in urban areas. It is clearly helpful when the program uses male staff to work with the fathers.

Staff in teen pregnancy and parenting programs are attempting to work with young fathers primarily because they believe it will bring positive benefits to the young mothers and their children. Studies still need to be mounted that will rigorously assess the effects of paternal or family involvement to determine if this belief has validity. In addition, studies need to assess the effects of father involvement especially when the father's needs are viewed as being independent of the young mother's needs.

It seems unlikely in the immediate future that resources will be sufficient to mount programs that offer a full panoply of services to meet the needs of unwed fathers or that program staff will be able to invest a great deal of time in outreach to them such as in the Teen Father Collaboration (described by Sander in Chapter 15). However, the two studies described in this chapter suggest that it is both feasible and desirable to expect teen pregnancy program staff to make it a routine practice to attempt to work with the baby's father in most cases (except for rape, incest, and very casual encounters). The focus of involvement ideally should be widened beyond helping the father provide support to the teen mother, to include the father's long-term responsibilities to his child as well as his own emotional, social, and economic needs.

Program staff can, as many do, invite the father to participate in many of the services provided to the young mother, but they can also provide him with counseling, do some couple and family counseling, and refer him to other services as needed. Many of the young fathers have service needs of their own pertaining to the pregnancy, as well as needs that shape their sense of responsibility to themselves, their child, and others.

In these two studies the difference between the programs which much more actively involved fathers and family members and those which did not seemed to rest more on questions of basic program philosophy and administrative leadership than on the availability of special resources, although there is clearly a reciprocal relationship between the two. Importantly, the program director must convey to the staff that working with the young father is important and valued by acknowledging the time spent in doing so and giving credit for it.

One major barrier is that program staff often have very little knowledge or training about how to work with young fathers, the young couple, and their respective families, particularly if the relationships are conflictual and/or the families are very dysfunctional. Staff report that they believe they should have more contact with the young unwed fathers than they do. Yet there is scant literature on the subject, and no training curricula. Considerable skill is required to overcome the initial resistance of the pregnant teen and/or her parents or the young man himself and to help them negotiate their conflicts with each other. Most importantly, program budgets need to include resources to pay for staff in-service training.

In spite of the interest at the federal level in promoting father and family involvement, neither public nor private funding sources have provided any program guidelines or technical assistance to grantees about how to involve families in their program. The Bank Street Teen Father Collaboration did publish an initial guide for programs, but much more is needed. This subject is ripe for development of some administrative guidelines and in-service training curricula.[5]

Policy Implications for the Future

Several aspects of the welfare reform legislation, the Family Support Act of 1988, have the potential to reinforce the gradual shift toward encouraging health and social service professionals to include unwed fathers in services. However, community-based nonprofit teenage pregnancy programs for the most part continue to have little contact with public welfare programs or youth employment and training programs, and their orientation is primarily to health care agencies and schools. It was not perhaps surprising then that very few of the program staff interviewed and surveyed in these studies volunteered any comments about the importance of establishing legal paternity, nor did they mention issues of child support or the need for linkages to employment and training programs for the young fathers and mothers.[6] Similarly, there was little emphasis on paternity and child support in the Teen Father Collaboration programs (see Chapter 15). Social workers' general lack of knowledge, their ambivalence, and at times even hostility, towards issues of paternity and child support were documented vividly in Esther Wattenberg's study in Minnesota (see Chapter 10). It is also true, however, that child support and AFDC–eligibility workers have little knowledge of, or contact with, teen pregnancy programs.

The requirements in the Family Support Act that all teen mothers receiving AFDC (the majority of AFL program clients) must attend school or its equivalent should, in theory, help bridge the gap between agencies and bring teen program staff and workers in the welfare system into closer contact with each other. In addition, as the states and localities move more assertively toward implementing the paternity establishment and child support provisions of the Family Support Act, teen pregnancy program staff can expect that they will be under some pressure from state public health and welfare authorities to reach out earlier and routinely to the unwed fathers to inform them of their responsibilities and rights and to encourage them to establish legal paternity.

Program staff will also be expected to be more active in cooperating to get child support payments made. This may place them in an uncomfortable role since it is their clear current preference and practice only to involve the young fathers on a voluntary basis, and only with the permission and support of the young mother, who may resist his involvement. The extent to which teen pregnancy program staff will actively and assertively promote legal paternity establishment and payment of child support is open to question. It will undoubtedly be largely a function of the education and training they obtain on these issues, the extent and manner in which they coordinate and collaborate with public sector agencies, and the leadership and support of their program directors.

In conclusion, the two studies discussed in this chapter indicate the need to view unwed fathers, and their families, as a heterogeneous group with varying influence on the ways in which the pregnant teens and teenage mothers make decisions about how to resolve their pregnancies and care for their children. However, broadening service delivery to include these significant others has implications for caseload size, cost of services, and clinical skills needed by supervisors and line workers. A supportive foundation within the agency at the administrative and supervisory levels is essential in broadening teen pregnancy and parenting services to teen fathers. In addition, recent policy developments, such as the passage of the Family Support Act in 1988, will put additional pressures on teen pregnancy program administrators and staff to work with both young parents, and their families, in order to accomplish the act's goals of enforcing parental responsibility.

Notes

1. In this chapter the term *young unwed father* is used to refer to the man who impregnated the adolescent woman and is the baby's biological father (if the pregnancy is brought to term). However, in the studies discussed in the chapter, teen pregnancy program staff volunteered that for a significant number of their teenage clients, the man in question is not young; he may be in his late twenties or even older. And in Hispanic communities the young couple are often married to each other.

2. For a general description of the recent history and development of teenage parent programs, see Forbush 1981; Hofferth 1987; Ooms 1981; Robinson 1988; and Weatherly et al. 1986.

3. The focus and design of both studies draw upon the authors' experience in conducting family systems training, program consultation, and evaluation in teen pregnancy and other family and youth programs.

4. Several situations that can result in a teen pregnancy are not dealt with in this chapter such as incest, rape, or a very casual sexual encounter, because in such situations it is generally not appropriate to involve the putative father. Such situations are complex and sensitive, requiring very skilled handling. When a pregnant teenager is very reluctant to involve the putative father, the counselor must be alert to exploring these possible reasons for her reluctance.

5. As a first step, and building on these two studies, one of the authors (Ooms) is preparing a *Guide to Family Involvement in Teen Pregnancy Programs,* which will be distributed by the Adolescent Family Life Office.

6. Neither study asked specific questions about how or whether issues of paternity were handled by program staff.

References

Burt, M., et al. 1984. *Helping Pregnant Adolescents: Outcomes and Costs of Service Delivery*. Final report to the Office of Adolescent Pregnancy Programs, Department of Health and Human Services. Washington D.C.: The Urban Institute.

Cervera, N. 1991. "Unwed Teenage Pregnancy: Family Relationships with the Father of the Baby." *Families in Society: The Journal of Contemporary Human Services* 72(1):29–37. January.

Elster, A., and M. E. Lamb, eds. 1986. *Adolescent Fatherhood*. Hillsdale, N.J.: Lawrence Erlbaum.

Forbush, J. B. 1981. "Adolescent Parent Programs and Family Involvement." In *Teenage Pregnancy in a Family Context: Implications for Policy*, edited by Theodora Ooms, 254–276. Philadelphia: Temple University Press.

Furstenberg, F. F. 1981. "Implicating the Family: Teenage Parenthood and Kinship Involvement." In *Teenage Pregnancy in a Family Context: Implications for Policy*, edited by T. Ooms, 131–164. Philadelphia: Temple University Press.

Hanson, S., et al. 1990. *Family Involvement in Adolescent Pregnancy Programs*. Final report of a study submitted to the Adolescent Family Life Office, Office of Population Affairs, Department of Health and Human Services. Washington, D.C. June.

Hendricks, L. E. 1980. "Unwed Adolescent Fathers: Problems They Face and Their Sources of Social Support." *Adolescence* 15:862–869.

Hofferth, S. 1987. "Effects of Programs and Policies." In *Risking the Future: Adolescent Sexuality, Pregnancy, and Childbearing*, edited by Cheryl Hayes. Vol. 2, Working Papers and Statistical Appendices, 207–263. Washington D.C.: National Academy Press.

Ooms, T, ed. 1981. *Teenage Pregnancy in a Family Context: Implications for Policy*. Philadelphia: Temple University Press.

Pannor, E., F. Nassarik, and B. Evans. 1971. *The Unmarried Father*. New York: Grune & Stratton.

Parke, R. D., and B. Neville. 1987. "Teenage Fatherhood." In *Risking the Future: Adolescent Sexuality, Pregnancy, and Childbearing*, edited by Cheryl Hayes. Vol. 2, *Working Papers and Statistical Appendices*, 145–173. Washington D.C.: National Academy Press.

Robinson, B. E. 1988. *Teenage Fathers*. Lexington, Mass.: Lexington Books, D.C. Heath.

Rosen, J., J. Sander, T. Rogers, and M. Cannon. 1988. *Teenage Parents and Their Families: Findings and Guidelines from a Collaborative Effort to Promote Family Competence*. Final report submitted to the office of Adolescent Pregnancy Programs, Office of Population Affairs, Department of Health and Human Services. Washington, D.C. January.

Rosen, R. H. 1980. "Adolescent Pregnancy Decisionmaking: Are Parents Important?" *Adolescence* 15:43–45.

Sachdev, P. 1991. "The Birth Fathers: A Neglected Element in the Adoption Equation." *Families in Society: The Journal of Contemporary Human Services* 72(3):131–139. March.

Weatherley, R. A., et al. 1986. "Comprehensive Programs for Pregnant Teenagers and Teenage Parents: How Successful Have They Been?" *Family Planning Perspectives*. 18(2):73–78. March/April.

Westney, O. E., O. J. Cole, and T. L. Munford. 1986. "Adolescent Unwed Prospective Fathers: Readiness for Fatherhood and Behaviors toward the Mother and the Expected Infant." *Adolescence* 21:901–911.

Young, L. 1954. *Out of Wedlock: A Study of the Problems of the Unmarried Mother and Her Child*. New York: McGraw Hill.

14   The Role of Unwed Fathers in the Abortion Decision

ARTHUR B. SHOSTAK

Unwed fathers are the least significant figures in the modern abortion drama: they are treated as second-class citizens by lawmakers and judges who respect only spouses, and they are scorned by a public that prefers conception be confined to married couples. On the rare occasion when they seek an injunction to delay a contested abortion, their position may be caricatured by the media. Since *Roe v. Wade*, 410 U.S. 113 (1973), and *Doe v. Bolton*, 410 U.S. 179 (1973), the man as an unwed or even a married, coinitiator of an unwelcomed pregnancy, has been relegated to the sidelines, a powerless observer of a choice reserved by the Supreme Court exclusively for the woman and her physician.[1] What role should the male sex partners be assigned—whether married to the pregnant woman or not—in the law, and how can it be promoted in practice? Should the unwed status of the male make a difference?

A scholar in 1979 concluded in exasperation that the voluminous body of abortion research literature available to him "often totally disregarded the male role, reported it in an implicit or covert manner, or at best reported it through the perceptions of the man's partner" (Smith 1979, 13).[2] Now, more than a decade later, the scene is much the same. One exception is the survey conducted by this author and his two collaborators (Gary and Lynn) in 1983–84, the largest body of information gathered to date. The sample consisted of 1,000 respondents located in the waiting rooms of 30 abortion clinics in 18 states. However, as we explained in our book, *Men and Abortion Lessons, Losses, and Love*, we were unable to secure the cooperation of males who had not accompanied their sex partners to clinics, a block equal to perhaps half of all clinic patients (or about 700,000 of 1,500,000 annual patients).[3] Nor were we able to find and survey unwed males who suspected a lover may have aborted a fetus they coconceived, but remained uncertain. As many as 15 percent of clinic patients in various studies indicate they have not told their sex partner of the conception or its termination (Shostak, McLouth, and Seng 1984). In addition, our data came only from males inclined to complete our questionnaire, and we lack answers therefore from others perhaps too embarrassed, indifferent, or embittered to tackle our 102 questions.

Above all, given the absence in 1983–84, as in 1979, of any scientific knowledge of the universe of relevant males (unwed and wed alike), my collaborators and I had to settle for this sample of convenience, an "available sample" of a previously unmeasured aggregate. In the absence of a random or representative sample, we urge utmost caution in generalizing beyond our data.

Consistent with findings of dissertation research conducted by others on single clinics, our sample of 1,000 males from 30 clinics included 180 husbands and a diversity of unwed types (60 percent had never wed; 12 percent were "living together"; and 10 percent were divorced). The 820 unwed males were overwhelmingly Caucasian (over 85 percent) and gentile (about 45 percent Protestant; nearly 33 percent Catholic; 2 percent Jewish; and about 14 percent agnostic). Only 5 percent were under 18, some 30 percent were 18 to 21, another 30 percent were 22 to 25, with only 8 percent over 36. About 35 percent were blue-collar, 28 percent were students, and nearly 20 percent were white-collar. Less than 6 percent were professionals (many of whose wives or lovers are thought to prefer the privacy of a doctor's office to the openness of an abortion clinic). Overall, perhaps 80 percent of our 820 unwed males fit the focus of this book, as they were 15 to 24 years old.

Most of the answers given on the 820 completed questionnaires and in over 120 personal interviews were thoughtful and serious. Only 20 percent of the respondents thought males in their position had an easy time of it; only 15 percent of the whole sample believed males escaped having disturbing thoughts about the experience afterwards; and 93 percent said they were convinced they would be more careful now about risking another pregnancy (even though 25 percent were repeaters). Naturally, the timing of the interview near the moment of abortion may have contributed to the seriousness of the reflections.

Given their minority representation in clinic waiting rooms (where the majority are mothers, sisters, and girlfriends), it was not surprising that most of the male respondents were caring and empathetic: some 37 percent had only been dating the female in the procedure room; 17 percent were in a "living together" set; and another 17 percent were engaged to that woman; only 10 percent were "frequent" or merely "casual" dates. 92 percent agreed females involved in an abortion did *not* have an easy time of it.

Consistent with this unsparing approach were the self-reports of the respondents about their initial responses to the news of the pregnancy. Forty-four percent of the never-wed males had offered to marry the mother and raise their child together, as had 58 percent of those living together and 44 percent of the divorced men. Twenty-eight percent of the never-wed males had offered to pay child support if the mother carried the fetus to term and raised the child, as had 30 percent of those living together. Twenty-one percent of the unwed males (versus only 11 percent of the husbands) had been open to having their offspring put up for adoption. Because some 85 percent felt they and their sex partner wound up equally favoring the abortion option, it was plain that much thought had gone into the matter.

What set the 820 unwed males apart from our 180 husbands came out far more clearly in personal interviews than in the relatively sterile format of our five-page questionnaire. In lengthy discussions with 120 single individuals we learned that the conception had been the first confirmation of virility for most ("I felt like a *man!*"); the conception had been unexpected, even though over half of the couples had not been using any form of birth control; the conception had stirred private fantasies about the rewards of impending fatherhood ("I knew I would make a helluva good father, certainly a helluva lot better than my old man"); and about desirability of "settling down" ("I figured that maybe now that we were about to start a family it was time for me to grow up, and start behaving like a family man"). Thoughts about the child that would not be born occupied the minds of 31 percent "frequently" and 54 percent "occasionally." Of these 85 percent, some 33 percent characterized their thoughts as a matter of curiosity; another 27 percent, as troublesome; and another 21 percent as sad. Typical of the thoughts shared were this comment, as quoted by a journalist from her own interviews:

> I don't think about what was happening in concrete terms like "This is my son," and I knew abortion was the only possible solution. But I still thought, What a shame! This is the combination of her and me . . . It could be such a beautiful child . . . (Mithers 1981, 321)

Again and again in our interviews unwed males volunteered moving words about fatherhood only glimpsed. This was in contrast to the husbands with a child or two already at home, most of whom dwelled on their relief at ending this unwelcome evidence of their continued fertility.

A related challenge to the self-esteem and role of unwed males involved the allocation of power in choosing abortion or childbirth. Our interviews revealed that the female had commonly conveyed both news of her unwanted pregnancy and her resolve to terminate it in the same distraught utterance and that the disclosure came couched as a test of the male's deference to his partner. Most unwed males had never before felt so much out of their depth, emotionally and spiritually.

The men also felt isolated because of the insistence by women that no one else be told about her pregnancy. Despite their obvious need for counseling help in dealing with their own stress, more than three in four unwed males discussed the situation only with their sex partner.

A good deal of anger surfaced in our research. While commonly kept from the sex partner, this repressed anger may help explain the "folklore" that holds that half of all relationships break up after an abortion (Francke 1978). Typical of the thoughts shared were those which focused on failed communications between the couple:

We didn't discuss it except for one argument over the expense of the abortion. . . . I felt like a chunk of me was going at the time. . . . I would have been happy with the kid, but she had the final say. . . . We were still arguing over the clinic this week, how much it bothered me. It might have been the only thing to slow me down from drugs, having the baby. She's under the impression that it didn't bother me, but it did, more than her, I think.

Others mixed grief and exasperation in talking of suspicion ("She was trying to trap me into marriage"), intimidation ("She was strong-willed; I had no say at all"), and incrimination ("She now claims that I forced the whole matter. She cries a lot, and insists I made her do it").

These negative feelings came out despite the fact that the vast majority shared the following three attitudes. First, the respondents essentially "graded" their performance, their role playing, in terms of how well it served the apparent needs of the female. They defined their role as secondary to hers, and took their cues from her expressed or apparent needs. Second, the respondents were decidedly pro-choice, and 85 percent opposed the outlawing of abortion. Third, most respondents rejected the moral arguments of the antiabortionists. Only 24 percent felt abortion was the killing of a child; only 18 percent felt life began at conception; only 15 percent condemned abortion as morally wrong. However, unwed males were in full agreement with the conventional pro-choice wisdom. Contrary to prevailing law and public policy, the 820 single men departed from the mainstream in five revealing ways:

1. 80 percent felt a husband should have as much say in the abortion decision as his wife; 19 percent, said less; 1 percent, more.
2. 58 percent felt an unwed male should have as much say as his sex partner; 41 percent, less; and only 1 percent, more.
3. 54 percent felt that abortion clinics should be required to notify a husband before performing an abortion on his wife.
4. 34 percent felt the law should require that a wife consult her husband before deciding to have an abortion; 30 percent, an unwed lover; 36 percent, however, felt neither male should gain this new legal right to participate in the decision.
5. 38 percent felt a woman should not have an abortion if her husband opposes it.

Policy Changes

Unwed males expressed unusually strong opinions about reforms in the clinic's procedures and practices based on their personal experiences. 93 percent urged clinics to stop barring males from accompanying patients during the one-hour post-abortion recovery period. 69 percent urged clinics to offer counseling and/or education about abortion and contraception to males in clinic waiting rooms. 64 percent urged clinics to offer waiting-room males a private session with a counselor. 93 percent also felt that "adolescents should get more information about birth control at school."

In all, then, unwed males urged reforms that would enable them to show more love and care throughout the process (even as nearly all fathers-to-be now have the right to help their partner through a childbirth) and that would prepare them to deal with their own turmoil over abortion.

One dilemma is that educational and clinic reforms that allow more involvement for men are far more likely to materialize if preceded by controversial changes in the law unacceptable to feminists. Three alleged rights of males have won enactment in a handful of state assemblies, only to be judged unacceptable in part or whole by the Supreme Court. The mildest would require spousal notification, and thereby oblige a provider (clinic, hospital, or doctor's office) to make a strenuous effort to notify a husband of his wife's request for an abortion. The second would require a provider to conduct at least one mediation session before permitting a disputed abortion. The most extreme would require spousal consent to the termination of a contested pregnancy.[4]

Legal experts see in this situation what they call the classic "faulty rights" dilemma: one set of rights (those of the pregnant woman) tends to cancel out another (those of an expectant father). The dilemma is discussed in the 1967 *Danforth* decision that denied men abortion rights, where the Supreme Court expressed sensitivity to the case that can be made for male involvement:

> We are not unaware of the deep and proper concern and interest that a devoted and protective husband has in his wife's pregnancy. . . . Moreover, we recognize that the decision whether to undergo or to forego an abortion may have profound effects on the future of any marriage, effects that are both physical and mental, and possibly deleterious (as quoted in Shostak, McLouth, and Seng 1984, 212).

The Court nevertheless concluded that one particularly repugnant variation of male involvement, spousal consent laws, was "not at all likely" to strengthen a marriage: "When the wife and her husband disagree on this decision, the view of only one of the two marriage partners can prevail (Shostak, McLouth, and Seng 1984, 212).

Proponents for another less extreme option, mandatory notification, have also evoked the situation of estranged married couples.

> In an era when the family has been rendered increasingly vulnerable to dissolution, we should not gratuitously add to the stress by enshrining in the law the starkly individualistic view that a child in the making, a future shared project of the family, is wholly, and completely a "private" matter for the woman to determine, with no concern at all for the wishes of the father—when he is her husband (Etzioni 1976, 58).

They argue that in order for a husband and wife to engage in sensitive give-and-take discussions, both parties must have legal sanctions and a stake in reaching an equitable decision.

For the purposes of this chapter, however, special note should be taken of the privileged treatment the proposed legal reforms offer husbands, while relegating unwed males to legal oblivion. Proponents of notification or mandated mediation, or even of the more extreme spousal consent, restrict their advocacy to husbands: they treat unwed males like pariahs. Opposition remains fierce to any legal change that would put unmarried and married males on the same plane. It would be an important step forward to win inclusion of a "males and abortion" component in public and private school sex education and pregnancy prevention curricula. Similarly, both males and females will have much to cheer when the nation's abortion clinics substantially enlarge caring options available to waiting-room males.

Should we eliminate this "second-class citizenship" of unwed males, we might finally be ready to tackle the legal puzzles of mandating child care payments *despite* male opposition to a contested childbirth. Unwed males in my clinic sample divided almost equally over the question of whether a man should be required to pay child support if a woman has refused his request that she have an abortion. Should the states gain the right to require notification and/or mediation for *both* married and unwed males, then the case feminists make for obligatory child support would be stronger. As lawyer Karen DeCrow (former president of the National Organization for Women) has argued in court:

> Justice . . . dictates that if a woman makes a unilateral decision to bring a pregnancy to term, and the biological father does not, and cannot share in the decision, he should not be liable for 21 years of support. Or, put another way, autonomous women making independent decisions about their lives should not expect men to finance their choice (DeCrow 1982, 383).

No discussion of rights is ever complete without a complementary consideration of responsibilities. Before risking conception, a man must assume his full share of the contraception effort and discuss the subjects of abortion and contraception with his lover. If each has an opposing view tightly held, the responsible course would seem to be to delay or even forgo lovemaking. On learning of an unwanted conception, an unwed male should seek professional counseling as commonly offered by pro-choice clergy, social workers, and even most abortion clinics (although this fact goes unknown by clinic and nonclinic males alike).

Finally, what will be the effect of the introduction of RU486, the new French abortifacient, on these issues? It may make it possible within five years to replace clinic-based abortion technologies with a home-based pill-reliant technology. Should this scenario unfold as proponents envision, it could result in the closing of many of the nation's 450 abortion clinics, the cessation of most antiabortion demonstrations, and the subsiding of related public acrimony, since abortions could now disappear into the privacy of conduct located at home.

Would these changes in fact recast the current questions concerning the relative rights and responsibilities of the parties? Should the law require notification of the natural father (spouse or lover) before a physician can prescribe RU486? Should the law require joint consultation with both prospective parents before authorizing access to the "abortion pill"? Should the law require child support payments from a man who earlier urged resort to RU486?

Above all, should the law get involved at all? Or is this an overdue opportunity for public policy to relegate the entire matter to the wishes of the woman, or the cohabitating couple? (See, for example, Sperling 1989, D-1; Anderson 1989, 12-C; Shostak 1991; and Shainwald 1989, 10-A.)

Notes

1. See, in this connection, Gilbert 1973, 442–445.

2. *Sociological Abstracts* had 118 citations for "men" or "males" and abortion, along with 635 for "females" or "women" and abortion, as of 14 June 1989. Very few of the male citations, however, referred to research on Americans, and all went as far back as 1963.

3. As recently as 1983, some 26 percent of all procedures were being performed other than in the nation's abortion clinics (Ory et al. 1983, 9); and the males involved thereby were also excluded from my sample.

4. In the twenty-four months immediately following the 1973 *Roe* decision, 62 efforts were made by 32 state assemblies to alter its significance. Twelve of these new laws provided a spousal consent provision, and the lower courts struck these down in eight states. Finally, in 1976, the *Danforth* ruling declared unconstitutional any absolute veto by a male over a female's assessment of her own needs.

References

Anderson, David E. 1989. "Yard, Smeal Push for Abortion Pill." *Philadelphia Inquirer*. 2 June, 12-C.

Blackwood, Rich, and Robin Blackwood. 1975. "What are the Father's Rights in Abortion?" *Journal of Legal Medicine* 3:28–36. October.

Callahan, Daniel. 1970. *Abortion: Law, Choice, and Morality*. New York: Macmillan.

DeCrow, Karen. 1982. "Letter to the Editor." *New York Times Magazine*, 9 May, 84.

Etzioni, Amitai. 1976. "The Husband's Rights in Abortion." *Trial* 12:58. November.

Farrell, Warren. 1988. *Why Men Are the Way They Are*. New York: McGraw-Hill.

"Father's Rights Cases Declined by Supreme Court." 1989. *Christianity Today*. 13 January.

Francke, Linda Bird. 1978. *The Ambivalence of Abortion*. New York: Dell.

Fuments, M. 1988. "The H Baby Incident." *National Review*. 24 June, 32–33.

Gilbert, Richard A. 1973. "Abortion: The Father's Rights." *University of Cincinnati Law Review* 42:442–445.

Jacoby, T. 1988. "Doesn't a Man Have any Say?" *Newsweek*. 23 May, 74–75.

Kapp, Marshall B. 1982. "The Father's (Lack of) Rights and Responsibilities in the Abortion Decisions: An Examination of Legal-Ethical Implications." *Ohio Northern University Law Review* 9:369–383.

Kaye, E. 1988. "The New Abortion Battle: Whose Baby Is It, Anyway?" *Mademoiselle*. December, 184–185.

Mithers, Carol Lynn. 1981. "Abortion: Are Men There When Women Need Them Most?" *Mademoiselle*. April, 321.

Ooms, Theodora. 1984. "A Family Perspective on Abortion." In *Abortion: Understanding Differences*, edited by Sidney Callahan and Daniel Callahan, 81–96. New York: Plenum.

Ory, Howard W., et al. 1983. *Making Choices*. New York: Alan Guttmacher Institute.

Sanger, Margaret. [1928] 1956. *Motherhood in Bondage*. Reprint. Elmsford, N.Y.: Maxwell.

Shainwald, Sybil. 1989. "Don't Betray Women Yet Again." *USA Today*. 7 June, 10-A.

Shostak, Arthur B. 1979. "Abortion as Fatherhood Lost: Problems and Reforms." *Family Coordinator* 28(4):569–574. October.

———. 1987. "Motivations of Abortion Clinic Waiting Room Males," In *Changing Men*, edited by Michael S. Kimmel, 185–197. Beverly Hills, Calif.: Sage Publications.

———. 1991. "Abortion in America: Ten Cautious Forecasts." *The Futurist* 25(4):20–24. July–August.

Shostak, Arthur B., Gary McLouth, and Lynn Seng. 1984. *Men and Abortion: Lessons, Losses, and Love*. New York: Praeger.

Smith, Mark R. 1979. "How Men Who Accompany Women to an Abortion Service Perceive the Impact of Abortion Upon Their Relationships and Themselves." Ph. D. diss., University of Iowa.

Sperling, Dan. 1989. "A Campaign for 'Abortion Pill' in USA." *USA Today*. 2 June, D-1.

Weiss, M. J. 1989. "Equal Rights: Not for Women Only." *Glamour*. March, 276–277.

Wishard, Bill, and Laurie Wishard. 1980. *Men's Rights*. San Francisco: Cragmont.

Woodman, Sue. 1984. "Your Body, but His Feelings, Too." *Self*. August, 140, 142–143.

15   Service Programs to Help Unwed Fathers

JOELLE SANDER

This chapter will discuss the Teen Father Collaboration, a two-year national research and demonstration project and the largest study on programs for adolescent fathers to date.[1] Aspects of this collaboration have previously appeared in several publications (Klinman et al. 1985; Sander 1986; Sander and Rosen 1987).

Although research on teenage fathers appeared as early as 1967 (Pannor and Evans), over the last two decades relatively few studies on adolescent fathers have taken place compared to those on teenage mothers. Nevertheless, research on young fathers has pointed up the importance of serving these young men not only to enhance their own competence as fathers but also for the good of the young mothers and children (Pannor, Evans, and Massarick 1968; Pederson and Robson 1969; Earls and Siegel 1980; Card and Wise 1978; Parke, Power, and Fisher 1980; and Klinman et al. 1985). Moreover, researchers on young fathers have also discussed the tremendous difficulties teen fathers face in becoming parents so early in their lives (Barret and Robinson 1982; Rumberger 1981; Sullivan 1984; Hendricks 1980; and Wattenberg 1983) and the cost to society of teenage parenthood (Moore and Burt 1982; and Alan Guttmacher Institute 1981). Several studies have also been published on the ethnic ramifications of adolescent parenthood in the lives of teen fathers (Gerschenson 1983; Stack 1974; and Hendricks 1983).

The author wishes to thank Debra Klinman, Project Director of the Teen Father Collaboration, and Jacqueline R. Rosen, Principal Investigator, for their contributions.

297

Teen Father Collaboration

In keeping with the increased awareness of the needs of teen fathers and the neglect they have experienced in the field of adolescent pregnancy and parenthood, the Ford Foundation and eight community foundations across the country launched the Teen Father Collaboration. Eight organizations participated in this unique venture, which was directed and documented by the Bank Street College of Education. These organizations included the Teenage Pregnancy and Parenting (TAPP) Project of the Family Service Agency of San Francisco; the YMCA of Greater Bridgeport, Connecticut; the Teenage Parent Program of the Jefferson County Public Schools, Louisville, Kentucky; the Division of Indian Work, Minneapolis; Face-to-Face Health and Counseling Service, St. Paul; the YWCA of Dutchess County, Poughkeepsie, New York; the National Council of Jewish Women; Insights, Portland, Oregon; and the Medical College of Pennsylvania, Philadelphia. In each situation the local community foundation funded the service delivery component of their chosen agency and the Ford Foundation funded the data collection component at the organizations as well as Bank Street College's role. Throughout the Collaboration Bank Street gave technical assistance to the sites, suggesting ways each site could enhance its program, writing and disseminating a newsletter describing the successes and the stumbling blocks each organization was encountering, and convening yearly conferences for all those participating in the Collaboration. Bank Street processed and analyzed the detailed data collection forms each site maintained and the data Bank Street itself kept from regular lengthy interviews the college's staff held with agency administrators, counselors, and teen fathers. All but one agency had a long history of working with teen mothers and chose to extend their services to include teenage fathers. The eighth site addressed itself to males exclusively.

Between 1983 and 1985 the Collaboration served 395 teen fathers and fathers-to-be. Housed in hospitals, schools, and social service agencies, the sites provided a comprehensive range of services to their male clients who came from a wide variety of ethnic backgrounds. These included blacks, whites, Hispanics, Asians, and American Indians. Given the lack of models for both reaching and serving teenage fathers, each agency designed and developed its own ways of meeting the needs of its male clients. However, despite the operational differences of each program, several overarching goals for the fathers and the collaboration were shared by all agencies:

1. To develop effective strategies for reaching young fathers and prospective fathers;

2. To provide these young men with services appropriate to their needs, with particular emphasis on their responsibilities as fathers;

3. To document and describe the development of agency services and the impact these services had on the lives of the young men and their families;

4. To draw attention locally and nationally to the need for programs for this previously neglected population;

5. To continue successful Collaboration programs beyond the duration of the demonstration.

From the outset of each program it was clear that these young men, who ranged in age from 15 to 19 years, needed a multitude of services. They battled problems, including low self-esteem and feelings of isolation, ignorance about how to parent their child, and confusion about finishing their education and finding jobs. It was necessary, therefore, to assess the needs of each young man and then to offer, either on or off site, those services that would most effectively help him in his plight as an adolescent father.

Essential Program Components

Core Services

As the sites began to develop their programs more fully, specific components of successful service delivery clearly emerged. A group of core services was developed at each site. These included: counseling (individual, group, and couples, or some combination of these), vocational training, employment placement, educational services (GED and support for obtaining a regular high school diploma), parenting skills classes, family planning services, and prenatal education. At the Medical College of Pennsylvania, birthing classes were also provided and several fathers helped in the delivery of their babies.

In each client's case at all sites it was necessary for the counselor and the young man to work out a realistic set of services that would enable him to take on his role as father both psychologically and financially, when the latter was feasible. Although steady child support was not the immediate goal of the service providers in any agency, given the age and lack of skills of their clients, every effort was made to find these young men either part-time or full-time jobs so they could contribute to their child's well being. This goal was in keeping with the goal many fathers had when they entered the program.

It should be mentioned that at only one site (the TAPP program in San Francisco) were fathers individually helped to establish paternity. The lack of knowledge about the process of establishing paternity and its frequently punitive stance toward unmarried young fathers prevented many agencies from becoming involved in the process. The time-consuming nature of the process made it particularly difficult for all but the TAPP project to help fathers navigate the system. This was the only site that had both sufficient staff to allow for the time the process took and a relationship with the local district attorney's office.

Over the course of the Collaboration TAPP staff did inform the other seven organizations about the importance of establishing paternity. Generally, this prodding was insufficient for the process to be carried out. However, staff did begin to counsel teen fathers about the benefits of establishing paternity, especially to their children. Data were not collected on the few adolescent fathers who did establish paternity.

The overall goals of all services to the young men were to keep them involved in their children's lives. This was best done by teaching them the rudiments of child care so they did not feel irrelevant as caretakers, by counseling them about their desires and fears in being or becoming fathers, and by assisting them in developing the educational and technical skills they needed to become financially supporting parents at the appropriate time. Much guidance was also provided to the adolescent father, and often to his partner, as a couple, on the issues of contraception and family planning.

Community Linkages

The key to a comprehensive program of services rested on the linkages made between the agency and other outside service providers in the community—another essential component of service delivery. These linkages included high school guidance counselors, housing officials, welfare workers, directors of vocational programs, directors of GED programs, day-care supervisors, family planning counselors, personnel at emergency shelters, food programs, and prenatal clinics. Programs not only used these organizations to refer clients to, but also received referrals from them. Strong linkages in the community also facilitated follow-up on the male clients.

Hiring Male Staff

In addition to the core services across sites and the establishment of community linkages, several other program components became critical in successfully working with this adolescent male population. One of the most important factors in well-run programs was the hiring of full-time skilled male counselors. Although some females did work well with male clients, it was crucial to hire at least one male at each agency for two reasons. First, the young fathers or prospective fathers who came into an agency needed to feel that males were a part of the world of social services, that it was natural for males to both receive and give services. Hiring male staff said to the young men that their concerns about being a good father were taken seriously and shared by other older males, who had chosen to help them with their responsibilities.

Secondly, these young men in their adolescent years needed positive role models, other males they could feel comfortable with and whom they could emulate. Especially with a population that frequently experiences father-absent homes or inadequate role models, a successful male staff member was instrumental in motivating these young men to come into the agency for help and to utilize appropriate services. It worked best if the male counselor was in his late twenties to middle thirties, from the same ethnic and cultural background as the majority of his clients, and was skilled at "connecting" with teenagers. This male worker also had to be sufficiently aggressive in recruiting young men into the program.

Strategies for Reaching Teen Fathers

Strategies for reaching young men were another crucial factor in successful programs for teenage fathers. Although each agency worked out the details of its recruitment techniques in its own ways, certain overall strategies emerged as particularly effective in building a viable clientele. The strategies for reaching this population can be broken down into on-site and off-site resources.

The most important on-site resource was the female partner of the young father or prospective father. Since all but one agency serving teen fathers already worked with teen mothers, often it was these young women who became the staunchest and most assertive advertisers for the male program. In many cases the counselor only had to describe the program to the young woman and to give her a flier for her partner's program. She was pleased to inform him about the services he, too, could receive. Because so many of these young women felt lonely and isolated in their plight as teen mothers, they were tremendously relieved to involve their male partner in their pregnancy and their shared parenthood. With coaxing and sometimes a bit of "nagging" on the part of the young woman, the male partner came into the agency first to "check it out" and often to stay.

In other situations, the young woman came into the agency with her partner. While the young man was in the waiting room, a counselor had an excellent opportunity to seek him out, to describe the program for fathers to him, and to encourage him to join the group. This kind of immediate on-the-spot contact was instrumental in reaching many young men at several sites. As one male client stated:

> I only came to the clinic to hear the baby's heartbeat. Then one day a social worker stopped me and told me about the program. Before I had a chance to say no, a counselor, who was sitting right next door, introduced himself to me and asked me if he could tell me about the program. I have to give him credit. It was the way he talked. He was frank. He told me about the benefits of the program. I have to be honest with you, if my counselor hadn't been there right at that moment, I might have told that social worker I'd come back, but I wouldn't have.

In almost all the settings, when a young woman telephoned the agency to make an appointment for herself, she was asked to bring in her male partner, too, if the relationship between them was amicable. If he did not come in, the young woman was asked for his name and some way to contact him directly. At that time the male counselor called the young man to make an appointment at the agency. It should be noted that one-third of the male clients came into agencies through their female partners.

Recruiting male clients off site involved other strategies. Outreach in the communities was vital. Often counselors gave presentations about their programs to schools, or made contact with the guidance counselors for referrals. They made personal contacts with staff at vocational training programs, GED programs, and at recreational centers. Or, in the case of some particularly aggressive outreach workers, contacts were made on basketball courts, in pool rooms, and on street corners. By becoming well known among teenagers in the neighborhood, word about a program for males spread rapidly, and clients came in because friends sent them.

The media, too, were helpful in bringing teenagers into programs. Television and radio spots, newspaper and magazine articles made the community aware of the services for these teens, and in turn created more referrals. Teens at many of the sites spoke on radio, television, and at schools about the programs in which they participated.

Obstacles to Service Delivery

But reaching and serving teen fathers and prospective fathers were by no means easy endeavors, especially in the initial stages of the Collaboration. A variety of formidable obstacles had to be overcome. These obstacles divided themselves into three major areas: problems with the teen male population itself, program staffing difficulties, and organizational issues.

Teen Males

Historically, social service agencies have offered assistance to females; this has been especially true in the area of teenage pregnancy and parenthood. Given this tradition of exclusion, when young men first learned about services for fathers, some were surprised, others skeptical, and still others wary. Service delivery staff needed to concentrate their efforts on overcoming the young man's expectations that he would be punished for his partner's pregnancy and held accountable for unrealistic child support. Young men needed to be convinced that Collaboration services were designed to help them cope with their own personal problems and to assist them in becoming capable fathers.

Some young men were difficult to engage because they took a "macho" independent stance. Others said they were willing to participate but demonstrated their age-appropriate adolescent self-centeredness in not always following through with what they promised to program staff. Some, for example, failed to show up for scheduled job interviews or counseling sessions. Others seemed to drop out of service programs, only to reappear after weeks or months had passed. As one counselor stated, "these young men have not formulated adult attitudes yet." Much patience was needed.

Other young men attended programs on an irregular basis, but had little choice in the matter. They were attempting to juggle an unrealistic and almost impossible array of responsibilities: school, work, regular visits with their partners and children. Many young men were poor, and found it difficult to afford transportation to get to the agencies. And some were fearful of going out of their "territories" to participate in services that were deliberately scheduled at night, so as not to conflict with their school and/or work lives.

Each of these obstacles was dealt with by agencies in the Collaboration. Program staff, aware of the developmental needs of adolescents, had to be flexible but direct in their expectations of the young men. Transportation money was often given to them, or vans were used to transport them to services. Some services had to be rescheduled to suit the needs of the majority of young men who wanted to participate in a particular activity.

Program Staffing

When an agency's financial resources did not permit the hiring of at least one full-time male counselor to work with males, the program had a greater chance of failing. As one administrator stated: "A program cannot be 'piggy-backed' onto another one. If there's not one person coming into the agency who wouldn't have a job if he wasn't working with teen dads, the program can't work."

In one program, for instance, a counselor was hired who spent more time working with teen mothers than with his male clients. His own personal discomfort with, and lack of skills in, serving a male population and the agency's insistence that he see a higher proportion of female clients undermined the program for teen fathers.

The importance of a good fit between counselor and clients cannot be stressed enough. A distant and formal staff person proved to be much less effective than someone whom the teen fathers felt was their advocate and confidant, someone on whom they could rely. Young men were quick to recognize when a counselor understood their needs and was prepared to offer them services. An agency not only suffered a serious number of dropouts when it failed to hire the right kind of counselor, but in time, the agency received no new referrals because other agencies heard the program did not work and teen fathers and mothers spread the word that the program counselor was unhelpful.

Agency Politics and Administrative Issues
Each service agency participating in the Collaboration had to do more than hire competent staff in order to execute their programs for teen fathers. The organization had to demonstrate a strong belief that providing services to adolescent fathers was essential to dealing successfully with the serious problems of teenage pregnancy and parenthood. When an organization was resistant to the ideas of working with young fathers, failure occurred.

Support for serving young male clients had to start at the top levels of an agency. Full commitment to serving young fathers had to come from the agency's board and especially from the head administrator, the person who hired and supervised the agency's staff, and who was responsible for fund-raising. Often this person was called upon to integrate the new teen father program into the larger existing program, not an easy feat. Frequently, staff attitudes about serving young men had to be addressed and sometimes changed to reflect more positive thinking about males in general. When this kind of support was lacking, or unsustained, the program became largely ineffective. In the case of one organization, for example, the administrator's constructive attitude toward serving young men was inconsistent. Although at first he expressed his commitment to beginning a program for teen fathers, he changed his mind when his counselor proved incompetent in working with a teen father population. Instead of hiring someone more adept, the head of the agency was outspoken in his intention to serve females over males:

> On a scale of 1 to 10, my own commitment to making this organization more focused on men is 5. I'm really dedicated to women. I can see the teen fa-

thers' stuff as being important because it lends to the growth and development of the child, but when it comes down to services to males for this agency, it's not a priority.

Messages from the head of an agency permeated the staff attitudes at all levels. The feeling of not being supported led to fear, anger, and eventual lassitude in bringing teen fathers into a program. "I'm feeling that what I'm doing in seeing teen fathers is wrong . . . or that it meets with consistent criticism," said one service provider. Another stated, "Especially in my advocacy work, I feel that I'm working at cross purposes with the agency's basic philosophy of protecting and serving women."

When agency politics were positive about serving men or became so over the course of the Collaboration, staff benefited in a variety of ways. Support was given by the administrator either in one-to-one supervision or in a group. The counselor's own personal issues in working with these young men were discussed, especially any issues dealing with difficulty in reaching these adolescents or in attempting to meet their many needs. Counselors, for instance, sometimes experienced a sense of fragmentation or even burnout if their caseload became unduly heavy or if their own expectations for these young men were unrealistic and they sought to solve an array of problems too quickly.

Staff also benefited from organized weekly case presentations. An administrator who was committed to serving young men realized that the whole staff, those working with mothers and those working with fathers, would gain from learning about each other's clients' problems. Shared cases often broke down the stereotypic thinking about adolescent fathers as negligent and uncaring among those workers who had a history of advocating for and serving only female clients. Presentations were essential in giving an overview to all counselors of a young family's stresses and the necessity of serving both teen males and females. Such presentations also served to facilitate cooperation among staff members in spreading the word about the program for males to the teen mother clients.

Overall, it can be said that when top level support was present, the counselor was more motivated to be aggressive in his outreach to involve fathers, was more active within the community in making the necessary linkages between his agency and others, and more confident in his work with the young fathers. Given the relatively untried ground of serving teen fathers, a consistent and reliable support from the head of an agency made for a solid pioneering spirit among the counselors toward their clients. Those that lacked that support constantly complained of "feeling out on a limb" in their work.

Profile of Teen Father Participants

In a profile of the 395 young fathers and prospective fathers who were served during the Collaboration's two years, data—both quantitative and qualitative—present a wide variety of backgrounds, and present-day circumstances.

Basic Demographics

At the time of initial contact with the Collaboration's eight agencies, the great majority of young men (90.1%) were first-time fathers or fathers-to-be. Slightly more were expectant fathers (54.7%) than fathers (45.3%).

The eight program sites served almost exclusively young men, ranging in age between 15 and 19.5 years. However, the majority of young men were between the ages of 17 and 18. These adolescents came from an ethnically diverse population: 37.7 percent were black, 25.2 percent white, 24 percent Hispanic (10% Puerto Rican; 7% Mexican American; and 7% other Hispanic), 7 percent American Indian, and 5.1 percent Asian. Many young men (43.7%) were from Protestant backgrounds, over one-third (38.8%) were Catholic, 12.3 percent claimed no religious affiliation, and a small portion of young men (6.2%) came from a range of other religious backgrounds, including Muslim, Rastafarian, and Mieng.

Living Arrangements

In terms of their living arrangements, 18 percent said they lived only with their partner or with their partner and child, 29.8 percent lived with their parent(s) (usually their mother), while the largest number (37.4%) said they lived in some kind of extended family arrangement (including grandparents, siblings, aunts, and other relatives). Only a small percentage (3.8%) lived alone.

Financial Support of Father/Employment Status

Over half (50.7%) of all respondents stated that they received all of their financial support from their families (occasionally supplemented by their own earnings); 21.9 percent relied completely on public assistance; and 9.7 percent reported some combination of family support, personal earnings, and public assistance. The remaining 17.6 percent either attributed their financial support to "other" sources or declined to answer this question. This financial picture is not surprising, given these young men's ages and their high rate of unemployment (65.5%). The remaining 34.5 percent did hold jobs; over half of these worked part-time. Those young men who worked generally were employed at entry-level jobs that required little specialized training. Many worked in service industries (such as fast-food restaurants, hotels, car washes), as janitors or maintenance workers, or in factories (on assembly lines, as machine operators). A few held clerical positions, while others reported working at a series of "odd jobs."

Education

In terms of the young men's education, relatively few young men of any ethnicity (8.2%) reported leaving school before completing the ninth grade. However, dropout rates increased subsequently in a pattern similar to national data on school dropouts among all young males (Rumberger 1981); 14.3 percent left after completing ninth grade, 21.3 percent after tenth grade, and 25.5 percent after eleventh grade. Less than one-third of the respondents said they had completed high school or obtained a high school equivalency diploma upon entering the agencies' teen father programs. When asked why they dropped out of school, answers varied, although of the 115 young men who responded to that question, 29 (25.2%) said they didn't like school or were bored and 32 (27.8%) said they needed a job or wanted to support their partner and child.

Relationship to Partner

Looking further at the profile of these young men who participated in agency programs, we find that nearly three-quarters of this group (73.3%) considered the young women their "girlfriends," 9.7 percent were married, and 4.0 percent categorized their relationships as "other." (Usually, this meant that the young couple was living together or engaged to be married.) Only 8.6 percent said the young women were "just friends," and 4.3 percent reported that they no longer saw the mother of their child.

It is particularly interesting to note that the average duration of these ongoing relationships was more than two years. Only 4.5 percent reported knowing their partners for six months or less, while 73.1 percent reported that their relationship had already lasted for more than one year. These data helped offset the stereotype that all teen fathers are hit-and-run victimizers of young women. There are adolescent fathers who are very much related to their partners and who seek help in continuing to support them and their children.

Frequency of Contact with Partner and Child

The young men were also asked how frequently they had contact with their female partner. The majority (72.5%) had daily contact, and another 12.5 percent saw her once a week. A close relationship between partners also resulted in the young man seeing his child frequently. The over-whelming majority of young men (81.6%) reported daily contact with their child. Those who were "just friends" had less regular contact, some-times because the young mother did not want the father to visit, other times because the maternal grandmother refused to let the father see the child, and in some situations, because the father himself felt awkward about seeing the child, given the tense partner relationship.

Financial Support of Child

Young men also indicated all of the sources from which their child re-ceived (or could receive) financial support. Out of the 328 young men who answered this question, most fathers (34.6%) and prospective fathers (33.7%) attributed the support of their child to both their own families and the child's mother's families. Many reported that they alone would be responsible for their child's support, and although this intention was highly unrealistic, it indicates the level of responsibility these young men wanted to assume in relation to their children. In fact, 74.1 percent of actual fathers reported that they did make monetary contributions. More-over, they also stated that they made in-kind contributions like food (15.6%), babysitting (15.2%), clothing (14.2%), diapers (11.5%), and toys and books (11.5%). In spite of their limited economic resources, these young men both wanted to and did provide their child with practical support as well as the psychosocial support that came when they visited their child and involved themselves in their child's life.

In sum, this overall profile of young men who utilized agency services indicates they came from a wide variety of cultural and ethnic back-grounds, were poor, often uneducated and unemployed, and committed to their female partners and children. They were also, as one counselor states, "not guys who were trying to rip off the world—they were not so caught up in their own anger that they couldn't see us helping them."

Highlights of Program Impact

In looking at the Collaboration's eight programs, what are some of the highlights of program impact? Of the 395 young men on whom the agen-cies kept detailed logs, the majority sought multiple services. Almost 85 percent availed themselves of at least two services, with more than three-quarters participating in three or more program components; the average length of time spent in a program was six months. The number of ser-vices used underscores the importance of offering a variety of services to young males in these circumstances.

Effects of Personal Counseling

From studying the logs, it was clear that counseling was the single most sought-out service. With very few exceptions (13), nearly all the young men participated in individual counseling sessions and dealt with issues which included their responsibilities as fathers, their relationship to their partner, and their attitudes and behavior in relation to family planning. In addition to individual counseling, 27 percent participated in group counseling, and 12 percent took advantage of couple's counseling. Counseling was conducted once or twice a week, or more often, if one counts the frequent phone contact participants had with staff.

For many fathers, counseling helped in crucial ways. It assisted them in coping with demands of early parenthood, in building stronger ties with their children, and in working on their ongoing relationship to their partner. Counselors, teen fathers, and teen mothers all stated how much more solid a connection these young men developed to their families when they participated in the agency program. The male adolescents themselves spoke about learning how to take care of their child, "even how to hold my baby, put on diapers and fix formulas," or as another said, "to get different viewpoints about how to properly raise my child," or as many stated, "to be a better father to my child than my father was to me." Moreover, many fathers spoke about learning what to expect from their child at different stages of the child's development. This knowledge was particularly helpful in reducing abusive behavior toward the child and in helping the father be more patient and controlled.

Being taken under the wing of male counselors—and sharing their experiences with other young fathers—also reduced the young men's tremendous sense of alienation from adolescence. "Seeing people in the same position as I was really helped," stated one father. "Before this I felt like I was one out of a million. I probably got through the whole thing knowing other people are in the same boat."

Effects of Educational Services

Other services were also crucial in the lives of these adolescent fathers. Collaboration participants who had dropped out of high school were assisted either to return to school, or to obtain their high school equivalency diploma. Of the 155 nongraduates who were also not enrolled in school, nearly half experienced positive educational outcomes. About one-third of these young men returned to high school, while two-thirds enrolled in and/or obtained their GED. Given the fact that dropping out of school early is known to lead to a higher rate of social and economic difficulty, the impact of these services may bode well for higher esteem, better job possibilities, and financial support.

Effects of Vocational Service

In regard to their present employment status, it was noted that about two-thirds of the 395 Collaboration participants were unemployed job seekers at program entry. Of the participants making use of vocational services available to them, including job skills training, vocational training, and referral for job interviews, a total of 148 young men (40%) experienced positive employment outcomes, with 56 (15%) obtaining part-time jobs and 92 (23%) obtaining full-time jobs. Thus, as a consequence of their participation in the programs, counselors reported that a preponderance of these young men were helped to contribute to their family's well-being and enjoyed a more positive attitude about their own competence and their role as providers.

The Documentation Process

Data Collection

Both qualitative and quantitative data were collected throughout the two years of the Collaboration. Bank Street College documented all aspects of the research. Reponsibility for data collection was shared by Bank Street staff and program staff at the eight local sites. Typically, the same site person who worked directly to provide services to male clients also kept all relevant records. While Bank Street staff collected most of the data concerning the process of program development at the sites, local staff members—after being trained at Bank Street—collected the bulk of the data describing the young men who participated in their programs. All data were forwarded to Bank Street for purposes of data analysis and report preparation.

Three principal kinds of information were collected. First, program staff gathered descriptive information about the agency's overall organization, staffing, and types of services delivered, and about the activities of the teen father program itself. Each year Bank Street staff conducted telephone interviews with the program staff about progress and setbacks in implementing the teen father program. Second, at the initial, follow-up, and exit interviews program staff collected basic background data directly from the teen fathers about their living arrangements, employment status, sources of support, relationships with their partner and child, contributions to support their child, and so forth. In addition, through ongoing logs, the program staff kept track of the extent of the young fathers' participation in specific services. Third, the Bank Street staff conducted on-site interviews with the teenage fathers each year, exploring the fathers' assessment of the program, their relationships with their partner, child, and others, and other problems that confronted them as fathers.

Several limitations must be noted concerning the evaluation of services. First, the young men who came into the programs were entirely self-selected. They were, by and large, men who wanted services, wanted to be responsible fathers. It was not clear therefore if or how these same services would affect young fathers who, for example, are referred to the programs by the court; who may not want to take on the role of father. Would they utilize such services? What effects if any would these programs have on them?

The difficulty in interpreting impact data is further compounded by the high rate of program attrition among participants. Often these young men, once they received the services they needed, left the Collaboration programs—sometimes forever, sometimes for several months—without informing their counselors. Outcome data were difficult to collect in these cases, and program effects had to be assessed using the logs which the counselors themselves prepared.

In an overall sense the Teen Father Collaboration was designed to explore the feasibility of services to adolescent fathers. Aside from a small handful of programs that existed prior to the Collaboration, it was not clear whether programs for teenage fathers would attract this population at all. The Collaboration's findings then support the important conclusion that programs for young fathers are crucial to those young male parents who want and need assistance in being skillful, knowledgeable, and nurturing parents.

Policy Implications

Although the Teen Father Collaboration officially ended in September 1985, five of the eight sites continued programs for teen fathers. The need for such programs is clear. In fact, at each of these locations more teen fathers are signing up for programs than can be adequately served. What is lacking, then, not only in these organizations, but in other cities and towns across the nation, are the resources to amplify those programs that already exist, and to create new ones where they are needed. An increasing number of service providers are now realizing the importance of working with both the teen mother and the teen father, and funds— local, state, and federal—are crucial if agencies are to hire the proper staff to serve all those young men who see the need for services. These services are necessary not only to help young men become better fathers, but even more so to ensure that they will not become fathers again prematurely.

Furthermore, as local communities begin to serve teen fathers, good coordination between those public and private delivery systems serving teenagers is vital. As stated in the 1986 report of the Select Committee on Children, Youth, and Families, *Teen Pregnancy: What Is Being Done? A State-by-State Look*: "A majority of states (28) cited a lack of coordination among state and local agencies as a serious problem in serving teenagers" (p. 43). Coordination between local and state agencies results in more comprehensive programs for this needy population. For example, while social service organizations may be able to offer certain on-site program components, there is often a need to supplement these services with those provided by the state-run organizations in that community. For instance, teen males face difficulties in meeting the needs of their partners and children for adequate housing, food, and medical care. Linkages with agencies that provide these services are crucial.

As the problems of adolescent pregnancy and parenthood have become more pronounced in the United States, the role of the state and federal government vis-à-vis this national epidemic needs more clarification. What, for instance, can be done about the laws regarding the establishment of paternity? These vary by state now, and according to many of the teen fathers and counselors interviewed in the Teen Father Collaboration, the process is often humiliating, punitive, and ineffectual for all concerned. Can the states humanize this process to encourage more fathers to establish paternity, thus increasing the benefits their children might receive? As it stands now, unrealistic child support is often so tightly linked with establishing paternity that many teen fathers do not acknowledge paternity for fear that they will not be able to meet payments, or that they will incur debts that they will be unable to settle. In Oregon, for example, when a young man establishes paternity, a percentage of his salary is assessed for child support. If he loses his job, which happens to many of these unskilled teenagers, the assessment continues and his debt increases.

The same disregard for the plight of these adolescents is shown in regard to their rights as fathers. Again according to the counselors at various sites in the Collaboration, and the teen fathers and mothers themselves, too many child support enforcement officers are concerned solely with the father's financial payments. They care much less that the father sees his child and has the opportunity, like other fathers, to form a good relationship with his offspring. Child support enforcement officers themselves need more education and guidance in working with young fathers.

In addition, in many social service agencies that serve teen parents, there is still a great need for information about the process of establishing paternity and about working with both male and female clients to ensure that this happens. Staff are often ignorant about the laws in their own state regarding paternity, and uninformed about the benefits that paternity has for the child (e.g., Social Security and Armed Forces benefits). Consequently, staff do not broach this important subject with their clients, and many fathers never become legal parents. States might better inform clients and social service providers about establishing paternity by writing and distributing pamphlets about the process and its benefits.

Another vital policy issue in regard to teenage fathers relates to the need for more job training and employment placement programs. At this time, there is a serious dearth of such programs, and federal and state funds are sorely needed to establish and administer more of them. Many adolescent fathers want to help support their families but need assistance in basic job seeking skills, vocational training, and in finding work. In those communities where such programs do exist, and where there is strong affiliation between social service agencies and these labor offices, teen fathers and their families do benefit. Young men are helped to find either full- or part-time work, which enables them to contribute money and goods to their children. These contributions raise the young man's self-esteem in relation to his role as a father. He is part of his family, rather than an outcast or an onlooker. Moreover, his female partner and her family are also often relieved by his monetary contributions and frequently encourage him in his role as a father because he is assisting his child in concrete ways. It should be noted here, for example, that many teen mothers served by sites in the Collaboration openly stated that their mothers allowed the young man access to his child only because they saw him as working and contributing financially. Employment is crucial then for many reasons, and a link between social service organizations and employment organizations is vital in helping these young men take on the parental responsibilities many of them yearn to.

In sum, federal and state governments need to allocate more funds in an effort to reduce adolescent pregnancy and to assist those adolescents who have become parents too early. More research is needed to ascertain what kinds of programs best meet the needs of the teen mothers, teen fathers, and those young people at risk for adolescent pregnancy and parenthood.

In the past several years, the Department of Health and Human Services, and in particular the Office of Adolescent Pregnancy and Parenting, has begun to recognize the serious consequences of early parenthood on this male and female population, on their offspring, and on their families as a whole. But more resources are badly needed by organizations seeking to serve more than the female and her child. At present, most organizations working with teenage mothers do not have the funds to develop services for the teen fathers, too, or for the larger family. These programs, therefore, cannot address the myriad problems of the family as a whole, and are forced to deal only with the mother and child, placing on the young woman more responsibility than she alone can handle. Not until adolescent pregnancy and parenthood are seen as family matters, and sufficient funds are made available to organizations seeking to deal with these problems, will the United States be able to overcome or at least reduce this serious national epidemic.

Note

1. The Teen Father Collaboration was funded by the Ford Foundation and eight local community foundations—the Bridgeport Area Foundation, the Louisville Foundation, the Minneapolis Foundation, the Philadelphia Foundation, the Oregon Community Foundation, the Area Fund of Dutchess County (N.Y.), the St. Paul Foundation, and the San Francisco Foundation.

References

Alan Guttmacher Institute. 1981. *Teenage Pregnancy: The Problem That Hasn't Gone Away*. New York: Alan Guttmacher Institute

Barret, R. L., and B. E. Robinson. 1982. Teenage fathers: Neglected too long. *Social Work*, 27:484–488.

Card, J. J., and L. L. Wise. 1978. Teenage mothers and teenage fathers: The impact of early childbearing on the parents' personal and professional lives. *Family Planning Perspectives* 10:199–205.

Earls, F., and M. D. Siegel. 1980. Precocious fathers. *American Journal of Orthopsychiatry*, 50:484–488.

Gerschenson, H. 1983. Redefining fatherhood in families with white adolescent mothers. *Journal of Marriage and the Family* 45:591–599.

Hendricks, L. E. 1980. Unwed adolescent fathers: Problems they face and their sources of social support. *Adolescence* 15(60):862–869.

———. 1983. Suggestions for reaching unmarried black adolescent fathers. *Child Welfare* 62(2):862–869.

Klinman, D. G., et al. 1985. *Reaching and serving the teenage father*. New York: Bank Street College of Education.

Moore, K. A., and M. R. Burt. 1982. *Private crisis, public cost: Policy perspectives on teenage childbearing*. Washington, D.C.: Urban Institute Press.

Pannor, R., and B. W. Evans. 1967. The unmarried father: An integral part of casework services to the unmarried mother. *Child Welfare* 46:150–155.

Pannor, R., B. W. Evans, and F. Massarik. 1968. *The unmarried father: Findings and implications for practice; effective service for unmarried parents and their children; innovative community approaches*. New York: National Council on Illegitimacy.

Parke, R. E., T. G. Power, and T. Fisher. 1980. The adolescent father's impact on the mother and child. *Journal of Social Issues* 36:88–106.

Pederson, F. A., and K. S. Robson. 1969. Father participation in infancy. *American Journal of Orthopsychiatry* 39:466–472.

Rumberger, R. W. 1981. *Why kids drop out of high school.* Program report no. 8184. Stanford, Calif.: Stanford University Institute for Research on Educational Finance and Governance.

Sander, J. 1986. *Working with teenage fathers: A handbook for program development.* New York: Bank Street College of Education

Sander, J. H., and J. L Rosen. 1987. Teenage fathers: Working with the neglected partner in adolescent childbearing. *Family Planning Perspective* 19: 107–110.

Select Committee on Children, Youth, and Families. 1986. *Teen pregnancy: What is being done? A state-by-state look.* Washington, D.C.: Government Printing Office.

Stack, C. 1974. *All our kin: Strategies for survival in a black community.* New York: Harper & Row.

Sullivan, M. L. 1984. Youth, crime, and employment patterns in three Brooklyn neighborhoods. Vera Institute of Justice. New York City. Mimeo.

———. 1985. Teen fathers in the inner city: Exploratory ethnographic study report to the Ford Foundation. April. Mimeo.

Wattenberg, E. 1983. *The project on paternity adjudication and child support obligations of teenage parents.* Report to the Ford Foundation, the McKnight Foundation, and the Center for Urban and Regional Affairs, University of Minnesota.

16   Employment Patterns of Unwed Fathers and Public Policy

ROBERT I. LERMAN

Fatherhood brings new financial responsibilities. Given the added cost of supporting a child, parents must increase their earnings or reduce their own material living standards. In principle both married and unwed fathers feel the heightened financial pressure. Married fathers living with their children see their families' rising expenses on a daily basis. Unwed fathers living apart from their children become liable for providing child support payments, while continuing to pay for their own households.

Yet the case of unwed fathers is complicated. Although some experience the same urgency as married fathers, others feel little or no financial obligations toward their children. In either case unwed fathers may differ in their capability to raise their earnings. If unwed fathers are very young, high school dropouts, and have little work experience, even the most sincere efforts can yield little increased income.

Until recently, public officials charged with collecting child support from noncustodial parents acted as if unwed fathers had little capacity to contribute support payments and the costs of collecting their modest potential payments exceeded their benefits. But recent legislative and administrative actions have made establishing paternity and support orders from unwed fathers a high priority. The 1988 Family Support Act (FSA) mandated new standards, requiring states to determine paternity for an

The author thanks the U.S. Department of Health and Human Services, Assistant Secretary for Planning and Evaluation, for financial support to carry out this research, and Theodora Ooms for comments and encouragement.

316

increasing proportion of out-of-wedlock children born within their borders. One rationale for this provision is the belief that unwed fathers have, or will have, sufficient resources from which to pay child support. However, acknowledging that unwed fathers sometimes lack enough earnings to pay child support, the FSA allows for waivers that permit five states to mount demonstration projects of employment and training services for unemployed unwed fathers.[1]

The deliberations over the FSA had to proceed without reliable information on the job market patterns of unwed fathers or on the relationship between their earnings and support payments. But efforts are underway to uncover these patterns and to consider their implications for policy.

This chapter begins by taking up a range of questions about the job market success of unwed fathers. Do young unwed fathers earn significantly less than other young men? If so, what accounts for their disadvantages? Are the differences between unwed fathers and married fathers caused by differences in worker capabilities, such as low education and limited work experience, or differences in worker effort? Do young unwed fathers eventually experience rapid earnings growth, or do their earnings stagnate?

The chapter next asks about the linkages between earnings and child support payments. A common assumption guiding public policy is that increased earnings among unwed fathers will generate increased support payments. But do high levels of earnings always translate into increased support payments? Perhaps the causation runs in the opposite direction; that is, maybe the willingness to pay child support influences earnings. A third possibility is that unmeasured attitudes, such as responsibility, influence both earnings and child support.

These findings bear on questions concerning the appropriate government role in dealing with earnings deficiencies of unwed fathers. Should public programs provide targeted employment and training assistance to these young men? How should programs link the fulfillment of child support obligations with job-related services? Do adjustments in government benefit programs make sense? The chapter concludes by reporting on demonstration projects aimed at learning more about unwed fathers, how to increase their earnings and support payments, and how to improve their fathering.

Earnings Patterns of Unwed Fathers

All young workers are in the early stages of their job market career. For some, it is a time to receive training and higher education; for others, it is a time for casual involvement in jobs; still others try to gain work experience to raise their long-term earnings. Given this variety of situations, current employment and earnings are not necessarily reliable indicators of a young man's performance in the labor market. At the same time, if the responsibilities of fatherhood ever affect earnings, the impact should be especially striking during an early stage of their job market careers.

Because marriage and fatherhood patterns vary significantly by race, we begin by examining job market indicators within racial groups. All the data for the analysis come from the National Longitudinal Survey of Youth (NLSY). As noted in Chapter 2, the NLSY tracks the experiences of nearly 13,000 young men and women who were between the ages of 14 and 21 in 1979. Table 16-1 reveals the differences among youth in hours and earnings during 1983 and 1987, by their marital and fatherhood status in 1984 and 1988. Note that unwed fathers worked only about the same hours as unwed young men without children. In contrast, married fathers as well as married young men without children worked much longer than either unmarried group. Thus, in terms of hours worked, unwed fathers resembled other unmarried young men rather than other young fathers. The earnings of unwed fathers were substantially lower than all other groups, including unmarried young men without children.

The job market outcomes cited in Table 16-1 show patterns for two different cohorts of young men. To see whether unwed fathers raise their earnings as they age, we can view the 1983–87 trends among those who were 20–24 years old in 1984 by their status in 1984. The results appear in Figures 16-1 and 16-2. Unwed fathers started the period working about the same hours and earning almost as much as single men without children. However, their earnings did not keep up with any of the other groups. By 1987 unwed fathers were working 400–500 fewer hours and earning $5,000–9,000 less per year. The severe stagnancy of earnings of unwed fathers suggests that, without some policy initiatives, their capacity to pay significant amounts of child support will be limited.

A close look at the trends indicates the importance of unwed fatherhood status rather than a young man's initial earning capacity in limiting earnings growth. Note in Table 16-2 that the 20 percent of unwed fathers who subsequently married achieved extraordinary gains in earnings. While their 1983 earnings (when they were unwed fathers) were nearly as low as those of other unwed fathers, they reached parity with other married young men by 1987.

These results capture the overall differences in the job market outcomes of unwed fathers and other young men, but they do not reveal how these differentials arise. Young fathers, especially those living with and

TABLE 16-1 Annual Hours Worked and Annual Earnings
for U.S. Males, Ages 23–27, by Fatherhood and Marital Status,
1983 and 1987

Family Status	Hispanic	Black	White
		1983 hours	
Single, no child	1,563	1,463	1,764
Married, no child	1,676	1,827	1,898
Unwed father	1,434	1,365	1,585
Married father	1,975	1,824	1,953
		1987 hours	
Single, no child	1,530	1,446	1,811
Married, no child	1,696	1,868	1,988
Unwed father	1,548	1,401	1,548
Married father	1,945	1,714	2,042
		1983 earnings	
Single, no child	$13,236	$10,906	$14,850
Married, no child	15,007	13,179	17,458
Unwed father	8,961	8,048	9,912
Married father	16,076	12,896	15,913
		1987 earnings	
Single, no child	$13,273	$11,033	$15,707
Married, no child	16,932	13,978	19,096
Unwed father	9,223	8,850	9,944
Married father	16,030	12,692	17,811

Source: Tabulations by author from National Longitudinal Survey
of Youth (NLSY) data.

helping to raise their children, may become more responsible and mature
in the process of building a family. These traits may encourage them to
work harder at their job and make special efforts (on and off the job) to
find high-paying jobs. The more pressing monetary needs of heading a
family may discourage young men from taking positions that pay less but
have other desirable characteristics. In particular, young single men may
spend more years at low earnings but investing in training so as to gain
higher earnings in the future.

A second possibility is that only young men with the capabilities to
earn an adequate income end up marrying and forming intact families.

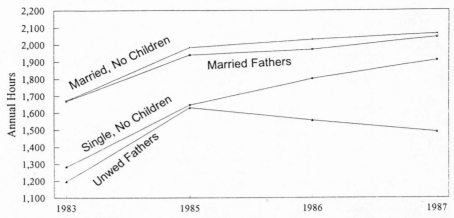

FIGURE 16-1 Trends in Annual Hours Worked for U.S. Males, Ages 20–24, by Marital and Fatherhood Status, 1984

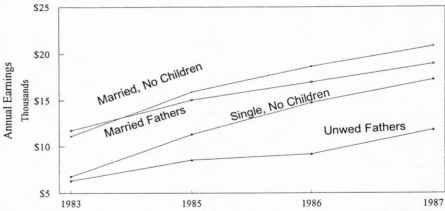

FIGURE 16-2 Trends in Annual Earnings for U.S. Males, Ages 20–24, by Marital and Fatherhood Status, 1984

Potential mates, including the mothers of their children, may decide not to marry or live with men who cannot financially support a family. A third possibility is that some outside event, like low area unemployment rates, might both create increased earnings opportunities and spur young men to marry and/or have children. A fourth possible linkage is that unwed fathers might avoid working very hard if a significant portion of their earnings went to the child's mother in the form of child support payments or to the government to offset the mother's welfare benefits.

TABLE 16-2 Hours Worked and Earnings in 1983 and 1987 of 1984 Unwed Fathers, by Marital Status, 1988

	Hours worked in 1983	Hours worked in 1987	Earnings in 1983	Earnings in 1987	Percentage unwed fatherhood	Unweighted number of fathers
Hispanic						49
Never married	981	1,491	$4,735	$10,413	65.8	
Married	1,476	1,982	7,835	18,409	28.9	
Separated/divorced	778	1,903	4,999	14,000	5.3	
Black						256
Never married	1,005	1,389	4,877	9,791	69.5	
Married	1,314	1,941	6,898	14,903	20.8	
Separated/divorced	1,923	1,185	8,944	10,696	9.7	
White						65
Never married	1,218	1,480	6,844	11,656	70.9	
Married	1,809	1,923	8,022	22,084	21.1	
Separated/divorced	1,634	2,645	6,607	11,958	8.0	
Total						370
Never married	1,078	1,428	5,552	10,485	69.7	
Married	1,496	1,939	7,370	17,669	21.5	
Separated/divorced	1,782	1,671	8,041	11,236	8.8	

Note: The sample consists of young men, ages 20–27 in 1984, who completed NLSY interviews in 1984 and 1988.

Source: Tabulations by author from NLSY data.

Alternatively, the need to provide child support payments might spur unwed fathers to increase work effort, largely through an income effect.

To examine these possibilities, we estimated the impact of marital and fatherhood status net of other characteristics of young men. Our analysis began with multivariate regressions on annual earnings and the proportion of the year that young men (ages 23–31 in 1987) were employed. Using the rich array of information from the NLSY, we isolated the effects of fatherhood and marriage from the impacts of education, prior or current military activity, other family income, race, local unemployment rates, and a set of aptitude measures (including paragraph comprehension, math knowledge, auto shop skills, and electronic knowledge). Table 16-3 reveals the net impact of each factor on earnings and employment relative to the base case of a white young man who was single, childless, a high school graduate, and with no prior military experience.

While education, skill, and other characteristics of young men have large and significant impacts, fatherhood and marital status continue to exert extremely large impacts. Note that married fathers living with their

TABLE 16-3 Effect of Fatherhood and Marital Status on
Earnings and Employment of U.S. Males, Ages 23–31, 1987

Predicted levels for young men with base-level characteristics	$17,550	.870
Change in earnings relative to base level associated with each status	Effects on earnings	Effects on employment
No child, married	3,791	0.11
Unmarried absent father	−478	−0.07
Married absent father	771	0.03
Married resident father	4,490	0.10
Unmarried resident father	−240	0.04
High school dropout	−3,719	−0.07
Some college	−809	−0.03
College graduate	1,654	−0.05
Postgraduate	−983	−0.13
Black	−1,599	−0.03
Hispanic	806	0.01
Past military experience	−1,505	−0.04
Active military	−758	−.003

Note: These results come from OLS regressions of 1987 earnings
and employment rates on the variables listed above, plus age,
other family income, scores on four tests from the Armed Forces
Vocational Aptitude Battery (ASVAB), and area unemployment.
All the impacts listed above come from coefficients that were statistically significant at the 1-percent level. The base level characteristics are young men who are white, age 27, unmarried, high
school graduates with no college, with median scores on ASVAB
tests of math, reading, electricity, auto shop, living in area with
no reported unemployment rate, and with other family income of
$10,000. The overall sample consists of young men, ages 23–31
in 1988.

The employment rate is equal to the percentage of the year the
young man was employed or in the military (i.e., weeks employed
plus any weeks in military service divided by 52). Thus, the − .07
coefficient for unwed absent fathers represents a reduction in employment of .07 × 52 weeks, or 3.5 weeks per year.

The full regression results with effects on earnings and employment are available from the author on request.
Source: Regressions by author on NLSY data.

children earned about $4,500 more than single childless men with similar
personal, family, and area characteristics. In contrast, unwed fathers living away from their children earned about $500 per year less and worked
about three fewer weeks. The few unwed fathers living with their chil-

dren had lower earnings but higher employment rates than single childless men.

Taking personal and family characteristics into account raised the position of married fathers relative to married young men without children. Note in Table 16-1 and Figure 16-2 that married young men without children earned more than married fathers did. However, the results in Table 16-3, which compare young men with the same personal characteristics and family backgrounds, reverse that pattern and show married men with children having higher earnings.

The impacts of explanatory variables other than family variables are interesting. Black young men earned $1,600 less per year than expected on the basis of observed characteristics, but Hispanic men earned about $800 more. Not surprisingly, high levels of other family income reduced earnings and employment, while high skill levels (as measured by the Armed Forces Vocational Aptitude Battery) raised earnings significantly. Both past and current military service lowered earnings; however, active duty in 1987 left employment rates virtually unchanged.

Skills and other job market characteristics might well affect earnings differentially by fatherhood status. For example, high levels of education might have a less positive effect on single childless men than on married fathers. One reason may be that those with fewer family responsibilities do more experimenting in the job market and give more weight to job quality than to current income. In fact, the effects on earnings of education, race, and employment conditions differed by fatherhood status. First, marriage had a substantially larger effect on fathers than on nonfathers. Even among fathers living away from their children, the earnings gain associated with marriage was higher than for childless young men. Divorced or separated young men generally earned more than those who never married, but the effects were much larger among absent fathers than among nonfathers. Apparently, the experience of marriage was most consequential for earnings of young absent fathers.

Education effects also varied somewhat by fatherhood status. Graduating from college had a large effect among childless young men, but none among fathers. In contrast, graduate education yielded big gains only for married fathers. Other surprising findings emerged from racial and ethnic impacts. Hispanic nonfathers and absent fathers actually earned more than whites with similar family and job market characteristics. The only negative effect of Hispanic status was among resident fathers, and even for this group, the effect was extremely small. For black young men, the largest earnings reduction showed up among nonfathers. Black fathers earned less than white fathers with similar characteristics, but the employment gaps were small or nonexistent.

Overall, the results point to large and independent effects of fatherhood and marriage. Living with one's child clearly matters as shown by the fact that absent fathers earn much less than resident fathers of the same marital status. However, marriage differences can override fatherhood effects; for example, married absent fathers have higher earnings than unmarried resident fathers with similar characteristics.

How are we to interpret these results? One possibility is that high potential earnings permit young men to marry, to live with and support their children, and to do well in the job market. However, the *observed* earnings advantages of married men and resident fathers cannot be due solely to higher skills and favorable employment conditions, since the positive effects of marriage and resident fatherhood were measured net of these differences.

Of course, some *unobserved* characteristic that helps young men do well in the job market might also influence them (together with their female partners) to marry and have children. Perhaps, some young men simply choose to take on more responsibilities than others. This responsibility trait could explain both why some men marry, have children, and remain married and why married men, especially resident fathers, work more of the year and achieve higher earnings than other young men. Another explanation is that the decision to marry or become a resident father is unrelated to job characteristics, but that the experiences of marriage and raising children influence young men to work harder and earn more.

What about the earnings disadvantages observed among unwed fathers? Does unwed fatherhood push some young men to raise their earnings, in order both to provide financial support for their children and to achieve an adequate living standard for themselves? Or do unwed fathers—most of whom do not pay child support—regard their dual responsibilities as more apparent than real?

Child Support Responsibilities and the Earnings of Young Absent Fathers

Support responsibilities are likely to interact with fatherhood in a variety of ways. Because unwed fathers are much less likely to face a legal support obligation than other absent fathers, the linkages between support payments and earnings may be less significant. Still, if unwed fathers view child support obligations as a tax, they may reduce their work effort because some of each dollar of earnings will have to go toward child support. Alternatively, they may increase their work effort because of the increased need for income. The interplay between child support obliga-

TABLE 16-4 Child Support Payments of Absent Fathers, by Marital Status and Race or Ethnic Group, 1986

	Mean support payments	Payments as percent of earnings	Percent making payments	Mean payment by those who pay	Number of fathers (thousands)
All races					
Single	$678	6.7	35.2	$1,928	690
Married	1,052	9.9	47.2	2,231	323
Separated or divorced	1,476	13.6	58.0	2,545	771
Hispanic	1,301	15.0	49.3	2,638	140
Single	458	4.3	24.6	1,866	37
Married	1,352	6.4	77.5	1,745	20
Separated or divorced	1,667	22.0	53.8	3,101	83
Black	770	9.4	40.6	1,895	726
Single	698	7.8	37.6	1,856	465
Married	1,152	19.6	55.2	2,086	106
Separated or divorced	724	7.2	39.7	1,824	155
White	1,312	10.2	52.1	2,519	918
Single	672	4.5	31.2	2,153	187
Married	969	5.1	39.8	2,434	197
Separated or divorced	1,664	14.2	63.9	2,602	533

Source: Tabulations by author from NLSY data.

tions and the formation of second families is especially interesting. The needs of children in a second family might compete with, or take priority over, the needs of dependent children from the first family and thus reduce the father's ability and willingness to make child support payments. On the other hand, young men who form second families may be more responsible and have added capabilities, which leads them to support both families.

Table 16-4 presents simple tabulations showing the child support paid in 1987 by unwed fathers and other absent fathers. Clearly, married absent fathers provided more in child support than did single absent fathers. The surprising element is that even the proportion of earnings spent on child support was higher for married than single fathers. However, the highest rate of spending on support payments was among divorced or separated fathers.

Racial differences were linked largely to differences in marital status. Hispanic young fathers paid the highest proportion of earnings for child support. Their high rate of contribution was the result of the 22-percent burdens experienced by divorced and separated fathers and the fact that this group made up about 60 percent of Hispanic absent fathers. White fathers had similar payment patterns, except that white divorced and separated fathers spent only about 14 percent of their earnings on child support. Blacks showed the lowest levels of support payments, providing only $770 per father as compared to about $1,300 paid by Hispanic and white fathers. The low payments among blacks were the consequence of the unusually small amounts provided by black divorced and separated fathers, as well as the high proportion of absent fathers who had never married. Black absent fathers who were married actually paid a substantial 20 percent of their earnings for child support.

The differences in payment performance had most to do with whether fathers made any payment at all. Among fathers making some payment, the average amount provided was almost as high among unwed fathers as among married, divorced, or separated fathers.

Earnings can influence child support payments in a variety of ways. High earnings tend to raise legal support obligations and thereby force many fathers to increase payments. A high capacity to earn will increase a father's ability to make payments without jeopardizing his own living standard. Fathers who have close relationships with their children or who feel a strong moral commitment will increase their efforts to earn in order to provide support for their children. Other factors may have direct effects as well as indirect effects related to earnings. Fathers who have started second families by marrying and having children in their current home might pay less in child support payments so as to maintain their current family's living standard. However, the presence of a spouse or their own children might stimulate fathers to earn more and thus avoid reducing payments. Still another possibility is that only those absent fathers who are most responsible are willing to start second families and this responsibility pushes more of them to pay child support.

Responsibility and necessity may also play a role among absent fathers who have been or still are in the military. Military experience, especially current active duty, can make fathers easier to locate, but also may increase the father's sense of the importance of fulfilling his obligations. Aging should increase a young father's maturity, and thus cause him to pay more. But, aging may also be associated with a drifting away from earlier relationships, including those with one's children. Income from other family members should also raise support payments, although this impact is likely to vary with family size. Finally, even after taking account of these job market and family obligation factors, there may be cultural differences between white, black, and Hispanic absent fathers in their capacities, willingness, and sense of obligation to pay child support.[2]

Given a young man's personal and family characteristics as well as area employment conditions, earnings and child support can interact in the following ways: (1) the earnings of a young father can largely determine the child support he pays; (2) the level of child support payments

TABLE 16-5 Factors Influencing Child Support Payments by Young Absent Fathers, 1986

| | Means | Change in child support payments with unit change in variable | | | |
		1	2	3	4
Married	0.17	487	78	210	2
Divorced, separated	0.37	560	362	411	192
Own child in household	0.15	91	306	179	175
Children not in household	1.52	176	221	255	126
Black	0.53	−311	−216	−222	−86
Hispanic	0.15	−133	−144	−156	−70
Age	26.0	−32	−57	−57	−35
Military experience	0.03		107	178	72
Active in military	0.10		368	373	175
Actual earnings	$11,461		0.05		0.02
Earnings in 1985	$9,924			0.05	
Predicted earnings					0.01
Other family income					0.004
Percent of impact on fathers who pay child support		32.8	30.8	30.5	22.5

Note: The numbers shown in columns 1, 2 and 3 reveal the independent effects on child support payments relative to the base case of a white, 26-year-old, never-married, childless young man, with no military experience and average earnings. For example, the impact of being married is to raise payments by an expected $487 per year in column 1. The bottom row indicates that part of the effect (32.8 percent in column 1) comes about through raising the amount paid by those young men making any payment. The remaining proportion shows how much of the effect is to raise the proportion of young men making a payment.
Source: Tobit equations estimated by author from NLSY data.

provided by the young father can strongly influence his earnings; and/or (3) the degree of responsibility can have a large impact on both the earnings and child support payments of the young father.

The main statistical tools for the analysis are two sets of multivariate tobit equations. The first set estimates the impact of earnings and other factors on child support, while the second projects how child support and other factors affect earnings.[3] Using transformations of the tobit coefficients, one can distinguish the impacts on the probability of making payments from the impact on payments, among those who made at least some payment.

The starting point is to estimate the impact of personal characteristics and family status on child support payments in 1986. Column 1 in Table 16-5 indicates that married and divorced fathers pay more than unwed fathers, that black and Hispanic fathers paid less than white fathers, and that support payments increased with added numbers of children outside the household. Surprisingly, fathers that started second families, via marriage and having children in their own homes, actually paid more in child support than other young fathers. Unwed fathers who did not subsequently marry provided the least support.

Column 2 reveals the effects of earnings as well as the impacts of family, race, age, and military activity variables *net* of earnings. Note that the child variables increased in importance, while the impact of marriage became weaker. By implication, the higher payments associated with marriage shown in column 1 must have been due to their higher earnings and not some unmeasured responsibility factor related to marriage. On the other hand, the larger positive effect of having an own child at home means that such fathers provided added financial support without any added earnings.

Involvement with the military raised support payments, independently of any impact on earnings. One can interpret the military variables in terms of being more willing to follow rules or to respect responsibilities and/or being an easier target for child support collection efforts. Note that while both military variables were positive, the current active duty variable was much larger and statistically significant. This suggests that it is the ease of collection that is playing the strongest role in the process.

The negative impact of age is surprising. Note that the negative age effects were net of earnings and family factors. Any maturation process that encourages paying child support either operates through increased earnings, increased family responsibilities, or does not take place at all. Not surprisingly, higher earnings were associated with higher child support payments by young absent fathers. However, each dollar increase in earnings raised support payments by only about 5 cents.

Interpreting the connection between earnings and support payments requires us to consider alternative mechanisms. One mechanism is simply that differences in earnings capacities generate differences in support payments, that those able to earn more because of higher education and variable job market conditions tend to contribute some of their increased earnings to child support. A second mechanism is that attaching a high priority to meeting support obligations stimulates fathers both to earn more and to pay more.

A two-stage procedure can distinguish between these mechanisms. The first stage predicts earnings on the basis of human capital and area job market variables; the predicted earnings variable is essentially independent of motivational influences on earnings associated with fatherly responsibilities. The second stage estimates the effects of both predicted earnings and actual earnings on support payments. If actual earnings continue to have a positive effect on child support payments even after taking

TABLE 16-6 Effects of Past and Current Child Support on Earnings of Young Absent Fathers, 1986

Explanatory variables	Means	Change in earnings with unit change in variable			
		1	2	3	4
Black	0.53	−1,465	152	589	451
Hispanic	0.15	1,700	2,040	2,254	2,060
Age	26.0	181	56	23	15
Married	0.17		5,831	5,883	5,400
Divorced, separated	0.37		3,279	2,842	3,119
Own child in household	0.15		−1,988	−2,379	−2,176
Children not in household	1.52		−279	−659	−308
Other income	5,902		0.010	0.000	0.000
Child support in 1986	1,018			1.25	
Child support in 1985	622				1.48

Note: These results come from tobit equations that include test scores (on reading comprehension, math, auto shop, and electricity), education, military experience, and unemployment rates in the father's local area. The full results are available from the author on request.

Source: Tobit equations estimated by author from NLSY data.

account of predicted earnings, one can conclude that some unmeasured characteristics—perhaps the father's effort to make adequate child support payments—is raising both earnings and support payments.

The right column (4) in Table 16-5 reveals that while predicted earnings exerted a positive effect on support payments, the impact was less than the impact of actual earnings. In fact, the effect of predicted earnings vanishes in the presence of the actual earnings variables. This pattern of results is subject to more than one interpretation. One possibility is that the predicted earnings variable shows the weaker impact because it is a less accurate measure of potential earnings than the youth's actual earnings. Another is that increased effort, which may be stimulated by the desire to pay child support, causes both actual earnings and support payments of the young father to rise, to differ from predicted earnings.

Direct evidence of the impact of child support payments on earnings shows up in Table 16-6. Column 1 includes only race and Hispanic origin, human capital variables (schooling, test scores, and military experience), and area unemployment variables. From columns 2 and 3 it is clear that fatherhood and marital status exerted extremely large impacts. Those married and/or separated or divorced earned $3,000–6,000 more than others with the same human capital variables. On the other hand, having his own child in a father's home and added numbers of children living away from home apparently were associated with lower earnings. Column 3 reveals the extremely high and positive impact of child support payments on earnings.

Endogeneity could easily arise between earnings and child support. The most natural explanation is that added earnings may cause added child support rather than the other way around. One way to limit the endogeneity is to measure child support payments with a lag of a year behind the year in which earnings is measured. This creates a type of exogeneity since the level of child support payments in 1985 cannot literally have been caused by earnings in a subsequent year. Of course, a third variable such as fatherly responsibility might have been at work in both years to stimulate higher earnings as well as child support. Whatever the explanation, the results in Table 16-6, column 4 clearly show that added child support in 1985 was associated with higher earnings in 1986, even net of human capital, area unemployment, race, and other family variables. These large and highly significant impacts indicate that the requirement and/or the desire to pay child support helped stimulate increased earnings.

Family variables again show large net impacts on earnings. Married absent fathers earned $5,400–5,900 more, and separated absent fathers earned about $3,000 more than never-married fathers with similar job market characteristics. On the other hand, fathers with their own child in their home or added children away from home earned less than other absent fathers. A few influences on earnings showed considerable sensitivity to the impact of family variables and child support payments. Note particularly the effects of race and age. When we include only human capital and job market variables in column 1, black absent fathers showed an earnings disadvantage in comparison with whites. However, with the inclusion of family variables and child support payments in columns 2, 3, and 4 of Table 16-6, the situation reverses itself as black absent fathers earn more than white absent fathers with similar labor market, human capital, and family characteristics. The age effects go in the opposite direction. The presence of family variables and child support payments reduces the importance of age on earnings.

Overall, the results show that unwed fathers paid less in support payments than other absent fathers and that their subpar support payments may have been the cause as well as the effect of the low earnings of unwed fathers. Both marriage and the willingness to make child support payments raised earnings by statistically significant amounts. This suggests that policies aimed at increasing the employment and earnings of unwed fathers should recognize that motivating young men to fulfill their financial responsibilities may be as important as providing training.

Policy Initiatives to Raise the Earnings of Unwed Fathers

Public concern over the job situation of unwed fathers has prompted the government and several foundations to create demonstration projects that stress training, placement, and remedial education. Two fundamental difficulties arise in any effort to structure job-related programs *specifically* for unwed fathers (as well as other low-income absent fathers). The first is that such programs offer special services on the basis of socially undesirable behavior and thus may encourage unwed fatherhood. Given the evidence cited in Table 16-2, any actions that deter unwed fathers from marrying are likely to harm earnings growth by more than the training programs help. Further, it may be inequitable to provide a training slot to an unwed father over an equally needy married father or childless young man wanting to enter the program. One way to mitigate these problems is to take measures to ensure that a large portion of any increased earnings induced by the program goes to support the unwed father's child rather than his own living standards.

But these actions run up against the second fundamental problem, the fact that a large part of the increased support payments by unwed fathers go to offset welfare benefits instead of raising the income of the child and the custodial parent. For women receiving benefits from Aid to Families with Dependent Children (AFDC) and food stamps, the income gain from added child support amounts to about $35–40 per month. Mothers now on welfare could reap larger benefits from added support payments only by moving off welfare rather than remaining on the rolls. Unwed fathers whose children remain on welfare might see themselves as doing more good by paying child support informally with earnings that are easy to hide from welfare authorities than by earning more in the formal sector and then having their child support simply offset AFDC and food stamp benefits.

Thus, providing special job training slots unlinked to support responsibilities is unwise and possibly inequitable, while requiring such a connection might deter fathers who see any earnings gains as going to the government.

The two national demonstrations both retain the connection between services that enhance earnings and provisions to collect added support payments. The larger effort is the Parents' Fair Share Demonstration organized by the Manpower Demonstration Research Corporation, with funds from the Departments of Labor and Health and Human Services, the Pew Charitable Trust, and the Ford Foundation. This is the demonstration called for under the Family Support Act, in which selected states can receive waivers to offer job-related services to nonresident fathers on welfare. The ten pilot projects began in the spring of 1992, and a full social experiment in five of the sites is to begin in mid-1993.[4]

The primary Parents' Fair Share model involves working with noncustodial fathers who report they cannot pay existing child support orders because of unemployment. In project sites judges can refer nonpaying fathers to the Fair Share program in lieu of jail or other penalties. As long as the fathers participate actively in the program, they are not subject to serious penalties. Agencies funded under the demonstration work with fathers by offering training, including on-the-job training positions that provide steady salaries. As fathers increase their earnings and agency monitoring ensures increased collections, fathers may encounter disputes with custodial mothers about visitations and other issues. In anticipation of these problems the operating agencies provide dispute resolution services. In addition, participants obtain peer support and counseling about issues of fatherhood, such as relationships with their own fathers, their expectations for their children, and the appropriate obligations of fathers toward their children. Some fathers referred by the court to Parents' Fair Share who never participate are likely to admit having an existing job and decide to comply with the support order. Others are subject to jail or other stiff penalties.

The early intervention component of the Fair Share demonstration involves unwed fathers. Here, the idea is for agency personnel to meet with young putative fathers at the hospital or in the community soon after the child is born and to encourage them to take advantage of the project's services and counseling. The goals are to increase paternity establishment, to establish formal support obligations, to increase collections, and to promote constructive fathering activities. Since spring 1992 the projects have been operating on a pilot basis in ten states. Although the states do not follow a uniform design, they are all expected to provide for enhanced child support enforcement, employment and training, peer support, parenting skills, and mediation. The sponsors presume that states will vary in the stage at which they intervene. Some will deal with fathers who have support awards but inform the courts they cannot pay because of unemployment. Others will identify parents for whom neither paternity nor a support order has been established. As of this writing, a social experiment under which fathers will be randomly assigned to treatment or control groups is to begin in mid-1993.

A second large national demonstration—the Young Unwed Father's Demonstration Project—began operating in early 1991. Public/Private Ventures (PPV), a nonprofit organization, developed the project with funding from the Charles Stewart Mott Foundation. The focus of the demonstration is to influence unwed fathers and expectant unwed fathers between the ages of 16 and 25 who are unemployed and eligible for services under the federal Job Training Partnership Act (JTPA). Each of six sites is serving a minimum of fifty young men over an eighteen-month period.[5] Sponsoring agencies are to offer employment and training services, parenting classes, mentoring, counseling, and referrals for legal and health services. The sites also encourage fathers to declare paternity, and work with fathers to assure child support payments. The sites have flexibility in the provision of services and approaches to recruiting fathers. Two sites take fathers whose participation is mandated by the courts or the state IV-D agency (the agency responsible for collecting support).

Once sites have operated for about one year, PPV plans to design a social experiment, using random assignment of young fathers to treatment and control groups. This experiment will attempt to answer questions similar to those posed by the Parents' Fair Share Demonstration. Does a combined program of employment services, fathering classes, counseling, and monitoring for support payments increase the earnings of fathers, their support payments, and their fathering activities? Will this array of services affect the marriage rate of unwed fathers?

Both demonstrations have a dual goal of increasing the father's responsibility toward his children and of raising the father's earning potential. A major question will be whether the projects are effective in promoting an increased sense of responsibility. If so, the efforts at training and job placement should be especially effective. However, as of this writing, the designers of the projects have not tried to distinguish between the role of components aimed at encouraging responsibility and the role of the education and job training services. Still, the results of these two demonstrations should generate solid evidence about the ability of their programs to raise the earnings and increase the support payments of unwed fathers and other noncustodial fathers. In addition, the projects will yield new information about the actual capabilities of fathers who claim they have too little income to pay their child support obligations.

Notes

1. The original Senate bill included a provision that would have permitted states to offer employment services to nonresident fathers of AFDC children. However, the House-Senate conference deleted the provision because of the lack of evidence documenting the benefits of such programs.

2. Mercer Sullivan argues in Chapter 3 that such differences exist in selected New York City communities with black, Hispanic, and white communities.

3. The tobit procedure is especially appropriate for continuous dependent variables truncated at zero. The model takes account of the fact that the observed zero values for a large number of observations mask an underlying distribution in

which a related latent variable varies among those with the same observed zero level. In the case of child support about 56 percent of absent fathers pay zero child support, but they differ in the likelihood of making positive payments.

4. The ten pilot sites are Mobile County, Alabama; Jacksonville, Florida; Springfield, Massachusettes; Grand Rapids, Michigan; Blaine–West St. Paul, Minnesota; Kansas City, Missouri; Trenton, New Jersey; Hamilton and Dayton, Ohio; and Memphis, Tennessee. At press time, the five full-demonstration sites had not yet been chosen.

5. The six sites are Fresno Private Industry Council, Fresno, California; Friends of the Family, Annapolis, Maryland; Cleveland Works, Cleveland, Ohio; Pinellas Industry Council, Clearwater, Florida; Philadelphia Children's Network, Philadelphia, Pennsylvania; and Goodwill Industries, Racine, Wisconsin.

References

Christensen, Bruce. 1988. "The Costly Retreat from Marriage." *Public Interest*: 59–66. Spring.

Garfinkel, Irwin, and Sara S. McLanahan. 1986. *Single Mothers and Their Children: A New American Dilemma*, Washington, D.C.: Urban Institute.

Garfinkel, Irwin, and Donald Oellerich. 1986. "Noncustodial Fathers' Ability to Pay Child Support." Discussion paper DP 815-16. Madison, Wis.: Institute for Research on Poverty.

Lerman, Robert. 1989. "Child Support Policies." In *Welfare Policies for the 90s*, edited by Phoebe Cottingham and David Ellwood, 219–246. Cambridge: Harvard University Press.

McDonald, John F., and Robert Moffitt. 1980. "The Uses of Tobit Analysis." *Review of Economics and Statistics*: 318–321. May.

Nakosteen, Robert, and Michael Zimmer. 1987. "Marital Status and the Earnings of Young Men," *Journal of Human Resources*: 248–268. Spring.

Ooms, Theodora, and T. Owen. 1990. *Encouraging Unwed Fathers to Be Responsible: Paternity Establishment, Child Support, and JOBS Strategies*. Washington, D.C.: Family Impact Seminar.

Robins, Phillip. 1987. "An Analysis of Trends in Child Support and AFDC from 1979 to 1983." Discussion paper DP 842-87. Madison, Wis.: Institute for Research on Poverty.

List of Contributors

ELIJAH ANDERSON is the Charles and William L. Day Professor of the Social Sciences and the associate director of the Center for Urban Ethnography at the University of Pennsylvania. His most recent book is *Streetwise: Race, Class, and Change in an Urban Community.*

SANDRA K. DANZIGER is assistant professor of social work at the University of Michigan. She was formerly with the Institute for Research on Poverty, University of Wisconsin at Madison and has published on the topic of single-mother families, teenage parents, and child support.

FRANK F. FURSTENBERG, JR., is Zellerbach Family Professor of Sociology and Research Associate in the Population Studies Department at the University of Pennsylvania. He has published widely on family issues including coauthoring *Adolescent Mothers in Later Life* and, most recently, *Divided Families: What Happens to Children When Parents Part.*

ANNE M. GONZALEZ is a family therapist in private practice in Bethesda, Maryland. She has consulted to many youth-serving agencies including a program for pregnant adolescents and their families.

GEORGE W. HARRIS is associate professor of Philosophy at the College of William and Mary. His publications have appeared in the *Journal of Philosophy, Nous, Ethics, The Monist,* and other philosophical journals.

335

KATHLEEN MULLAN HARRIS is assistant professor of sociology and fellow of the Carolina Population Center at the University of North Carolina at Chapel Hill. She is currently completing a book on the life course of teenage mothers and their experience with welfare dependency (to be published by Temple University Press).

RUTH-ARLENE W. HOWE is associate professor of law, Boston College Law School. Her special interests are family law, child welfare, and adoption, and she is reporter for the drafting Committee of the Uniform Putative and Unknown Fathers Act promulgated by the National Commissioners on Uniform State Laws in 1989.

CAROLYN K. KASTNER is the director for state and local policies at the Center for the Support of Children, Washington, D.C. In this capacity and in her previous work at the National Conference of State Legislatures, she has assisted thirty-seven states with improving their child support laws and policy.

LEIGHTON C. KU is a research associate at the Urban Institute in Washington, D.C. He has been recently collaborating in research on teenage men and is especially interested in behaviors relating to the risk of HIV transmission.

M. LAURIE LEITCH divides her time between program evaluation, training, and her private psychotherapy practice in Washington, D.C. Her special program interests include adolescent pregnancy, AIDS, sexual abuse, and bicultural approaches to service delivery.

ROBERT I. LERMAN is chair of the Department of Economics at the American University. Dr. Lerman has written widely on poverty and welfare programs, youth employment programs and patterns, family formation of young people and, most recently, the case for youth apprenticeship programs. Among his recent publications are "Income Stratification and Income Inequality" in *Review of Income and Wealth* and "The Compelling Case for Youth Apprenticeship" in *The Public Interest*.

LINDA M. MELLGREN is a policy analyst in the Office of the Assistant Secretary for Planning and Evaluation, Department of Health and Human Services, where she is responsible for the oversight of child support policy, evaluation, and research.

TERRI J. NICKEL is senior associate for the Center for the Support of Children, a nonprofit organization based in Washington, D.C. She has worked on a number of national training and technical assistance projects concerned with child support, paternity establishment, and programs for young families.

THEODORA J. OOMS is director of the Family Impact Seminar, the policy unit of the Research and Education Foundation, American Association for Marriage and Family Therapy in Washington, D.C. Previously she worked as a family therapist and administrator at the Philadelphia Child Guidance Clinic. Among her many publications is the edited volume *Teenage Pregnancy in a Family Context: Implications for Policy*.

MAUREEN A. PIROG-GOOD is associate professor of Public Policy Analysis in the School of Public and Environmental Affairs at Indiana University. Her principal research interests include teenage parenting and child support enforcement.

JOSEPH H. PLECK is research associate at the Wellesley College Center for research on Women. In addition to his work on adolescent male sexual and contraceptive behavior, his other research interests include men's work and family roles, and attitudes towards masculinity. He is author of *The Myth of Masculinity* and *Working Wives, Working Husbands*.

JOELLE SANDER is associate director of continuing education at Sarah Lawrence College. While working at Bank Street College of Education, she was coordinator of the Teen Father Collaboration and the Adolescent Family Life Collaboration. She has recently published *Before Their Time*, an oral history of a four-generation family of women, all of whom were teenage mothers.

ARTHUR B. SHOSTAK is professor of sociology at Drexel University in Philadelphia. He is principal author of *Men and Abortion: Lessons, Losses, and Love*.

FREYA L. SONENSTEIN is senior research associate at the Urban Institute in Washington, D.C. She directs the project that conducted the National Survey of Adolescent Males, and was formerly codirector of the Family and Children's Policy Center at the Florence Heller School, Brandeis University.

MERCER L. SULLIVAN is an urban anthropologist and senior research associate at the Community Development Research Center of the New School for Social Research in New York City. He is author of *Getting Paid: Youth Crime and Unemployment*.

ESTHER WATTENBERG teachers in the School of Social Work, University of Minnesota, and is research associate with the Center for Urban and Regional Affairs. She is currently the principal investigator of the Ford Foundation study "Paternity Decisions of Young Unmarried Parents."

Index

ABO blood-typing system, paternity testing, 163

abortion: fathers' right to notification of, 179–80, 288–95; premarital sexual activity and, 7; RU486 pill and, 294; spousal consent laws, 292–95; Supreme Court decisions regarding, 166n.9

absent fathers: accuracy of data on, 29; defined, 28; overlap between unwed fatherhood and, 32–37; racial differences among, 35; social problems of children and, 14–15; welfare laws and, 2–3

absent parents, defined, 19n.3

actual rights: conflicts regarding, 172–73; nonpatriarchal conception of, 173–74. *See also* prima facie rights

Adams, Charles, 211n.2

adjudicated father, defined, 143–44

administrative structure: as barriers to child support collection, 15–17, 239–41; in Teen Father Collaboration program, 304–305

adolescent: defined, 19n.3; well-being, outcome measures of, 135–36

Adolescent and Young Adult Fathers: Problems and Solutions, 207

Adolescent Family Life Collaboration (AFLC), 278–79, 283

Adolescent Family Life (AFL) program, 8; demonstration projects under, 270–71; goals of, 204–207

Adolescent Fathers: Directory of Services, 203

Adolescent Pregnancy Act of 1978, 268

adoption procedures: Supreme Court rulings regarding, 150–56; unwed fathers' involvement in, 267–71

Advocacy Center for Child Support, 207

AFDC (Aid to Families with Dependent Children): Adolescent Family Life (AFL) program and, 204–207; as barrier to earnings opportunities, 331–33; child support payments and, 261–63; demographics of recipients, 215–16; goals of, 199–201; La Barriada dependency patterns and, 64–66; paternal contributions and, 71, 261–63; paternal rights and obligations, 157–59; paternity determination and, 220; Projectville support patterns and, 62–64; reimbursement incentives, as barrier to child support, 238–39; TAPP program individuals in, 256; teen pregnancy programs and, 9–10, 284–85; traditional child support enforcement in, 252–53; unemployed parents program, 208–209; unmarried mothers as percentage of recipients, 20n.15

AFDC-Unemployed Parent (AFDC-UP), 19n.4, 200–201

African Americans: marriage and fatherhood patterns, 34–36; spread of unwed fatherhood among, 46–48; unwed parenthood among, 17. *See also* racial differences

age as determinant: child support compliance and, 327–30; of children, decline in visitation patterns and, 45–46, 48; marital status and, 31–32; procreation rights and, 174–76; role of, in sexual activity, 94–96; rights and responsibilities of unwed fathers and, 182–83; of unwed fatherhood, 41–42, 285n.1; of unwed motherhood, 174–76

Aid to Dependent Children (ADC), 7

AIDS epidemic: contraceptive use and, 104–106; sexual activity and, 100

alcohol abuse, unwed fathers' patterns of, 37, 39

alternative school programs, for unwed mothers, 7–8, 63

American Indians, marriage and fatherhood patterns, 34–35

Anderson, Elijah, 44